P9-DYZ-626

Birth of a Salesman

Walter A. Friedman

Birth of a Salesman

The Transformation of Selling in America

Harvard University Press

Cambridge, Massachusetts, and London, England · 2004

Library of Congress Cataloging-in-Publication Data

Friedman, Walter A., 1962–
    Birth of a salesman : the transformation of selling in America /
Walter A. Friedman.
        p. cm.
    Includes bibliographical references and index.
    ISBN 0-674-01298-4 (alk. paper)
    1. Sales management—United States.   I. Title.

HF5438.4.F75 2004
381′.1′0973—dc22   2003065235

To my family

Contents

Prospect: "My old car is worth at least $100.00 more than you offer me."

Salesman: "Your old car, Mr. Prospect, has given you a lot of pleasure and service. You are thoroughly familiar with its condition and I can understand how it may appear to you to be worth more. But the price of a used car, just like anything else, is determined by the demand for it. It is impossible to offer you more for your old car, much as we would like to do so, but we can offer you many quality features that cannot be duplicated in any other car at or near the price of a new Chevrolet." (Show him features and ask for the order—often.)

From General Motors'
Selling Chevrolets: A Book of General Information for Chevrolet Retail Salesmen
(1926)

Prologue, 1916

The First World's Salesmanship Congress

On the morning of July 10, 1916, over three thousand salesmen, managers, and executives from many industries gathered in Arcadia Auditorium in Detroit for the first World's Salesmanship Congress. President Woodrow Wilson, the keynote speaker, urged his audience of salesmen to travel the globe and promote the goods that, he believed, had come to symbolize prosperity and the promise of America itself. "Lift your eyes to the horizon of business," he began. "Do not look too close at the little processes with which you are concerned, but let your thoughts and your imaginations run abroad throughout the whole world. And with the inspiration of the thought that you are Americans and are meant to carry liberty and justice and the principles of humanity wherever you go, go out and sell goods that will make the world more comfortable and more happy, and convert them to the principles of America."[1]

The event was the brainchild of D. M. Barrett, editor of *Salesmanship* magazine. The previous September, Barrett had organized a Detroit sales club, which operated under the slogan "Business betterment through betterment in salesmanship." He hoped to build a national organization and gained the support of Norval A. Hawkins, Ford Motor Company's sales director, and Edward A. Woods, head of

Equitable Life Assurance's largest agency.[2] The event's "constitution" pledged to "promote the dignity of Salesmanship by the elevation of the rank of the salesman to a higher plane" and to "encourage contributions to the science of Salesmanship in the form of books, lectures, courses and publications."[3]

The Salesmanship Congress brought together some of the best-known businessmen in the country. Henry Ford met with Wilson on the morning of the president's talk. Not surprisingly, many of the businessmen attending the Salesmanship Congress came from companies that relied on salesmen. The audience was made up of representatives of Burroughs Adding Machine, National Cash Register, and other office-machine manufacturers; automobile makers, such as Packard and Cadillac; and insurance and real-estate companies. The weeklong event offered a wide selection of lectures, covering everything from the daily tasks of management to the qualities of good salesmen. Demonstrations of expert sales ability were provided. Edgar F. Roberts, a local realtor, overcame an obstinate buyer onstage to sell a Detroit property for $4,925 in fifteen minutes. In the evening, attendees listened to sermons on ethics and salesmanship at local churches, watched boat races, and enjoyed the melodies of the Studebaker band.

The speakers at the weeklong event included sales managers, like Richard H. Grant of Dayton Engineering Laboratories (later head of Chevrolet) and Frank H. Dodge of Burroughs Adding Machine, and company presidents, like William R. Malone of Postal Life Insurance, Harry M. Jewett of Paige-Detroit Motor Car, and Alvan Macauley of Packard.

Academics, consultants, psychologists, and advertising executives shared the stage as well. James Samuel Knox, president of the Knox School of Salesmanship in Cleveland, Ohio, spoke about how to teach modern sales techniques. Charles Wilson Hoyt, author of *Scientific Salesmanship*, discussed ways to make selling more efficient. Walter Dill Scott and Walter Van Dyke Bingham, both of the Carnegie Institute of Technology, performed "mental alertness tests" on twenty-five young salesmen at the Statler Hotel to predict which ones would most likely succeed.

Some "experts" at the World's Salesmanship Congress were of dubious merit. The phrenologist Grant Nablo instructed his audience of managers to look for a high forehead when hiring, as this supposedly denoted imagination, and to avoid applicants with "a flat back head" because they would be "quick starts but slow finishers." "Look around you," said Nablo, in what must have been an uncomfortable moment. "And you will see heads like that."[4]

Like many other public celebrations of the Progressive Era, the World's Salesmanship Congress was both a celebration of the past and an effort to gain distance from it. Speakers—businessmen, academics, and politicians—expressed enthusiasm about a new era of salesmanship, in which selling would be conducted according to systematic principles.

The days of the backslapping, hard-drinking drummer were over, speakers proclaimed. No longer the pursuer of farmers' daughters, as depicted in popular jokes, the modern salesman was, one business executive argued, "a man of stability, character and regular habits—he must be married."[5] Salesmen now exhibited loyalty to the employing "house" and a good relation with "the boss." Moreover, salesmen of the new era were expected to play a beneficial role in society. They would "overcome obstinacy, soften prejudice and let the light of reason into dark places," said a representative from the National Cash Register Company.

The Salesmanship Congress revealed the cross-section of individuals fascinated by salesmanship and its possibilities in the early twentieth century—a mixture of businessmen, politicians, scientists, pseudoscientists, and promoters; they were organization-builders, reformers, managers, entrepreneurs, researchers, theorists, and motivators. They ushered in modern salesmanship and its consequences, both economic and cultural, creative and destructive.[6]

Introduction

The Science of Selling

The development of modern sales management is a uniquely American story. The intense effort to standardize salesmanship distinguished the growth of capitalism in America from that in other countries. All European nations had peddling networks, some of which had existed for hundreds of years, but none created organized sales forces to the same degree as did the United States. There are several reasons for this. First, the emergence of salesmanship depended on a stable currency, the rule of law, the protection of private property, and the availability of credit—all aspects of the American economic system. More important, the scale of American firms was greater than elsewhere. The massive manufacturing concerns of the early twentieth century, which produced tremendous numbers of business machines, appliances, and cars, hired salesmen in the hundreds (and even thousands); and these goods, all pushed by aggressive salesmanship, distinguished the American economy by their early appearance and widespread purchase. British industry, which produced on a smaller scale, and German manufacturers, which were rooted in craftwork traditions, seldom exhibited a similar interest in mass selling campaigns.[1]

Organized selling in America flourished also for cultural reasons. In a country that, from the outset, held dem-

4

ocratic elections and had no established church or hereditary aristocracy, salesmanship provided political and religious groups with a way to compete for followers. Moreover, with more fluid class boundaries than in European countries, the skills of salesmanship, especially beginning in the late nineteenth century, seemed to offer a pathway to personal success. In the early twentieth century, Americans read how-to-sell books and turned Bruce Barton's *The Man Nobody Knows* (1925), which portrayed Jesus Christ as a successful sales and advertising executive, into a best-seller.

The birth of modern salesmanship occurred in the decades around the turn of the century. Entrepreneurs at the vanguard of selling, who developed modern sales techniques, created procedures for management that paralleled those of the new science of mass production. With the rise of mass manufacturers in the United States, salesmanship became of interest to psychologists, economists, ministers, and politicians. The country, as envisioned by the pioneers of modern selling, now comprised sales "territories." Citizens were not steelworkers, bankers, or housewives, but "prospects." Other nations around the globe were not allies or enemies, but trade "opportunities."

In 1904 businessman P. W. Searles, writing in *System* magazine, summarized the changes he had seen in selling over the past several years—changes resulting from the imposition of managerial systems at large manufacturing companies. Earlier, as he put it, a salesman traveled "as his own boss." Now his routes were planned, his customers evaluated before his departure, and a trail of sales slips and reports established a record of his every move.[2] Sales managers at large corporations assigned salesmen specific territories and gave them monthly or weekly quotas to meet. They aimed to make salesmanship uniform, predictable, and capable of being taught to new recruits. They even instructed salesmen on such minutia as how to stand while talking with a customer, or how to hand over the pen at "closing."

Managers also tried to redefine the image of their sales force by adopting a new vocabulary. Only after the turn of the century did the terms "salesman" and "salesmanship" come into vogue, carrying with them parallels to "workman" and "workmanship," but also signaling that selling was a male-dominated occupation.[3] While the late nineteenth century had had a small tradition of female book canvassers, most large companies in the early twentieth century hired only men for their sales forces. Managers wanted the members of their sales force to appear professional, neat, responsible, and masculine.

The revolution in selling had consequences beyond the firm. The growth of systematic methods of sales management gave rise to a number of products and services that supported sales managers, including trade journals and popular magazines, such as *Salesmanship* (founded in 1903), *Salesmen* (1909), *Salesmanship: Devoted to Success in Selling* (1915), *Sales Management* (1918), and *Salesman's Opportunity* (1923). The Dartnell Corporation of Chicago began collecting empirical data on selling and produced scores of reports for sales managers on topics ranging from "Modern Methods and Tendencies in 259 Different Lines of Business" to "Plans for Building Up a Spirit of Loyalty in a Sales Organization" and "Enlisting the Cooperation of Salesmen's Wives and Families."[4]

The creation of methods of sales management also opened up new branches of academic inquiry, such as marketing, consumer behavior, and industrial psychology.[5] After the turn of the century, economists and professors of sales management at business colleges analyzed costs and methods of distribution. In 1913, Harvard's Bureau of Business Research published its first bulletin, which concentrated on the selling of shoes. The bureau followed with studies of the grocery trade, retail hardware dealers, and department stores.[6]

Psychologists sought to make sense of the way that salesmen created demand in the minds of customers. In *Psychology in Personal Selling* (1926), A. J. Snow attempted to explain the physiological changes that occurred to nerve cells in the brain when customers made a decision to buy: Were consumer wants largely instinctual? Were they built up through habit and suggestion?[7] In 1916, the Carnegie Institute of Technology (now Carnegie Mellon University) founded a Bureau of Salesmanship Research to create psychological tests for salesmen. The embrace of sales-management systems by large corporations encouraged new ways to make sense of the role of salesmanship in the economy. The promoters of modern sales techniques described an economy in which demand was malleable, language was expedient, and enthusiasm—demonstrated by salesmen selling products—was a powerful economic force. Charles Bennett, whose book *Scientific Salesmanship* (1933) grew out of a doctoral dissertation at the University of Missouri, referred to salesmanship as the "expansion of meaning." Bennett argued that salesmanship, rather than merely gaining a greater share of the economic pie for one company or another, increased the size of the pie overall.[8]

All the transitions in selling methods—organizational, strategic, and ideological—were central to the growth of the U.S. economy in the late nineteenth and early twentieth centuries. Sales and marketing were not afterthoughts to the coming of industrialization, but were part and parcel of the same phenomenon. Large firms were capable not only of production on a great scale, but also of persuasion, pressure, and the fostering of an evangelical exuberance. The "visible hand" of management, to borrow a phrase from historian Alfred D. Chandler Jr., could not have succeeded in many industries without the "visible handshake" of a team of salesmen out on the road.

This book highlights the work of entrepreneurs and managers who were especially fascinated by selling and who devised innovative and effective sales strategies. It emphasizes the entrepreneurs, managers, and system builders, rather than salesmen themselves. In relating the story of salesmanship "enthusiasts" and the rise of modern sales management, it follows a rough chronology, from the years following the Civil War to the end of the Great Depression.[9] Each chapter offers an example of a particular type of salesmanship: the selling of General Grant's memoirs by book canvassers; the wholesaling of hardware by traveling drummers; the beginnings of sales management by mass-manufacturing companies like Singer Sewing Machine and Heinz; the formation of a comprehensive system of management at National Cash Register; the development of methods to analyze selling at the Carnegie Institute of Technology; and the building of consumer marketing strategies at Ford, General Motors, and Fuller Brush. Together, these examples illustrate the growing scale of sales organizations and the increasingly sophisticated implementation of sales strategies.

Among the people featured in the book are Albert ("Fine and Dandy") Teetsel, a sales manager at Fuller Brush and an exponent of positive thinking; Saunders Norvell, a long-time traveling salesman for the nation's largest lumber company and editor of the *Gimlet* newsletter; Walter Dill Scott, an industrial psychologist who became director of the Bureau of Salesmanship Research; Norval Hawkins, author of several popular books on selling and head of sales at Ford; and Arch Shaw, who lectured on marketing at Harvard Business School, published *System* magazine, and advised the Hoover Administration on how to conduct a national survey of distribution methods. While emphasizing business strategists, I also look at economists and other academics who examined the role of salesmanship in the larger economy, such as Thorstein Veblen, Charles Bennett, and Harvard Business School professor Harry R. Tosdal. At the center of the book is a chapter on John H. Patterson, president of the National Cash Register Company, who did more than anyone else to systematize salesmanship.

The work of entrepreneurs and managers at large manufacturing companies is given the most attention. The firms that these businessmen built, like Burroughs, Coca-Cola, and General Motors, operated with resources far beyond those available to independent peddlers or petty canvassers. They employed a range of new technologies to facilitate communication with salesmen in the field and to gather information about the marketplace that helped them predict future demand. They also used new advertising outlets—newspapers, magazines, and, after 1920, radio—to complement the work of their sales forces. These resources enabled them to launch strategic sales campaigns and create demand on a scale unseen before.[10]

The focus is on mass producers because they devoted the most attention to standardizing methods of selling and techniques of sales management. The firms that created modern salesmanship included office-machine manufacturers, automobile companies, and makers of soap, canned goods, and paints and varnishes. Companies that made these types of products hired sales forces to conquer their markets and take trade away from competitors. Manufacturers that sold branded goods in great quantities, or made perishable products or complex machines that were difficult for independent wholesalers to handle, also tended to build their own sales forces. They generally manufactured a high volume of output and sold their goods across a vast geographic area.

Salesmen for these companies knocked on doors, waited outside offices, dropped off samples, shared good stories, offered special rates, and in other ways informed, persuaded, and cajoled "prospects" as they ceaselessly promoted their goods. They pressured customers to compare, buy, and then "trade up."

Salesmen were trained to answer specific questions about a product and were often able to grant credit to buyers and make arrangements for delivery. They were particularly good at promoting new products— they played an essential part, for instance, in the introduction of cash registers and adding machines. Through their demonstration of products, relentless sales pitches, and ability to sell goods on credit, highly managed salesmen encouraged a shift in the type of items that consumers purchased by urging them to buy appliances, cars, and other expensive products.

As manufacturers of cash registers, refrigerators, and many other goods knew, low prices did not always create demand. People bought for a variety of reasons, including their own rational decision-making and the preferences of taste. They also bought because they were "sold."[11] Sales workers played a role that was both informative and persuasive. They worked to overcome what they saw as the inertia or procrastination of buyers.

In designing and rehearsing their sales pitches, sales managers, and salesmen themselves, mastered the mechanics of persuasion: What types of arguments worked best on prospects? What emotions triggered a "buying impulse"? When were logical appeals most effective? Manufacturing companies invested a great deal of money in standardizing methods of selling, because they felt that salesmen could lead "prospects" to make purchases that they might not otherwise have made, or that might have gone to the competition. As *Fortune* magazine observed in the mid-twentieth century, "Mass production would be a shadow of what it is today if it had waited for the consumer to make up his mind."[12] Salesmen persuaded customers to make purchases. They also gathered information, wrote credit reports, and often even serviced products.

The most ardent believers in the power of salesmanship were those, around the turn of the century, who tried to make selling a "science." Since the earliest days of trade, selling had been viewed as something of an "art." It had been the province of peddlers who endured the hardships of life on the road and used wit and skill to make sales. In the years following the Civil War, however, selling had become increasingly systematic, as publishing houses organized teams of canvassers to sell popular books, and large wholesalers such as Marshall Field's sent out traveling salesmen to stock general stores throughout the nation.

With the coming of mass production and the formation of highly managed sales forces at Heinz, National Cash Register, Burroughs Adding Machine, Ford, General Motors, and other firms, entrepreneurs and businessmen began to refer to a "science" of selling. Entrepreneurs at mass-production companies set up sales departments to systematize the promotion and distribution of their products. Makers of inexpensive goods, like soap and condiments, used salesmen to promote brandname products. Manufacturers of sewing machines and of office machinery, such as typewriters and adding machines, hired salesmen to explain their products and to provide credit so that customers could purchase these items. Companies that sold to consumers often had large sales forces, larger than those that sold to businesses. In 1923, Fuller Brush had 3,400 salesmen going door-to-door.[13] That same year, Ford Motor Company sold its cars through a network of 9,451 automobile dealers.[14]

Like their colleagues in production, the pioneers of modern sales-manship followed the ethic, if not the methods, of Frederick W. Taylor's scientific management movement, whose aim was to divide work into efficient routines and place the pace of labor under the control of managers. In *Scientific Sales Management: A Practical Application of the Principles of Scientific Management to Selling*, Charles Wilson Hoyt explained, "Scientific Sales Management believes in the proper training of the salesman. This training even goes down to the individual motions and work of the salesmen. It goes so far as to insist upon the substitution of exact methods of work by the individual salesman for scattered efforts. This is carried out even to the matter of standardizing, in some propositions, the salesman's talk, his manner of approach, etc." Hoyt described the transformation from independent peddlers to manufacturer-controlled employees as one from the "big me" salesman to the "little me" salesman; at mass-manufacturing companies, the manager was in charge.[15]

More generally, Hoyt's use of the word "science" revealed the increasingly common urge to systematize and standardize methods of selling. It also indicated the direction for the future: the need to gather ever more empirical information about sales costs and gain a greater understanding of consumer behavior. NCR, Heinz, Coca-Cola, Burroughs, and other mass-manufacturing companies did indeed develop comprehensive and systematic methods of sales management. They devised procedures to recruit and train sales workers and published large sales manuals and newsletters (*Pickles* at Heinz, for example) to keep salesmen informed and motivated. They also established systems to gather information from salesmen about specific customers and relied on public and private sources for statistics about individual credit ratings or overall economic conditions.

Not all manufacturers developed highly managed sales forces, however. Many salesmen in the early twentieth century acted with little or no managerial oversight and with the independence of a peddler. Hucksters sold items along the boardwalk in Atlantic City, and horse traders carried out deals in Mississippi.[16] Many manufacturers, operating on a small or medium scale, built strong sales forces but did not standardize their activities to the same degree. And companies that relied on "batch" methods were not as pressed to match uniform production and distribution schedules. They were less likely to launch large, persuasive sales and advertising campaigns, and more inclined to tailor approaches to individual customers.[17]

But the history of the effort to make a "science" of selling by entrepreneurs at large companies, managers, and consultants provides a model of how old economic practices were modified and incorporated into new forms of capitalism—in this case, how old traditions of selling, persuasion, prediction, and motivation were brought into the rationalized world of managerial capitalism.

The coming of modern salesmanship, then, is the story of a search for order. It is part of the broader history of America's Progressive Era, as the country moved from what historian Robert Wiebe has described as a series of rural, isolated communities in the 1870s to a modern, urban, and bureaucratic society after the turn of the century.[18] The difficulties of rationalizing sales processes make this a story of a *search* for order, rather than of the establishment of order.[19] Though the drive to build organizations, draft formulas, and train teams of salespeople was relentless, the results were not always successful or predictable. The divide between old and new methods of selling was not always clear, nor was highly managed salesmanship as "scientific" as its spokesmen claimed. With an emphasis on persuasion, motivation, and theatricality, twentieth-century sales management drew on the older techniques of peddlers, patent medicine men, and drummers, not to mention the ideas of a cadre of self-proclaimed experts and authorities. More important, aspects of the spontaneity and improvisation of the face-to-face economy persisted, despite managers' efforts to orchestrate the daily moves of their sales forces.

Unlike other reform impulses in the late nineteenth and early twentieth centuries, efforts to systematize selling originated in domestic strategies for commercial and personal success, rather than in the European intellectual movements that influenced, for instance, city planning, modernist architecture, and social insurance.[20] Entrepreneurs and managers drew on trends and ideas in American culture. They enlisted contemporary diet and exercise fads in shaping (literally) the salesmen on their force. They also incorporated the ideas of America's leading political figures and intellectuals in their sales equations. For instance, the pages of sales manuals and house organs often reprinted the self-help philosophies of Benjamin Franklin and Teddy Roosevelt. Even the writings of psychologist and philosopher William James appeared in sales books; business writers popularized James, not for the purpose of forming a highbrow metaphysical club, but rather to create a "motivational club" as they watered down his ideas and reduced them to inspirational slogans and speeches. Finally, entrepreneurs and managers responded to changing ideas about gender as they tried to redefine selling as a masculine profession, dependent on hard work and determination, rather than on feminized skills of seduction.

While the book focuses on entrepreneurs, managers, and salesmen, it also says a lot about the people on the other end of the equation: shopkeepers, wholesale buyers, and consumers. Salesmanship and consumption were opposite sides of the same coin. Entrepreneurs, salesmen, and sales experts carefully studied "prospects," observing their tendencies and inclinations. Sales scripts relied on the premise that consumers acted in somewhat predictable ways when talking with a salesperson. Prospects, salesmen found, were often risk averse, skeptical, status conscious, afraid of being duped, and easily distracted. They were also eager to improve their bargaining position by gathering product information from consumer advocates, ingredient labels, and other sources. Managers and salesmen tried to keep pace with the shifting wants, demands, and tastes of consumers by offering brand-name items, easy credit terms, and guarantees, and by endlessly adjusting their sales talks and promotional strategies. As the history of modern salesmanship shows, the consumption-based economy of the early twentieth century originated in the face-to-face selling strategies of peddlers and book canvassers of previous generations.

Hawkers and Walkers

1

The Independent Peddler

Leaving his native Vermont in 1818 at age twenty-one, James Guild decided to pursue life as a peddler, trading in a seventy-dollar bank note for a pack and some merchandise. He wanted to escape the drudgery of his Vermont farm life, just as later in the century others became traveling salesmen to avoid factory labor. "My disposition would not allow me to work on a farm," Guild confided in his diary.[1] He went wherever he could find goods to trade and customers to take them, traveling for several years through New England and upstate New York and then venturing as far south as Charleston, South Carolina.[2] During his career, he sold a number of different items and performed a variety of services, serving stints as a tambourine player, silhouette cutter, portrait painter, and teacher of penmanship.[3]

Guild's diary reveals the independence of peddlers in early America. He traveled on his own, formulating sales strategies to overcome the suspicion and hostility that greeted him when he approached a farmer's home. Exchanges were not always pleasant: "Get out of my house in a minute, or I will horse whip you, you dam profiters and pedlers, you ought to have a good whipping by every one that sees you," said one farmer.[4]

Guild was one of a number of Americans who, in the

decades following the Revolution, were eager to travel and to engage in commercial activities, and looked to advance themselves through competition in the marketplace.[5] Peddling was a popular occupation among young unmarried men, for it required little initial investment. Bronson Alcott and other Americans took to the road to learn the rules of trade and to explore the country.[6] Peddlers carried trunks filled with goods; some pulled a wagon or traveled on horseback. Those with skills for entertaining played music or told stories.

Guild had doubts about taking up work as a peddler, for it required long treks down dirt paths and crossing woods and rivers in all kinds of weather. Moreover, peddling was not a highly respected trade. "I not only had the disagreable sensations of leaving my friends, but I wondered why I should stoop so low as to follow so mean a caling," he wrote. Despite days of cold and isolation, Guild persevered, writing: "You must know it was awkward for a farmer boy who had been confined to the hoe or ax to put on a pedler[']s face, but I believe I was as apt as any one, I got my things in rotation pedler form, so when I went into a house, [I asked] do you wish to buy some harecombs, needles, buttons, buttonmolds, sewing silk, beeds?"[7]

Peddlers had to gain the trust of farmers and other buyers. This was not easy, for peddlers were, essentially, strangers coming to town to make a series of trades and then leave. Unlike door-to-door salesmen of the twentieth century, they did not represent well-known companies or sell brand-name goods. And because peddlers would likely only see a prospect a few times, they were eager to make a sale on their first encounter and were less concerned about any future consequences if buyers were dissatisfied with the purchases. The goal of such peddlers engaged in "transactional" selling differed from that of salesmen working for companies later in the nineteenth century, who called upon the same customers repeatedly, often over many years.

Guild found that customers bargained to get the lowest possible price. Bartering and bargaining were a common part of antebellum New England merchant culture. Three-fourths of the American labor force worked on farms in 1800, where bartering was a way of life. While there were tobacco plantations in some southern states, most Americans at this time cultivated crops for their own consumption.[8] Many produced their own soap, candles, leather, beeswax, and furniture, trading the surplus to local merchants for other goods or services. "If they [the customers] wished to purchase, they would want to banter untill they could get it for nothing," Guild complained.[9] The constant bargaining and persuading led some peddlers to want to leave their occupation, especially as the size of the peddling population grew in the antebellum period and trading became more competitive. The U.S. census listed 10,669 peddlers in 1850 and 16,594 in 1860; most came from the states of New York, Pennsylvania, Massachusetts, and Ohio.[10]

Guild worked out his own methods to overcome the resistance that greeted him—and he delighted in the process. Wit and humor were his allies when visiting farms. He discovered numerous ways to make his pleas successful, including playing to people's rising social expectations and their desires to own decorative goods. He altered his approach according to the type of person he met. For example, in Troy, New York, he attended a dinner party with the city's wealthy citizens. At first he felt conspicuous but then realized that he could pass himself off as one of the elite. "I was capable of niping and twisting and deceiveing them by affectation," Guild wrote. "Soon I was waited on in great stile." He adopted a philosophy: "Now I begin to learn human nature. I find people are not alway[s] what they seem to be . . . I find by experience if a man thinks he is something and puts him self forward he will be something."[11] Guild's sentiment of projecting confidence—of "putting oneself forward" in a bold way—became common advice in how-to-sell books of the late nineteenth and early twentieth centuries.[12]

The techniques he gathered were based on his own observation and experimentation and on hints passed along to him by other peddlers whom he met on the road.[13] He realized that there was economic value in entertaining and in using less orthodox ways of sparking interest. He even traveled with a bison at one point to attract attention.

Guild also saw selling as a form of seduction. Peddlers were almost exclusively men, at least until the emergence of women book agents by mid-century; but historians have suggested that selling was traditionally viewed as something effeminate because it required skills that had long been associated with femininity, such as courtesy and politeness, verbal dexterity, and a familiarity with decorative and stylistic aspects of objects.[14] Guild flirted and joked with his female customers, who saw an opportunity to trade their rags, food, or currency for tinware and other goods. He managed to sell one woman a portrait of herself, even though he confessed in his diary that it looked like a "strangle[d] cat."[15]

Traveling through New England one winter, Guild hoped to sell scissors quickly at the low price of twelve cents a pair. To his dismay, he found customers reluctant to purchase them. Most felt that, at the price he was charging, the scissors could not be any good. Guild tried an experiment. He divided the scissors—all of the same quality—into two packs, keeping some at twelve cents and raising the price on others to twenty-five cents. This improved his sales, as he found when he sold a pair to a mother and daughter who chose the higher-priced scissors:

> When I went into a house it was, do you want any tin cups tin pans tin or puter dishes of any kind mended and do you want to buy some sissors? Yies, if you have got some good ones. Well, marm, I have got some good ones and some poor ones; my best come at 25 cents and the other at 12 cents. So I would show them, to them, and they would look of them. Now mother you must get me a pair of sissors for me, for you never got me a pair. O well dear child I suppose you must have a pair or I shall be teased to death. Now the girl would say mother which is it best to get 12 or 25 cents one? O it is best to get a good pair if any; so they would try them by cutting out paper, and if they cut wet paper, they were good; and in this stile I was spending my time which I thought was a meaner caling than I deserved, but I felt at this time as mean as my employ.[16]

The passage revealed the peddler's keen awareness of the nature of the relationship between the mother and daughter and how to cater to it through his price. He found that the way he presented the scissors determined their price, rather than some objective sense of what they were worth, or, in other words, that a good sales strategy could trump logic.

The value of the object depended on how it was "sold." This was something that Guild felt uncomfortable about, or "mean" as he put it, and this issue, of what constituted the actual value of a good, is one that recurs throughout the history of selling.

Peddling Clocks and Other Inventions

The knowledge that Guild gathered—knowledge of how to talk about scissors, books, tin utensils, and other items, and how to present oneself in commercial exchange—occupied a growing place in American culture and economy in the nineteenth century. Peddlers like Guild traveled with no training, making observations on their own about how to sell and gathering tips from more experienced itinerants. Their work was not easy, for they had to overcome the hazards of hard traveling and the difficulties of bartering in a country without a national currency. They also encountered the antagonism of shopkeepers, who resented their arrival in town and pushed for taxes on out-of-state traders, and they met cultural hostility in the form of folklore that portrayed peddlers as swindlers and cheats.[17] The issues that confronted Guild, such as how to overcome suspicion, how to talk to different types of customers (such as women or children, northerners or southerners), and how to make sense of the occupation itself, also challenged other peddlers.

Despite these problems, peddlers and peddling networks flourished in America. During the colonial period, peddlers often obtained manufactured goods directly from urban merchants and artisans, or from sailors who smuggled them to shore. Others received goods to trade from rural storeowners, who had purchased items from importers or manufacturers.

In the years after the Revolution, Americans increasingly pioneered new enterprises and expanded overseas trade—traveling as far as China. Entrepreneurs took risks, settling land, borrowing, bartering, and manufacturing.[18] And printers helped spur a literacy revolution and a passion for reading. In addition, methods of transportation and communication improved in early America. Canals became a principal method of moving freight in the 1820s and 1830s. The Erie Canal, the most extensive inland water route, allowed passage from Lake Erie to New York City by 1825, and an extensive system of other, smaller canals served cities like Akron, Ohio; Lowell, Massachusetts; and Chicago.[19] Railroad mileage also increased, so that by 1840 the United States had 2,800 miles of railroad track.[20]

Peddlers were an indispensable part of early America's market revolution, carrying manufactured goods, imports, books, and broadsides. They formed networks that tied together the agricultural areas, hinterlands, and cities. Peddlers and artisan-entrepreneurs were partners in the transformation of rural life. They not only brought manufactured goods to farmers and townspeople; they also introduced a market culture. They carried buttons, cloth, brooms, chairs, clocks, books, paintings, and decorative objects—all of which served as "emblems of affluence."[21]

There were three types of peddlers: those who traveled independently, like Guild, purchasing goods with a bank note or bartering for them; peddlers who worked for an artisan-entrepreneur or storekeeper on some kind of salary or commission; and a third type, who were hired by peddling organizations that distributed manufacturers' or merchants' goods. These organizations could be as small as two people and as large as more than a dozen, and were operated under the direction of a master peddler. Morillo Noyes, working out of Vermont, employed twenty or, at times, even fifty peddlers. Peddling networks were important, for they brought together artisans, banks, shipping and transportation companies, and warehouses into an effective distribution system.

While some peddlers carried a wide range of goods, others specialized in selling a single type of item, such as tinware, clocks, or books. Tin-smithing had its origins in Connecticut before the Revolution and remained concentrated there for several decades. Peddlers sold pots and pans and introduced farmers to new devices that saved time or made life and work easier. Throughout much of the antebellum period, the sole means of power for tinware production came from human and animal labor, or from waterpower. This limited the scale of production, but as small factories were founded, the rate of production outgrew local demand, and artisans and manufacturers looked for ways to distribute their goods to new places.

The tin peddler became a quintessential "Yankee," carrying pots, pans, boxes, pails, and utensils. Morillo Noyes was both manufacturer and general wholesaler. Selling tinware and other items, his peddlers were middlemen, connecting farmers and factories: they brought manufactured goods to customers and, at the same time, carried reusable products back to factories.[22] Wages for successful tin peddlers in the early nineteenth century ranged from about $25 to $50 ($360 to $730 today) per month, with their annual employment running from six to nine months. This rate was higher than agricultural laborers, who might earn $8 to $15 ($120 to $220 today) in the summer months.[23]

Specialized peddlers also carried goods that were relatively new or that required some explanation or promotion, such as clocks and, after mid-century, sewing machines. Clockmakers turned to peddlers to distribute their wares, especially after Eli Terry began factory production of clock mechanisms, or movements, in the early nineteenth century.[24] Beginning around 1802, Terry used waterpower to manufacture his wooden clocks and was able to make several hundred annually. Using peddlers to hawk his clocks throughout New England, Terry was able to expand his production to about four thousand clocks per year by 1806. In 1816, Terry invented the shelf clock, which was easily transportable, being less than two feet high and attractive, with decorative scenes painted on the casing and face. It was also relatively inexpensive for a clock then, selling for about ten dollars (about $125 today).[25] Clock peddlers preferred to get bank notes or coins for their goods, while peddlers of lower-priced items, like tinware, were more likely to receive barter.[26]

With improvements in design and production methods, Terry and the other regional entrepreneurs produced a total of 15,000 clocks per year by 1820, establishing Connecticut as the clock-making center of the country.[27] Producing in such volume, manufacturers were depen-

The tactics of the lightning-rod agent, 1879. The top panel shows the smooth-talking canvasser describing the marvelous lightning rod, which he promises will safeguard the farmer's family and property. The bottom panel shows the burly "settler," who has come to collect the huge bill after numerous, unnecessary, lightning rods have been installed on all buildings. Note that even the dog's house has received one.

dent on peddlers to distribute their timepieces throughout the country. Some were shipped to shopkeepers or master peddlers in other states, who then sent canvassers around to sell the clocks to local farmers and townspeople. Other peddlers traveled out from Connecticut in early autumn, making new sales and collecting unpaid notes from the previous season before returning home in the spring.

The lightning-rod peddler also became a familiar figure beginning in the antebellum period. The device, invented by Benjamin Franklin, was common on rooftops by the mid-nineteenth century, particularly in the Midwest and regions prone to thunderstorms. The rods were made of brass or iron, adorned with decorative glass balls, and were mounted on the highest part of the roof in order to attract lightning and direct the bolt's current through a connecting wire safely to the ground.[28]

One of the largest lightning-rod manufacturers was Cole Brothers, of Mount Pleasant, Iowa. The company was founded by four brothers in 1849 and was originally known as the Franklin Lightning Rod Works. Cole Brothers hired teams of salesmen to comb farmlands and sell lightning rods, eventually securing representatives in Iowa, Missouri, Indiana, and parts of Nebraska, Kansas, Kentucky, and Texas.[29] Salesmen worked in the spring and summer, when rainstorms threatened and barns, filled with livestock and crops, were vulnerable. The newspaper *Prairie Farmer* commented on the seasonal nature of the job and revealed the popular image of the lightning-rod peddler as a man on the make: "In autumn, when muttering thunders retire southward . . . the lightning 'regulator' calls in his forces, his traps, his wagons and horses, disposing of the latter, or putting them out to board for the winter . . . But as soon as the zigzag streams of light dart athwart the spring clouds, and awaken the fears of the nervous, he, like the circus man, gathers his retinue and takes possession of the field of operations decided upon."[30]

Book Peddlers and Evangelicals

There were various other "hawkers and walkers" in early America whose work prefigured modern salesmanship. The selling, promoting, and preaching of ideas had an important place in a country with no established religious institutions and in which competition between political parties was intense. Traveling preachers, in particular, promoted the theme of self-transformation that would also be taken up by patent-medicine salesmen and peddlers of self-improvement guides.

Pamphlets and books, especially the Bible, were popular items for peddlers and preachers to carry. Evangelical preachers pioneered many techniques that salespeople would later adopt. George Whitefield, a famous eighteenth-century preacher, was indeed a "pedlar in divinity," as one of his contemporaries called him, traveling the country giving impassioned sermons and circulating his message in newspapers, pamphlets, and journals. Whitefield exploited the commercial revolution, made possible by improvements in printing and transportation, to advance his evangelical goals.[31]

In the late eighteenth and early nineteenth centuries, populist preachers revolted against the formal church hierarchies and polite styles of preaching.[32] Religious leaders used techniques of publicity and advertising to appeal to citizens.[33] Methodist circuit riders, in particular, invented a form of traveling salesmanship that had immediate commercial potential. By 1800 Methodists had established remarkable networks to spread their message. Their strategy relied on an army of over three hundred traveling salaried preachers, each working a circuit.[34]

The published reminiscences of James Erwin reveal the similarities between the Methodist circuit rider and the peddler, for Erwin preached as well as sold books on his travels. He started out as a traveling preacher in the early 1830s. "A 'plan' was given me [by church officials], which called for at least *thirty-six sermons* in four weeks, beside *extras* and *funerals*," he wrote. "This plan gave the name of each appointment, . . . the class leader's name at each place and any other church officer living there."[35] Erwin received an allowance for food and transportation and was given a standard salary of one hundred dollars; if he had been married, he would have received twice that amount. He earned additional money, as traveling preachers often did, by selling books on his trip.[36]

Circuit riders thought deeply about how to reach and convert souls in ways that foreshadowed how salespeople would talk about gaining customers. In his memoirs, which were intended to guide young missionaries, Erwin described his techniques. In one case, his fellow preachers encountered a farmer who was hostile to their cause. The preachers "opened their batteries" against him and challenged him to repent and pray, but they failed to persuade him. Erwin took another path, choosing to conquer the man with kindness. "One morning I went to visit him; found him alone working in his hayfield," Erwin wrote. "He gave me rather a rough reception, but I paid no attention to his ravings, inquired about his farm, how much hay he cut to the acre and so on. I told him that I needed physical exercise, and if he would get me a rake I would help him while I remained." Erwin worked hard until evening, and then was asked to stay for dinner. After eating—and gaining the man's confidence—Erwin then asked the man and his wife to pray with him, which they did, and so gained a follower.[37]

Erwin even sought to teach more general principles of persuasion, or conversion, in his book. At one point, a fellow minister told him that to convert souls it was better to go about his sermons with care and less impassioned rhetoric—that it was best to "catch fish" with "a silk line and a small hook" than a splashy large one baited with worms. Erwin, however, was an experienced fisherman who realized that "different kinds of fish required different" approaches: "If I wanted trout I would move quietly, but if I wanted chub I would splash in the water, because noise attracted them to the place and they preferred substantial bait."[38] Such commonsense lessons were similar to those in popular secular how-to-sell books published later in the century.

Some of the best-organized booksellers were those who worked for Bible societies. Both the American Bible Society and the American Tract Society maintained large sales forces that sold or gave away their publications. Russell Salmon Cook (1811–1864), an itinerant preacher, directed the activities of the American Tract Society for many years. Cook joined the society, which had been founded in 1841, and carefully trained a force of salesmen to sell religious publications. In 1856, the American Tract Society had 547 colporteurs working full-time.[39]

The American Bible Society, founded in 1816 in New York City, employed a large canvassing force beginning in 1820. Through the nineteenth century, the Bible society continued to strengthen its control over agents. In 1853, it produced a twenty-four-page manual of instructions.[40] The manual advised agents to keep a journal of their transactions. It also told them to send monthly statements to the home office and to include "a view of your proceedings of interesting incidents, good effects with Bible and Bible Societies, objections to the Bible Causes and kinds of oppositions met with, so that parts of this journal can be published. Treasure up interesting incidents and give them to us for the Record."[41]

Secular peddlers, as well as preachers, carried Bibles and spiritual tracts to sell. Religion dominated the antebellum book market.[42] But peddlers also carried the *New England Primer,* Webster's *American Spelling Book,* and the *Farmer's Almanac,* as well as some scandalous titles, such as the eighteenth-century novel *Fanny Hill; or, Memoirs of a Woman of Pleasure.*[43] They offered a wider selection of books than many stores, often loading them onto a wagon that could be opened up for display.[44]

As early as 1805, the Philadelphia publisher Matthew Carey, who hired peddlers to sell his books, noted that it was no longer possible to rely on simple retail sales in his own shop to stay in business. Instead, he had to turn to the "forced trade" by taking orders for books through traveling agents—he employed the colorful Mason Locke Weems, the most famous peddler in early America.[45]

Parson Weems, like Erwin, embodied the connections between traveling preachers and booksellers. Weems, who was born in Maryland, became an ordained minister in England before beginning his work as an itinerant preacher and book agent in the 1790s. For much of his career, he worked for Carey, not only selling books but also providing him with valuable information about demand and usually recommending that the publisher provide more colorful fare and a range of self-improvement literature.[46] Weems himself wrote many of the books he sold, including patriotic tales like his *Life of Washington* (1800), which popularized the fictitious story of Washington and the cherry tree, and moralizing tracts like *The Drunkard's Looking Glass*. But his stock in trade was the Bible. He wrote to Carey in 1800: "Thank God, the Bible still goes well; better, I think, than Washington . . . I am *agreeably surpris*[*e*]*d* to find among the multitude such a spirit of veneration for the Bible. Good old Book! I hope we shall live by you in this world and in the world to come!!" In many of the other letters to Carey, Weems pestered his publisher to raise his commission rate and to pay him more quickly.[47]

Other peddlers and itinerant salesmen, besides those carrying religious works, viewed their occupation in evangelical terms. The connection between selling and evangelism was particularly clear in sales of life insurance, a business with antecedents in church-operated societies that pooled money for the indigent. An agent for Connecticut Mutual viewed his task in such terms. "I returned yesterday morning from a short visit to Portland and Colchester during which time I have agitated the subject of Life Insurance," he wrote. "At Colchester I found the people (in the language of the missionary) in the most heathen darkness on the subject of Life Insurance, and very much in want of the stated preaching of the principles of our *faith*."[48]

An evangelical model of selling—in which selling was a form of conversion—helped salesmen steel themselves for the frequent rejection they inevitably faced and infused them with zeal for pursuing their targets. The idea of selling as a form of religious or spiritual conversion continued to exist alongside more secular approaches to selling. The roots of commercial salesmanship, argued Thorstein Veblen in 1923, were found in the history of evangelism: "The Propaganda of the Faith is quite the largest, oldest, most magnificent, most unabashed, and most lucrative enterprise in sales-publicity in all Christendom."[49]

Economic and Cultural Impediments to Trade

There were many obstacles, both economic and cultural, to the work of peddlers carrying tinware, clocks, books, lightning rods, and other items. Despite advances in canal and railway travel in early America, transportation and communication capabilities were still fairly limited.

Goods that were shipped might not arrive on time or might be damaged in transport. For instance, sending all-wooden clocks along water routes often resulted in swollen or warped parts. One peddler sent a note back to his employer in the 1830s: "Respecting the 30 Clocks Ship[e]d last fall they arrived in Ohio late this Spring . . . wires very rusty and many of them were Swelled So that they will no run until I whittle & Smooth the wheels."[50]

Along with difficulties of shipping and receiving goods, trade was also inhibited by the lack of a federal currency; until the National Banking Acts of 1863–1864 and the printing of greenbacks, state and private banks printed their own notes. It was difficult to know if the bank notes issued in one region would be accepted in another. In any case, the notes would be discounted a percentage of their face value when used in a state that was not home to the issuing bank. With notes being printed by many different banks in various styles, counterfeit currency was also an acute problem.[51] This, too, tended to increase the desire of parties to barter for goods or to sell and purchase them on credit.[52] In stores, clerks knew how to drive hard bargains, trading butter, eggs, or other items for goods, rather than using currency. Caveat emptor was the rule of the day.[53]

Another problem for peddlers was the imposition of state and county taxes on their trade. Regional storekeepers, who often resented the incursion of itinerants in their area, lobbied state legislatures to impose license requirements on out-of-state salesmen; these tariffs had the effect of inhibiting a national marketplace. As early as 1806, Virginia merchants complained that peddlers from other states were draining money from the commonwealth.[54] Pennsylvania passed a law requiring all peddlers selling goods of "foreign" (that is, out of state) manufacture to carry a license.[55] And Massachusetts enacted a hawkers-and-peddlers license act of 1846. While most licenses allowed peddlers to operate within an entire state, some fees were set at the county level. For example, the license to sell in Madison County, Alabama, was $39 in 1825.[56] The presence of these fees encouraged peddlers to move about surreptitiously to avoid having to pay them.[57]

Peddlers also faced cultural critics, and because they symbolized the growing market-based economy, the criticism leveled against them illuminates the cultural context in which they worked. Folklore recorded Yankee peddlers to be especially adept at swindling, selling fake nutmegs or hams that were made out of discarded wood from New England factories, or other deceitful items. Indeed, the word "Yankee" became used in the South as a verb meaning "to cheat."[58] Anti-Semitic attacks on peddlers increased as German Jewish peddlers became more common in the 1840s. Shopkeepers and other merchants who resented the incursion of Jews into their towns were among those who agitated for the enforcement of license laws.[59]

The peddler's rootless lifestyle and constant deal-making were among the reasons that some denounced the vocation. Writing in 1823, Timothy Dwight, president of Yale College, argued that the consequences of a life of peddling were generally "malignant." Dwight complained that too many young men from his home state of Connecticut were heading off in horse-drawn wagons loaded with goods. "Men who begin life with bargaining for small wares will almost invariably become sharpers," he wrote. "The commanding aim of every such man will soon be to make a good bargain, and he will speedily consider every gainful bargain as a good one. The tricks of fraud will assume in his mind the same place which commercial skill and an honorable system of dealing hold in the mind of the merchant."[60]

Henry David Thoreau found salesmanship an unnatural, wasteful force. In *Walden* (1854), Thoreau described the attempts of an Indian to sell baskets in Concord. The Indian strolled up to the house of a well-known lawyer but was turned away. The lawyer declined, saying he did not want any. The Indian found this unfathomable. "Do you mean to starve us?" exclaimed the Indian as he left the gate, thinking that he had done his part in making the baskets and that it was the lawyer's obligation to buy them. In short, the Indian did not understand salesmanship. Explained Thoreau, "He had not discovered that it was necessary for him to make it worth the other's while to buy them, or at least make him think that it was so, or to make something else which it would be worth his while to buy." Thoreau resented the need for such an ex-

change and the seller's attitude that propelled it: "Instead of studying how to make it worth men's while to buy my baskets, I studied
rather how to avoid the necessity of selling them."[61] For Thoreau, self-
reliance made salesmanship, with its attendant deception, chicanery,
and confrontation, unnecessary. The excessive consumption encouraged by salesmen was enervating and corrupting; it distracted individuals from the vital pleasures of life, like walking, reading, and con-
versing.[62]

Some criticized peddlers of a specific type. Thomas C. Haliburton
and Herman Melville singled out peddlers who introduced new products or technologies, like the shelf clock, into rural communities, or sold
goods whose efficacy was hard to prove, like lightning rods, insurance,
or patent medicines.

Haliburton, a Canadian who created the fictitious character Sam
Slick, delighted in satirizing the techniques of clock peddlers. He first
introduced Slick in 1835 in *Clockmaker; or, The Sayings and Doings of
Sam Slick, of Slickville*, which was followed by further adventures, such
as *The Attaché; or, Sam Slick in England* (1843), and *Sam Slick's Wise
Saws and Modern Instances* (1853). The stories of Sam Slick popularized
the image of the Yankee peddler as an overly clever tradesman. As Slick
himself admitted, the key was not to have great goods, but to know how
to sell them: "It is done by a knowledge of *soft sawder* and *human
natur*."[63] Slick used "sawder," or flattery, and other devices to sell his
wares. In one story, when the clock peddler reached the house of a
church deacon, he immediately began to praise the beauty and expanse
of the property and the deacon's health and vigor ("Why you are worth
half a dozen of the young men we see, nowadays"). One of the clock
peddler's tricks was to ask a farm couple simply to store a clock for him
while he went on his rounds. He would wind it up and place it on their
wall, knowing that by the time he came to retrieve it in a few months,
they would be accustomed to its presence and want to buy it. "We can
do without any article of luxury we have never had, but when once obtained, it is not in 'human natur'" [*sic*] to surrender it voluntarily," said
Slick.[64]

One of the most formidable critics of Yankee peddlers was Herman Melville. Melville described the tactics of a lightning-rod salesman in a short story published in *Putnam's* magazine in 1853—supposedly after a real-life encounter.[65] During a night of "grand irregular thunder," the lightning-rod peddler banged on the door of a farmer, avoiding the more "delicate" knocker. He was a "lean, gloomy figure" who carried his "polished copper rod, four feet long" in hand and looked like the Roman god Jupiter. Once inside, the gloomy salesman would not be swayed from his goal of raising the prospect's anxiety. "'For Heaven's sake,'—he cried, with a strange mixture of alarm and intimidation— 'for Heaven's sake, get off the hearth! Know you not that the heated air and soot are conductors—to say nothing of those immense iron fire-dogs? Quit the spot—I conjure—I command you.'"[66] Eventually the farmer decided he had heard enough and threw the peddler back out into the storm.

Melville created an even darker impression of itinerant salesmen in the 1857 novel *Confidence Man*, in which he depicted a satanic traveler aboard a Mississippi riverboat posing as an herbal medicine salesman, an agent of a coal company, and a collector for an Indian charity. In each of these guises, the traveler secured money from strangers by making false promises: the medicine would heal sickness; the stock in the coal company would appreciate; and the Seminole widows and orphans would be saved from starvation. Melville was writing about more than selling, of course. He saw an evil side to canvassers, equating their deceptions with false promises. For Melville, the trust and confidence of peddlers' victims were ultimately achieved through false or idealistic promises—such as guarantees to protect a house from heaven's thunderbolts or offers to cure illness with herbs.[67]

Legal records revealed that peddlers were, at times, capable of the worst types of swindling. In one state court case, an agent for Cole Brothers, the lightning-rod manufacturers, was sued for taking advantage of a farmer who was unable to read a contract without glasses. According to the case, the canvasser had "read, or pretended to read, the paper, but did not read anything about the price to be paid for the rods." The agent sold the farmer a lightning rod for a moderate price, but he charged an exorbitant per-foot rate for the wire to connect it to the ground. Using as much of this connecting wire as he could, the agent ran his bill up to an astonishing $404.25.[68] Other court cases reveal the "tricks" of atlas peddlers, who promised carefully drawn maps but delivered only hasty sketches, and nursery agents, whose seeds never sprouted.[69]

Peddlers were, therefore, seen as disruptive and disturbing figures by regional merchants and politicians, as well as by writers and clergymen. Unlike criticisms of selling and advertising in later decades that commented on the ubiquity of institutions that promoted products (through magazine advertisements, billboards, and a range of other methods), mid-nineteenth-century attacks on peddlers tended to concentrate on the work of individual agents combing the countryside. Here the peddler was an outsider, acting on his own initiative, and his actions—bringing in competitive goods from out of state, selling items of uncertain merit like lightning rods, and demanding trust (the true coin of the realm) in face-to-face encounters—had dangerous implications.

Fascinating Peddlers

Many peddlers, probably most, were hardworking and honest, but fictional accounts and legal records seldom recorded their side of the story. The diary of Abraham Kohn, who worked as a peddler in the early 1840s and later founded a Jewish congregation in Chicago, reveals that the farmers he encountered, like those faced by James Guild in 1818, were themselves shrewd bargainers who forced his prices down on every sale.[70]

Beginning in the 1840s, several entrepreneurs sought ways to overcome the impediments and suspicions that hindered peddlers' work. They began to study selling more closely and gave salesmen detailed instructions, while at the same time gathering more information from the field.

As mentioned earlier, in 1853, the leaders of the American Bible Society produced a twenty-four-page manual for their agents, which advised them to keep a journal of their transactions, send monthly statements to the home office, and collect descriptions of incidents that would be helpful to other Bible salesmen.[71] The "Instructions to Agents" was periodically updated. During the Civil War, a new 1864 edition came to nearly fifty pages.[72] This represented a transition from diary writings like Guild's to something more permanent and planned.

Salesmen and their employers in this period tried to make sense of the rules of persuasion. Even the critics of peddlers expressed fascination with their ability to sway an audience. Nathaniel Hawthorne recalled seeing a peddler holding the attention of a crowd at a college commencement. "I could have stood and listened to him all day long," he wrote.[73] Both Melville and Thomas Haliburton, author of the Sam Slick stories, made the peddler's techniques and language central to their stories. As one historian wrote, Melville portrayed the peddler's words as being like coins: exchanged so often, and so expertly, that they themselves became a medium of commercial exchange.[74]

The success of P. T. Barnum also testified to a general interest in the mid-nineteenth century to understanding methods of persuasion, trickery, and "salesmanship." Barnum was the most popular impresario of the period. He had learned to drive hard bargains in the early nineteenth century, when he had worked as a clerk in a country store and was required to accept payments in the form of butter, eggs, and hickory nuts.[75] His American Museum, in New York City, was packed with curiosities, such as the Feejee Mermaid, "a small amalgamation of dried and wrinkled skin, hair, and scales that looked as if it had once been alive."[76] Crowds flocked to Barnum's museum, not out of gullibility—the belief that they would actually see George Washington's 165-year-old nursemaid—but because they delighted in seeing his elaborate concoctions. His shows were intended to make people wonder if the exhibits were fraudulent or not; and if so, how the fraud was perpetrated.[77]

Both popular and professional interest in salesmanship and promotion continued to increase in the years after the Civil War, as manufacturers in several industries hired large canvassing forces and undertook to overcome impediments to canvassing. They harnessed new technology, tried to defeat interstate tariffs, drafted rules for successful selling, and put more salesmen on the road.

Selling Ulysses S. Grant 2

The Art of the Canvasser

After the Civil War, more specialized canvassers traveled through the landscape, visiting farmers or working out of stores. There were 53,500 hucksters and peddlers in 1880 according to the census: of these, 51,000 were male and 2,500, female (with many women working as book agents).[1]

Salesmen of petty goods—small, inexpensive, and easily manufactured items like books, atlases, and lightning rods—began to perfect their techniques. Traveling from farmhouse to farmhouse, they gained notoriety, especially in agricultural newspapers, for their aggressive sales pitches. "Atlas men work upon the vanity of the public; book men hold up the attractive bait of pictorial contents, and set forth the fact that the world is simply crazy over the particular work they may be selling," complained a contemporary critic. "Then there are the lightning-rod agents. People are often frightened into signing blind contracts full of hidden catches, which these agents present to them for their wares."[2]

Itinerant salesmen from other industries joined these petty-goods sellers on the road. Manufacturers of more expensive machinery, such as weighing scales, sewing machines, and harvesting equipment had begun to deploy canvassers by the mid-nineteenth century. These products were complicated to make and to operate, and they required explanation and service. The early sales strategies of these machinery manufacturers influenced selling methods at large companies throughout the twentieth century.[3]

But petty-goods manufacturers deserve attention, for they were particularly rigorous in working out intricate sales strategies designed to push farmers, or more often farmers' wives, to make a one-time purchase—or "transactional" sale. Several firms, especially in the publishing industry, developed large canvassing organizations that operated in several states.

Manufacturers who relied on canvassers tried to organize and control their sales force as best they could. Selling, like most aspects of business, was bound by a series of formal relationships—whether verbal agreements or written contracts—between employers and workers. Manufacturers hired salesmen either on salary or on commission and made alternative financial arrangements with them, sometimes paying for a cart or other equipment. Some manufacturers simply sold products to peddlers at a discounted rate. Others allowed them to purchase goods on credit. Such arrangements were common in the sale of items, such as books, that were ordered in advance and then paid for on delivery.[4]

But selling was also about the ability to navigate a series of informal rules, such as codes of human conduct and behavior and customs of politeness and courtesy. Canvassers had to master, and exploit, common customs of human interaction. After mid-century, manufacturers and other employers began to rely less on the wit of canvassers and adopted more systematic approaches, publishing sales scripts for distribution to their sales forces. These scripts codified the techniques (or, as critics said, the "tricks") of canvassing. The intention of the sales scripts was to help canvassers overcome the suspicion and reluctance of farmers. Such scripts revealed the canvasser's shrewd insights into the psychology of selling.

Book publishers and other manufacturers of small goods gave canvassers elaborate instruction kits, which both described the formal aspects of the job (compensation rates, territories to work, methods of shipping goods) and offered hints on how to handle the informal ones (how to talk to "prospects"). In a sense, these petty-goods merchants were manufacturers not only of products but of sales arguments as well. The sales scripts, with their cleverly imagined dialogue, describe a literary understanding of selling that resembled traditions of folklore and humorous stories, rather than the more analytical and quantitative approaches developed by sales managers in the twentieth century. These instruction kits, and particularly the sales scripts they contained, were an important step in the evolution of modern salesmanship. The scripts reveal the pressure on companies to train large numbers of canvassers quickly, and also, due to their length and complexity, underscore the difficulty in convincing customers to make a purchase. They show that the clear intent of canvassers was to persuade, rather than merely to provide information about the items they carried.

Manufacturers also introduced the idea of a sales campaign, which they adapted from the military model used in the Civil War: a large organization of soldiers, supported by wartime propaganda and vigorous money-raising efforts. For example, Philadelphia banker Jay Cooke organized several thousand agents to persuade Americans to invest in bonds in support of the Union cause.

In the early nineteenth century, the model for organizing large teams of canvassers had often been an evangelical one, based on the work of Methodists and other religious groups that had organized teams of preachers to proselytize. Instructions to book agents and other canvassers preserved the evangelical language, describing canvassing as requiring faith and a sense of duty. After the Civil War, instruction books were also often infused with the language of military campaigns, as manufacturers sought to rally canvassers to conquer reluctant buyers. Mark Twain mounted one of the largest such sales campaigns in his effort to sell the memoirs of Ulysses S. Grant.

Canvassers on the Landscape

Of the 13 million adult workers who made up the U.S. economy in 1870, more than half (about 53 percent) worked directly in agriculture as farm owners, managers, and laborers.[5] Not surprisingly, much of the commercial exchange of the period involved trading and shipping agricultural products. Farmers, agents, and merchants made use of the telegraph, steamship, and railroad to ship grain, cotton, and food products from individual farms to wholesalers and retailers. Beginning in the mid-nineteenth century, entrepreneurs and merchants established networks of warehouses and grain elevators and founded commodity exchanges, which facilitated the distribution of agricultural products.[6]

Canvassers frequently sold goods that promised to lighten the burdens of agricultural work, such as mechanical butter churners and incubators. They also sold packaged seeds, bulbs, roots, shrubs, fruit trees, and patent medicines. Printers and publishers, like Jacob Monk of Philadelphia, employed salesmen to sell books, maps, and atlases.[7]

Salesmen went by a variety of names in the years following the Civil War. *Canvasser* and *agent,* the most common terms, usually signified a salesman working on commission. Often, agents were employed to represent a publisher in the book trade, or, as in the case of insurance, to operate a regional office. After mid-century, *canvasser* became the term of choice for salesmen carrying petty goods door-to-door. These terms were applied loosely; *peddler, canvasser,* or *agent* could refer to any type of itinerant salesman. The overlapping of terms is understandable, for they all had a common goal: selling inexpensive goods directly to consumers.

The strategy of many small manufacturers was to hire large numbers of canvassers, pay them on a commission basis, and provide them with general instructions. Some of the more established manufacturers, like book publishers, hired general agents to supervise the selection of canvassers in specific regions; others simply advertised for canvassers in newspapers and hired them by mail. Salesmen went from farm to farm, often targeting the farmer's wife for the sale of their goods.

Book Agents

One of the most common figures on the landscape was the book agent. A number of eastern publishers began to hire canvassers to sell books by subscription—that is, to take orders for delivery at a later date, a practice that stretched back at least to John James Audubon, who sold his *Birds of North America* that way.[8] Tycoon Jay Gould, writer Bret Harte, and President Rutherford B. Hayes all peddled books in their youth. Daniel Webster sold Tocqueville's *Democracy in America* as a canvasser.[9]

Hartford, Connecticut, was by far the most important city in the subscription book-publishing industry.[10] At least a dozen subscription houses were located there in the 1860s and 1870s. Together they employed as many as fifty thousand agents per year.[11] The Hartford-based American Publishing Company advertised for disabled soldiers to act as representatives—it also employed youths, teachers, and retired clergymen.[12]

Books sold by subscription were often long, running six hundred to seven hundred pages, to give readers "their money's worth."[13] The staples of the subscription trade were religious books and self-help guides on home health care and legal procedures. Canvassers also carried new "success manuals"—large, illustrated, elaborately bound books that promised to teach young men how to succeed in life. They were written by ministers, educators, and professional success writers and had titles like *The Royal Path to Life.*[14]

Book peddlers also sold volumes that had to do with the Civil War and other historical events, such as Horace Greeley's *American Conflict*, Thomas Prentice Kettell's *Rebellion*, and Harriet Beecher Stowe's *Men of Our Times.*[15] Hubert Howe Bancroft hired canvassers to help him sell his multivolume histories of Central America, Mexico, and Texas. Bancroft schooled his canvassers in sales techniques and supported their efforts through newspaper advertisements and the distribution of pamphlets.[16]

Subscription book publishers transferred much of the financial risk onto the book agents. Most agents had to purchase the books they sold at discount and pay their own expenses in a job that entailed not just traveling through the countryside once, but also tracking down customers after the initial sale in order to collect payment.[17]

Many canvassers worked part-time, having answered advertisements in newspapers. And several book canvassers were women. Annie H. Nelles, who described her experiences in *The Life of a Book Agent* (1868), began her selling career by responding to a newspaper advertisement. She was given the territory of Peoria County, Illinois, and after paying $2.50 for her first book she received, for free, pamphlets, circulars, and an order book showing different bindings that were available for each book she sold.[18] She then began her rounds. Once a customer had agreed to purchase a book, Nelles placed an order with the printer, who sent books via express delivery. Nelles paid for the books at the express office and then went to collect payment from the customer. She kept the difference between what she paid to the publisher and what she collected from the subscriber, earning about one dollar on each book.[19]

The subscription book publishers competed directly with the retail trade. Agents were forbidden by their contracts from selling any copies to store owners. Through their persuasive methods, book canvassers were able to sell books for higher prices, sometimes getting $5 to $7 (or around $65 to $100 today) for a volume, when the retail trade generally sold books for closer to $3.50 (or under $50 today).[20] In 1874 the retailer George A. Leavitt and Company discussed how the presence of itinerant agents was demoralizing the retail book trade. "Where *we* reach 5 towns, *they* reach 500 or 1,000, and sometimes half-a-dozen agents in a town at once."[21]

Like other petty canvassers and peddlers, the book agent became a subject of criticism. The rural areas, some claimed, were flooded with cheaply made "gyp" books.[22] In *The Mossback Correspondence* (1889), Francis E. Clark noted: "Next to the long-suffering mother-in-law, the book agent probably is made a target for more cheap wit of the average newspaper variety, than any other modern mortal."[23]

To train an army of book peddlers, publishers mailed recruits a packet of instructions. "Canvassing outfits" included a cover letter, a contract between the canvasser and the publisher, a certificate of agency, a handbill of advice, a description of particular volumes, certificates of agreement and calling cards for customers, weekly report forms, order forms, envelopes addressed to the publisher, posters, and pamphlets with other titles. They also contained sample books and order books.[24]

The sales scripts, included in the outfits sent to canvassers, mapped out the different directions the sales process could go, predicting various customer objections and providing the salesman with handy responses. *Success in Canvassing: A Manual of Practical Hints and Instructions, Specially Adapted to the Use of Book Canvassers of the Better Class* was originally published in 1875 by Ebenezer Hannaford, who himself wrote books about the Spanish-American War. The manual was divided into sections that reveal the tone and direction of the account, taking cues from the military: "Organizing Victory," "Opening the Campaign," the "General Canvass," "Securing the Order," "General Management," "Practical Hints on Soliciting," "Weaknesses to Be Avoided," "Hints for Special Cases," "Answering Objections," and "Delivering Books."

The manual emphasized that salesmen needed to project a professional image and to consider themselves representatives of the company. It advised that success came only through persistent work and careful preparation. Agents were told to study the eighty short sections of the manual and "mark with pencil on the margin the paragraphs that strike you particularly."[25]

The sample books that canvassers carried to show to farmers were designed to whet the appetite. They never contained the entire text. If they had, not only could a customer have demanded to keep the copy, but he or she also would have had the opportunity to thumb through the volume and see the whole of its contents. Instead, by showing only a portion of the book, the salesman sold the mystery of what the book might contain.[26]

The key to a good canvass, the manual suggested, was to maintain control by holding on to the sample book. The agent was supposed to handle the "prospectus"—the name usually given the sample book—and not allow the prospect to touch it; doing so, according to the manual, would surrender control to the prospect. Language itself was not to be flowery, but "concise, direct, forcible." It was also important that the agent avoid discussion of the price. "NEVER mention the price until you have done your best in showing the Prospectus. If previously asked, *pleasantly evade* the question, (or, still better, *ignore* it). Say something like this: 'Well, most books, you know, of this size and finish sell at $— to $—; but we don't ask any such price as that.'"[27]

If the prospect offered any objection during the sales pitch, the manual contained ready answers. The agent was usually advised to handle these complaints by agreeing with the prospect—by stating that the objection was a reasonable one—but then turning the negative comment to the seller's advantage. It was not useful to argue with the prospect or to be too eager to dismiss a complaint. Winning arguments often meant losing sales.

The manual paid particular attention to lowering the suspicion of people who had been cheated by agents before. A number of objections, like the one quoted below from *Success in Canvassing*, indicate the number of cheaply made books on the market.

"*I bought* (some worthless book) *once, and was completely sold.*"

"Yes, that *was* a poor affair. No Agent of *good sense* and *good principle* ever could handle *that* book. That is one of the kinds of books we are *crowding* out of the market. People *discriminate* in buying books now, and I am *glad* of it; for it gives this work the *preference*. You will see (then go right on to show your book)."[28]

Note that the "answer" was not written about a specific book—in fact, the book itself was irrelevant, as the parenthetical remarks in the script make clear.

The details in these scripts underscore the differences between selling and advertising. Advertising reached a mass of people, delivering the message of the manufacturer or advertising agent. It produced no conflict and demanded no direct response. Selling, however, was predicated on give and take. Salesmen realized that people expressed themselves in predictable ways that were conditioned by politeness and other social conventions. When a prospect said "I need to think it over," she may have meant just that, but she also may have meant that she did not want to buy under any circumstance and simply wished the salesman would go away. Book agents were trained to counter these traditional methods of expression. The salesman might ask, for instance, "Just what is there to think over?"

Sales scripts reveal the types of argument that salesmen found most effective in countering popular conventions of speech. Often, in the years following the Civil War, sales pitches were designed to increase the anxiety of a "prospect," in particular the fear of loss of property. Lightning-rod salesmen told stories of families left indigent after a house and barn caught fire; life insurance solicitors recounted the plight of widows and orphans left penniless because the family was uninsured. Self-improvement was also a popular theme in sales pitches. Book agents sold success manuals as well as reference books on the law and health. Provoking status anxiety was another common ploy. Frequently when selling an item, salesmen mentioned that the prospect's neighbors had all already purchased it.

Taken together, the sales scripts of petty canvassers show that farmers, and other prospects, were particularly concerned with preserving their property and their status quo. This can be interpreted as a message about a specific historical context: in a time of great mobility, both social and economic, the fear of loss was more compelling than the promise of riches. But it also indicates a tendency that salesmen continued into the twentieth century (and one recognized by psychologists and behavioral economists): people are more risk averse when faced with the possibility of a loss than with the promise of a gain.

Sales scripts were heuristic devices, written to help salesmen solve the "problem" of selling. They also reveal, however, that selling was hard and that mere memorization of pat answers was not enough. The seller had to have something else—something harder to define: an energy, confidence, and enthusiasm. This was at the very heart of selling; the salesman had to be part "soldier," following orders, and part "evangelist"—not only a believer, but also one who would get others to believe. The salesman's tone was important, for it needed to be cheerful and not tiresome. The agent could not appear awkward or indifferent. "Aim to make your influence a *controlling* one," the manual advised.[29] Persuasion was a subtle art; gesture and nuance were critical. Little things, like twitches or hesitations, could break the sale.

The Campaign to Sell Grant's Memoirs

All the elements of standardized canvassing were employed in the campaign to sell Ulysses S. Grant's memoirs. Mark Twain helped to orchestrate the sales effort, which became one of the largest and most successful campaigns of the nineteenth century.

For the first thirty years of his writing career, Twain used subscriptions alone to sell his books, including *Innocents Abroad* (1869), which won him a national reputation, *Roughing It* (1872), *The Adventures of Tom Sawyer* (1876), and *Life on the Mississippi* (1883). Twain was not a sequestered writer but was actively involved in marketing his books. He paid attention to the cost of production and to the illustrations, making sure that the final product would be appealing, or at least intriguing, to the public.[30] Twain's nephew, Charles Webster, served as the general agent for some of Twain's books, and the author occasionally wrote him about canvassing strategy. On April 14, 1884, Twain instructed Webster: "Get at your canvassing early, & drive it with all your might, with the intent & purpose of issuing on the 10th (or 15th) of next December (the best time in the year to tumble a big pile into the trade)—but if we haven't 40,000 orders then, we simply postpone publication till we've *got* them. It is a plain, simple policy, & would have saved both of my last books if it had been followed. There is not going to be any reason whatever, why this book [*Huck Finn*] should not succeed—& it shall & *must*."[31]

Subscription selling could bring high financial returns. Twain's contract for *A Tramp Abroad* (1879) called for him to receive 50 percent of the profits. The American Publishing Company printed and sold 62,000 copies of the book at $3.50 apiece (about $60 today), bringing in a total revenue of $218,000 (about $4 million today). The company paid out to its general agents $112,000 of this; that is, they paid them on average around 51 percent. The general agents then passed along a portion of that money to the canvassers they had hired to sell the book. The company itself earned $106,000 from the book, or about $1.70 per copy. Out of the $106,000, the company had to pay its manufacturing costs, which were $41,540. This left a profit of $64,460, which, in turn, was split with Twain, who received about $32,000 (about $590,000 today).[32]

In 1884 Twain formed his own publishing house in Hartford with his nephew, naming it after Webster.[33] Twain was eager to earn more money from his own works and to publish and promote other projects—the first of which was Grant's memoirs. Twain learned that General Grant had agreed to publish, with the Century Company, an account of his experience during the Civil War but had not yet come to final terms with them. Grant's motives for writing the memoirs were largely financial; his brokerage company, Grant and Ward, had failed in May 1884 after his partner Ferdinand Ward engaged in fraud, and the failure had left Grant nearly broke. Twain visited Grant in New York to try to get the rights to the memoirs for his own company, and he told the former president that the terms offered by Century were inadequate. Continuing his feat of salesmanship, Twain eventually persuaded Grant to sign with Webster, promising him an astonishing 70 percent of the profits.

Grant started writing his memoirs in the summer of 1884, after learning he had cancer, and finished the two-volume project in less than a year. It was a tour de force. He worked on them, initially, at his house on 66th Street in New York City and, as his health declined, at a resort outside Saratoga Springs, New York. He usually wrote them himself, often in longhand; at other times he dictated passages to a member of his family. He was assisted by his son, Frederick, and by Twain and Adam Badeau, a former aide to Grant and an author of military histories. While there has been speculation about the relative contributions of Twain and Badeau to the text (Badeau himself brought an unsuccessful lawsuit, claiming he should have received greater credit and a larger share of the profits), most historians have concluded that Grant completed the task largely by himself. The *Memoirs*, which tell in great and personal detail of the Mexican War and the Civil War, are of outstanding literary merit. Twain himself, hardly impartial, thought them to be the best memoirs written by any general since Caesar—and others have agreed.[34]

While Grant wrote, Webster took long trips to secure agents in cities throughout the country. He sought out information on the character and financial standing of potential general agents, dismissing one who seemed "like a drinking man" and another who already seemed to have "too much on his hands."[35] Finding good salesmen who would stick with a campaign even after facing numerous rejections was difficult and would remain a problem for sales managers. Twain instructed Webster to concentrate on hiring veterans and encouraging them to wear their Grand Army badges, as they supposedly would be harder for prospects to turn away, given the subject matter of the book. He wrote to Webster, for instance, to make one well-known war veteran the general agent for the state of Kansas: "There are *80,000* Grand Army veterans resident in Kansas & Homer Pond is *Grand Commander.*"[36] Webster and Company ended up employing sixteen general agents and roughly ten thousand canvassers, two hundred of whom worked in New York and Brooklyn.[37] Twain wrote: "Canvassers must be given streets or *portions* of streets in New York—all outlying districts to be canvassed *first*—then the cream of the city to be given to those canvassers who have done the best." Twain also advocated for a script: "Furnish canvassers a list of truthful & sensible things to say—not rot."[38]

Canvassers took orders for the sets beginning in March 1885. Meanwhile, the situation for Grant and his family became increasingly dire as Grant's cancer advanced. Throughout the spring, the public was acutely aware of Grant's declining health. Grant hurried to get the book done, once dictating ten thousand words in one sitting. When he died that summer, the nation was plunged into mourning and canvassers went to work throughout the country.

Canvassers employed by Webster and Company carried a manual entitled *How to Introduce the Personal Memoirs of U.S. Grant,* which outlined a series of sales arguments. It was a thirty-seven-page booklet of instructions, which, the company advised, should be kept out of the prospect's sight.

"I called to give you an opportunity to see General Grant's book, of which so much has been said in the papers," the canvasser was instructed to begin.[39] The booklet told the canvasser to produce the sample edition, which showed the illustrations and selected text—but not, again, the whole thing. The pitch continued: "Each volume will contain 600 large octavo pages. Here is a fine steel portrait of the General, from a daguerreotype, taken when he was twenty-one years of age, and Second-Lieutenant in the United States Infantry."[40]

The canvasser then went on to discuss binding options, which began at a few dollars and went all the way up to $12.50 (about $230 today). "I presume it is simply a question with you as to your choice of bindings, as no American will want to have it said that he has not read General Grant's book, a work that will descend to your children and will increase in value with every generation."[41]

Canvassers could offer terms for partial payment and were instructed to remind the prospect of the pitiful need of the Grant family. "Get the prospect seated, in a fence corner, behind a stump, on the plow beam. Put the book right in his lap, but *you* turn the pages." Remember, the manual advised: "In leaving a house be careful not to turn your back to the family; retire sideways, keeping your eye on the good people, and let your last glance be full of sunshine." The booklet advised the agent to have "complete confidence" in himself and to remember that "enthusiasm is an essential ingredient in the composition of a salesman"—information repeated in almost every manual on selling.[42]

It also suggested that the canvasser compliment the farmer on his home and possessions, and it gave other general advice:

One of the strongest arguments that can be used to get a man's order is by telling him of his influence, and other means of flattery, or rather compliments, which should always be used in such quantities as will take well, and to be successfully done you must thoroughly inform yourself about the man before calling on him. If he has fine stock that he is proud of, mention what you have heard about them. Take a great deal of interest in them, and even express a desire to see them. Find out a man's weak points, and you can work upon them; and men who would not at first listen to you can often be thus interested.

Avoid men in groups as you would poison. It is better to lie still and do nothing than to go into a group of men to canvass. You seldom sell to a man you meet away from home or his own neighborhood, as when you call upon a man at home he is personally addressed, especially called upon, and his attention required, which is not the case if you run across him away from home.

A man living on a four corners or a crossing is quite an important man to get, for you can go in three different directions and you have an order from the last house.[43]

There were also instructions for collecting the money when the book was finally delivered. Here, the canvasser encountered an imaginary "Mrs. Higgins."

Mrs. Higgins: "You will have to take it along with you, sir, as I haven't the money to pay for it, and can't get it."

Salesman: (who has previously refused to be seated on the plea that he had some thirty or forty to deliver that day, and must be very expeditious.) "Very well, Mrs. H., I will sit down and rest a moment, while you go or send little Johnnie back to Mrs. Smith's and borrow the amount. Mrs. S. has just paid me for her copy and seemed to have plenty of money. She appears to be a most estimable lady, and is, no doubt, an intimate friend of yours, and would take pleasure in accommodating you. I can assure you, Mrs. H., that it would seriously inconvenience me to call again, and a number of my subscribers have borrowed the money for me, rather than put me to any trouble, or disappoint me." With this last remark, the salesman settles himself down into a chair, crosses his legs, takes his order book and pencil, and begins figuring up his accounts, as if he had not time to lose, and yet was determined to sit there all day.[44]

Canvassing in Towns.

Make a thorough canvass. See every family from whom there is a possibility of obtaining an order, on each street before leaving it, even if you have to call several times at some residences. It is not policy to canvass one whole side of a street before canvassing the other side; you should canvass one side of a street until you reach a crossing, then cross over and canvass the other side. The object in doing this is to keep within the influence of your names. Only a systematic, *careful* canvass *pays* and permits the agent to canvass a long time in a place.

What Door to Enter.

Always go in at the front door; it shows that you have respect for yourself and your business. Entering back or kitchen doors advertises a salesman's work as fit only for the less honorable parts of the house. Advertise your work as fit for the sitting-room, the library, or the parlor, by seeking to enter and introduce it there; show that you are a gentleman, and at home in the most honorable part of the house.

While on the steps of the house, soliciting admission, keep the hat on the head, merely touching it to the lady, until invited to cross the threshold. Upon entering the house, remove your hat as soon as you are inside. Be very easy and agreeable in your manners, but do not go to the extreme of making yourself too agreeable.

How to Leave the House.

In leaving the house be careful not to turn your back to the family; retire sideways, keeping your eye on the good people, and let your last glance be full of sunshine. When salesmen do not receive an order they feel like saying " Good day " and immediately turning their back to the family. This will never do. It is not retreating in good order, with colors flying. The proper way is to retire backwards or sideways, saying: "I think you will yet conclude to order a copy, and when you do you can drop me a line in the post office." While doing this shower smiles on the people as bountifully as though you had received an order for ten copies—then walk off treading the ground as though victory sat enthroned upon your brow; to do this will require much effort upon your part at first, but practice will make perfect, and it must be done. Though some hours, or even days, may prove financially fruitless, yet time will show all to be well at the close of the week, if you push steadily on.

A page from *How to Introduce the Personal Memoirs of U. S. Grant* (1885), instructing canvassers on how to enter and leave a house (go in the front door and, when exiting, never turn your back to the prospect), and reminding them to leave a good impression.

A strange and irritated man, camped out in the house, was no doubt threatening—and effective.

The campaign was a great success. Sixty thousand two-volume sets had been ordered by May 1885.[45] Of the 200,000 copies at the disposal of agents on publication day, 19,000 were shipped to San Francisco, 60,000 to Chicago to service the Midwest, 40,000 to New England, and 50,000 to Delaware and Pennsylvania.[46] By early 1886, the sale of Grant's memoirs had reached 325,000 in the United States. The sale in the South was moderate but in the West was enormous. Much of the profit went to Grant's widow. Twain wrote in December 1885: "We've bound & shipped 200,000 books; & by the 10th shall finish & ship the remaining 125,000 of the first edition."[47] In 1886 Charles Webster gave Julia Grant a check for $200,000 (just under $4 million today); the family eventually received a fortune of between $420,000 and $450,000 (over $8 million today) from sales of *Personal Memoirs.*

Other Petty Canvassers

Canvassers of other small goods received advice from their employers much like the instructions publishers gave to book agents. Dewey's *Tree Agents' Private Guide: A Manual for the Use of Agents and Dealers* (1876) included a dictionary of horticultural terms and a guide to the pronunciation of the names of plants and flowers. It instructed agents on the rudiments of salesmanship, which, the manual suggested, required making a good impression and the ability to separate oneself from the typical peddler: "An agent should feel the nobleness of his vocation, as if he was conferring a benefit rather than asking a favor." It reminded the agent that his "time belongs to his employers" and that he must not be "lazy." The canvasser's goal, the manual suggested, was to create a desire for planting various fruit trees by describing their beauty and value and by showing pictures of the trees in plate books. "Your *success depends* not on the demand which you may find for trees, but on your power to *convince* your fellow-men that it is the all important work of life, and one that should not be neglected another day."[48]

Some veterans formed canvassing companies. Captain T. H. Thompson and Major L. H. Everts started an atlas business at the end of the Civil War; they hired canvassers to travel through counties in Iowa to sell county maps—each map, on purchase, could be personalized with a depiction of the farmers' houses and land. The Thompson and Everts Company later expanded the business to other states and advertised heavily in newspapers, selling not only maps but also drawings of farmhouses and property.[49]

Other industries that employed canvassers also went through growth and standardization and conceived of selling as a military-style campaign. Henry B. Hyde, founder of the Equitable Life Assurance Society, devoted a great deal of time to developing the competitive spirit of his agency force. Once employed, agents received a stream of inspirational letters. Hyde gave special incentives to agents for developing new business, as he did in this 1869 letter, in which he promised a gold watch to the agent subscribing the most insurance. "The importance of making the new business of the Equitable Life Assurance Society for the year 1868 much greater even than it was last year, cannot be properly estimated," wrote Hyde. "My only solicitude is lest our matchless company of Agents, like a valiant army flushed with victory, should lapse into a condition of inactivity, through the very sense of invincibility, and make no steps in advance."[50] Subsequent letters continued to press home the same theme: persevere.

To gain further control over the sales process, Hyde and other insurance executives provided their agents with advertising support. Among the most common forms of advertising were short pamphlets published by independent insurance writers or trade magazines. These pamphlets told short, usually tragic, stories in which the main character suffered dire consequences for failing to purchase life insurance—wives ended up in the poorhouse, children were forced to forfeit an education. They were purchased in bulk by the major insurance companies, which would stamp their own name and logo on the cover sheets for distribution to potential customers.[51]

In his letters and his own book, Hyde warned of the dangers of remaining idle and reminded his agents that life-insurance solicitation was "dignified" and "important."[52] He equated sales success with extraordinary effort. In his own book, *Hints for Agents* (1865), Hyde wrote sales pitches to match every imaginable situation and instructed agents to insure all of their friends, persuade local clergymen to help insure their flock, and view all marriages and funerals as possible sales situations.[53]

One of the best-known figures on the road was the patent-medicine salesman, who carried such items as Lydia E. Pinkham's Vegetable Compound, Bliss Cough Syrup, Merchant's Gargling Oil, and Herrick's Sugar Coated Pills. These peddlers greatly increased in number following the Civil War. Medicine salesmen had been frequent visitors to the battlefields, hawking their remedies, which often contained a fair amount of alcohol, to wounded or traumatized soldiers. After the war's end, patent-medicine salesmen sought customers among the troubled, incapacitated, ill, and forlorn in both northern and southern society.[54] Some medicine salesmen worked as mere canvassers, carrying their products door-to-door, but others were entertainers who presented elaborate Wild West shows, menageries, bands, and pie-eating contests, all of which allowed them to deliver their message to crowds. The Kickapoo Indian Medicine Company held torch-lit shows that featured impassioned orations on the curative capabilities of ancient Indian remedies. In 1859, the patent-medicine industry's output was valued at $3.5 million (about $75 million today) according to the census figures; by 1904, it was more than twenty times that amount.[55] As historian James Harvey Young noted, these salesmen were true pioneers in modern sales and advertising, handing out almanacs, putting up roadside signs, and printing their claims in joke books and songbooks. "The big-scale patent medicine maker . . . was the first promoter to turn out a multitude of psychological lures by which people might be enticed to buy his wares."[56]

Canvassing and "How 'Tis Done"

As these examples and the case of Grant's memoirs show, the formal and informal aspects of door-to-door canvassing were well worked out by the 1880s. During the decades after the Civil War, there occurred not only attempts to standardize selling but also a growth in the literature warning against canvassers and increased legislation to address petty swindling. South Dakota, for example, passed a statute against wearing a badge of the Grand Army of the Republic "if not entitled to."[57]

Yet underlying much of this criticism was an interest in standardizing methods of canvassing and, more broadly, techniques of persuasion—or, as it was most often called, "influence." The word was a common one in late-nineteenth-century sales manuals. One book agent's manual pressed this point home: "It is recorded of St. Augustine that, being asked, 'What is the first step in religion?' he replied, 'Humility.' 'The second step?' 'Humility.' 'The third step?' 'Humility!' If you should ask the progressive steps of success in canvassing, we should have to answer with similar iteration, *influence,* Influence! INFLUENCE!! You can convince the most obstinate, mollify the most prejudiced, and win the most crabbed, if you can only bring to bear *enough* Influence *of the right kind.*"[58]

There were practical steps to gaining influence. One was to get a few leading names to head your list: "The majority of people are afraid to trust their own unaided judgment about buying a book; but show them that Dr. A. and Rev. Mr. B., or Judge C. and Professor D., or Colonel E. and Squire F.—have taken your work, and you will decide them immediately."[59] The manual advised securing orders from prominent townspeople and obtaining testimonials.

It also presented a theory, called "the philosophy of canvassing," about three basic steps of selling:

First—Gaining a Hearing
Second—Creating Desire
Third—Taking the Order.[60]

The "philosophy" is of interest because it assumes the need to "create" demand. The economy, from the viewpoint of the book agent, did not follow Say's Law, which states that supply creates its own demand. Demand was generated by sales agents and their clever arguments.

While sales manuals presented "influence" as a powerful economic force, the word had negative connotations in most late-nineteenth-century writings. "Influence" was a common subject in advice manuals written by clergymen and other moralists early in the nineteenth century to warn country boys who ventured to cities of the impending dangers that awaited them, and to suggest ways that they might avoid trouble. These advice books offered lessons on morals and personal appearance and, as well, gave tips on where to live and eat. They warned, in particular, about the dangers of confidence men and "painted" women and of the negative "influence" these types could have on their lives. Wrote historian Karen Halttunen: "As a force for good, influence was spoken of as a moral gravitation, a personal electricity, a cosmic vibration. But as a force for evil, influence was compared to a poison, a disease, a source of contamination and corruption."[61] Under the wrong influence, young men could fall into a life of luxury and sin.

The subject of influence was also a common one in books on pseudoscientific subjects like mesmerism. Itinerant mesmerists were familiar figures in nineteenth-century America. Loosely following the teachings of the Austrian physician Franz Anton Mesmer (1734–1815), who speculated that a person's health was affected by the flow of an invisible fluid throughout the body, mesmerists claimed to have the ability to heal. In highly dramatic and even emotional ceremonies, they would pass magnets or wave their hands over an individual to gain control of the magnetic fluid within. Talented mesmerists could sometimes lead their clients, often women, into trancelike or hypnotic states. Mesmerists, like confidence men, were often dismissed as masters of influence. In *"Confessions of a Magnetiser" Exposed!* (1845), for instance, La Roy Sunderland claimed to "set forth the real nature of that form of human *influence* hitherto most generally known under the name of 'Mesmerism,' and the useful purposes to which it may be applied."[62]

"Influence," like salesmanship, was a subject of fascination for critics as well as proponents—for many, the curious part was figuring out how it worked. This simultaneous fascination and criticism was apparent in Bates Harrington's *How 'Tis Done: A Thorough Ventilation of the Nu-*

merous Schemes Conducted by Wandering Canvassers (1879). On one
level, the exposé resembled the standard complaints of the agricultural
press. "For years designing men have preyed upon the rural sections of
the country, draining it of a large proportion of its wealth, as tribute to
cunning, lazy canvassing agents and downright criminal swindles of all
kinds," the preface states. "These men have become adept in the business of hatching schemes and setting traps, that are so shrewdly manipulated that their victims are in every community and almost every
household in the land." Harrington described in detail the tricks of the
subscription-book agent, the patent-right sellers, the fruit-tree vendor,
and the jewelry peddler. The nature of the crime rested not only in the
choice of victim (the poor farmer, mechanic, and laboring man), but
also in the calculated effort by the salesmen. "The work of canvassing
has been reduced to a *science*," wrote Harrington.[63] He used the word
"science" ironically, indicating either a carefully calculated "swindle" or
else the mastery of techniques of exerting "influence."

On another level, Harrington's book was as much an instruction
manual (as its title, *How 'Tis Done*, suggests) as an exposé. While the
book was presented as an antidote to designing men, it also served as a
guide for would-be salesmen and swindlers.[64] While condemning the
work of canvassers, Harrington's jeremiad revealed a great interest in
making sense of salesmen's methods. He viewed selling as a step-by-step
process, much like subjects described in the how-to manuals that were
so popular in the late nineteenth century.

Harrington's book was similar to a handful of other confessional accounts intended to make money through public curiosity. These books
included S. James Weldon's *Twenty Years a Fakir*, J. H. Mortimer's *Confessions of a Book Agent; or, Twenty Years by Stage and Rail*, and Jack
Greenberg's *Confessions of an Industrial Insurance Agent: A Narrative of
Fact*.[65] Weldon's *Twenty Years a Fakir* celebrated his years as a lightning-
rod salesman, book agent, and dealer in "notions." The choice of "fakir"
for the title suggested Eastern opulence and mysticism as well as "faker."
A fakir, he informed, was anyone who can "talk up" a product without knowing much about it. Together, these books defined tactics for

one-time selling: asking open-ended questions, using descriptive language or anecdotes to raise the anxiety of prospects, citing various prices (both high and low) to arouse desire, and holding or displaying in ways to excite curiosity.

Harrington's book summed up the ambivalence about salesmanship in this period. It showed not only the interest in methods of selling—out of which would grow the fascination with selling in the 1910s and 1920s—but also the need to camouflage this interest with moral outrage. Here the outrage was about the assault of urban values on rural life, the rehearsed and calculated nature of the salesman's pitch, and the larger issues of consumption—a continual contest pitting neighbor against neighbor in an endless cycle of envy and acquisition.[66]

Forging a National
Marketplace

3

The Traveling Salesman

At the same time that canvassers and book agents were testing their sales pitches on farmers, another kind of salesman was also traversing the landscape. Known as commercial travelers, traveling salesmen, or drummers, they were employed by large wholesale houses, though many also worked independently on commission.[1] They pursued a different type of customer than the canvasser, for they sold to businessmen and they favored a different strategy, being less interested in the psychological aspects of the quick transactional sale and more concerned with cultivating long-term relations with customers. Yet like the petty canvasser, they played an important role in the development of modern salesmanship.

Throughout much of the nineteenth century, most manufacturers did not distribute their own products. Instead, they sold their wares through large wholesale companies. Doing so relieved manufacturers of having to establish widespread distribution networks. Moreover, it allowed them to devote all their resources to improving production. Wholesalers were usually "jobbers"—that is, they did not sell goods on commission, but took title to them. They had traditionally operated in large cities along the eastern seaboard, but in the years after the Civil War they were able to operate in interior cities, such as Cincinnati, St. Louis, and most of all, Chicago. The railroad, telegraph, and steamship allowed the wholesalers to build large buying networks, which could gather goods from manufacturers in any part of the country and even abroad. The new modes of transportation enabled wholesalers to create far-flung distribution networks, which could send a range of manufactured goods, repackaged and divided into smaller lots, or "jobs," to distant corners of the nation.[2]

Working for the large New York and Philadelphia wholesale houses, traveling salesmen went south and west after the Civil War, armed with catalogs and trunks filled with samples.[3] They carried dry goods, whiskey, groceries, patent medicines, jewelry, chemicals, hardware, and leather goods.[4]

Collectively, these drummers sold the goods that stocked the general stores found at country crossroads. Such stores carried a tremendous range of items, including fruit and candy, nails and hinges, horse collars, lamps, cloth, wire, netting, cord, alcohol, paint, and leather goods. They were so densely packed with goods that even the ceiling was used for display.[5] The growth of these stores helped bring an end to the general pack peddler in the United States.[6]

Traveling salesmen came into prominence in the decades after the Civil War. Prior to the growth of the railroad, wholesalers did not send out agents. Instead, regional storekeepers and merchants would themselves visit large northeastern cities to select their goods. Representatives of the wholesale companies usually met the rural shopkeepers at train depots and tried to lure them to their employer's "house" or to a nearby hotel to show their wares. These "drummers" or "borers," therefore, remained in the cities waiting for regional merchants to come to them. It was only in the final decades of the nineteenth century that the large wholesale houses sent them on the road to "drum up" business.[7]

The number of commercial travelers increased with the growth of dependable railroad transportation. According to census figures, which tend to undercount itinerant workers, the number of traveling drummers increased from 7,000 in 1870 to 60,000 in 1890—though most estimates put these figures higher. The *New York Times* claimed that there were 95,000 commercial travelers in 1882.[8] There was increasing competition on the road. One hardware salesman who began traveling in the 1860s commented that he had encountered few salesmen on the road when he first ventured out: "All were glad to see me."[9] But as the hardware trade became more competitive in the ensuing decades, sales-

THE SALESMAN'S SNARES FOR HIS ANNUAL VICTIMS.

An 1881 cartoon from *Puck*, showing drummers from urban wholesale houses competing for orders from rural buyers. Drummers congregated at railway stations, hoping to persuade incoming shopkeepers, who came to town once a year to visit their wholesale houses. In order to secure orders, drummers took buyers for drinks or to the theater, before "carting" them off to look at goods. Things were changing by the time this cartoon appeared, however, as improvements in the railroad and telegraph enabled drummers to take to the roads themselves and seek out buyers around the country.

men bumped into one another more frequently on the road and on railway cars.

Drummers were relentless in their search for new stores to carry their lines. A couplet of the late nineteenth century testified to their resourcefulness: "Commercial travellers will find their way / Where wolves won't dare to stray."[10] They were the link between countryside and city and between wholesaler and retailer. By distributing manufactured goods, drummers hastened the growth of large wholesale houses and also of the factories that supplied them.

The wholesale firms that hired drummers operated at the center of the nation's economic activity. The goods they bought and sold came from all over the world. Improvements in transportation and communication facilitated the distribution of a range of new products that were invented or became popular in the late nineteenth century, including ready-made clothing, canned goods, and refrigerated foods. In 1860 it took three days to ship dry goods from New York to Chicago; in 1880 it took less than twenty-four hours.[11] Drummers connected the urban and rural areas, working out of their urban wholesale houses, collectively selling lumber from Wisconsin, cotton from Mississippi, guns and steel from Illinois and Pennsylvania, and cloth from Massachusetts.[12]

Unlike canvassers, traveling salesmen were the "nobility" of the sales trade, or at least they claimed to be, calling themselves "knights of the grip" and "ambassadors of commerce." In 1869, the Society of Commercial Travellers of New York City produced *The System of Commercial Travelling in Europe and the United States: Its History, Customs, and Laws*. The booklet recounted a history of a profession that extended from ancient civilizations to the present, chronicling a tale of increasing efficiency and freedom in the distribution of goods. "We all know that the history of commerce is but the record of the gradual advance of mankind from a condition of probation and barbarism to that of national well-being and civilization. We know that the earliest civilization—that of Egypt—flowed from commerce, and that the two great nations of antiquity, the Phoenicians and Syrians, were as distinguished in arts, inventions, and letters, as in trade."[13]

Commercial traveling was an occupation that defined itself as being "manly" and, indeed, was almost entirely filled by men. This was true in 1890 (when 99 percent of those in the profession were male) and continued to be so in the decades afterward. This was a higher percentage than the number of men in the labor force in 1890 (82 percent). Nearly all commercial travelers were white (more than 99 percent), and the overwhelming majority of commercial travelers were native-born (85 percent in 1890). In contrast, the number of foreign-born within the category of "hucksters and peddlers" was much higher (53 percent in 1890).[14] While canvassing had been taken up by Jewish peddlers and female book agents, traveling salesmen were almost exclusively white, Protestant men.

Working as a traveling salesman brought more prestige and money than did canvassing. In 1874 a lightning-rod canvasser gave up that line of work to become a traveling salesman, saying, "I am going from house to house selling something that I can never sell again. I tell them goodbye and never see them again. I want a business that will enable me to sell to a customer something that he will continue to use as long as he lives."[15] In the final decades of the nineteenth century, when skilled workers earned $500 to $800 per year (about $8,500 to $14,000 today), traveling salesmen made an average annual income of $1,200 to $1,800 (about $20,000 to $31,000 today). The very top salesmen with high commission rates earned much more—at a place like Marshall Field's in the 1870s and 1880s, talented salesmen earned $2,000 and the best, $6,000 (about $35,000 to $100,000 today).[16]

Backed by large wholesale houses, traveling salesmen developed extensive buying and distribution networks.[17] Successful drummers amassed a fair amount of power through their personal connections with retailers. When drummers left the employment of a wholesale concern, they were sometimes able to take their clients with them; they regarded the customers as their own, rather than as belonging to the firm.[18] Drummers also knew a lot about business trends and the workings of credit. Indeed, commercial traveling served as a school of business for young merchants. William H. Baldwin, president of the Young

Men's Christian Association of Boston, said in a speech that commercial traveling promised great opportunities for the country's youth.[19]

For traveling salesmen, selling had a large geographic and logistic component. Rather than gaining a single sale, drummers spoke of "making" a town, which entailed venturing to a new destination and capturing the trade there.[20]

Commercial travelers redefined the image of salesmen. Seeing each other frequently on train cars or hotel lobbies, they formed associations and clubs of traveling men and also joined late-nineteenth-century fraternal organizations, such as the Masons and Odd Fellows. They celebrated the "manliness" of their trade in rituals, jokes, and stories. Their work, as they saw it, was about conquering towns and building up the nation's commerce by packing and unpacking their heavy trunks filled with a cornucopia of goods. To their critics, the overt emphasis on manliness meant that traveling salesmen were aggressively shouldering out local businesses and seducing farmers' daughters at every opportunity.

Drummers also helped to draft new rules of salesmanship, which they regarded as a form of commercial adventure that could have great reward. Skillful selling was not based on trickery but on establishing trust with the customer—trust that had to be developed over time and through offering advice about business. This, at least, was the lesson offered by Saunders Norvell, a hardware agent profiled in this chapter. The most important requirement, wrote Norvell and other drummers, was experience. Years on the road taught drummers how to judge people; a good traveling salesman was widely thought to be capable of "reading faces." Some authors tried to capitalize on this by publishing guides for novice traveling salesmen that were based on physiognomy and phrenology. But for traveling salesmen, salesmanship was still something of an art, based on knowledge of their product and of human nature. For them, the "science" of selling meant more the creation of a "system," which combined their own experience and personal connections with practical details of commerce, such as credit reports, shipping schedules, and express costs.[21]

Knights of the Grip

The largest wholesalers, like Marshall Field's (now a large retailer), were major businesses in the late nineteenth century. They often had a common structure, with departments for the purchase, storage, sale, and shipment of goods. Wholesalers had extensive, even international, buying networks that purchased products from a range of manufacturers.[22] Buyers usually set the price to be paid for goods and the price at which they were to be sold—though salesmen often had leeway in setting final prices. Wholesale houses also hired operating managers who tracked the actual shipment of goods—sometimes from hundreds of small manufacturers to thousands of customers.[23] A credit and collections department gathered information from the credit-reporting agencies and from company salesmen in order to determine the terms to set for individual customers. By the 1870s, the credit-rating agencies R. G. Dun and the Bradstreet Agency (which were later to merge) were active enterprises. Dun's agency employed some ten thousand reporters or investigators (one of whom was Abraham Lincoln) and received about five thousand requests per day for information.[24]

Salesmen were monitored and evaluated by a general sales manager. Large wholesale houses hired assistant sales managers to be in charge of different territories. Wholesalers tended to employ much smaller sales forces than those used by the canvassing organizations that sold directly to farmers, for they had far fewer customers—comprising storeowners and regional wholesalers. A sales department often included an advertising office that put together the company catalogs and occasionally placed ads in newspapers.

Unlike petty canvassers, who were often hired by mail or after a quick interview, drummers often worked their way up through the wholesale house in another capacity. This was necessary, for wholesalers entrusted drummers with far greater responsibility than canvassers, including the authority to grant credit to retailers. Also, unlike the petty canvassers, traveling salesmen were often given a large territory to work.

The "formal" arrangements between wholesalers and drummers featured territorial assignments, compensation rates, and credit allowances. Drummers were responsible not only for ensuring the flow of goods, but also for supplying information. They filled out order forms and credit reports, sending information back to the wholesalers. Their work combined selling and advertising and included distributing flyers and hanging posters at crossroads, at church gatherings, or whatever location they could find.[25]

When commercial travelers visited shopkeepers, they left behind trade cards. Some of the techniques used on these brightly colored cards were eye-catching examples of "salesmanship in print." For instance, in 1880, Buckingham's Dye for the Whiskers trade card featured an illustration with a pull tab that switched the color of a man's beard from white to brown.[26] Traveling salesmen also helped shopkeepers set up store counters and window displays and offered advice on promotions.[27]

Sales managers created compensation schemes to motivate traveling agents and induce them to work in ways that would satisfy the interests of the firm. This often called for a mixture of salary and commission. Agents working solely on commission tended to call on "sure bets" and were less likely to strike out into new territory. They neglected writing reports and doing promotional work, or they tried to overstock merchants in order to collect a big paycheck. For these reasons, by the late nineteenth century many houses came to prefer paying salesmen a salary, with some additional compensation based on commission. If they wanted salesmen to push a particular item—say, a new style of cloth—they could attach a higher commission rate to its sale. Many employers also came to favor reimbursing salesmen for expenses rather than giving them a set daily allowance, a strategy that encouraged them to skimp by staying in cheap hotels or taking less expensive trains.[28]

The sales techniques, or "informal" rules, governing the work of the traveling salesmen were subtler than those regulating the canvasser. Unlike book canvassers, traveling salesmen tended not to work from transcribed sales scripts, and their pitches were not nearly as intricate. One former traveler recalled:

I had, before starting on my first trip, asked my employer for instruction regarding the most satisfactory method of approaching a prospective customer. My employer declined to give me any advice or instructions, remarking that there could be no fixed rules, and that if I were guided by circumstances, I would doubtless find out for myself the most successful method of introducing myself to secure a favorable hearing.[29]

Nor was there much further instruction from the home office while the drummer was on the road—and drummers were often traveling for months at a time. According to George Olney, who traveled for a paper and stationery wholesaler in the mid-nineteenth century, "Sometimes you'd get instructions which were not plain or which didn't fit the case and which to-day you'd get straightened out in a few hours. It used to take as many days to unravel the tangle."[30]

Wholesale drummers, then, developed a particular sales strategy that suited their goals. While petty canvassers formalized techniques for one-time selling, wholesale drummers sought to build a lasting relationship with customers. Olney noted, for example, that traveling salesmen had to be sociable. "The traveler who was a good mixer, had an engaging manner, had the arts of popularity, was the man as a rule who got the most merchants coming to his house in the city," he wrote. Olney's territory comprised the entire South. "The main stores . . . were at the crossroads in those days," he noted. "I'd drop in on one of them that I had never seen before and introduce myself and present my card. Then a bottle of something would be brought out and we'd get acquainted."[31] Drummers were "big personality" sellers, in part because the goods they sold were often undifferentiated from what other salesmen had to offer—hence, they felt, their own personality could make the difference. The latest joke and tale picked up on an overnight Pullman or culled from a drummers' magazine was a tool of the trade.

Drummers' efforts to make lasting connections with customers were as much a strategy as the "hard sell" approach of the petty canvassers who brought their goods directly to the consumer. It was perhaps the cleverest strategy of all: not trying to sell anything at first, but merely having a drink or a chat. *Commercial Travelers Magazine* noted that the drummer's "smile, so well-known by experienced merchants and so often noticed by press wits, has become, in a way, a trade-mark."[32]

Moreover, the idea that they would be calling on the same customers repeatedly over the years encouraged drummers to be careful in their dealings, and not, for instance, to overload merchants with merchandise that would sit unsold—though, of course, there were many who engaged in unethical practices.

"I developed into an excellent salesman," explained the main character in Abraham Cahan's *The Rise of David Levinsky* (1917). "If I were asked to name some single element of my success on the road I should mention the enthusiasm with which I usually spoke of my merchandise. It was genuine, and it was contagious."[33] But there was more to drumming than enthusiasm. In their work, drummers relied on many small publications to facilitate trade, such as town directories of businesses, credit reports, hotel guides, and train schedules. By developing a form of salesmanship based on geniality, on the one hand, and gaining a mastery of the flow of goods through the marketplace, on the other, they helped standardize methods of selling goods. In doing so, they built commercial networks that became the most important distribution channels in the economy.

The Variety of Wholesalers

Mid-century wholesalers, and the drummers they hired, tended to specialize in distributing one line of goods—such as, for instance, dry goods, groceries, hardware, liquor, or paints and varnishes. Salesmen for these concerns typically sold all the products in that particular field, which often added up to hundreds, or even thousands, of items.

Almost every industry had its own trade journal. Grocery wholesalers and drummers read the *Grocer's Criterion* (1873–1912), or one of its competitors; confectionery wholesalers leafed through the *Confectioners' Journal* (1874–1953) and *Candy and Ice Cream Retailer* (1889–1927). Most of these trade journals began publication during the late nineteenth century as wholesalers came to dominate the economy: *Dry Goods Guide* (1898–1921); *Dry Goods Reporter* (1871–1929); *Shoe Trade Journal* (1893–1910); *Boots and Shoes* (1882–1901); *American Furniture Gazette* (1880–1902); *Chicago Lumberman* (1897–1929); *Music Trade Indicator* (1878–1915); *Hardware Dealers' Magazine* (1893–1929); *Implement Age* (1892–1918); *Wine and Spirit Bulletin* (1886–1918); *American Pharmacist* (1885–1890); *Bulletin of Pharmacy* (1887–1928); *Drug Bulletin* (1879–1933); *American Jeweler* (1882–1929); and *Jeweler's Weekly* (1885–1900).[34]

These journals carried stories celebrating commercial traveling—and carefully avoided the term "drummer," which sounded unprofessional. In 1875 the *Confectioners' Journal* noted:

> Commercial travelers are more numerous today in all lines than ever before. Whenever you see a smart, active man going from store to store in suburban cities talking with the proprietor confidentially, and producing a memorandum book in which he makes notes from time to time, that man is a commercial tourist, as we call ourselves for fun, and is doing as much business in his way for his house as they do for themselves. No firm can get along without them.[35]

The magazines also contained articles about new machinery or popular products, and they featured want ads for salesmen and business directories.

The frequency with which drummers visited their customers varied according to the type of commodities they sold: those selling groceries tended to see their customers once a month; drugs and other pharmaceuticals, once every two months; dry goods, two to four times per year; and shoes and leather goods, twice per year.[36] If the products were small, drummers carried samples from store to store. Otherwise, travelers set up a display in a hotel room, using either their own room or a special one reserved for that purpose—and many late-nineteenth-century hotels had drummers' showrooms. Because of the variety of goods sold, the sample cases and trunks were often quite large and burdensome. George Marshall, in *O'er Rails and Cross Ties with Gripsack*

(1892), wrote, "Often a commercial traveler has to carry around with him as many as twenty trunks, weighing from 4,000 to 5,000 pounds."[37]

Drummers for confectionery wholesalers carried catalogs as well as samples of candy. Confectionery wholesalers, such as M. E. Page of Chicago, sold a range of goods that included glucose, grape sugar, potato starch, nuts, oils, and vegetable colors. E. Greenfield's Sons and Company of Philadelphia sold mixed candies, gumdrops, and penny specialties. Davis, Warner and Merritt, also of Philadelphia, dealt in what were considered "foreign" fruits—oranges, bananas, pineapples, coconuts, and grapefruits.[38]

As in many other industries, drug wholesalers did not send out traveling salesmen until after the Civil War. But they then began to rely on traveling salesmen to advertise medicines as well as chemicals and extracts.[39] Wing and Evans of New York City specialized in sodas and bleaching powders; the Missouri Chemical Works of St. Louis, oil vitriol and acids. Drug salesmen carried catalogs and sample cases of pills, chemicals, powders, herbs, roots, and seeds.

The best-known and most powerful wholesalers were in dry goods. Their extensive merchandise included linen, flax, velvets, silks, twills, and cottons.[40] Alexander T. Stewart's, in New York, was the nation's largest dry-goods distributor at mid-century. It opened both wholesale and retail departments. By 1870, the firm had annual sales of $50 million (about $685 million today), $8 million of which were in retail; at the time it employed two thousand people. H. B. Claflin and Company, also of New York, was of comparable size. Chicago, with Marshall Field's, and Philadelphia, home to Hood, Bonbright and Company, were other dry-goods centers.[41]

Though the Marshall Field's Company was somewhat late in employing drummers, it developed an organized wholesale sales force that proved critical to its success. When Marshall Field himself first arrived in Chicago in his early twenties, he worked as a clerk for the city's largest dry-goods wholesale house—Cooley, Wadsworth and Company. Field was soon sent out as a salesman, traveling through southern Iowa on horseback from town to town. He proved adept at this trade and eventually rose to be a partner in the firm before the company dissolved in 1864. The following year, Field and his partner, Levi Leiter, took over the management of the well-known dry-goods wholesale house of Potter Palmer. Palmer had gained a good reputation in Chicago through his frequent advertisements in local papers and his courteous policies to customers, such as a then-unheard-of "money-back guarantee of satisfaction"; Field and Leiter continued these policies. They also separated themselves from the bartering process that many shoppers found distasteful by instituting a one-price policy.[42]

In 1867, the two partners bought out Palmer, and the business became Field, Leiter, and Company—although Palmer remained important, renting them a prominent building on the corner of State and Washington streets. Field and Leiter continued to operate both a retail and a wholesale business: in 1867, total sales were $9.1 million (about $110 million today), of which $7.6 million were wholesale; in 1872, total sales were $17.2 million (about $250 million today), of which $14.0 million were wholesale.[43]

Marshall Field's used its sales organization to compete with New York dry-goods wholesalers. At first, Field insisted that shopkeepers come to Chicago to examine goods at his store. In 1877, however, he started a small-scale sales force of three people to sell carpets. Field's carpet salesmen proved a great success, and the money the company spent on "country traveling" increased to $142,940 (about $2.8 million today) in 1893. Historian Robert W. Twyman described a typical traveling salesman at Field's:

> Setting out with his grips, a couple of trunks-full of samples or "swatches" of goods, and his vest bedecked with lodge emblems, the Field traveling man journeyed patiently and laboriously from one town to the next within his allotted territory. Arriving in town, he engaged a room at the local hotel and one of the other hotel rooms. Having several days earlier sent an advance card to each of the merchants in town notifying them that he would be there, he was now ready for business.[44]

Eventually Field came to employ two types of traveling salesmen—the "general lineman," who sold a great variety of goods, from cloth to toys to jewelry, and covered a discrete territory; and the "specialty sales-man," who sold a particular high-quality product, such as lace, linen, or leather goods.[45]

Despite the various types of traveling men, many interests drew them together to form associations and clubs. Traveling salesmen's associations lobbied for legislation against unsanitary conditions in hotels, such as the use of unsanitary roller towels in common restrooms, and for well-lit train platforms.[46] According to a contemporary source, the worst of the hotels were "dirty and noisy, the food musty and loath-some, the servants negligent and supercilious, the bedding greasy and foul, the sheet unchanged from the last occupant, and the guest goes to bed in his drawers and with a haunting of vermin. The office and ad-joining bar-room is often a loafing place for the 'Smart Alecks' of the town, who criticize each arriving guest."[47] The Associated Commercial Travelers of America sought other transportation improvements, such as lighted stations. "It is a positive catastrophe to have to wait for a late train at night in many of the smaller towns," wrote one member. "The stations are usually so dimly lighted that it is out of the question to read anything. In the Spring and Fall these same stations are very apt to be without heat. This means positive discomfort; sometimes it means pneumonia and death."[48]

Among the most important undertakings of travelers' associations was their successful fight to overturn licensing laws—the same laws that hampered the work of peddlers and canvassers.[49] A Baltimore merchant described the severity of these fines in 1886, noting, "If we send a man from Baltimore to go through the South we have to pay over a thousand dollars in annual licenses for him." Drummers did their best to circum-vent these laws. Some mailed their sample cases ahead so as not to ap-pear like salesmen and then set about their practice surreptitiously. Antilicensing groups, such as the New York State Commercial Travellers Association, the Michigan State Commercial Travellers Association, and the Western Commercial Travellers Association, lobbied for an end to such fees. The Supreme Court proved to be their ally, ruling against the imposition of licenses in *Ward v. Maryland* (1871), and again in *Robbins v. Taxing District of Shelby County* (1887). The latter case came about when Robbins, a Cincinnati drummer selling stationery in Memphis, sought the right to sell to customers outside Ohio without having a license. Though the Court ruled against license requirements in both instances, it did not entirely put an end to them.[50]

The Society of Commercial Travellers (New York) and the Merchants and Commercial Travellers Association (Chicago) were formed as anti-licensing groups in 1869. The Society of Commercial Travellers published a report arguing their case, which stated: "The history of commerce is but a record of the gradual advance of mankind." In trying to overturn license laws, "the question we seek now to discuss, is that of hampering, binding, stifling, and preventing, not only the operations of trade, but the very interchange of ideas and intelligence between two different sections of the same country."[51] The report was one of the earliest, fullest celebrations of the commercial traveler. It expanded the claim for the drummer's role beyond trade to the promotion of a national culture through the exchange of ideas among regions of the country.

The increase in the numbers of commercial travelers spawned a number of additional organizations, among them fraternal insurance societies such as the United Commercial Travelers of America (UCT) and the Travelers' Protective Association of America (TPA), as well as societies created to provide homes for indigent and retired travelers. Each of these had their own trade magazines, including *Sample Case: The Journal of the Order of the United Commercial Travelers of America* (Columbus, Ohio, 1891); *T.P.A. Magazine: The Journal of the Travelers' Protective Association of America* (St. Louis, 1897); and the *Commercial Traveler's Home* magazine (Syracuse, New York, 1893).

Drummers' groups served a social function in a lonely occupation. In January 1902, roughly a decade after its founding, the UCT had a membership of 17,143. Members paid roughly two dollars every three months for accident insurance. But membership in the "Grip and Crescent" brought more than coverage; it provided, or at least promised, what drummers so actively pursued: "social prestige," manly ritual, and the "unqualified respect of the best citizens, regardless of faith or creed"—but evidently not race, because membership was limited to whites.[52]

The UCT held frequent conventions. On Saturday, December 28, 1902, a "brother" from St. Paul, Minnesota, reported of one event: "After the initiatory ceremonies were concluded we were highly entertained with music, songs, dancing, and an all-round high-class vaudeville. The merriment started promptly at 8 o'clock and continued until long after midnight." These notices cast the image of the drummer as a man with a great appetite. One noted, "The way cold turkey, cold ham, baked beans, hot coffee, etc., disappeared would have surprised any one but a traveling man." The commercial man was also temperate; no alcohol was served.[53]

Fictional stories in *Sample Case* reinforced the idea of the traveling salesman as responsible and honest, more often swindled than swindler—a theme adopted by sales managers at manufacturing concerns when referring to their own forces. In the story "The Reformation of Bonner," it was the commercial traveler who was plotted against. Bonner was "reformed," having given up drinking and gambling. But two thieves aboard a Pullman stole Bonner's sample case, filled with jewels, and switched it for an identical one, containing worthless rags, while the drummer was busy reading the train schedule.[54] Fictional stories in trade journals also told of drummers' remarkable energy. They would know everyone in town two days after arriving; according to one tale, on a two-hour layover, a drummer made five sales, joined the local fraternal club, courted a girl, got married, noted that it was election day, campaigned, and got elected mayor by eight votes.[55]

Like members of other fraternal orders and societies that flourished in America from 1865 to 1900, those in commercial travelers' organizations forbade alcohol at their meetings and engaged in rituals, which at times included medieval imagery (knights, swords, crowns, and shields) and hierarchical titles for officials (masters, nobles, and chancellors). Members also participated in elaborate initiation rituals, which were intended to show their commitment to the society and prove their manly courage.[56] One applicant to the UCT earned his membership by walking along a rocky and foul-smelling path (the odor reminded him of "stale eggs") before reaching a summit containing the messages of the UCT—in this case, "Unity, Charity, Temperance." The secretary of the local order explained the purpose of the ordeal: "Bro. Kitch was reminded of some of the hardships which a salesman encounters when he is guilty of unbusinessmanlike methods, and tries to make a customer believe that cabbage is good when it is rotten."[57]

Drummers' groups thus began to recast the role and image of the salesman and answered some of the common criticisms of middlemen and nonproducers. The traveling salesman was not a "nonproducer." His economic contribution did not grow up out of the soil, like the farmer's, but spread across the nation with the circulation of goods. Fraternal orders of drummers also equated the selling of goods with the spreading of Christian civilization. The Gideons, a group organized in Wisconsin by traveling salesmen in 1899, pledged to band together for personal evangelism and service for the Lord; in 1908, using funds from churches, they began to place Bibles in hotels, ships, schools, and penal institutions as they toured about the country for work. Former Kentucky governor J. Proctor Knott, at a speech to the Louisville Commercial Club in the 1880s, described the salesman as a "Commercial 'Evangelist' . . . who puts aside the endearments of home and family, and goes bravely out into the world on his Master's work, defying discomforts, disease, danger and death."[58] Unlike canvassers, who sometimes used the term "evangelist" to describe their role in converting individual customers, drummers' organizations preached the advantages of commerce itself.

Saunders Norvell, Hardware Drummer

Saunders Norvell worked as a traveling salesman, and later as manager, at the Simmons Hardware Company of St. Louis. Simmons was a large company, with seventy salesmen in the 1880s and two hundred by the turn of the century; it eventually operated in all parts of the world and had assets of $16 million in 1915. Simmons, like other Midwestern wholesale houses, fought especially hard to supply western markets with lumber for the growing cities.

In the early nineteenth century, most hardware wholesalers were located in eastern seaboard cities, but, with each passing decade, they began to operate farther from the coast. By the 1850s, hardware wholesalers had emerged in Cincinnati, Pittsburgh, St. Louis, and Chicago.[59] Many of the early hardware houses had three partners, such as Farwell, Ozmun, Kirk in St. Paul; Kelley-How-Thomson in Duluth, Minnesota; and Hibbard, Spencer, Bartlett in Chicago. Typically, each partner carried out a different function, one handling sales and marketing, another controlling the purchase of goods and operation of the warehouse, and a third running the office and overseeing the accounting and finance.[60]

As in other industries, the sale of hardware was affected by improvements in transportation and communication technology. In the early nineteenth century, hardware wholesalers generally remained sedentary and let customers come to them. In the years after 1870, however, hardware wholesalers began to rely on salesmen to travel to customers. Hardware drummers were common in the mid-1880s, when Saunders Norvell started to travel. By 1896, according to the National Hardware Association, 75 percent of hardware merchants' sales were made by traveling salesmen; the remainder was accounted for by retailers, who either visited the wholesale houses themselves or ordered products by mail.[61]

Like other members of his traveling fraternity, Norvell made seasonal trips. In the late summer and early fall, hardware drummers supplied goods for harvesting and hunting. In the early spring, they sold farm implements for planting and construction materials for building. Most hardware salesmen carried only catalogs, though some supplemented them with samples. They provided services to the retail merchants, particularly those just starting in the hardware business, for they were knowledgeable about products, credit, and techniques for tracking inventory.[62]

Norvell spent most of his life in hardware wholesaling. He was born in Canada in 1864 and grew up in St. Louis. At age seventeen he began working as a clerk at the Simmons Hardware Company, then a local concern. He remained at the same firm for thirty years, eventually becoming its vice president. During his years at the company, he worked as a traveling salesman (1883 to 1892) and sales manager (1892 to 1898). He enjoyed his work on the road, was a "good mixer," and was also devoutly religious.[63]

Simmons listed thousands of items in its catalog: all kinds of ammunition, anvils, augers and bits, awls, axes, balances, and bells—handbells, doorbells, cowbells. Blocks, bolts, boring machines, and braces made up just the beginning of the list. There were more than thirty different types of hammers and over eighty kinds of hinges, as well as dog collars, drawing knives, egg beaters, paints, wires, and assorted wrenches. Hardware was a large category of goods. As the saying went: "If you can't eat it, and it don't pour or fold, it's hardware."[64]

The company earned a reputation for paying its salesmen well. Like Marshall Field's, Simmons employed general salesmen as well as specialty salesmen to handle cutlery, sporting goods, and other lines. It became one of the largest hardware wholesale companies in the country.

Norvell began working as a traveling salesman at age nineteen. His first assignment was to replace an ailing drummer who worked out of the nearby Mississippi River town, Cape Girardeau, Missouri. Norvell was excited about the prospect of selling—or, more particularly, of traveling from town to town. "I bought a very large grip, a mackintosh coat, a large umbrella and other things I thought I would need on my journey," he wrote—though he soon learned to travel light. In the beginning he took the Iron Mountain railroad, choosing to save two dollars by not purchasing a berth and instead sitting up all night near the cast-iron stove and being continually re-awakened as they arrived at each stop and the doors opened to the cold air.[65] He did not skimp on train fare again. He found some of the adventure he sought sailing on skiffs down the Mississippi River and moving, as his territorial assignment changed, to Alabama, Kansas, and, finally, Colorado.

Like other drummers, Norvell received only limited advice and training in general sales techniques before going on the road. "Mr. [R. H.] Stockton took me to the cutlery department and gave me my first lesson," he wrote. "He especially advised me to always carry my samples to the customer's store, to open up the samples and show them, whether the customer needed any goods or not."[66]

Norvell did, however, occasionally get advice about building bonds with customers. Here E. C. Simmons, who had earned the nickname "No. 8" because the "S" in his signature resembled an "8," taught him how to hand out lapel pins in a way that would have influence:

I remember that "No. 8" . . . handed me a dozen . . . gold axes wrapped up in tissue paper and then said to me, "Now show me how you would present one of these axes to a customer." I took the package of axes out of my pocket, unwrapped the tissue paper and then, holding the package in my left hand, I held out the gold axe in my right. "No. 8" shook his head with a disgusted expression and remarked, "Wrong, wrong, all wrong." Why let the customer know that you have a dozen axes to distribute? He will want one for every clerk in the store. He will not attach any value to it. Pin one axe on your own lapel and when you call, take it off and pin it on your customer's coat. You don't have to tell him that you have any more, and he will certainly appreciate the gift and wear the axe longer if you do it this way.[67]

With such techniques, Norvell learned to make the customer feel special.

Norvell was able to set final prices himself and found that the amount of profit he could make varied depending on the product. Standard items, like nails or tools, were often competitively priced and brought in only a small profit, while specialty items—whose value was less well known—could bring in a higher one. Norvell also found that he could afford to grant a lower price to large retailers and charge a premium to those who were usually slow to pay. At Cape Girardeau he received the following advice: "When I left Mr. Search [the ailing drummer] the only instructions he gave me in the way of selling were to average about 20 per cent profit above the cost, 'and if they don't kick, you will know it is all right.'"[68] The flexibility of prices could have drawbacks, however. Shrewd retailers could tell drummers that a salesman from a competing concern had promised a low price on a particular good, which would then have to be matched.

Communication with the office was relatively infrequent, though greater than at many other wholesale houses. E. C. Simmons, the president of the company, sent the salesmen a monthly report that often included encouraging words. This role, as motivator, became a common one for managers, and they adopted methods of communicating inspirational messages. "Mr. Simmons was a great believer in encouragement," wrote Norvell. "Whenever it was possible, he wrote something encouraging on my reports and even when he thought it necessary to jack me up a bit about my small sales he usually said something friendly to take the sting out of his criticism . . . He made the salesman feel that he was invincible."[69]

Norvell placed his orders on Saturday so that they would arrive in St. Louis on Monday morning. The orders were then filled and shipped out Tuesday or Wednesday, and the customers would have the goods in their stores the following Saturday, or within about one week.[70]

The money proved fairly good, especially after Norvell was assigned to Kansas, which like many western areas experienced a building boom in the late nineteenth century. Norvell worked on a flat salary of $1,800 (about $35,000 today) and earned a share of the profits, minus his salary and expenses. His sales were about $60,000 per year (just over $1 million today). The profits on actual cost ranged from 25 percent to 30 percent, with his share being 33 percent. If, for instance, his gross profits for one year were $12,000, his share was $4,000. From this he deducted his salary ($1,800) and expenses ($1,200), leaving about $1,000 in commission for the year. His total income, therefore, was about $2,800 (about $55,000 today), being the total of his salary ($1,800) and his commission earnings ($1,000).[71]

Norvell took advantage of the inefficient methods of the regional retailers to ingratiate himself with his customers. At one general store in Charleston, Missouri, he asked the proprietor if he could stay after closing to sort out the stock and ended up working all night to clean his shop and create an inventory of goods; this allowed him later to present the owner with an order form for items the store should have been carrying.[72]

Norvell spent much of his time packing and unpacking his heavy cases of samples. At the end of the day he hauled them to the train, spent the night in the sleeping car, and rose early to lug his hardware samples to a new town. Endurance was critical for success, particularly in the decades of acute competition in the construction industry, as occurred in Kansas during the 1880s and 1890s.

Malone Wheless also worked for Simmons Hardware and had experiences similar to Norvell's. He was born in Nashville, Tennessee, in 1870—just a few years after Norvell. A recollection from his youth was the sight of colorful drummers, who came into town in their horses and buggies, sporting "natty" attire. Before working for Simmons, Wheless spent several years at a smaller business. He began as a clerk, filling orders sent in by traveling salesmen and shelving the products delivered by manufacturers.

Like Norvell, Wheless started out as a traveling salesman after another drummer had failed. Again, communication with the home office was slight and provided little instruction. "The few letters I had received during my [first] two months['] absence offered *no* comment on my work in general or my results in particular; in fact, they came mighty near saying *nothing*, so far as offering advice or help was concerned." Letters arrived handwritten on thin paper. He was paid no salary in the company and had to cover his own expenses, though he was given a share of profits. When first starting on his travels, he had to go into debt to buy a horse, buggy, and harness. Yet, after a year, he was making more money than many of the store workers, even the billing clerk. In the 1880s, the clerk received $100 per month, while Wheless came to earn about $150 (about $2,600 today). This arrangement encouraged him to push goods that had the highest profit margin.[73]

After a dispute over his pay, Wheless left the smaller concern to work for Simmons. Simmons was well managed compared with his previous employer and even had a department that created attractive carrying and display cases for the merchandise. When Wheless arrived at

Simmons, he was asked to go through the catalog and draw up a list of samples he would like to take with him. He found that carrying samples gave him an advantage over the hardware salesmen who sold through the catalog alone. But it meant that he had to haul heavy trunks.[74]

Wheless discovered that, despite his hard work, the status of traveling salesmen remained low. Most of his customers, he wrote, had no idea of the arduous aspects of his life:

> [They did not understand that] I was carrying eight to ten trunks of samples, opening and displaying, repacking them all, day by day and every day—nor that some days, or rather, nights, I would get through with my last customer at one o'clock in the morning, and after two more hours of packing, catch a milk train for my next town, and unpack again, without having seen a bed. Nor did they have any conception of the heavy duty of writing up all the orders, or of answering the enormous amount of mail I received each day and a double dose on Saturday nights.[75]

Furthermore, Wheless worked far from his family; his wife and children lived in St. Louis, while his territory covered part of Virginia and the Carolinas. Norvell had come to a similar realization: "Some of my friends seemed to think I was in the same class as a peddler, while several times I was asked how I liked being a 'drummer.' I thought then, and I have often thought since, that the *general public* needs quite a little education as to just what a traveling salesman does do and what his standing should be in the estimation of the business and social world."[76]

Both Wheless and Norvell eventually became managers, and their supervisory experiences revealed the difference between commercial traveling and office work. After traveling for nine years, Norvell was promoted in 1892 to sales manager for Simmons Hardware. This required moving back to St. Louis and working primarily in the office, which he did not like. "I had been accustomed to almost absolute freedom. I had worked exactly according to my own ideas. Nothing had been asked of me except results. I had led a life of perfect individualism."[77]

As manager, Norvell had to master a new set of relationships: not merely between salesman and customer, but also between manager and salesman. He began to keep memorandum books on his salesmen and their "peculiarities," as he had once done for customers. He spoke frequently with the other executives of the firm. He consulted with the head buyer, who played a pivotal role in the company by maintaining contacts with the many various manufacturers who supplied goods and by overseeing the construction of the catalog of products. Norvell also met frequently with the head of bills payable, who handled customer accounts. He was in charge of two hundred salesmen traveling "in almost every part" of the country. He saw each salesman only about once a year; they came individually to the office for lunch or dinner, and Norvell was urged to spend as much time as possible with them. He found the work "very strenuous," because it called for many late nights of entertaining.[78] Unlike other occupations, the rise up to management meant a drop in pay, for Norvell was no longer entitled to receive a commission.[79]

Norvell himself published an inspirational booklet entitled *That Devil: Doubt,* and later his own magazine, named the *Gimlet* after the small woodworking tool.[80] They presented his view of commercial traveling as a forward-looking, optimistic profession, with almost limitless opportunity—a job constrained only by an individual's lack of confidence, effort, or imagination.

Handbooks, Jokes, and the Tools of the Trade

Working out of large wholesale houses and having storekeepers for clients, traveling salesmen developed a form of salesmanship distinct from that practiced by canvassers. Though they did not usually work from scripts, traveling salesmen were aided by a variety of pamphlets, instructional books, and charts. During the late nineteenth century, several guidebooks were published to give traveling salesmen practical advice about the marketplace, including handy train schedules, credit reports, hotel guides, and indices of shipping rates. Wholesalers and drummers were also dependent on reliable information about the financial health of shopkeepers. The reports of Dun, like that of its rival and eventual partner, the Bradstreet Agency, provided essential information to wholesalers, allowing them to decide how much credit, if any, to extend to shopkeepers or other businesses wishing to purchase goods.[81]

Handbooks written for commercial travelers presented information to facilitate travel and to help create distribution schedules—for instance, L. C. Breyfogle's *The Commercial Traveler: Being a Hotel Guide and Gazetteer of the United States* (1881).[82] L. P. Brockett's *The Commercial Traveller's Guide Book* contained railroad route information, lists of local hotels with prices, postage and tariff rates, and tables that displayed the types of businesses operating in each town.[83] These various charts, schedules, and reports helped to standardize the flow of goods through the economy.

During the late nineteenth century many books were also published about the techniques of traveling salesmen—books often written by retired drummers reflecting on their careers on the road. Among them were the anonymously written *Twenty Years on the Road; or, The Trials and Tribulations of a Commercial Traveler, by One of Them* (1884), N. R. Streeter's *Gems from an Old Drummer's Grip* (1889), Charles S. Plummer's *Leaves from a Drummer's Diary; or, Twenty-five Years on the Road* (1889), and George L. Marshall's *O'er Rail and Cross Ties with Gripsack* (1892).[84]

These books presented the life of a salesman as an alternative to the boredom of both farm and factory work. But drummers also described the marketplace as a series of personal relations and knowledge built up from experience. As drummers traveled from town to town, met with different types of shopkeepers, spent nights on trains or in hotels, they developed a conception of the profession as one requiring great persistence and energy as well as an ability to maintain an optimistic outlook.

They did not describe selling as comprising a set of rules (as later salesmen would), but rather as an accumulation of anecdotes. They tended to make sense of selling in narrative form. An anonymous booklet, *How to Succeed on the Road as a Drummer* (1891), offered tips on selling by making general observations:

TABLE I.

CITIES, TOWNS, AND VILLAGES, OF MORE THAN 500 INHABITANTS, WITH THE RAILROADS IN WHICH THEY ARE SITUATED, THEIR DISTANCE AND DIRECTION FROM R.R. TERMINI, POPULATION IN 1870, THE NUMBER OF STORES (DRY GOODS, GROCERIES, HARDWARE, JEWELRY, BOOK, DRUG, BOOT AND SHOE, AND GENERAL), AND MANUFACTORIES.

☞ In this Table we have adopted the plan, after mature consideration, of arranging the towns under their natural railroad centre, as most convenient for the use of Travellers. By this arrangement the Traveller, at whatever railroad centre he may be, finding that place in the distance and direction column, will be able to ascertain without difficulty all the towns on the railroads radiating from it which it is desirable for him to visit.

We have been obliged, in some instances, to estimate the population of small towns in some of the Western and Southern States, as it was impossible to obtain the census returns of these places either from the Census Office or from the marshals of the several districts, to all of whom we made application in person or by letter. The population of *Canadian towns*, except a few leading ones, is not given, as the Canadian census is to be taken in the summer of 1871.

The railroad centres are given in the distance and direction column in small capitals.

NAME OF PLACE.	State.	On what Railroad.	Distance and direction from.	Population, 1870.	Dry Goods Stores.	Groceries.	Hardware Stores.	General assortment.	Manufactories.	Drugs.	Books.	Jewelry.	Shoes.
Yonkers	N.Y	Hud. River R. R.	15 N. N. Y. CITY.	18,818	18	20	6	4	18	3	2	2	8
Hastings	"	"	19 "	1,250	...	3	1	1	4	..	..	..	1
Dobbs' Ferry	"	"	21 "	1,240	...	6	...	...	...	...	...	...	...
Irvington	"	"	23 "	920	2	6	1	1	2	..	..	..	..
Tarrytown	"	"	26 "	5,123	5	14	1	4	3	4	...	...	...
Sing Sing	"	"	32 "	6,351	9	14	4	6	10	4	1	2	7
Croton	"	"	35 "	251	...	1	...	1	...	...	...	...	...
Crugers	"	"	38 "	160	...	3	...	...	...	...	...	...	...
Peekskill	"	"	42 "	4,500	18	20	5	6	19	4	2	2	6
Cold Spring	"	"	53 "	2,770	9	6	2	6	2	2	1	..	..
Fishkill	"	"	59 "	1,500	2	1	2	5	1	1	1	3	5
NewHamburgh	"	"	65 "	553	2	4	1	...	1	..	..	..	1
Poughkeepsie	"	"	73 "	20,148	41	45	14	1	30	9	6	10	23

L. P. Brockett's *The Commercial Traveller's Guide Book* (1871) provided handy charts for traveling salesmen, showing the population and principal businesses of large towns and cities.

Never complain about the dullness of business. Nothing succeeds like success.

The power of entertaining men in a proper, yet interesting way, tells much for the salesman.[85]

Unlike canvassers, drummers operated in a business world that was almost exclusively male—both the salesmen themselves and the customers they met—and drummers' memoirs comment on the need for a courageous and "manly" frame of mind. "There are some who are constitutionally timid," wrote drummer Edward Briggs. "They are always afraid and, without confidence either in themselves or their fellow men, they hesitate and are lost to the road." The "fighting spirit" was imperative to the commercial traveler.[86] In 1878, the *Confectioners' Journal* derided the "Nervous Traveler," who constantly worried about the food he was likely to be served, fretted over the dampness of his bed, and feared that "the 5.40 will run into the 6.20 at Clasham Junction, and, as a consequence, three distinct whistles from the engine will send him into a cold seat, and his head out of the window." The same article praised the "Comic Commercial" who "is at home everywhere." He "starts every journey with a laugh, and finishes up with a guffaw . . . He is at home with you at once . . . his continued jollity overcomes you."[87]

Engaging in small, or informal, talk with a merchant could be extremely useful. It was a subtle form of salesmanship that allowed commercial travelers to check up on the general tastes of a particular customer and of a community.[88] Salesmen gained a reputation for good storytelling. Old-time drummer George Olney recalled the stories and fabrications he had witnessed in the smoking car: "The smoking room of the Pullman is the scene of probably more story-telling exploits than any other place. And—say!—the lies, the blowing, the gassing I have heard in my years in the smoking room of the sleepers! There's no place like those smoking rooms for exaggerated statements."[89] Memoirs of commercial travelers played up their ability to deliver a good yarn, especially when it involved securing huge orders or beating the competition.

They were collected in publications like *A Drummer's Diary: Twenty-five Stories as Told by a Traveling Man* (1906).

Joke books written for drummers around the turn of the century helped pass long hours on the train, but they also provided salesmen with useful stories to tell on the job. Often the jokes were intended not only to break the ice but also to make a connection between the drummer and the shopkeeper through their subject matter—overbearing mothers-in-law, drunken Irishmen, and other topics both could, supposedly, find amusing.[90] *New Drummer's Yarns* (1913) by a "Knight of the Grip" offered a variety of jokes intended to establish links between the salesman and customer, including ones about mothers-in-law ("What's the extreme penalty for bigamy?" "The extreme penalty for bigamy, I should say, is two mothers-in-law"), wives ("Does your wife choose your clothes?" "No, she only picks the pockets"), and the Irish ("Phwat are yez lookin' fer, Mike?" "Oh, nothin'," says Mike, who is searching for a bottle of whiskey that Pat has gotten to first. "Well, Mike," says Pat, "ye'll foind it over there in the corner of the bottle").[91] Other similar books helped the drummer to perform when needed, such as Henry Williams's *Here's to Ye!; or, Toasts for Everybody* (1903), which included 150 after-dinner stories suited to all occasions.

Experience, in the end, was what drummers claimed to be the most important part of learning to sell. In *On the Road to Riches* (1876), William H. Maher wrote that the traveling salesman had to learn to "read faces" and master "human nature." Maher highlighted the importance of spending years on the job, rather than, as marketing professionals would later claim, learning a particular strategy or analyzing market statistics.[92]

Occasionally there was an effort to codify the drummer's goal—to read faces—drawing on phrenology and physiognomy.[93] F. B. Goddard's *The Art of Selling: With How to Read Character; Laws Governing Sales, etc.* (1889) included general principles of selling that would be useful for any product or situation and were based on science—or, in this case, pseudoscience. Unlike Bates Harrington's *How 'Tis Done* (1879), which

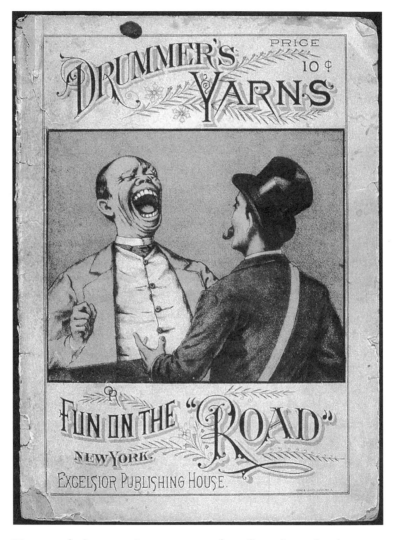

Humor and wit were an important part of traveling salesmen's culture. Joke books, like this one from 1886, helped pass the time on a train and provided some clever remarks that could come in handy when trying to establish a relationship with a merchant.

"exposed" the tricks of canvassers while at the same time explaining how they worked to all interested parties, Goddard's book was explicitly to instruct. He told salesmen to master the art of physiognomy, or the reading of facial structure. Faces, wrote Goddard, were "legible as books." Square faces denoted firmness and good judgment; oval, sensibility; oblong, melancholy and weakness; round, sensuous or animal natures. Careful observation revealed not just the broad strokes of personality, but the "finer shades and crossings." The salesman needed to pay attention to the customer's face—to the forehead, eyes, teeth, hair, and chin—to get a sense of the customer's temperament and tendencies. "A long, broad, thick, bony chin, is only found in harsh, proud, violent and over-bearing persons," he wrote. "The pointed chin signifies acuteness or craft. The soft, fat, double chin marks the epicure; the round chin with a dimple speaks of benevolence."[94] The ability to judge from physical appearance was essential, wrote Goddard, because men try their best to conceal their true nature and their emotions. In the swirling comings-and-goings of society, physical features offered a map to an individual's true character and temperament.

The work of phrenologists and physiognomists in deciphering the elements of salesmanship continued into the early twentieth century, long after these "sciences" had been discredited. The work helped spread the idea that buyers and sellers could be categorized into a series of types, which became a common device for writers and academics to analyze selling. More than anything else, however, the early appearance of these books revealed the growing desire to find applicable laws of salesmanship, even though there were no reliable methods for doing so.

The Drummer's Passing

All these aspects of the traveling salesmen's work and culture—guidebooks, memoirs, and associations—defined modern selling as something greater than the scripts and practices of canvassers. Selling was a "system," combining logistics and personal connections. But despite the role that drummers played in the growth of commerce, they eventually faced harsh criticism, just as peddlers and canvassers had. They were seen as unnecessary middlemen. Moreover, the drummers' lifestyle on trains and in hotels—drinking, playing cards, and storytelling—made them easy targets for satire. According to one critic, the drummer was a "fellow who affected fancy clothes, kept his pocket stuffed full of cigars and his mind full of questionable stories with which to regale customers, and was a first hand advisor to every bartender."[95]

Theodore Dreiser took a special interest in the drummer—a type of businessman he sensed, rightly, that was vanishing by the time he wrote *Sister Carrie* (1900). "Lest this order of individual should permanently pass, let me put down some of the most striking characteristics of his most successful manner and method," he wrote. "Good clothes, of course, were the first essential, the things without which he was nothing. A strong physical nature, actuated by a keen desire for the feminine, was the next."[96] In *Sister Carrie,* Dreiser introduced the character Charles Drouet as a quintessential drummer and took special care to describe Drouet's clothing: He wore a "striped and crossed" patterned suit, a stiff white shirt with pink stripes, yellow agate cufflinks, several rings, and a watch bearing the seal of the Order of the Elks; on his head, a gray fedora; and on his feet, polished tan shoes. Drouet was a "masher," out to seduce susceptible young women. He prowled the parlor cars on trains, taking a seat next to the most promising candidate. He would then ask the woman if she would like to have the shade lowered, and would command the porter to bring her a footstool. "At the next lull in his conversational progress he would find her something to read, and from then on, by dint of compliment gently insinuated, personal narrative, exaggeration and service, he would win her tolerance, and, mayhap, regard."[97] Here Dreiser suggested the drummer's methods of using guile, humor, and storytelling to win others over—not unlike the techniques used on merchants, or, significantly, by Dreiser himself.

In 1879 a high percentage (about 70 percent) of manufactured goods in the economy flowed through wholesalers.[98] In the years afterward that figure would drop as manufacturers in several industries began to sell goods directly to retailers or to consumers. There were many reasons for the drummers' demise. In the late nineteenth century, mail-order houses challenged the wholesaler's dominant position in the economy.[99] Dry-goods wholesalers faced competition from mail-order companies like Montgomery Ward and Sears Roebuck. Montgomery Ward sent out a single sheet listing products in 1872, which grew to a thousand-page catalog two decades later.[100] And hardware wholesalers competed with catalog sales from Sears.[101] By the turn of the century, Sears had become the leader in the mail-order field, with annual sales of $11 million.[102]

Department stores also cut into the drummers' sales, because they bought directly from manufacturers. Macy's, founded in 1858, became a colossal emporium that sold jewelry, chinaware, sporting goods, clothing, furniture, leather goods, bedding, and virtually everything else. The store's annual sales exceeded $8 million before the turn of the century, and it employed over three thousand people.[103]

But a more important reason for the decline of drumming had to do with the increasing number of manufacturers who chose to distribute their products themselves, rather than rely on a wholesaler. The growth of mass manufacturing and brand-name marketing toward the end of the nineteenth century diminished the drummer's power and also that of his employer. Shopkeepers could demand a specific brand-name product, advertised in national magazines and known to their clientele, rather than take the unbranded goods of a trusted drummer.

Ironically, many of the steps that drummers took to improve the reliability and efficiency of distribution hastened their demise in certain industries—though by no means all. In addition, the emergence of national magazines allowed manufacturers to take over the advertising of their own goods. The new business organizations that emerged in the late nineteenth century and practiced mass manufacturing called for a different approach, one that made selling more of a "science," combining production and distribution.

Fifty-Seven Varieties

4

Sales Managers and Branded Goods

In the 1880s the agricultural canvasser and the wholesale drummer were at their peak. Canvassers toured from farmhouse to farmhouse, either on foot or in a wagon, carrying books or other small items, taking instruction from a sales outfit, and selling goods on commission. At the same time, drummers worked for wholesale houses, which bought goods from a range of small manufacturers, sorted and repackaged them, and sold them to retail stores or to other, usually smaller, wholesalers. Wholesale drummers traveled on trains and wagons, hauling trunks filled with merchandise samples or carrying thick catalogs, and were usually paid a mixture of salary and commission.

But in the late nineteenth century, a newer, more aggressive, and highly managed form of salesmanship emerged. Mass manufacturers began to build their own cadres of salesmen, and in doing so, developed the first modern sales forces—"modern" because their use of salesmen set the pattern for companies in the decades that followed.

The final decades of the nineteenth century were an unusually fertile period for American business. The economy was changing rapidly, propelled by the emergence of large industrial manufacturers. Several companies grew from small entrepreneurial concerns to large enterprises before the turn of the century. National Cash Register, Eastman Kodak, Coca-Cola, Westinghouse Electric, and Carnegie Steel were all founded in the 1880s; in the following decade came Wrigley's Chewing Gum, General Electric, Burroughs, and Pepsico.

These mass-manufacturing companies, and others like them, helped to end the dominance of the large wholesaling houses. Several companies launched large, expensive sales campaigns, which cut into the distribution paths established by drummers. The development of a strong sales department was essential for the success of these large firms, helping them to generate demand and to prevent competitors from entering the industry. Firms that produced in high volume also had to sell in high volume.[1]

The sales strategies of large industrial manufacturers were different from those of wholesale drummers. They linked the work of their sales forces with their production schedules and sold branded products, rather than generic ones. The effective use of brand names allowed manufacturers to differentiate their goods from the many generic items carried by wholesalers. In the 1870s only a handful of registered trademarks existed (about 170 according to one source), but their numbers multiplied rapidly in the final decades of the nineteenth century.[2]

The entrepreneurs who founded these large manufacturing companies frequently had forceful personalities. They organized the production and distribution facilities and selected managers and other executives. They hired and deployed the sales force and often continued to lead the organization, or at least to maintain their own stamp on it as the company grew. Several entrepreneurs invented the product that their company sold, including Cyrus Hall McCormick (the mechanical reaper), Isaac Merritt Singer (the sewing machine), and William S. Burroughs (the adding machine). A number of them had experience selling; both William Wrigley Jr., chewing-gum magnate, and C. W. Post, inventor of Postum (later Post) breakfast cereals, worked as traveling salesmen, and others (McCormick, Heinz, Burroughs, and cigarette baron James B. Duke) went on the road to promote their companies' products when they were starting out. Several of these entrepreneurs—

including Heinz, Kellogg, Duke, and Post—also attended local schools for business, learning accounting and other aspects of commerce.

Many of the entrepreneurs were interested in reform of one sort or another: William K. Kellogg and C. W. Post advocated nutritional and dietary reform; Henry Heinz lobbied for the Pure Food and Drug Act of 1906; John H. Patterson, of National Cash Register, pioneered in "welfare work," or the creation of healthy work environments, with parks, exercise facilities, and public lecture halls. This did not mean that these businessmen were not primarily interested in profit, but rather that they harbored a deep enthusiasm and personal zeal for their enterprises, which they communicated to their sales forces. At times, they viewed an entire industry as their personal calling.

Drawing on their own experience, entrepreneurs made sense of selling in different ways. Henry Heinz came out of a peddling tradition, selling vegetables off the back of his wagon, and built an organization that sold ketchup, pickles, baked beans, and other packaged food around the world. Asa Candler, a devout Methodist and pharmaceutical salesman, combined the zeal of his religion with the advertising acumen of patent medicine makers in his promotion of Coca-Cola. William S. Burroughs, grandfather of the writer of the same name, was a tinkerer and inventor who fielded a team of salesmen to hawk his ingenious adding machine and explain its many features.

Still, these entrepreneurs—peddlers, evangelists, and inventors—shared many characteristics. They built large businesses that combined production with mass distribution. And they usually complemented the work of their sales force with advertising and other promotional devices. Significantly, the salesman's role in promoting goods was very different from that of advertising. To use a military analogy common in the early twentieth century, advertising was a weapon for waging an air war, while salesmen were deployed as foot soldiers in a ground campaign.

To orchestrate their sales campaigns, entrepreneurs increasingly turned to sales managers, who had control over the intricacies of the sales process. Managers oversaw every detail of selling—assigning territory, setting up sales quotas, and establishing compensation schemes.

These efforts transformed selling in ways equivalent to Frederick W. Taylor's scientific management movement, which had revolutionized production. Taylor instructed managers to analyze and standardize all work routines, making them as efficient as possible and giving workers clear guidelines and timetables for the completion of tasks. Taylorism was a way for managers to seize control of every aspect of the production process. Around the turn of the century, "scientific sales management," as one business writer called it, had somewhat similar implications for selling.[3]

In many ways, large manufacturing companies "branded" their salesmen, just as they had their products. Mass manufacturers were not only trying to turn out uniform sales arguments, as book companies had done by distributing detailed manuals, but uniform salesmen as well. They did not hire "canvassers" or "drummers," but rather Remington salesmen, NCR agents, or Heinz salesmen. The company name, or brand, was paramount in the salesmen's identity, for they represented the manufacturer, not themselves. They were integrated into a large corporate system that began with gathering raw materials and continued through to the sale of products.

Systems of sales management at large companies altered not only the day-to-day responsibilities of the occupation, but also, at times, the appearance of the salesmen themselves, as employers demanded conservative dress and a healthy diet to distinguish their representatives from the stereotypical corpulent traveling salesman.[4] Manufacturers tried to raise the status of their salesmen by belittling the common "drummer"—often their main competitor for the attention of shopkeepers. One article in a Heinz company newsletter in 1905 claimed that the loudly dressed and vulgar drummer was a thing of the past. "Specimens of this type should be stuffed and mounted and exhibited in museums, simply as a matter of historical record, along with stage coaches, muzzle-loading guns, and other relics." The modern salesman bore no relation, it claimed. "He is polished, intelligent, energetic; a man of affairs; a student of human nature; an observer of conditions; alert, affable, dignified, enthusiastic. He is trained for his work."[5]

The sales force remained a male preserve. Women seldom were hired for sales work, but occasionally were hired as demonstrators at machinery companies like Burroughs and Singer Sewing Machine. Yet the masculinity of the manufacturer's salesman, as revealed in house journals, was supposed to be restrained and professional, rather than exuberant and aggressive.

The increasing numbers of these "branded" salesmen, however, did not mean a decline in petty canvassers or drummers. The numbers of each group increased. According to the census, which tends to undercount itinerant salespeople, the number of "hucksters and peddlers" increased from 59,083 in 1890 to 80,415 in 1910, and the number of traveling salesmen grew from 58,691 to 163,620 during the same period.

While the subscription book industry declined, some late-nineteenth-century canvassers of other small items began to sell to the growing urban and suburban markets. In 1886, for example, David Hall McConnell, a former book salesman, founded the California Perfume Company (located in Brooklyn, New York), which eventually grew into the global concern Avon Products. Canvassing also flourished in the industrial insurance industry, which was introduced in the United States in the late 1870s by Metropolitan Life of New York, Prudential Life of Newark, New Jersey, and John Hancock of Boston. These companies sold policies in small units (from $50 to $1,000), with premiums ranging from only a nickel to sixty cents collected weekly by door-to-door agents. They proved so popular that, by 1909, two of every nine people in the United States were covered by industrial policies. Around this time, Metropolitan had over 13,000 agents making weekly calls on subscribers.[6] There were also several African American industrial insurance companies, such as North Carolina Mutual Life Insurance Company (1898) and Atlanta Life Insurance Company (1905), which catered to markets that white-owned companies ignored.[7]

Wholesale drummers continued to distribute many generic products after the turn of the century, including liquor, leather, groceries, jewelry, and furniture—undifferentiated, unbranded goods that were sold through many small retail outlets.[8] Some wholesalers increased their efforts to monitor their salesmen by having drummers write reports more frequently or by creating a network of contacts in the field. William Castelow wrote in *Only a Drummer* (1903), "Many a drummer has been asked when he returned home from a trip about certain things that happened in cities where he had been that he was concerned in, and he never dreamed his house would find them out, but it did."[9]

But in the decades around the turn of the century, the entrepreneurs most devoted to systematizing selling, and most enthusiastic about the promises of salesmanship, were located in large manufacturing concerns. Many of these mass manufacturers were based in New York or one of several growing cities of the Midwest, like Chicago, Dayton, Detroit, or Pittsburgh. Over time, the companies that spent the most on maintaining a sales force included makers of sewing machines, office equipment, drugs and pharmaceuticals, paints and varnishes, and heating and electrical equipment.[10]

As shown in the previous chapters on canvassers and drummers, the nature of the product and the type of customer shaped the sales strategy. Such characteristics were critical, for instance, in determining whether salesmen looked for a transactional sale or a longer relationship with the customer. They also suggested the amount of advertising to use and the form it should take, whether in trade journals, newspapers, or national magazines. Salesmen for mass manufacturers sold branded goods to a number of customers—including to the public, retailers, and business offices—and often advertised widely in magazines, on billboards, and in newspapers. The experiences of salesmen of sewing machines, brand-name foods, and office machinery reveal the varieties of sales strategies at large firms.

Selling Sewing Machines

Many well-known mass-manufacturing companies established sales forces in the 1880s and 1890s, but, as noted earlier, a handful did so before then. Several of these established sales organizations sold directly to farmers and small business owners. Singer Sewing Machine, in particular, had built an especially large and effective sales force by the mid-nineteenth century. It made distinctive contributions to selling by introducing a network of branch offices, by offering to sell its product on installment, and by setting up demonstration centers that let potential customers try out the machine. All these advancements were essential to the future role of salesmen in the sale of increasingly complex merchandise, such as automobiles, to the public.

Though founded by Isaac Merritt Singer (1811–1875), the company was effectively headed by Singer's partner and lawyer, Edward Clark (1811–1882), who became president following Singer's death. At first, Singer Sewing Machine relied on full-time, independent agents to sell its machines, granting these agents exclusive rights to specific U.S. territories, sometimes counties or even entire states.[11]

Beginning in 1852, Singer opened its own retail branch offices—in Boston first, and then in Philadelphia and New York. These offices were expensive to maintain, for the company had to pay rent and advertising expenses and had to install machines for display. Setting up branch offices also required an office staff, which usually consisted of a demonstrator, a mechanic, a salesman, and a manager. There were fourteen branch offices in U.S. cities by 1859, stretching as far west as Chicago and south to Charleston.[12] Despite the expense, the branches proved essential to the company's success and gave sales agents the opportunity to educate customers. They also enabled the company to keep track of regional inventories and to make informed assessments of prospects' credit.[13] Clark soon began to reduce the company's reliance on independent agents, shifting resources to the branches.[14]

As an invention, the Singer sewing machine was truly revolutionary. Inventors had been trying to develop a mechanical sewing machine since the mid-seventeenth century. Singer's machine, which made use of a foot pedal for power, brought a remarkable increase in productivity over hand sewing. Because sewing machines were expensive, Clark, well ahead of his time, came up with the idea of "renting" machines to women, and then applying the payments toward the eventual purchase of the machine. In 1856 he began a program whereby purchasers would pay $5 down and $3 to $5 monthly until the price of the machine, plus interest for the credit loan, had been paid. Sales tripled the following year.[15] Singer's marketing organization, which included advertising and the deployment of canvassers, allowed the company to dominate the market, even though it did not always have the most technologically advanced machine.[16]

The American Civil War boosted sales of Singer sewing machines to over ten thousand per year. The company built its first large factory in Elizabethport, New Jersey. It also established assembly plants in Great Britain in the 1860s and then built entire factories in Scotland.[17]

Many of the important innovations in the company's marketing strategy came from its offices in Britain and then were imported to America in the years after the Civil War.[18] Singer had made a strong, early commitment to Britain. Beginning in 1864, George Baldwin Woodruff, who had headed Singer's New Haven and Boston branches, became the company's general agent in Britain. The selling situation in London was more complex than in the United States, where the company enjoyed patent protection. Under Woodruff, the London office developed an aggressive sales strategy that targeted both the commercial and consumer markets. Woodruff began using door-to-door canvassers in the late 1860s. He also set up a system of sales branches and small district offices, which provided operating bases for canvassers. Woodruff offered sewing lessons to customers, printed illustrated catalogs, and counted on large volume sales, with only a small margin per unit. After the introduction of door-to-door canvassing in Britain, sales increased from 30,000 (1875) to 60,000 (1880) machines per year.[19] Clark began establishing a similar system in the United States in the late 1870s.[20]

In 1874, Singer controlled about 37 percent of the U.S. market for sewing machines, selling 219,758 machines that year.[21] Agents were held to a twenty-two-point contract that outlined their exclusive right to sell in a particular territory and their obligation to be conscientious in filling out the forms and paperwork that tracked daily transactions. The contract instructed agents that they could exchange new machines for old ones (though at a lower commission) and could sell machines for "farm products, stock and other marketable commodities" in lieu of cash.[22]

Singer found itself encumbered by regional licensing fees that forbade the sale of goods made out of state—these were the same laws that hamstrung peddlers as they went from state to state. Singer, however, launched a successful fight against them. An agent for the company in Missouri, M. M. Welton, was charged with selling a product of "foreign"—that is, out-of-state—manufacture without a license. Singer appealed the case to the U.S. Supreme Court, which in *Welton v. Missouri* (1876), found that interstate commerce should be "free and untrammelled."[23] The decision was pivotal for American commerce, because it prevented the balkanization of American domestic trade, although it did not completely end the ability of counties and towns to pass ordinances designed to restrict canvassing and door-to-door sales.[24]

In 1878, Singer president Edward Clark issued a reorganization plan, hoping eventually to build a global network of branch retail offices out of which canvassers would operate. The plan established a hierarchical sales and distribution system containing agents, subagents, canvassers, and assistants. The New York headquarters directed the work of three controlling offices (in New York, London, and Hamburg); these in turn supervised the district offices, which monitored the retail outlets that served as home bases for canvassers.[25] Managers received a salary; canvassers received a small weekly salary and commission of 15 percent on sales and 10 percent on collections.[26]

The Atlanta branch office prepared a *Canvassers' Manual of Instructions, with Hints and Suggestions Concerning the Art of Canvassing*. It reminded canvassers to use standard forms in processing orders and to make sure to state correctly the style of machine ordered and the proper part numbers for servicing. It explained in detail the methods of leaving machines for a test trial and for taking leases. The manual also included a section entitled "The Art of Canvassing," which did not contain a script, but offered general advice. "Always learn the name of a family before you enter a house. Introduce your business at once, in a pleasant way," it said. "Do not immediately ask them to purchase, but proceed to show your machine, its usefulness and points of excellence, and the economy of having one. When they become interested, teach them how to use it, and then try to effect a sale." Largely it told agents to follow the directions of management, to take care in processing reports, and to work their territories thoroughly.[27]

The sewing-machine industry remained, in percentage of total sales costs, among those that spent the most, per product, on face-to-face selling—until the twentieth century (after 1940, when selling expense exceeded 30 percent of total net sales, the strategy was changed).[28] The sale of the sewing machine paved the way for other expensive or intricate machines, including the vacuum cleaner and the automobile, to be sold to consumers at their homes as well as through branch sales offices. Cars, as will be discussed in a later chapter, depended on door-to-door selling in the early twentieth century as a supplement to franchised dealerships. In these industries, salesmen played a vital role, explaining the products, providing information about servicing them, arranging for credit purchases, pointing out differences between competing machines, and persuading customers to overcome their "inertia" and spend large sums of money.

Selling Brand-Name Foods to Storekeepers

Unlike Singer, most mass manufacturers in the late nineteenth century did not sell goods directly to consumers. Instead, they made products to sell to businesses: some sold to retailers—general stores, grocers, tobacco shops, restaurants, pharmacies, and soda shops—and others, depending on the nature of their product, sold to business offices or to manufacturers. The goods they made were integral to the industrialization and urbanization of the country in the late nineteenth century.

Salesmen for American Tobacco, Heinz, and Kellogg's sold their goods to retailers, much as wholesaler drummers had; they developed sales forces to solicit orders for their products, but relied on wholesalers to distribute them. These firms produced in great quantity, making use of high-speed machinery that churned out items continuously.[29] In

THE SALESMAN.

OUR PASSWORD---HUSTLE.

VOL. 2.   ST. LOUIS, MO , SATURDAY, OCTOBER 18, 1890.   NO. 2.

The Salesman,

PUBLISHED AT THE

OFFICE OF THE SINGER MFG. CO.

Issued every other Saturday. Correspondence of general interest to our readers solicited.

All communications should be addressed to EDITOR "THE SALESMAN," 1124 OLIVE ST., ST. LOUIS, MO.

SUBSCRIPTION TERMS.

One copy postpaid to every Singer agent in good standing in the St. Louis territory.

ADVERTISING RATES

Special mention will be made of good results when the small reports are sent us. No reports, no mention.

Go for full payments.

Back numbers and suspended debts *must go.*

A faint heart never won a fair lady, or any other prize.

Bird hunting and money hunting don't go well together.

Oh! What will our harvest be? Just what our money gatherers make it.

It is amusing to see how lively a "lame duck" can get up stairs, when a collector calls.

The fairs are over. Will you now make good your very fair promises for big remittances.

Verily! Verily! a soft answer turneth away wrath, but our wide awake collectors are not all named *wrath*

When you go for a collection, stay until you get it. This is not the season of the year to be put off with a promise.

"Suspended debt" is no man's friend. The person who makes it his associate must be judged by the company he keeps.

The man who permits himself to be found loaded up with back numbers must not be surprised at finding himself a back number also.

Our "Arkansas travelers" will have a money pic-nic during the balance of the year if they take advantage of the good things in store for them.

The agent who fails to remit enough money to pay for the machines he sells, can hardly expect to ever be entrusted with greater responsibilities.

Don't propose to a girl whose mother has tried to beat you out of the payment due on her sewing machine. What the mother is, the daughter will be.

The agent who at this season of the year is satisfied with a ten or fifteen dollar payment on a fifty or fifty-five dollar note can never expect to win a prize.

Some of our sub-branch officers are making excellent records, at least twenty of these officers have a splendid fighting choice for second prize. Who is the man to wear the laurels?

We suspect that the editor of the *Chicago Skirmish Line* has, of late, been living on fish food. At any rate the last issue of that bright paper shows there has been a remarkable improvement in brain work done in the editorial sanctum.

Chicago has a live set of boys, and they are dead set on cleaning up our hustlers this year. Can they do it? Oh, no! Our first brigade, of twenty strong, can knock out the world on this year's record. Who will the twenty be? We shall see when the battle ends.

Farmers have had excellent weather for seeding. The wheat acreage is probably larger than ever before known all over our territory, and with the fine start it is getting, an immense crop is promised for next year. This will encourage every person and should double your half cash sales from now on.

Make the last week of October a great week for sales and collections. The rain in some sections during the early part of the month delayed cotton picking and other farm work, which naturally retards our collections, but the latter half of the month has given the boys a fine chance for hustling through the country. So make up for any loss in the early part of the month by a unanimous effort during the next week.

Every man who succeeds in life has always a prize in view, and then works to obtain it. The man who has no ambition to satisfy, never gets out of the old easy way of doing things. It is not always the intrinsic value of the prize that makes it desirable, but it is the desire to excell in whatever we attempt that brings out our best efforts in all contests, whether in the schoolroom, business, politics, profession, or in any other endeavor of life. The man who has no desire to excell in whatever calling he may labor, will never make a great success of his business or profession; what a splendid opportunity we give this fall for every agent to test his own personal powers.

Make November the Boomer Month.

November will have five Saturdays, and as our month's business always ends on the last Saturday of each month, you will see that our November report to New York will contain the results of five weeks' work. We are especially anxious to make November the largest month in the history of this office, and second to no other office in the United States. We are particularly anxious to make it a great money month, cash sales and collections, are the things to work for; of course do not lose any half cash sales, but above all, give special attention to collections We want *one hundred volunteers* who will agree to remit individually during November not less than $200; that is only an average of $40 per week. We take pleasure in publishing the names in our next issue of all those who have the courage to answer to this call. Remember we ought to have at least 200 agents who can do that well or better, and while our call is only for 100 volunteers we will welcome three times that number. Agents who show an interest in such calls as this are the men who come up in the business. We hope every agent in the territory will write us at once something like this: "I hereby pledge myself to use my best efforts to get in not less than—sales and $—remittance during the month of November." Now boys, don't be afraid to show your hand. Make your own estimates of what you hope to do and then strive to exceed it, and we will feel sure of making November the boomer month in the history of the St. Louis office.

"The world stretches widely before you,
A field for your muscle and brain,
And though clouds may often float o'er you,
And often come tempest and rain.
Be fearless of storms which o'ertake you,
Push forward through like a man,
Good fortune will never forsake you,
If you do as near right as you can."

HINTS TO SALESMEN.

" Self Help and Home Study."

When trade is brisk push all the harder.

Selling ability depends on common sense, energy, courtesy, patience and tact.

The salesman will find it greatly to his advantage to cultivate a memory for faces and names.

Good salesmen seldom ask a man if he wants to buy goods; he doesn't come at him that way.

It is a misfortune for a young man to receive an exalted idea of his own ability and importance.

The weightiest arguments a salesman can use are, in general, those which appeal to interested motives.

The successful salesman knows how to talk, what to talk about, and more especially when to stop talking.

If a point can be made clear at all, it is all the clearer by brevity, and sensible people prefer brevity to eloquence.

The salesman should be keen, bright and ingenious, and at the same time truthful and open. Frankness invites frankness.

Josh Billings said, "When you strike ile, stop boring. Many a man has bored klean thru and let the ile run out at the bottom."

If the salesman cannot bring himself to believe in himself, his house, and his goods, he is either very badly placed, or he has mistaken his calling.

There is a magnetism in rich, low, and well-modulated tones, which express respect for the person addressed and they go far towards securing for the speaker an attentive and favorable hearing.

One of the best faculties of speech for a salesman, as it is for any person who has to convince others, is that of short, plain and pithy illustrations. It strikes home. Long-winded stories are tedious, and so are hobbies.

The eye may be eloquent. It is the chief medium through which a man fires off whatever personal magnetism he possesses. There is a maxim: "When you buy, keep one eye on the goods, the other on the seller; when you sell, keep both eyes on the buyer."

Collections.

Quick, sharp action is what is now necessary for collections. The next nine or ten weeks will stamp every agent and every office as a *success* or *failure;* collections will determine which it will be. The person who makes accounts that he cannot collect is an unsafe business man. Bankruptcy and failure follow in the tracks of bad debts. Bad debts are the children of prodigacy, looseness, dullness and indifference. A bright salesman never allow his accounts to become and remain bad. What is known as a "smart" salesman may do so, but a man may be "smart" and yet not *bright.* Brightness illuminates to some extent the future, smartness never shines but momentarily. The full collections will enable us to distinguish the bright agents in our field. Accept no excuses, avoid being put off, call on every customer promptly, and you will succeed; remember that success admits of no criticism, and failure is the companion of incompetency and disgrace.

1881, a cigarette-making machine was patented that could produce over seventy thousand cigarettes in a ten-hour day; in the same year, another new machine made matches by the millions each day and packed them into boxes.[30] Unlike the products carried by wholesale drummers, these items were often sold under the brand name of the manufacturer. By 1900, many goods, like sugar, molasses, vinegar, and ammonia, were coming out in colorful containers with the manufacturer's name on them. Indeed, innovations in printing and packaging brought great changes to the promotion of goods. Food, in particular, was wrapped more neatly and cleanly, in tidy packages and bottles that replaced the cracker barrel, molasses keg, and sugar bin; the new ideal was to have neatly lined shelves of merchandise. Advertisements for these products ran in nationally distributed magazines and were printed on posters and billboards. Retailers also reorganized their stores to allow for self-service and began to publicize that they carried nationally advertised, brand-name products.[31]

After a customer had tried a branded good a few times, he or she became familiar with its qualities. This increased the manufacturer's visibility to the consumer. It also strengthened the manufacturer's position over the wholesaler, for when customers wanted "Ivory," rather than generic soap, wholesalers had to go to Procter and Gamble to get it.[32] Moreover, the use of brand names allowed companies to compete against one another on terms other than price; this was essential in goods like candy or chewing gum that sold for only a few cents. Manufacturers promoted brand names primarily through advertising, but salesmen also helped establish brand familiarity by putting up promotional displays, gaining good shelf space, and giving away calendars, glasses, and other items bearing company slogans and trademarks.

Opposite page: Manufacturing companies often put out newspapers or magazines to instruct and inspire their sales forces. *The Salesman* (1890), published by Singer's St. Louis office, offered news, tips ("go for full payments"), sayings ("bird hunting and money hunting don't go well together"), poems, and even a password—"hustle."

Henry John Heinz, a leading entrepreneur of his day, developed a sales force and marketing campaign to transform his small vegetable-peddling business into an international organization.[33] Heinz (1844–1919), born in Pittsburgh, Pennsylvania, was the son of German immigrants. He attended the Allegheny Seminary in Sharpsburg, Pennsylvania, with plans of becoming a Lutheran minister, but decided to enter business instead, learning bookkeeping at nearby Duff's Business College. He was affiliated with different churches throughout his lifetime, at one time aligning himself with Lutherans, Methodist Episcopals, Methodists, and Presbyterians. He was a superintendent at a Sunday school for five years and was once president of the Pennsylvania State Sabbath School Association.

After working for a brief time in his father's brick business, Heinz turned his attention to selling food. In his youth, he peddled vegetables from his family's garden and took an active interest in the cultivation of crops. Heinz sold his own horseradish to grocers throughout the city in the early 1860s and soon entered into a partnership with his neighbor L. Clarence Noble. The idea of prepackaged condiments and vegetables was quite new; many families grew their own food or bought the produce of local farmers. But Heinz showed his marketing sense by selling his products under a brand name, Anchor, and distributing them in glass bottles to allow customers to see the contents. Heinz slowly gained customers and the company expanded, building a headquarters on the south side of Pittsburgh. The firm prospered until 1875, when, due in part to low agricultural prices and credit problems, Heinz was forced to declare bankruptcy.

Undeterred, Heinz started again, this time forming a partnership with his brother and cousin. The F. and J. Heinz Company, founded in 1876, began to market sauerkraut, ketchup, and pickles. Making use of new technology, Heinz also began to sell a range of canned fruits and vegetables.

As the new company grew, Heinz established branches in cities outside of Pittsburgh. His team of salesmen visited grocers to solicit orders, which were then filled by regional warehouses. Heinz salesmen were paid on commission. In the early 1880s, wagon salesmen were paid a commission of 2.5 percent to 5 percent, depending on the item.[34] Heinz's sales force grew from 2 in 1877, to 125 in 1893, to 952 in 1919.[35] The size of the sales force was a fraction of Singer's, which numbered in the tens of thousands. This was due in part to Singer's being a larger company and in part to the nature of the customer. Singer sold to consumers as well as to industry; it wanted salesmen knocking on every door. Heinz sold only to storeowners and therefore needed fewer salespeople.[36]

Heinz was a creative promoter, handing out pickle-shaped pins at the 1893 Chicago World's Columbian Exposition and allowing the public to tour his spotless factories. He came up with the slogan of the company, "fifty-seven varieties," simply because he liked the sound of the number; in 1896, when he coined the phrase, the company was making far more than fifty-seven products, including chili, tomato sauces, baked beans, pickled onions, and a wide variety of ketchups. Unlike the independent drummers, Heinz salesmen were aided by extensive advertising that promoted the product to consumers. In 1900 Heinz erected New York City's first electric sign; it made use of 1,200 light bulbs and stood at the corner of Fifth Avenue and Twenty-third Street. He also promoted his products at the 1902 World's Fair in Buffalo, and in Atlantic City he built a pavilion on a 900-foot pier as a giant advertisement.[37]

The example of Heinz, because of its size, reveals how carefully companies with high-volume production had to balance their output with distribution. Around the turn of the century, the company employed 3,000 regular workers and as many as 40,000 seasonal laborers to harvest crops. Its main plant in Pittsburgh was composed of twenty-five brick buildings whose floor space covered twenty acres. There were sixty-one salting houses to prepare pickles, and massive rooms to bottle and label products. The baked-bean department produced 36,000 cans per day—each one automatically filled with beans, weighed, and topped with tomato sauce before being sealed. Another set of bottling machines filled, corked, and washed 2,500 dozen bottles of ketchup a day.

The firm had a preserving department, a mustard department, and a to-mato soup department. It had its own glass factory and horse stables.[38]

To distribute its products around the world, Heinz set up an international system of warehouses in Europe, Asia, Africa, and Australia, and had twenty-six branch distributing houses in prominent cities in the United States and England. The shipping department managed its own refrigerator and railway tank cars, which traveled out of the plant on railway spurs connected to all the major railroad lines in Pittsburgh.[39]

Just as the operation of the packing and bottling plants was highly managed, so too were the functions of the salesmen, who filed forms and reported to supervisors. Heinz started a company magazine, *Pickles*, to inspire and instruct his sales force. His "travelers," as he called them, visited grocers, inspecting merchandise displays and advising retailers on methods of keeping and ordering Heinz stock. Getting good shelf space was a primary concern. "As the salesman covers his territory, it is his duty to see that our goods are in a salable condition; do not allow the grocer to scatter our bottled goods all over the store, but get him to give you a tier of shelves and devote them to our line; you can do it," advised *Pickles*.[40] Heinz urged his salesmen to concentrate on building lasting business relations by gaining the merchant's trust and not over-selling items that would bloat his inventory. He noted: "When once a salesman has established such relations between himself and the dealer that the merchant believes in him, almost any suggestion made by the salesman will be accepted by his customer as a good one, because he believes that the salesman is working for the interests of both."[41]

Heinz salesmen tried to present a professional image. In 1898, when salesmen from each of the branches posed for formal pictures, they wore black suits and white shirts with neckties. Captions underneath these portraits told something about the salesmen, such as P. H. Jacobs of Pittsburgh, who was the "best kraut salesman in the territory."[42] The key was to know the retailers—their stores, customers, and needs. "Sell your man, don't sell the goods" was the "war cry" of the sales force around the turn of the century.[43]

Heinz built swimming pools and lecture halls on the company grounds. Shortly after the turn of the century, the small brick house in which Heinz had launched his condiment empire in 1869 was floated down the Allegheny River aboard a barge and relocated at the company's large headquarters in Pittsburgh. The house served as a museum at its new location, holding works of art collected by the founder. It celebrated the company and its originator.[44]

Other entrepreneurs also "skipped the middleman" to sell soda, chewing gum, and breakfast cereals—though many of these firms continued to rely on wholesalers to ship their products after salesmen had taken the orders. Asa Griggs Candler (1851–1929) exhibited an evangelical zeal in the marketing of Coca-Cola. Like Heinz he transformed a relatively small business into a global organization through face-to-face selling.

Candler hired salesmen to promote the sale of Coca-Cola at a variety of venues, including soda fountains, hotels, restaurants, delicatessens, green grocers, and elsewhere. Salesmen gave away clocks, glasses, and trays, and in the early days, even stock in the company. They instructed retailers on how to best serve the drink. Under Candler's leadership, sales of Coca-Cola went from $1,500 in 1887 (a year after its founding), to $228,600 in 1897, to $3,363,100 in 1907 (about $64 million today).[45]

By the turn of the century, salesmen were being brought to Atlanta for training during the late winter or early spring. They received instruction in the policies of the company, watched the manufacture of Coca-Cola, and were told how to approach customers and handle them. Salesmen left Atlanta with names of towns to visit and businesses to see.[46] Candler, who also served as a vice president of the American Bible Society, melded his own Methodist beliefs with salesmanship. While he was not an inspirational speaker, Coca-Cola salesmen were known to accompany him in singing "Onward Christian Soldiers" at sales meetings.[47]

Other manufacturers of processed foods and agricultural products also built sales forces to solicit orders from grocers and other retailers. James Buchanan Duke (1856–1925), founder of the American Tobacco

Company, built a sales organization after he began using high-speed cigarette-making machines in his plant. Because his Bonsack cigarette machines were able to turn out thousands of cigarettes per day, the real challenge for Duke was selling—introducing Americans to the idea of smoking and setting up a widespread organization. This was quite difficult, because the cigarette was little known in America in the 1870s. Duke toured the country, and then the globe, signing up agents and visiting tobacco shops. He marketed relentlessly, handing out trade cards and other promotional items, and cutting the price of his product from ten cents a pack (the industry standard) to only five cents in 1883. Duke relied on salesmen to distribute handbills, trade cards, and other promotional material to tobacco shops and drugstores. He built a network of sales offices throughout the country and made arrangements with wholesalers and dealers around the world to promote his cigarettes.[48] By 1889, Duke was producing 834 million cigarettes annually and realizing sales of $4.5 million (about $87 million today).[49]

Finally, William Wrigley Jr., the chewing-gum magnate, also organized a force of salesmen in the late nineteenth century. Wrigley had little formal education and worked initially as a salesman in his father's business, Wrigley's Scouring Soap. He borrowed money from his uncle in 1891 and went into business, starting out with soap and baking powder before changing over to chewing gum. At the time, there were more than a dozen other American companies manufacturing chewing gum. Wrigley came up with Juicy Fruit in 1893 and Spearmint in 1899. In 1907 he spent $284,000—a huge sum at the time—in advertising the brand, and he mailed free samples of his gum to consumers. Wrigley sent salesmen out to encourage grocers and soda shops to carry his gum and to give away promotional lamps, razors, and scales. The company established sales branches outside the United States in Canada (1910), Australia (1915), Great Britain (1927), and New Zealand (1939).[50]

There were many enthusiasts of salesmanship in the branded food, tobacco, and candy industries. They depended on a combination of national advertising, branded products, and face-to-face selling to achieve their goals. The personalities of the founders shaped the culture and management of the sales force. These companies tended to spend heavily on advertising and on selling (together the two expenses accounting for perhaps 15 to 20 percent of their net sales).[51] Many of these companies were so successful that their brands have survived to this day. In part, their long-lasting success was due to the role that salesmen played in the distribution of these goods: they secured shelf space, arranged promotional material, gave away premiums and samples, and devised ways to defeat the competition.

Selling Business Machines to Offices and Stores

While makers of branded foods developed aggressive sales forces to court shop owners, other manufacturers sent their salesmen to two expanding business frontiers—the factory and the business office. Manufacturers of finished and semifinished products increasingly began to build their own sales forces in the late nineteenth century. In the 1880s, Carnegie Steel began building its own branch offices after it had shifted from making rails for railroads to manufacturing structural steel for buildings. In the early years of Carnegie Steel, sales were made through commission merchants. In the late 1880s, Carnegie opened its own sales office in Boston and, by the end of the nineteenth century, had branches in New York, Philadelphia, Chicago, Montreal, Pittsburgh, Cincinnati, Cleveland, St. Louis, New Orleans, Atlanta, Denver, Buffalo, and other cities. A general sales agent from Carnegie sent weekly letters to sales agents, urging them to push slow-moving items.[52]

After establishing his electric company in 1879, Thomas Edison also set out to construct a sales force.[53] The Edison electric lighting system had two kinds of users: central stations that produced and sold light, and firms. Of the latter type, early common customers were textile mills, breweries, mining operations, printing shops, and furniture factories, which found incandescent light superior to arc light and gaslight because it did not emit heat or fumes.[54] Eventually individuals began to install electricity in their homes. Initially Edison and his competitors, chiefly George Westinghouse, faced the problem of overcoming popular

You'll appreciate that porch light all the year round

It's just as convenient in winter as in summer. While its cheerful glow welcomes your friends and guests, it is also the best burglar protection against tramps and other undesirable callers. It is a striking example of the superior convenience of *electric* light.

His Only Rival

EDISON
MAZDA LAMPS

With Edison Mazda Lamps you can enjoy all the other conveniences of electric light—the cellar light the attic light, the closet light, the all-night light—because EDISON MAZDA lamps take so little current that you can afford all these electric comforts at no greater cost than you paid for the more ordinary uses of old style electric lamps. Tell us what you want and we'll tell you the best size of lamps for the purpose. We supply all sizes of the famous EDISON MAZDA Lamps.

Get our prices before buying elsewhere.

(Insert dealer's name here)

Ed-7

In this 1914 advertisement, a salesman for Edison's Mazda lamps tells a homeowner of electric lighting's year-round benefits, including protection against "undesirable callers."

concerns about the safety of electricity—during the 1880s and 1890s several disastrous fires resulted from careless operation and installation. Electricity salesmen, many of whom held engineering degrees, were trained to allay fear as well as to explain the versatility of this new form of lighting.[55]

Makers of new office machinery, such as adding machines, typewriters, and cash registers, built their own sales forces to give detailed explanations of the machines' uses and features. Traveling wholesale drummers did not know enough about these complex products to explain their features or to repair them. The products' expense also made them hard to sell and often required an installment purchase plan to be worked out—something that independent wholesalers or their traveling salesmen were not always able to arrange. The real pioneer of this type of selling was John H. Patterson, whose company, National Cash Register, dominated its market. But other manufacturers of business machines also developed sales forces around the turn of the century.

The Burroughs Adding Machine Company (known as the American Arithmometer Company until 1905) was founded in 1886.[56] After finishing secondary school, William Seward Burroughs (ca. 1857–1898) worked in a bank in Auburn, New York. There he became familiar with the tedious task of recording financial transactions. He conceived of a machine that could perform simple addition and subtraction, and that would not only alleviate the drudgery of the work but also help avoid errors. After moving to St. Louis, Burroughs began to develop his invention. He found backers in two dry-goods merchants and teamed up with another inventor, Joseph Boyer, to help with the project. By 1890, Burroughs had solved the mechanical problems and was able to produce a reliable machine. His own health, however, was never good, and he died from tuberculosis in 1896, just as the company was taking off.[57]

Alvan Macauley, a former patent attorney for National Cash Register, became president of Burroughs and relocated the company to Detroit. After trying to sell the machine through independent dealers, Burroughs created its own agency force. Agents were instructed to devote all their time and effort to sales of Burroughs machines within a specified territory. Machines and supplies were to be sold only for cash (no credit), at prices set by the company rather than by agents, with agents receiving one-third of the selling price as commission. In 1908, the company had 54 offices around the country, 166 salesmen, 39 junior salesmen, and 24 office managers. Altogether they sold over 13,000 machines that year. The largest agencies were New York, with eleven salesmen; Dallas, with ten; Philadelphia, with eight; and Chicago, with seven.[58]

Selling the adding machines was not easy. Salesmen had to make repeated calls to a single customer. "I believe it takes six calls to make a sale of a machine," said one salesman. "I don't mean it takes six calls to sell every machine for I don't think you can sell some in six calls but I think on an average all the sales made are just about in proportion to the number of calls you make."[59] Most sales calls did not result in a sale that day or ever. Even the percentage of sales following trials was fairly low, rising as high as 19 percent and falling as low as 8 percent. On average, only 14 percent of trials resulted in sales.[60]

One obstacle salesmen had to counter was the prejudice of clerks, who resented the new machine and thought it posed a threat to their jobs. This challenge was similar to that faced by cash-register salesmen, who had to persuade clerks that the register did not suggest a distrust of their ability or honesty in handling sales transactions. Also, when the adding machine was introduced, Burroughs and other companies had to send out a circular explaining the features of the new device and suggesting applications that might justify its cost.

At sales conventions, the salesmen and agents provided feedback about the product's design, describing how the machine's glass broke during shipping, the release keys stuck on a particular model, the paper was difficult to load, or the height of display stands was awkward. "Since they have been sending the machine out without these felt pads . . . I have . . . noticed that the paper around the rolls was compressed so that the paper does not feed in but rather behind on these rolls or rings," reported one salesman.[61]

They also discussed the best way to sell the machine. One salesman spoke of his "whirl of talk." He was a former adding-machine representative for the Standard Company, who had previously sold its machine at the price of $185 (about $3,800 today), half the amount of the Burroughs. "I come in with a whirlwind of talk. I talk. I do all the talking. I rush in with a regular cyclone of talk. In fact I really do all the talking. I do not know the Standard. My talk is the only thing on earth. It is the finest thing on earth. She is a cracker jack. It is all right, and I will give you for $185, everything that costs you $375 essential in an adding machine and that kind of talk, and not a detailed talk, and that is

A 1914 class for Burroughs salesmen, teaching them the proper operation of the adding machine as well as the elements of salesmanship.

SPECIAL ALL STAR CONVENTION ISSUE
of the
BURROUGHS SALES BULLETIN
NUMBER 1468—AUGUST 3, 1917

A 1917 All Star Convention for Burroughs salesmen who had made their annual quota. Conventions offered a mix of pageantry, patriotism, and positive thinking. They also gave companies a good way to gather feedback from their sales force and to introduce new products.

the way I had my success with the Standard machine." To sell the Burroughs, he recommended the salesmen develop a "circus whirl of talk" to overwhelm the prospect.[62] A rational-argument approach was favored by C. A. Forster, who referred to his own logical sales presentation as "building a fence around the customer." Frank H. Dodge, an agency manager, gave a demonstration to "build the fence" around a "Mr. Saxton." Dodge began: "Mr. Saxton, this is the latest model machine. You cannot realize the full benefit of this machine, until you can realize the uses to which it may be put."[63] He then proceeded to work methodically through the adding machine's features.

Another salesman, who sold to small banks and to farmers, noted that the physical size of the machine, its smallness, made it seem unworthy of such a large amount of money. "If it was as big as the side of a barn they wouldn't kick so much on the price," he said. To confront them, he asked: "How much [do you] pay for a binder?" The answer was usually $100 to $140. "How many weeks in a year do you use it?" Four to six weeks per year, the farmer would say. "What is the life of it?" Five years. "Thirty weeks' work for $140, when here is a machine that works 52 weeks in the year for 20 years for $375. Isn't it worth it?" the salesman asked, not forgetting to close with a question that would elicit a positive response. The minutes of the convention show that his reasoning was greeted with applause.[64]

The office-machine salesman was critical for the development of American selling. The methods of salesmanship established at Burroughs, NCR, and other companies greatly influenced methods of selling at IBM and other computer companies. Here, more than with other types of selling, salesmen played the vital roles of arranging credit, leasing, and serving as consultants to businessmen. These roles offered particularly important lessons for computer salesmen in the twentieth century, as well as for salespeople of business services.

The Dynamics of Sales Management

By the turn of the century, entrepreneurs at manufacturing companies had come to rely on a great range of promotional lures, including billboards, brand-name promotions, and giveaways. Some of the biggest campaigns synchronized the movements of salesmen with the placement of advertisements in nationally circulating magazines. By 1911, Heinz was using its sales force to change seasonal displays in 25,000 stores in coordination with magazine advertising. Procter and Gamble introduced Crisco in 1912 with an elaborate sales and advertising campaign, in which they pretested different promotional plans and mailed free samples to grocers throughout the country.[65]

As these companies grew, the key figures in charge of selling became sales managers. They wanted to make salesmanship as uniform and predictable as possible and to find ways of teaching it to new recruits. Some companies, especially those selling goods to consumers, trained salesmen to make quick, transactional sales. Door-to-door brush salesmen, for instance, were content with making a single sale and then moving on to the next house. Other companies, like those that sold to retailers and businesses, trained their sales forces to develop long-lasting relationships with customers. Salesmen of branded food products, for instance, tried to do business with the same grocers and shopkeepers over the years.

In pursuing their sales strategies, managers dictated the formal and informal aspects of selling. The formal aspects included quotas, territorial assignments, and compensation rates. Salesmen were frequently paid a mixture of salary and commission. Commission rates varied, depending on the product, the strategy of the company (an effort to introduce a new type of product, for instance, might require a lot of promotion and call for a high rate), and the salesman's position within the firm. At least one company employed newly hired salesmen on a salary basis so that they would not become too discouraged and quit. Then, as they learned more and increased their contacts, they worked on commission.[66]

While there was considerable variation in rates of commission, some patterns were apparent. Often the highest commissions were on office machines and other complex items that required a lot of explanation and instruction and that sold in relatively low volume. The commission for Burroughs Adding Machine agents was about 30 percent of the sale price of the machine; this would go to the regional agent, who then paid the salesman, who actually made from the sale only some portion of this amount. The commission rates for salesmen who sold branded grocery items, such as Heinz pickles, to retailers, were much lower. In the case of Heinz, they were about 5 percent of total sales.

The informal aspects of selling included methods of developing the salesman's confidence, improving sales talks, and building enthusiasm for the job. In many ways, salesmanship proved more difficult to standardize than production procedures. Managers had to contend with the desires of customers, the threat of competitors, and the psychology of the salesmen themselves. Because the sales force worked off-site, managers could not directly oversee their work. In order to ensure that sellers remained motivated, they created various compensation schemes, and they also pursued other strategies designed to increase pressure, such as setting up contests like the "NCR Derby" or the Burroughs "Auto Rally."[67]

Managers also tried to motivate salesmen by appealing to their sense of competition and manliness. In doing so, they continued some of the gender policies of the large wholesale concerns. They tended not to hire women as sales workers, but rather as clerks or secretaries—the "masculine" office jobs were considered to be managerial or executive positions. Managers also tried to cultivate a sense of manliness about selling—a job that, with its emphasis on verbal skills, persuasion, and care for the design of objects, had many characteristics traditionally described as feminine. In sales contests, managers played up the idea that selling was a manly activity. Companies assumed salesmen would compete most vigorously in contests in which they imaginatively shot deer, chopped trees, or threw touchdowns with each sale. Martial themes were also common—as they had been in the campaign to sell Grant's memoirs and in the sale of life insurance at Henry Hyde's Equitable. But by the early twentieth century they became more elaborate: The American Multigraph Sales Company, for example, staged a mock war between the salesmen and an imagined "State of Depression." The war game, a three-month sales campaign, was launched with a special "War Extra" edition of the house newsletter. Bronze, silver, and gold crosses were given to those performing "Signal Sales Service." And those who sold less than a specified minimum ($500) were considered "wounded, crippled, sick, [or] exhausted" and sent to the "Base Hospital" for recovery.[68]

To ratchet up pressure on salesmen, manufacturers sent details of a sales contest home, or made the prize something intended to appeal to a salesman's wife, such as china dinnerware or new furniture. A survey in the late 1920s found that nearly 20 percent of all sales companies had contacted their salesmen's wives, and over half were in favor of doing so. The wife was enlisted as a managerial accomplice, spurring the salesman to greater achievement.[69]

Believing that salesmen needed to feel inspired, confident, and "wide awake" in order to succeed, managers also held motivational lectures, prayer meetings, and theatrical conventions, which made the sales department become the most inspirational, even spiritual, component of the new multiunit enterprises—and gave these enterprises an appropriately evangelical feeling. Often these spiritual expressions reflected the theological underpinnings of what William James described in 1902 as the religions of "healthy-mindedness" (mind cure, New Thought, and to a lesser degree, Christian Science), which promoted a "refusal to feel" unhappiness, rejection, and despair.[70] Sales departments of the early twentieth century launched the careers of professional motivational speakers and helped formalize the type of advice that Dale Carnegie later popularized in *How to Win Friends and Influence People* (1936).

As salesmen went to work for large, multiunit companies, the nature of their jobs changed, and in some of the same ways that production workers' jobs did during this period.[71] Sales managers dictated the pace of work (through quotas), supervised their force carefully, and sought to control work methods by describing in detail a set of procedures to follow. Salesmen working in the sales departments of the large manufacturing companies found that their position held both power and powerlessness. They represented far more wealth and importance than before and were supported by advertising and office staff. Yet they experienced their subordinate position in the firm daily, when, for instance, they filled in reports or attended meetings and got their quota assignments.

The introduction of contests, scripts, and other routines in an occupation that had once celebrated independence, travel, and wit did not occur without conflict. Salesmen, for instance, expressed anger when management seemed to be tying their hands. A salesman from a St. Louis company complained of the imposition of a constraining managerial system. He had previously worked with autonomy, he noted, and then the company put in a "detail" man. The new manager "began to 'systematize,' and being a hound for detail he tied me to a desk until noon every day making out reports and a lot of other foolish stuff. I couldn't make calls on my distributors. I had to clear everything through the house. I had built up a reputation for the house for quick service. Now everything was delayed. I began to lose money."[72]

Salesmen were especially annoyed with managers who set themselves apart and considered themselves better than the men on the force. "The worst session of knocking that I ever sat in on was after a dinner at a New York hotel," wrote one salesman. "The sales manager we were with, sat at a table with some of the other executives of the company and let us eat at another table. Perhaps he meant nothing by it, but somehow it made us all feel resentful, until finally one of us opened up with some complaints we had on our chest. Then we all got into it, and from that time on, we made life miserable for that boss."[73] Every sales manager grappled with the expensive problem of turnover. A leading insurance executive estimated that of the 150,000 licensed insurance agents in the United States in 1915, half would leave the business before the end of a year.[74]

The creation of sales departments at large firms had the potential to transform selling, yet it also raised new problems. How could salesmen best be managed? How could the success of individual salesmen be measured? How high should quotas be? How should territories be determined and assigned? How much should salesmen be paid? What were the most effective ways to train and motivate salesmen? In short, how could a system be imposed on the sales process? Modern sales management, the most ardent enthusiasts of salesmanship claimed, should be run according to scientific principles. No one pursued this idea more vigorously than John H. Patterson at National Cash Register.

The Pyramid Plan   5

John H. Patterson
and the Pursuit of Efficiency

The salesman's life in a large manufacturing company was
a mixture of heaven and hell: heaven during the conventions and pep rallies, and hell when he missed his quotas.[1]
Nowhere were these extremes more evident than in the
managerial policies John H. Patterson developed at National Cash Register. Patterson created a global system
of management that pressured salesmen to seek out new
customers (and sell replacement merchandise to existing
ones) and to quash competitors. He spent lavishly to build
his organization, encouraged salesmen to view the company's interests as indistinguishable from their own, and
then pushed the goals to emotional extremes.

Patterson (1844–1922), a contemporary of Heinz,
Candler, and Burroughs, had great enthusiasm for the
possibilities of salesmanship to transform his business.
Patterson in some ways resembled the peddler James
Guild, who delighted in the cleverness of a sales pitch, and
the drummer Saunders Norvell, who saw salesmanship
as crucial for building lasting business connections. Like
other executives at large manufacturing companies,
Patterson sought to build a system of sales management
that would coordinate production and distribution. But
Patterson went further, by striving to make an all-encom-
passing science of selling. Because of his influence on the

117

coming of modern sales management, this chapter examines this single sales "enthusiast" in detail.

Beginning in the mid-1880s and continuing to his death in 1922, Patterson promoted "scientific" salesmanship more than anyone else ever had.[2] Like Frederick W. Taylor, the founder of scientific management, Patterson divided business processes into uniform procedures that could be taught to the mass of men who would undertake them. Also like Taylor, he placed the pace of work under managerial control by demanding that salesmen meet monthly quotas. But Patterson, in his efforts to reform selling, faced different challenges than Taylor.[3] He had to confront the unpredictability of the sales transaction as well as the problem of keeping off-site salesmen motivated. Patterson's ideas about how to run a large sales campaign were no doubt shaped by his military experience. Yet his own interests, or even fascination, with systems led him to become enamored of even the fads and pseudosciences popular in the late nineteenth century. His own faith in these ideas, and more generally in esoteric science, gave him the zeal of a missionary. Patterson believed in the need to break men down, treating them cruelly at times, and then to rebuild them as good agents or executives for NCR.[4]

Patterson's faith in salesmen's ability to create demand and to stifle competition shaped his entire managerial strategy. He paid salesmen an extraordinarily high commission and spent a great amount of time motivating his sales force through company newsletters and conventions. Patterson developed managerial methods that, to some extent, made motivation itself replicable and predictable; in portraying the cash register as an instrument of security and accurate accounting, he attempted to turn his salesmen into evangelicals for the company. Perhaps more than anything else, as one article noted, he "sold the salesman on the economic importance of his job, and in so doing gave him religion."[5]

Patterson saw sales and advertising as *driving* production, rather than the other way around, and he had great faith in the ability of his salesmen, imbued with the proper technique, to persuade "prospects" to purchase the NCR brand. These techniques of persuasion did not stop with highlighting the features of machines; they also relied on methods of speech (such as frequently asking questions that elicited a positive response) and gestures (such as handing customers a pen to pressure them to sign an order). Moreover, the case of NCR demonstrates the cumulative value of individual sales; although there were other, similarly advanced, cash registers on the market, NCR was able to garner sale after sale.

Patterson was determined to create a class of white-collar representatives—salesmen who dressed conservatively, were well rehearsed in company procedures, and issued daily reports to the home office. His goal was to create a system that did not depend on any individual, but could train new recruits to replace the old ones who were no longer effective or had grown too ambitious, or rebellious, for Patterson's tastes and so were fired.

The managerial system he developed included methods to train salesmen throughout the globe in company policies and products, to track the flow of money from a vast number of transactions, and to measure the demand of the marketplace town by town. In a sense, Patterson combined the canvasser's persistence and the wholesale drummer's cultivation of long-term relationships: he worked out a detailed script for salesmen to follow while encouraging his salesmen to develop lasting connections with businessmen and storeowners.

While Patterson was not typical, he exhibited many aspects of effective sales managers in the extreme. His success, and his knack for self-publicity, made him influential in the formative period of sales management. One of his loyal employees, Thomas J. Watson, developed a similar sales force at IBM—and Watson was only one of several well-known, well-paid executives who learned from Patterson.

Building the Cash-Register Business

Beginning in the late nineteenth century and continuing into the early twentieth, the invention of the typewriter, cash register, and adding machine changed the daily routine of the secretary, shop clerk, accountant, and bank teller. With their quick and accurate processing of information, these and other small business machines were the computers of their day. More than mere appliances, they came to symbolize the essence of modern business practice. George F. Babbitt, in Sinclair Lewis's eponymous novel, dreamed about office machinery as he passed through downtown Zenith: "At the Simplex Office Furniture Shop, the National Cash Register Agency, he yearned for a dictaphone, for a typewriter which would add and multiply, as a poet yearns for quartos or a physician for radium."[6]

Manufacturers of such machinery discovered that their product was not always an easy sell. Businessmen were reluctant to purchase expensive machines that they had never needed before; they had to be persuaded that the new equipment would result in improved efficiency and saving. Critical to a manufacturer's success was an effective sales force, and office-machine makers were among the first businesses to develop their own sales organizations.[7]

Patterson did not enter the cash-register business until he was forty years of age. He was born in 1844 on a farm in Dayton, Ohio, the seventh of eleven children. He served briefly in the Civil War as a hundred-day enlistee in the 131st Ohio Volunteer Infantry, then attended Dartmouth College, graduating in 1867. Patterson had a driving interest in building efficient organizations, and, like others who perceived selling as a "campaign," he admired military order. As he wrote years later, "I believe that a business ought to be like a battleship in many respects—in cleanliness, in order, in the perfect discipline of the men, in the readiness for use of every part of the plant."[8]

Patterson's first job was as a toll collector along a canal in Dayton. He soon started a side business selling coal and wood, eventually developing it into a full-time pursuit. In 1879, he formed a partnership with one of his brothers, and the two came to operate several coal mines and retail coal yards. The business failed a few years later, but in the meantime Patterson had become one of the earliest owners of a cash register. As he later recalled, he purchased the machine after he suspected a clerk of stealing from the cash drawer; the register provided him with an accurate list of the day's receipts. The machine Patterson bought was made by the National Manufacturing Company of Dayton under a patent held by a former saloonkeeper named James Ritty. In 1883, Patterson purchased 8.5 percent of the company's stock for $1,250; the following year, using the money he had left after settling his debts from the coal company, he bought a controlling interest for an additional $6,500. Soon thereafter he changed the firm's name to the National Cash Register Company.[9]

When Patterson took control, NCR had thirteen employees. He quickly expanded both the factory workforce and the number of salesmen. He persuaded salesmen who sold registers part-time to become full-fledged National agents and devote all their energy to the firm. Agents were paid by commission, the standard method of compensation at many concerns, but one made disreputable by its association

John H. Patterson, ca. 1882, two years before he founded National Cash Register Company.

with insurance solicitors, itinerant book salesmen, and other canvassers from whom Patterson wished to distance himself.[10] In the 1880s, agents kept about half the money they made on a register sale. As Samuel Crowther reported, agents were shipped registers on consignment. The list price of registers ran from $150 to $200 for the most popular models, and agents were entitled to a high 50 percent discount on the purchase price; several of the early NCR agents made fortunes. The rate of commission would not remain this high, however, and by 1919 it averaged 31 percent.[11] In part, resorting to commission pay in the company's early days was done out of necessity, for there was not enough money to pay salaries, but it also fit with Patterson's belief in the need to motivate salesmen. Agents were expected to open a retail office and were given a "guaranteed territory" that awarded them the whole commission in a particular area; this strategy was different than just assigning salesmen territory to cover, for it prevented them from competing against one another for the same customers. Patterson was convinced that such a plan would make salesmen more likely to share selling techniques.[12] Agents hired salesmen to help cover their territories. Whereas agents were employed directly by NCR, salesmen were legally the employees of the agent. They could be paid on either a salary or a commission basis, as the agent saw fit.[13]

By May 1888, the company had agents working in thirty-four U.S. cities, from Pensacola, Florida, to Portland, Oregon. The most productive agencies at the time included Dayton, Ohio, which took orders that month for 45 registers; Chicago, 35; New York, 18; and Boston and Philadelphia, 15 each.[14] The New York and New England area produced the most revenue for the company. Total domestic sales for 1896 were 9,600 registers, with a noticeable concentration in the Northeast, especially New York (11 percent of the total) and Boston (7 percent).[15]

From the time he founded the company in 1884, Patterson hoped to build an international sales organization. Singer had been the first modern American manufacturer to conduct an overseas business, and by the 1880s it already had three decades of foreign sales experience. It was followed by McCormick, Kodak, and other companies.[16] As Mira Wilkins noted, expansion abroad usually went through predictable stages. Companies first used the services of an international exporting firm, then appointed a salaried representative or constructed an international sales branch, and finally, established an overseas manufacturing plant. By 1886, NCR was already in the second stage, having appointed agents in London, Liverpool, and Berlin.[17]

In 1893 the company magazine, *NCR*, reported, "The tinkle of the National Cash Register bell is heard around the world," although, in fact, NCR's overseas business at this time was restricted mostly to Europe. In Germany the company was expecting to sell one hundred registers per month. In Great Britain, with its recent invention of a machine specifically to accommodate British currency, NCR hoped to sell twice that number. Holland and Belgium accounted for eight to ten sales per month. The company had agents working in Norway, Sweden, and Denmark, and recorded sales in France, Austria, and Italy as well.[18] By 1896, 23 percent of total sales were made outside the United States and Canada. Great Britain had 9 percent of total sales; Germany, 8 percent; and Australia and South Africa, 2 percent each.[19]

Because of the high price of NCR cash registers, sales agents had to convince proprietors that the machine would eventually pay for itself. NCR's early advertisements resembled the contemporary flyers of life-insurance companies. In both, the aim was to heighten customer fear and uncertainty. In the cash-register trade, the fear centered on stolen revenue. One of Patterson's advertisements, proclaiming "Stop the Leaks," depicted shop owners ruined by clerks who stole from their cash drawers.[20] This marketing strategy posed problems for NCR, because clerks and bartenders resented the implication that a mechanical "thief-catcher" was a necessary coworker. Some even organized protective associations to keep the product out.[21] In instances of intense opposition by clerks to newly installed registers, Patterson sent detectives to supervise the machine's operation. *NCR* for June 1888 printed a letter from a merchant in Detroit whose store had been watched by an NCR-hired detective. "Your operative's report relative to my man not registering is at hand. I was very much surprised, as it caught a man, above all others,

I have relied upon, not only in the bar but in other matters in the house."[22]

As cash registers became more common, the company entered a new marketing phase, adding sophisticated features to the machine and presenting it as essential to modern, efficient methods of accounting and inventory control. Rather than emphasizing the shopkeeper's fear of thievery by a trusted employee, NCR advertisements began to highlight the fear of losing profits through sloppy record-keeping and inaccurate data.[23] The company also targeted a wider range of clients. As late as 1896, saloons still accounted for 24 percent of its sales, but NCR was also selling to general merchants (17 percent of total sales), drugstores (11 percent), and grocers (9 percent).[24]

To ensure that salesmen communicated all the benefits of the register, Patterson gave them scripts to memorize. The first NCR sales script was the creation of Patterson's brother-in-law, Joseph H. Crane, in 1887. *How I Sell National Cash Registers,* which became known as the *Primer,* contained instructions not only on what salesmen should say but also on what they were to do while saying it.[25] In the *Primer,* an asterisk indicated that the salesman was supposed to point to the item he was referring to:

This,* Mr. Merchant, is a National Cash Register of the most approved pattern.

To appreciate what a help it would be to you, we must see what things you do in your store of which you keep a record.

I think the ordinary daily transactions with your customers may be arranged in five classes, thus:

1. You sell goods for cash.

2. You sell goods for credit.

3. You receive cash on account.

4. You pay out cash.

5. You change a coin or bill.

Am I right?

Now, sir, this register* makes the entries.

The indication* of the transaction shows through this glass.*

The amount* of the last recorded transaction is always visible, and the records are made by pressing the keys.[26]

The *Primer* divided a sale into four steps: approach, proposition, demonstration, and close. In the *approach*, the salesman made no mention of the cash register. Instead, he explained that he wanted to help the businessman find ways to increase profits—that he wanted, in effect, to act as a consultant. In the *proposition*, the salesman described the regis-

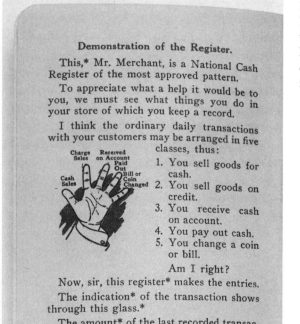

Demonstration of the Register.

This,* Mr. Merchant, is a National Cash Register of the most approved pattern.

To appreciate what a help it would be to you, we must see what things you do in your store of which you keep a record.

I think the ordinary daily transactions with your customers may be arranged in five classes, thus:

Charge Sales Received on Account Paid Out Bill or Coin Changed Cash Sales

1. You sell goods for cash.
2. You sell goods on credit.
3. You receive cash on account.
4. You pay out cash.
5. You change a coin or bill.

Am I right?

Now, sir, this register* makes the entries.

The indication* of the transaction shows through this glass.*

The amount* of the last recorded transaction is always visible, and the records are made by pressing the keys.

*Point out what is referred to.

4

Page from original NCR sales *Primer,* telling salesmen how best to introduce the cash register, 1887.

ter for the first time and explained how it would prevent theft and give an accurate account of the day's receipts. The goal of this stage was to schedule a demonstration of the machine in a nearby hotel where the salesman had set up a display, or, if convenient, in the local NCR branch office. During the *demonstration,* the salesman carefully led the customer to the point of a purchase. When the moment seemed right, he attempted to *close.* This was the toughest part of the sale. The *Primer* offered a number of techniques, including the following:

> After you have made your proposition clear and feel sure that the merchant realizes the value of the register, do not ask for an order, take for granted that he will buy. Say to him: "Now, Mr. Blank, what color shall I make it?" or "How soon do you want delivery?" . . . Take out the order blank, fill it out, and handing him your pen say, "Just sign here where I have made the cross." . . .
>
> If he objects, find out why, answer his objections and again prepare him for signature . . . Make the merchant feel that he is buying because of his own good judgment . . . find out the real reason why [he objects] and your chances are that that is the very reason why he should buy . . . Concentrate your whole force on one good strong point, appeal to judgment, get him to acknowledge that what you say is true, then hand the pen to him in a matter-of-fact way and keep on with what you were saying. This makes signing the logical and obvious thing to do.[27]

The *Primer* instructed salesmen to exert pressure in a forceful yet subtle manner. The key was to prevent a prospect from feeling manipulated. "Avoid giving the impression to the merchant that you are trying to force him to buy. No man likes to feel he is being sold."[28] At the same time, it was important for the salesman to exude confidence and honesty. Chief among the rules of salesmanship at NCR was the ability to demonstrate "sympathy [toward] . . . the business and interests of the P. P. ["Probable Purchaser"] and sincerity in presenting [the] machines to the P. P."[29] These were skills to be honed. After an agent named John T. Watson had given a demonstration at the 1895 sales convention, one audience member praised Watson's "sincerity" and another commented, "The best thing I noticed in the demonstration was that Mr. Watson's manner indicated that he thought he was telling the truth."[30]

Even careful use of the *Primer* could not, of course, guarantee a smooth sale. The process of selling remained a cat-and-mouse game. When A. T. Webb, the agent for Portland, Oregon, set out to sell a machine, he began, as the *Primer* advised, by studying the prospect and gaining his "confidence." When confronting an objection, he acknowledged the legitimacy of the complaint and then tried to counter it.

> My method of taking orders, I presume, does not vary much from that of other managers. If the party calling is a stranger, the first thing is to learn and know my man, his residence, business, etc., and get his confidence; then, I settle down, and will sell him the register best adapted to his wants and business; or, if he has made up his mind that he wants one like his neighbor's, I sell him that one, no matter if, in my judgment, it is not entirely best suited to his business. After I have his order in black and white, I then, if I think it advisable, undertake to educate him on the different registers, and see that he gets one best adapted to his work.
>
> High prices, of course, are one of the hard things to contend with. On this point I generally say, "to you, no doubt, the price seems high, and I don't blame you one bit for thinking so, because you lack experience and the knowledge of what our register will do." . . . Frequently, in the course of my talk, I will tell the P. P. that I don't want to sell him a register, and will not, if I think he has no use or don't care to use the register according to our instructions. As a reason for this, I tell him that one register misplaced might possibly spoil the sale of a dozen.[31]

This pattern—of first acknowledging the customer's complaint, and then trying to counter it—was typical of formulaic sales pitches.

Over the years, the *Primer* was frequently revised. Shortly after being introduced, it was supplemented by a *Book of Arguments* that contained a catalog of answers to frequently asked questions. In January 1894, NCR produced a more formal *Sales Manual* that combined the two.[32] The *Manual* reached its maximum size in the edition of 1904, with nearly two hundred pages. After that it was condensed so salesmen could master it more easily. The 1910 edition was a booklet of fifty-six pages.[33] Changes to the *Primer* were regarded like alterations in the register—both were part of an effort to continually improve and keep up with shifting customer needs.[34]

While the *Primer* provided a way of standardizing the salesmen's approach, Patterson also looked for new methods to regulate and monitor their day-to-day activities. He had salesmen write out daily reports that were then sent to Dayton. These provided a picture of how thoroughly a territory was being covered and how well competition was being suppressed (or "knocked out").[35] An NCR agent in Cleveland recalled writing such reports in the early 1890s: "The report contained the customers we called on, the sales we made—knockouts that we made; in fact, general history on a daily report to the Company regarding our business done that day, and calling on prospective customers and users, and opposition . . . The salesman would turn over his daily reports to the sales agent he was under, and the sales agent forwarded it to The National Cash Register Company. The sales agent reported the same day."[36]

Most important, Patterson assigned quotas to each agency. Initially quotas were set according to the population of the territory. Patterson had calculated that one cash register could be sold for every four hundred people living in a given area.[37] In time, however, quotas came to be based on the previous year's volume of sales. The actual quota numbers were not set by the number of registers to be sold, but by a point system based on the value of transactions, with each point equaling $25. In 1898 a moderately sized agency operating out of Toledo, Ohio, had a monthly quota of 70 points, or 840 points per year, and was expected to transact $21,000 (about $450,000 today) in merchandise during the year. The New York agency, meanwhile, had a monthly quota of 630 points, or 7,560 points per year, and was expected to bring in annual revenues of $189,000 (about $4 million today).[38]

Quotas were in place as early as April 1892 and were difficult to meet. Of twenty-five agents whose statistics were printed in *NCR* that month, only four had made 100 percent of their monthly quota.[39] Once in place, quotas were never lowered, reflecting Patterson's belief that the market would never be truly saturated and that customers could be induced to buy replacement machines. To increase the pressure on salesmen, the company held thematic sales contests, like the NCR Derby, in which salesmen competed for additional prizes in a race to make the quota.[40]

Not only were individual agents' sales records printed in *NCR*; so too were their records for collecting payments. Regular, on-time collections were critical at NCR, which remained a family-owned company dependent on internal financing. Salesmen often had to pressure customers to pay delinquent accounts.[41] The report of the Legal Department for April 1893 showed 511 overdue accounts, amounting to over $53,000 (about $1 million today). The company blamed its agents for the mounting debt. NCR advised: "Some of you think that all you have to do is to take orders and we will do the rest . . . We want Sales Agents to instruct their Salesmen to hustle collections just as hard as they hustle for orders."[42]

The Charismatic Leader

Essential to the company culture was Patterson himself—a small, wiry man who exhibited a ferocious temper, kept his executives on edge, and lectured his employees on selling and a range of other topics both professional and personal. The sociologist Nicole Woolsey Biggart, in her study of direct-selling organizations published in 1989, highlighted the role that "charismatic" leaders often played in such companies. This type of leader encouraged a sense of mission among sales agents and fostered a spirit of individual initiative within the corporate structure. Alfred C. Fuller, who founded the Fuller Brush Company in 1906, and Mary Kay Ash, who established her cosmetic company in 1963, both maintained a highly personal presence in their corporate leadership, sending inspirational letters to employees and offering advice on personal topics. Biggart found that employees in such enterprises often described their job as a "way of life" and participated in spirited public celebrations of the company.[43]

While Patterson did not head a door-to-door sales operation like those of Fuller and Ash, he did place his personal stamp firmly on the National Cash Register Company. Patterson aspired to be more than a mere business executive: he also attempted to create a model working environment at NCR by improving conditions in the Dayton factory. He built a brightly lit facility that included a cafeteria, hospital, library, and recreational facility, and he showed movies to employees and hosted lectures at lunchtime.[44] To advertise these innovations, Patterson opened the factory to the public. Visitors passed landscaped gardens of flowering plants and green lawns. They saw mock grocery stores and butcher shops, each displaying a shiny cash register, and teams of workers in front of well-kept machinery.[45]

Through newsletters, journals, and speeches, Patterson incessantly communicated his theories about work and life to NCR agents and factory laborers. His messages reveal a deep interest in popular science and pseudoscience, including numerous health and diet fads. *NCR,* for instance, frequently ran articles on the work of Horace Fletcher, the advocate of thorough mastication, and John Harvey Kellogg, director of the Battle Creek sanatorium.[46] And in 1905 Patterson hired a director of physical culture, Charles Palmer, who displayed an active interest in phrenology and physiognomy.[47] Stanley Allyn, who joined NCR in 1913 after graduating from college and rose to become the company's president, recalled that Patterson "was for a time obsessed by the numeral five, and for days on end we prepared variations on the theme. These took such forms as a notice to salesmen of five things they must do, five things they must avoid."[48] Such interests caused some to dismiss Patterson as a "lunatic," but for others they added a veneer of science, or at least special insight, to his directives and contributed to a sense of order and efficiency within the company.[49]

Workers in a traditional bureaucracy experienced a different type of environment than people who were employed in sales organizations under a "charismatic" leader.[50] Those laboring at conventional bureaucracies tended to receive financial reward in the form of salary. Charismatically led organizations, by contrast, had "missions" and a belief in the "moral superiority" of entrepreneurship. For compensation, em-

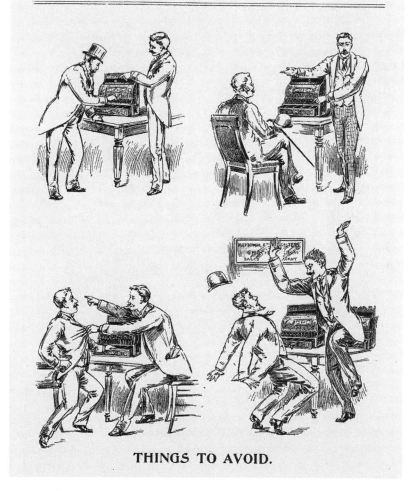

A September 1893 cover of *NCR* shows salesmen what to avoid: allowing the prospect to touch the machine, pointing, grabbing, and gesturing.

Vol. XIII.   Dayton, Ohio, October 1, 1900.   No. 19.

"Ready for the Road."

In an October 1900 issue of *NCR*, the salesman is portrayed as well dressed, robust, and "ready for the road."

ployees received a combination of material and "purposeful" (or symbolic) incentives. Moreover, under charismatic leadership, people were encouraged to transform themselves in order to achieve personal success. Biggart wrote that people in (direct) sales organizations were committed to positive thinking—"a belief that if one imagines success then success will follow, and that failure is the result of poor thought habits." The presence of a leader created "ideological focus" within the organization.[51]

Beginning in the 1890s, Patterson became interested in the pyramid, a common symbol in contemporary spiritual and pseudoscientific literature. His draft of an organizational chart for the company took that shape. "Mr. Patterson was extremely fond of his complex organizational pyramids," noted Allyn, "with names arranged in a fine flow downward from his own eminence."[52] The company was subdivided into one pyramid containing the board of directors, three "originating pyramids" (the legal, publishing, and labor divisions), and three "operating pyramids" (the so-called making, recording, and selling divisions). Most important, the organizational shape emphasized the place of Patterson at the top. "Through that pyramid plan, the entire business of The National Cash Register Company was conducted," explained Hugh Chalmers, second vice president and general manager.[53]

The pyramid was a prominent symbol in the late nineteenth century, particularly in Rosicrucian and Theosophical traditions. Theosophy founder Madame Blavatsky claimed that mathematical, scientific, and astrological truths could be discerned in the geometry of the Great Pyramid of Egypt. Two popular works of the late nineteenth century also used the Great Pyramid to comment on biblical scripture—John Taylor's *The Great Pyramid: Why Was It Built? And Who Built It?* (1859) and Charles Piazzi Smyth's *Our Inheritance in the Great Pyramid* (1864). Smyth's work inspired the founding of the International Institute for Preserving and Perfecting Weights and Measures in Boston in 1879, which aimed to use the measurements of the pyramid as standard units; the institute had an auxiliary branch in Patterson's home state of Ohio. Taylor and Smyth both emphasized the importance of the pyramid's five-sided shape. One of Smyth's disciples elaborated on this point: "This intense *fiveness* could not have been accidental, and likewise corresponds with the arrangements of God, both in nature and revelation. Note the fiveness of termination to each limb of the human body, the five senses, the five books of Moses, the twice five precepts of the Decalogue."[54]

In time, Patterson came to render nearly all his strategic and instructional charts in the pyramidal shape. One such pyramid plan, labeled the "Science of Selling," described the five qualities of successful salesmen: health, honesty, ability, industry, and knowledge of the business. Typical of much of the writing in *NCR*, this "plan," with its mention of "magnetism" and "animal spirits," exhibited the language of popular pseudoscience and emphasized connections between health and busi-

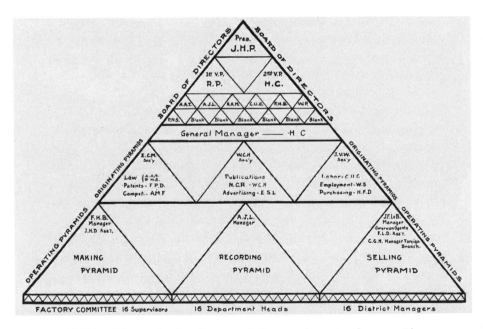

NCR's 1903 organization chart reveals Patterson's passion for pyramids. Naturally, he ("J.H.P.") sits at the top.

ness success. "A sickly, nervous man cannot exert that personal magnetism which unconsciously cuts such a large figure in the success of every salesman," it explained. "Not only the practical manager of the sales department of every large corporation, but as well the professors who write on the psychology of salesmanship, insist that good health and abundant animal spirits are perhaps the most important qualifications a salesman can have for his work."[55]

Patterson's most direct method of communicating with his agents was through motivational sales conventions. He convened the first such meeting in the Phillips Hotel in Dayton in 1886.[56] Agent A. T. Webb was in attendance that winter and recalled: "It was the convention which swung me into line and made me a National Cash Register agent."[57] By the late nineteenth century, conventions had become big, company-boosting affairs, with factory tours, sales-training workshops, lectures by engineers and inventors, and territory-by-territory reports from all the agencies. Conventions provided a way for the company to communicate its culture to agents, many of whom labored far from Dayton. They also provided a forum for agents to discuss strategy. An NCR salesman from St. Louis remembered meeting agents "from all over the country" who talked "about different systems and merchants they had sold; for example, a particularly hard case that they thought might help us overcome some objection from some merchant in our part of the country."[58] Conventions were episodes of emotional extremes, as company executives greeted salesmen with rousing speeches and martial music and assigned them quotas for the coming season.

Conventions also gave the company the opportunity to send a message to sales agents, reminding them of its high expectations. This was done in dramatic fashion. One agent recalled a not-too-subtle message at a convention lecture in 1895: "Over the center of the platform of the chapel was a clock. Upon the dial at each hour was painted a bag of money. Each bag was marked $500. On the face of the clock was the motto: 'The time of this convention is worth $500 an hour. Do not waste it.'"[59]

The convention summarized NCR's somewhat contradictory approach to its agents. On the one hand was the impulse to break a man down by reminding him of his quotas or testing him on his sales speech. On the other hand, the company encouraged agents to see themselves as independent businessmen who could earn virtually unlimited commissions. At an NCR convention, for instance, salesman John M. Wilson—quite likely planted by Patterson himself—gave the following address: "I want to thank you, Mr. Patterson, for the fine job *you* are doing working for *me* . . . My stock of merchandise, my inventory, was furnished by the company on consignment, costing me nothing. I needed no advertising manager, for Mr. Patterson, working with a big advertising department and printing plant at the factory, took on that job for me."[60]

A recurrent lesson put across by Patterson was the power of positive thought and determined effort. Edward Deeds, an engineer who was hired in 1899 and later became company president, recalled a convention at which Patterson ordered an entire building on the NCR grounds to be taken down in one evening and a patch of grass put in its place. With extraordinary effort and a crew of men, Deeds was able to accomplish the task while the salesmen slept. The next day Patterson used the magical disappearance of the building to illustrate that anything could be done if people set their minds to it.[61]

For Patterson, the greatest inhibitors of success were cowardice, discouragement, and lack of confidence. This was the message he emphasized to agents at conventions as he raised their quotas year after year: a territory could never be saturated if a salesman simply put his mind to it, worked hard, kept pressuring prospects, and made sure the competition was kept down. "Don't be satisfied," Patterson wrote in the *NCR*. "It is a great mistake for a man to rest on his laurels and pat himself too much on the back every time he does something."[62] Mottoes were chiseled into the walls of the NCR factory: "We progress through change." "Good enough is the enemy of the best."[63]

Patterson perceived himself as the founder not only of NCR but of the entire cash-register business. As he told one business associate who had invested some money in a rival cash-register concern: "Get your money out of it; I will break up any set of men that go into the register business; I own these patents; I developed the business; and I have spent about twenty years of my life to do it; and I don't propose that any man shall reap the fruits of it."[64] His managerial style was to convince agents to feel that they, too, were self-starters who had developed their own agencies and received compensation according to their efforts and abilities. Yet at the same time, he reminded them that they were part of something much bigger: the ever-watchful "pyramid" headquartered at Dayton.

The NCR Schoolhouse

NCR had been the pioneer in the cash-register industry and remained dominant through the early years. In the mid-1890s it faced new challenges, however, including an economic depression, that led Patterson to expand his marketing efforts still further.

The depression that began in 1893 was dire in a number of sectors of the economy, from farming to business; it was not a period of low production but of falling prices. Businessmen had several responses to the economic conditions: they introduced new managerial policies designed to decrease their dependence on skilled labor, and they devised marketing strategies for finding customers overseas.[65] The 1890s were also a period of industrial consolidation. The merger movement, which commenced between 1890 and 1893 and had lagged during the depression, revived in 1898 after the financial markets improved and following several Supreme Court decisions that seemed favorable to consolidation.[66]

Patterson undertook a number of initiatives. He introduced tighter methods of sales management, increased the number of salesmen at home and abroad, and suppressed competition, either by forcing competitors to fail or by purchasing them outright. Meanwhile, he repeatedly voiced a theme common in the literature of salesmanship—that the way out of hard times was simply to redouble effort. "When times got duller, we advertised the more and worked the harder," he later recalled.[67] Patterson had prepared for the depression by reading the prophecies of the "Ohio farmer" Samuel Benner, a homespun philosopher and economist who, beginning in 1875, published his predictions of economic cycles in *Benner's Prophecies; or, Future Ups and Downs in Prices*. Patterson was an ardent follower of Benner, and he reprinted his writings in *NCR*. Benner, who based his market forecasts on pig-iron prices, predicted dire economic news for 1891 and the six years following it. To some of Benner's followers, these forecasts signaled the need to retreat from commerce. Patterson chose instead to adopt a "lifeboat" view of the economy, hoping to survive while his competitors sank.[68]

Beginning in early 1893, Patterson intensified his efforts to monitor and train the sales force. From March until June 1893, he and E. D. Gibbs, NCR's advertising manager, visited the domestic agencies. The two stopped in all major American cities and held ad hoc conventions. They examined each agent "on his selling methods, his style of approaching a storekeeper, his ways of closing sales, his personal appearance, his attitude towards the prospect, and [then] . . . put in considerable time inspecting the showrooms and finding out how registers were exhibited and sales made." During the trip, Patterson wrote out new rules for agents and salesmen. Roll call was held each morning at 8:15 A.M., at which time the prior day's reports were to be turned in; by 9:00 A.M. all agents were expected to be out in their territories and to work them all day. Every Monday morning at 8:00 A.M. the heads of the agencies were required to hold a meeting to review the week's goals.[69]

Patterson issued a warning in the *NCR* to agents who were unable to memorize the *Primer:* "We do not propose taking any excuses, hereafter. We have demonstrated, on this trip, the advantages of using the 'Primer' and carrying out the instructions of the Company. The Agents who fail to do so, for any reason whatever, will have their contracts cancelled without any further cause."[70] For those who complained that they liked to sell the register in their own style, Patterson asked: "How would it do for a good actor like Booth, every time he plays Hamlet, to play it in a different way?"[71] To help maintain Patterson's standard approach, Patterson assigned agent Joseph H. Crane the task of testing agents around the country on their knowledge of the *Primer* and reporting the results by name in *NCR*.[72] The testing had become necessary not only because of fears of hard times but also because the number of registers NCR offered had increased, and salesmen were required to know much more about individual models than before. By the turn of the century, the company was offering over one hundred different styles of machines and accessories.[73]

To improve skills further, Patterson in 1894 inaugurated a sales school in Dayton. The initial course lasted six weeks and taught basic retail accounting skills, methods of demonstrating the register, and issues of good health and manners.[74] The first "NCR Schoolhouse" was a cottage that stood on the old Patterson family farm property, but the company soon set up makeshift schools throughout the country and abroad. In 1896 there were seven classes and 106 pupils at the Dayton school. Of these, 70 were still with the company at the year's end. NCR found that 30 percent of the graduates nonetheless did not stay with the company for a full year, due to what it termed "natural" causes, including discouragement and a lack of ability.[75] In 1901 the school program was expanded to include a tour through the factory, a luncheon at the Officers' Club, and addresses by the president and vice president.[76]

J. H. Stacey, an agent for NCR in Missouri, recalled his experience in 1907 at an NCR school at his local agency.

> I was put in a school at St. Louis, along with twelve or thirteen other men, and was kept in the school for about thirty days and then put out in the city territory to work. At the school we had a regular instructor who called us in about 9 o'clock in the morning and kept us until 5:30 or 6 in the evening . . . He got up before us like any other teacher would, and gave us a talk about some certain machine that would be on the line for a display that day. Then he gave us examination papers to be filled out. We filled those papers out at night and came back the next day and turned them over to him. He gave us a regular percentage of efficiency each day, marked our papers to show how well we learned our lesson.[77]

For some salesmen the relentless rehearsing of arguments raised troubling issues. Former salesman T. C. Henry described his experiences at an NCR school in his scathing book, *Tricks of the Cash Register*

Trust (1913). "There was never an argument of any kind brought out by any merchant against the use of cash registers, which has not been thoroughly thrashed out by the selling force in the schools and conventions of the NCR company," he wrote. He described NCR as a "shark," which trained salesmen to prey on small storeowners and competitors with manipulative arguments. "No merchant can meet the shark . . . And all the shark wants is an argument, in order that he may entangle the merchant."[78]

The demands of selling at NCR increased after the turn of the century. Pressure was not confined to work hours but went home with the sales agent as well. Unlike many peddlers or even a large share of traveling salesmen, most agents were married, and Patterson enlisted the support of the wives in improving performance. He did this by encouraging the wives' interest in their husbands' success. In addition to the previously mentioned dining tables or china offered as contest prizes,[79] sometimes Patterson invited wives to come without their husbands to Dayton for their own convention, where NCR put on plays and lectured on dress and diet.[80] At one such convention he posted a banner proclaiming the ten things a wife could do to help her husband succeed:

1. Serve simple well-cooked food.
2. Keep him cheerful.
3. Give him plenty of fresh air.
4. See that he gets enough sleep.
5. Lend encouragement at the right time.
6. See that he takes regular exercise.
7. Be economical and save for a rainy day.
8. Take a real interest in his sales record.
9. Read NCR advertising matter.
10. Be cheerful yourself.[81]

Patterson promoted the use of such techniques in the business press, publishing "Wives: Assistant Salesmen" in the magazine *System*, the precursor to *Business Week*.[82] A Dartnell report included a section on "Reaching the Salesmen [*sic*] through His Wife." The section mentioned

NCR and featured a letter written by a woman who attended an NCR wives' convention. Another letter advised: "Never appear disappointed when he returns home late. Compliment him always on the good business he has secured during the day and week. Talk over with him the importance of using simple language in his demonstrations. Be more particular to serve nutritious food at every meal."[83]

The establishment of relations between a company and the wives of salesmen was not uncommon.[84] A survey in 1921 noted, "Sales managers are utilizing the salesman's home ties more and more in developing him into a bigger business producer." The "married salesman is usually susceptible to the influence of his wife, and various plans are in use to win her co-operation."[85] Another survey, later in the decade, found that nearly 20 percent of all sales companies had contacted their salesmen's wives at one point. Often the effort was to enlist the wife as a managerial accomplice—checking up on the salesman's progress, spurring him to greater achievement.[86]

Such managerial tactics extended the supervision of salesmen beyond their peers at the company into the home. Just as contest themes were selected to provoke salesmen by challenging their manliness, the involvement of wives forced the salesman to prove his role as a husband and father; his success in these events established his standing in the company and in the family.

Starting in 1906, NCR salesmen who made their quota were allowed to join the newly formed One Hundred Point Club, which held its own annual celebration.[87] Members were given $150 in gold and a trip to the factory with expenses paid (normally salesmen had to pay their own fares to attend conventions in Dayton). Membership in the club was limited to those who had sold one hundred points a month for the entire year. The conventions lasted a week and featured talks by Patterson and the officers of the company.[88] According to a report of one such convention: "When the '100-Pointers' came into the factory the flags flew from every corner of the mammoth plant, and bulletins posted everywhere told the six thousand employees of the sales prowess of the men in whose honor the flags were flying."[89]

By the turn of the century, the company was expanding and capitalizing on economies of scale. From January 1902 to April 1903, four new factory buildings were erected and two other factory buildings were enlarged; plant size doubled during that time.[90] The sales force grew from 128 in 1890 to 750 in 1910, while sales of registers in the same period jumped from 9,091 to 83,333. Thus, while the number of salesmen increased by about six times, sales jumped more than ninefold.[91]

Along with sharpening methods of training at home, Patterson improved the sales organization overseas. In June 1897, he began a three-month European tour to visit agencies, much as he had done in 1893 in the United States. The 1897 trip took him to Liverpool, London, Paris, Berlin, St. Petersburg, Moscow, Sevastopol, Odessa, Vienna, and Kraków.[92] Patterson laid out for NCR employees his global strategy by drawing a large circle to represent the earth: losses on one side of the globe, he explained, could be made up by gains on the other side.

NCR's international reach was part of its corporate culture and was celebrated in company publications. The outside walls of the Dayton factory at the turn of the century were inscribed with the names of countries from around the world.[93] By 1903, NCR was selling registers in twenty-seven countries: Great Britain, Ireland, France, Germany, Italy, Spain, Holland, Norway, Sweden, Russia, Belgium, Austria, Turkey, Denmark, Portugal, Australia, New Zealand, the Philippines, South Africa, Puerto Rico, Mexico, Cuba, Costa Rica, Argentina, Chile, Brazil, and Uruguay.[94] Three years later, foreign sales accounted for 38 percent of total sales, with Germany selling the largest share (at 14 percent of total sales).[95]

The National Cash Register Company, Ltd., of London was formed as a subsidiary in 1895; and the National Cash Register Company, m.b.H., was established in Berlin in 1896. In 1902, a factory was built in Berlin largely to make register cabinets, which faced an import duty in Germany and were therefore cheaper to make domestically. It also manufactured a few of the simpler model cash registers.[96]

The London-based company maintained its own house organ and

faced its own economic ups and downs. In 1899, the *British NCR* noted that the Boer war in South Africa had hurt business, as had a downturn in the pub and saloon trade.[97] The sales of the London office showed a steady increase around the turn of the century, from 3,710 registers in 1898, to 5,617 in 1903.[98] Forty-seven sales agents and salesmen worked in Britain in March 1900, and that month they sold 176 new machines and six secondhand registers.[99] As in America, the cash register was most popular with saloonkeepers and liquor-store owners. The logbook of a London agency revealed that 22 percent of the customers who came to the store were in those trades, the highest of any group.[100] In 1908 Patterson traveled again to the London office and remained for approximately two years, managing its affairs himself.[101]

In the aftermath of the Spanish-American War, NCR increased its presence in Asia and the Pacific Islands. The agent for the Sandwich Islands (Hawaii) lamented, "Five-sixths of the retail business is in the hands of Japanese and Chinese merchants who have not yet been induced to adopt the use of the register, but I think this will come later on through persistent solicitation."[102] Classes were held to teach local salesmen, as well as transplanted American ones, the ways of the company. In 1906, J. A. M. Johnson was head of the NCR business in Japan; he noted of his sales force: "These men have been in training for over three weeks and every one of them can give a complete *Primer* demonstration, emphasizing the most important points."[103]

In the 1890s, while Patterson was improving agents' training and increasing the number of salesmen working overseas, he also stepped up his campaign against competition, enlisting salesmen for this challenge, too. Competition was not as pressing in 1888 as it would become later, yet even at that early date Patterson showed a determination to keep the industry all to himself. He wrote that year in *NCR:* "We have no serious competitors yet, and we do not propose to have any formidable ones if we can help it. But before any of the weak ones get strong we must crush them out."[104] One company that did attract his attention at the time was the Hopkins and Robinson Company of Louisville, Kentucky. To defeat them, Patterson put "knockers" on the market. These were look-alike copies of the Hopkins and Robinson machine, built in such a way as to avoid patent violation and priced below the Hopkins and Robinson version. "The intention of introducing this register is not to sell it, but only to prevent the sales of the Hopkins and Robinson's registers," Patterson explained. "We do not want the 'knocker' sold except where the P. P. won't buy our other registers and insists on buying an H. & R. register on account of the price."[105]

The use of knockers became a major part of NCR's marketing strategy, and the company even developed knocker catalogs to display their replica machines alongside the originals. When a new register came on the market, sales agents were instructed to buy it and send it to the factory to be examined by patent attorneys and mechanical experts for three reasons: to build a knocker; to see if an infringement on NCR's patent had occurred; and to see if it could be "beaten" in any way—that is, manipulated to ring up the wrong amount and thereby be proven faulty.[106] The use of "knocker" registers freed Patterson from having to compete on price with his standard line of machines. It was only with these ersatz machines that he undersold his competitors.

In the early 1890s, competition became increasingly burdensome and expensive to fight.[107] The Lamson Company had offices in Cincinnati, Toledo, Cleveland, and Detroit; the Sun-Simplex sold its relatively simple machine through jobbers across the country; and the Union Company was offering inexpensive machines. In all, NCR faced sixty-three competing companies.[108] Consequently, an "Opposition Department" was formed by November 1891.[109] The department oversaw NCR's aggressive use of patent legislation against competitors. It also had its own staff of salesmen, who worked in regions where competitors were emerging. These men were employed on salary and were called "company men" or "special men."[110] One of their assignments was to follow the salesmen of competitors from shop to shop and attempt to secure cancellation of the orders they had just placed. A Colorado shopkeeper recalled the techniques of one such NCR salesman:

> In 1909 I was in the novelty and confectionery business. On May 20, 1909, I contracted with The Aldridge Selling Company, of Denver, to buy

a cash register from The American Cash Register Company. The price was $120. I signed a contract to buy but did not make a payment down. The amount agreed upon as the first payment was $20. After making the contract . . . an agent for the National people at Boulder, came in to sell me a National cash register. He told me I was paying too much for the American cash register, that it was not any good. I didn't talk very much the first time he came in. He came later and showed me letters from different men in Colorado, different merchants in different parts of the country, that claimed the American cash register was no good, that it became inaccurate. Later he came in and took me over to the O'Connor hotel, and showed me the two cash registers, with the cases off, and explained the workings.[111]

These "special men" were trained in methods of beating competing machines.[112] James R. Waller worked in such a capacity for National in Los Angeles in 1900. He took a night class that demonstrated how to make Hallwood cash registers ring up an inaccurate total by running through a complex series of maneuvers—pressing several keys simultaneously while opening and shutting the machine drawer.[113] Many deeds of these "special men" transcended salesmanship.

To be fair, NCR was not the only company engaging in underhanded activities. In November 1892, the Boston Cash Register Company instructed its agents on how to use a thin piece of steel to open the drawer on an NCR register.[114] The efforts to crush competitors led salesmen to unethical behavior in other industries as well. United Fruit, Standard Oil, and Burroughs Adding Machine, to name but a few, used salesmen to gather information on competitors and undermine their efforts to sell. They intimidated salesmen from competing companies, undersold competitors' products, and threatened customers or clients. For instance, the sales director at Burroughs received frequent letters from the head of sales at the Felt and Tarrant Manufacturing Company, makers of the Comptometer adding machine. The Felt and Tarrant manager complained that Burroughs salesmen were dropping sand into the gears of Comptometers they encountered out in the field and pulling other tricks. In October 1919, he wrote: "Your repairman, or salesman, attempted to show the George W. Blabon Co., Philadelphia, that their two Comptometers recently purchased were out of order by jiggling a 9-key, and then placed two of your calculators on trial. He evidently succeeded in persuading them that they were out of order, because the two Comptometers were returned to us for repair and we found them to be in perfect order."[115] Such tactics, along with more legitimate practices, enabled companies to garner large sales.

NCR acquired those companies it did not put out of business, purchasing nineteen manufacturers or agencies between 1893 and 1906: Kruse Cash Register, Lamson Cash Register, Boston Cash Indicator and Recorder, Osborn Cash Register, Toledo Cash Register, Henry Theobald Agency, Luke Cooney Agency, Ideal Cash Register, Brainin Cash Register Exchange, Metropolitan Cash Register, Sun-Simplex Cash Register, Globe and Century Cash Register, Isaac Freeman Agency, Foss Novelty, Chicago Cash Register, Weiler Cash Register, Southern Cash Register, A. J. Thomas Cash Register, and Union Cash Register.[116] Most of these acquisitions (seventeen in all) occurred between 1900 and 1906.

Such activities, coupled with NCR's tremendous market share—estimated at 80 percent in 1892 and 95 percent a decade later—brought the company legal difficulty on several occasions.[117] Twice NCR faced antitrust charges under the Sherman Act of 1890, which had been passed six years after the company's founding. The first federal case, *The United States v. Patterson et al.* (1893), charged the company with conspiracy in restraint of trade. It was a conspiracy not by means of contract or combination, but "by means of destroying or preventing the trade of others," so that "the monopoly sought was to be secured by driving other people out of business."[118] The case never came to trial; the suit lapsed after one of the complaining companies, Lamson, joined National.[119] NCR again faced antitrust charges in 1912, during the Taft administration's invigorated pursuit of antitrust violations.[120] A civil antitrust suit was brought against the company in December 1911, and a criminal suit was issued the following February. This time, Patterson and other National officials were found guilty. The court imposed fines and prison sentences on Patterson and twenty-six other employees; Patterson himself received a $5,000 fine, plus costs, and one year in jail. But again the sentences were not served; NCR appealed, and the criminal convictions were reversed.[121]

Most accounts of the reversal credit Patterson's efforts during the Dayton flood for improving his credibility in the eyes of the public and the federal government. The flood had come in March 1913 and had devastated the city. NCR, under Patterson's direction, turned from building registers to making flatboats, which were sent out to rescue people. Such actions may indeed have contributed to the final outcome of the case. A more likely factor, however, was that NCR's lawyers had put together a thorough appeal, challenging the admissibility of evidence and protesting competitors' infringements on National's patents. In the settlement of the civil suit, NCR was enjoined by a consent decree from acquiring control or ownership of the business, patents, or property of competitors without approval from the U.S. District Court in Cincinnati and the U.S. attorney general.[122]

In the long run, the decree was not too burdensome for the company. In many ways it proved beneficial, because it pushed the company to diversify into other product areas.[123] The trial also forced NCR to temper the most egregious activities of its sales force. William Benton, who later founded the Benton and Bowles Advertising Agency and became a U.S. senator, took his first job at NCR in the period following the consent decree. "My first day as a salesman I had to read a booklet telling all Patterson Salesmen what they must not do, because if they did any of this the boss would go to jail," Benton recalled. "One of the things I couldn't do as a salesman was blackjack [coerce] the salesmen of competitors. Another was bribe freight agents to hold up shipments, or drop sand in competitors' machines to put them out of order, open offices next door to competitors and cut the prices 50 percent to knock them out of business—these were all things that his knockout squad had been doing which I was prohibited from doing."[124]

Patterson's Legacy

Although Patterson was surrounded by talented executives—many of whom got their training at NCR—he jealously kept the apex of the pyramid to himself. When executives seemed in any way to challenge him, they were fired.[125] After the consent decree, Patterson dispensed with most of his top managers, whom he blamed for getting the company in trouble; several of them took top positions elsewhere.[126]

In 1917, Patterson abdicated the day-to-day running of the company. At age seventy-three, he set out to travel for nearly a year. Stanley Allyn, who had for many years produced accounting reports for the company, claimed that Patterson, still angered by the antitrust trial, did not want to be accused of profiteering from war work when the company was reorganized during World War I to make airplane parts and pistols. In the final years of his life, Patterson became a proponent of Woodrow Wilson's attempt to bring the United States into the League of Nations and attended conferences in Europe on the matter. During his absence, the company was run by the general manager, John H. Barringer, and by Allyn, who worked as Barringer's assistant. In 1921, despite Patterson's declamations against nepotism, he bequeathed the presidency of the company to his son, Frederick, and took the title of chairman of the board. Frederick, however, left the daily running of the corporation largely to Barringer and Allyn.[127]

John H. Patterson's managerial style was in some sense inimitable, being so closely tied to his own personality.[128] Nonetheless, through his own speechmaking and self-promotion, Patterson had tremendous influence on methods of salesmanship and sales management. His business methods were described in articles and books that were written about him, most of which were excessively laudatory. Beginning in 1911, *Printers' Ink* ran a series of eight articles on Patterson's life.[129] The standard biography, *John H. Patterson* by Samuel Crowther, appeared in 1926, with the subtitle "Pioneer in Industrial Welfare."[130]

More significantly, the executives who worked under Patterson spread his managerial methods as they went to work for different companies—usually after being fired from NCR. Alvan McCauley, who was employed as a patent attorney for Patterson, later became president of Burroughs and created an organization to sell adding machines that paralleled the sales organization at NCR. Like salesmen at "the Cash," those at Burroughs were instructed to approach prospects as consultants and analysts, rather than as mere salesmen.[131] They kept track of "p. b.'s" (potential buyers), rather than "p. p.'s" (probable purchasers). Like NCR, Burroughs divided the marketplace into manageable territories and assigned quotas, motivated its sales force with dramatic contests, and used salesmen to counter competition.[132]

Indeed, a remarkable number of former NCR executives became presidents of other mass-production companies, many in the fields of automobiles and office machinery. NCR alumni included Charles F. Kettering of General Motors, Hugh Chalmers of Chalmers Motor Company, and Richard H. Grant of Chevrolet. William F. Bockhoff of National Automatic Tool also worked at NCR, as did Joseph E. Rodgers of

A sales convention at NCR, Dayton, 1920. The flags around the room represent countries with NCR offices.

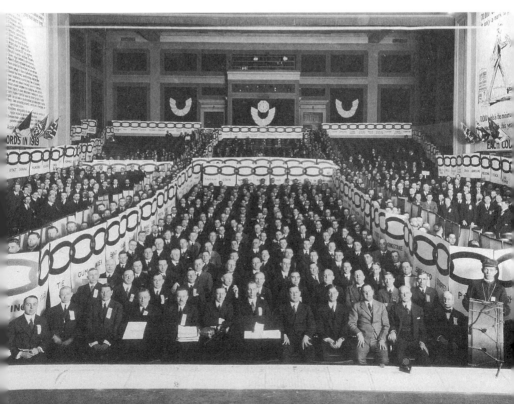

Addressograph-Multigraph, Henry Theobold of Toledo Scale, William Sherman of Standard Register, and Thomas J. Watson of International Business Machines (IBM). In a very direct way, the blue-suited salesmen of IBM were linked to the sales strategies worked out at NCR. The well-known IBM motto "Think!" first appeared on an NCR trade card, apparently at Watson's suggestion.[133]

Early-twentieth-century analysts of salesmanship also revealed Patterson's influence. E. St. Elmo Lewis, who worked for both NCR and Burroughs, wrote one of the best-known general guides to selling skills. In *Creative Salesmanship* (1911), Lewis praised Patterson and explained the sales process in a step-by-step manner that echoed the approach-proposition-demonstration-close sequence of the *Primer.* He declared that NCR's sales manual was "one of the fruits of the scientific attitude towards the problem of gaining greatest efficiency in selling goods."[134] Lewis formulated the slogan: "Attract attention, maintain interest, create desire." The theory, which he elaborated in his book, maintained that during the sales process, salesmen led prospects through progressive states of consciousness, beginning with attention, followed by interest, and ending with desire. These states, following in sequence, would stimulate the "action" of buying.[135] Lewis's model was frequently copied by other authors and, according to the industrial psychologist Edward Kellogg Strong, exerted "a very profound effect on the selling world"—most likely because it gave people a way to talk about the sales process.[136]

Patterson's efforts, and those of Lewis, were part of a larger movement, undertaken across a widening spectrum of people in the early twentieth century, both to bring a "scientific attitude" to bear on the problems of salesmanship and to give selling an air of professionalism. As salesmanship became increasingly analyzed, its study was no longer confined within the boundaries of individual firms, but was undertaken by a range of experts at powerful institutions.

Salesology

6

Psychologists, Economists, and Other Sales Experts

Many elements of modern sales management were in place by the early twentieth century. John H. Patterson was a great spokesman for systematizing selling. But other entrepreneurs and managers were also ambitious in building efficient and effective sales forces. W. K. Kellogg led the "cornflake crusade" against his competitor C. W. Post's Grape-Nuts cereal. Robert W. Woodruff, installed as head of Coca-Cola shortly after his father purchased the company in 1919, excelled at salesmanship, keeping the product unchanging and steadily linking it with American themes in his advertising.[1] William Cooper Procter, of Procter and Gamble, brought out new products, such as Crisco, which was launched in 1911 with a large door-to-door promotional campaign, premium giveaways, and advertising. He also reorganized the sales structure of the company in 1920, cutting out wholesalers and selling directly to retailers.

Spurred by promoters of scientific selling like Patterson and by their own experience, executives began thinking about salesmanship in a different way—as an opportunity to create new markets as well as sell to existing ones. For many mass manufacturers, the problem was not how to sustain high levels of production, but how to stimulate demand for the products they churned out in great volume.[2]

Entrepreneurs in several industries searched for new markets by diversifying their product offerings and increasing their sale of goods in the international market. Heinz and Kellogg's sent exports to many countries, including Britain; the British especially liked baked beans and breakfast cereals.[3]

In line with its growing economic role, sales acquired the trappings that other aspects of business—such as accounting and finance—had already received: professional associations, trade journals, academic books, and courses at business schools. Business writers, publishers, economists, and psychologists began to analyze selling after the turn of the century. These "experts" became the next wave of sales enthusiasts, following the book campaigners, wholesale drummers, and entrepreneurial mass manufacturers.

Academics and analysts sought to understand how salesmanship worked—or, "how 'tis done," to use an earlier phrase. They paid special attention to the problems faced by sales managers: how to set quotas, organize sales forces, determine the right compensation rates, reduce turnover, and keep morale high.

Businessmen, at the turn of the century, proved to be a receptive audience. Not only were they eager to make selling more efficient, but they also hoped to improve their image by aligning themselves with professionals and experts. Public trust of big business reached a low point after the "great merger movement" of 1895–1904 had increased the number of truly giant concerns in America.[4] Critics denounced the huge monopolies—including old ones like Standard Oil and American Tobacco, and new creations like U.S. Steel—as well as the "robber barons" who led them: John D. Rockefeller, James B. Duke, and J. P. Morgan. Some argued that soon all industries would be dominated by huge enterprises, even though, as it turned out, such concerns only emerged in some industries, particularly those with high barriers to entry.[5]

To make matters worse for entrepreneurs and managers, during the early twentieth century there were several scandals, some of which involved salesmen. In 1905 New York State launched a thorough investigation of the insurance industry. Chief prosecutor Charles Evans

Hughes exposed the unethical procedures of a number of sales agents, such as rebating (when the agent offered to share part of his commission with the prospect as an inducement to buy), and twisting (when agents pressured insurees to switch their existing policies from competing companies). Hughes argued that there could be no "social need" for a product that required such aggressive salesmanship to persuade people to buy it.[6] The activities of NCR and its salesmen also made front-page news during the company's antitrust trial. In February 1912, a grand jury indicted Patterson and twenty-one other company executives, charging them under the Sherman Antitrust Law with criminal conspiracy to restrain trade and attempt to form a monopoly. Some of the charges focused on NCR salesman Thomas J. Watson, future head of IBM, who set up a bogus secondhand cash-register shop to undersell competitors.[7]

The new experts and specialists promised to help entrepreneurs and sales managers confront the problems of low efficiency, high turnover, and public suspicion; they encouraged businessmen to turn to them for answers. Their cause was helped by the pioneering work of Frederick W. Taylor, a trained engineer and founder of "scientific management" who had promoted the idea that business processes, particularly production, could be improved through experimentation and observation. Taylor advocated "time and motion studies" to analyze the work routines of manufacturing laborers. Carefully watching workers perform their tasks, and recording each physical movement in his notebook, Taylor claimed to figure out the "one best way" to work. He became a spokesman for a comprehensive system of management, which included, along with time-and-motion studies, cost accounting, incentive-based pay scales, and systematic approaches to storage, inventory, and purchasing. The overall idea of scientific management, as Taylor often put it, was that whereas in the past "man was first," in the future "system would be first."[8]

While few companies followed all Taylor's recommendations, many developed systematic approaches to production management, which transferred control away from laborers to managers and streamlined

business processes. In the early twentieth century, too, some businessmen and writers thought to apply Taylor's ideas to distribution. In the
Journal of Political Economy (1913) Amasa Walker claimed, "In manufacturing plants under scientific management nearly every useless motion has been eliminated." Why, he wondered, "does scientific management end when goods are loaded into a freight car?"[9] Charles Wilson
Hoyt wrote directly about the application of Taylorism to selling in his
book *Scientific Sales Management* (1913). "Scientific Sales Management
believes in the proper training of the salesman," Hoyt claimed. "This
training even goes down to the individual motions and work of the
salesman. It goes so far as to insist upon the substitution of exact methods of work by the individual salesman for scattered efforts. This is carried out even to the matter of standardizing, in some propositions, the
salesman's talk, his manner of approach, etc."[10]

But while the sales experts of the early twentieth century followed
Taylor's goals of increased systematization and improved efficiency,
most formed their own ideas about how to turn selling into a "science."
Publishers conducted surveys of sales managers and profiled executives
at successful companies. Economists and other academics at newly established business schools analyzed the different economic functions of
salesmen and gathered empirical data about the costs of distribution.
Psychologists tested the effectiveness of sales scripts and used their theories of human behavior to make sense of selling; they also tried to dis-
cern the qualities of successful salesmen by studying their techniques,
intelligence, and personalities.

The rise of a class of specialists had many effects on the field. It
helped spread the idea that selling could be conducted more systematically, even scientifically. It added an air of legitimacy to the field, as
economists, psychologists, and other elite figures wrote and lectured on
the subject, elevating "selling" and "sales management" to academic dis-
ciplines. Finally, the rise of sales experts—and, more specifically, the
publishing houses, colleges, and even government agencies that employed them—helped forge an "institutional matrix," in the words of
one historian, linking large companies with a range of powerful allies.[11]

The various experts and institutions shared information and theories about a range of economic activities, including production, trade, advertising, and selling, as well as ideas about worker motivation, consumer behavior, and other important elements of modern salesmanship. They helped turn ideas about salesmanship into a full-blown system of beliefs, and, at the same time, opened the door for some legitimate as well as questionable authorities to step forward.

Business Writers and Publishers

Printers' Ink, founded in 1888, was one of the first journals for sales and advertising professionals, and remained in circulation for almost a century. Unlike the earlier specialized trade journals that had existed for decades in the fields of dry goods, leather, grocery, and drugs, it catered to a specific business *function.* It was followed by a number of competitors; there were approximately fifteen magazines covering the subject of sales and advertising from 1900 to 1909, and nineteen from 1910 to 1919. The number of books on the subject of salesmanship and sales management purchased by the Library of Congress rose steadily as well: from six in the years 1890 to 1900, to thirty-six from 1900 to 1910, to 220 from 1910 to 1920.[12]

Several books and magazines displayed the word "science" on their covers. *Salesmanship* magazine, which premiered in 1903, was published in Meadsville, Pennsylvania, by former salesman Frank H. Dukesmith and was "devoted to advancing the science of salesmanship in its relation to the art of selling."[13] Arthur Frederick Sheldon's *The Science of Successful Salesmanship* (1904), written for a YMCA course, was one of the first sales books to use the word "science" in the title. Other titles included W. A. Waterbury's *Book on Selling: What Makes Up the Science of Salesmanship* (1907) and Hoyt's *Scientific Sales Management: A Practical Application of the Principles of Scientific Management to Selling* (1913).[14]

Several publications were intended to teach the rudiments of salesmanship. These twentieth-century offerings differed from the memoirs of traveling salesmen that were written in the late nineteenth century.

One of several popular magazines about selling published in the 1910s and 1920s, *Salesology,* promised its readers success through the mastery of salesmanship. The February 1923 cover, "Smart Boy Wanted," preached that it was never too young to start.

The earlier works—like Charles S. Plummer's *Leaves from a Drummer's Diary; or, Twenty-five Years on the Road* (1889) or George L. Marshall's *O'er Rail and Cross Ties with Gripsack* (1892)—described selling anecdotally, whereas the newer ones portrayed selling as a series of fundamental principles or tactics.[15]

Among the most popular books were Charles Lawrence Huff's *Huff's Talks on Real Salesmanship* (1912), Burt Clifford Bean's *How to Persuade and Convince* (1913), Thomas D. Rust's *The ABC of Salesmanship* (1914), Norval Hawkins's *The Selling Process: A Handbook of Salesmanship Principles* (1918), and Orison Swett Marden's *Selling Things* (1916). These works taught general rules of business etiquette, which could be especially helpful for would-be salesmen coming from a background in manufacturing or agriculture. This was a common need as a growing portion of the labor force became involved in the distribution, rather than the production, of goods, and in service occupations; the number of employees in the labor force engaged in these activities rose from 24 percent in 1870 to 46 percent in 1930.[16] Sales manager W. T. Wright wrote of farm boys he had trained to be salesmen: "I have sat and taught them not to put their knife in their mouth. How to act around a hotel."[17] *Principles and Secrets of Advanced Modern Salesmanship* (1926), published by San Francisco's Auto-Science Institute, described in detail methods of greeting someone and shaking hands—the right stance, grip, and duration.[18]

The goal of these how-to books was something more than passing along rules of commercial etiquette, however. They aimed to teach readers how to recreate themselves as salesmen, thereby becoming more confident, enthusiastic, and ambitious.[19] In *Selling Things* (1916), popular writer Orison Swett Marden described salesmen as aggressive go-getters ("men with vigorous initiative and lots of pluck and grit"), who were a dynamic force in the economy ("men who can go out and get business") and understood the "science of salesmanship." A demanding skill, salesmanship had to be practiced every waking hour. Wrote Marden, "The hours we spend *off* the job should all be put in *on* the job. There are forms of recreation that increase efficiency . . . Let your development stop and you go backward or conditions leave you behind . . . Use all your recreation time *re-creating* yourself, physically, in mind, and in spirit."[20] Like other contemporary books inspired by mind-cure theories, Marden's taught the idea that discouragement was the greatest reason for failure in the new economy, rather than a lack of skill or knowledge.[21] Such books were the precursors of the sales-oriented writings of inspirational authors like Og Mandino, Norman Vincent Peale, and Tony Robbins.

These books on salesmanship also speculated about the nature of the sales process—how it worked and how it could be made more effective. As mentioned earlier, E. St. Elmo Lewis, claiming inspiration from his years at NCR, wrote that good salesmanship followed a simple formula: "Attract attention, maintain interest, create desire."[22] This simple theory, or even slogan, proved influential, for it provided a blueprint for the majority of sales books that described selling in the 1910s and 1920s. It posited that selling was a process of simple steps in which the salesman led the prospect to make a decision to buy; the sequence of the steps could not be altered, but must be followed one to the next. Arthur Sheldon, who founded his own school of scientific salesmanship, added a fourth step, "secure satisfaction," to Lewis's three in an effort to make the routine seem more ethical. According to one writer of the time, the slogans of Lewis and Sheldon "had a very profound effect on the selling world." The new formula, with Sheldon's addition, "caused order to come out of chaos," the writer claimed (with, perhaps, some salesmanship of his own), and was cited in "90 per cent" of articles and books on the subject written afterward.[23]

Indeed, from the turn of the century to the 1920s, business writers offered variations on the theme of selling as a discrete series of steps.[24] The most thorough elaboration of this was provided by Norval Hawkins, head of the Sales Department at Ford Motor Company. Hawkins, in *The Selling Process* (1918), described successful selling as following a sequence of preparatory steps (preparation, prospecting, approach, and audience); presentation steps (sizing up the buyer, gaining attention, and awakening interest); convincing steps (persuading and creating desire, handling objections); and closing steps (securing decision and obtaining signature). These steps were further subdivided. To gain the right type of "attention," for instance, required moving the prospect through three stages (compulsory attention; curiosity to some degree; intentional or spontaneous attention). The same method was applied to interest, which was broken into attentive interest; associating interest; and personal interest. Hawkins even provided a detailed chart of the types of knowledge salesmen needed to be successful in their efforts, and it contained over 150 items, from the "history of [the] goods" to "pleasure values."[25]

More significant for the professionalization of salesmanship (and likely more useful) than these efforts to draft rules of selling were publications that spread the principles of sales management. Among the journals specifically intended for managers were *Salesmanship: The Journal of the World's Salesmanship Congress* (founded in 1916), *Sales Management* (1918), and *Sales Manager's Magazine: Devoted to Increasing Efficiency in Selling* (1919). These magazines carried articles on compensation methods, quotas, pricing, sales conventions, sales campaigns, and selecting salesmen. There were also many books: Walter H. Cottingham's edited collection, *Book on Selling* (1907); E. H. Selecman's *The General Agent; or, Methods of Sales Organization and Management* (1910); John G. Jones's *Salesmanship and Sales Management* (1917); Harold Whitehead's *Principles of Salesmanship* (1918); and *System* magazine's series *The Knack of Selling* (1913).[26] These books' authors were enthusiastic about the possibilities of reforming and improving methods of management. In his *Salesmanship and Business Efficiency* (1915), James Samuel Knox proclaimed in the introduction that great progress was already under way: "Ten years ago there was no such thing as a Science of Business, a Science of Salesmanship or a Science of Advertising. To-day these Sciences are recognized everywhere."[27]

Chicago businessman Arch W. Shaw was perhaps the most influential publisher of magazines and books on sales management. Earlier in his career, Shaw and his partner, Louis Walker, had started a manufacturing company that sold office equipment and card-filing systems. The

Shaw-Walker Company sold products to cereal manufacturer William K. Kellogg and to Patterson at NCR, among other clients. Shaw's experience in this field convinced him to become a consultant and publisher. He was confident that he could "get a magazine out every month and take these ideas that we found in the Cash Register Company."[28] Shaw's company became well known for publishing a range of business books, including *Selling: The Principles of the Science of Salesmanship* (1905). In 1900, he founded *System* magazine, which printed articles by many well-known businessmen and writers and promoted efficiency in all aspects of commerce. The magazine also published in serial form Samuel Crowther's biography of John H. Patterson.

Another Chicago publisher, John Cameron Aspley, also specialized in sales management, printing spiral-bound reports on trends in sales management and sales strategy.[29] In 1917, Aspley founded the Dartnell Corporation, which conducted surveys of sales managers on topics ranging from popular convention themes to ideas about quotas. *Effective Quota Plans of Three Hundred Notably Successful Concerns,* for instance, listed the equations used by managers to calculate annual sales quotas.[30] Other titles included *Plans for Building Up a Spirit of Loyalty in a Sales Organization* and *Enlisting the Cooperation of Salesmen's Wives and Families.*[31]

If Dartnell's surveys had a grand theme, it was the use of statistics and other information to make selling more manageable and predictable. The company instructed managers to encourage salesmen to gather information on their rounds, and prompted them to do so with forms, questionnaires, and other tools. Dartnell even suggested that companies arm salesmen with cameras to take photographs of both the interior and exterior of customers' stores. The photos could be studied to see what inventory the store carried and what room was available for promotional display, and, eventually, could be framed and given back to the customer as a gift.[32]

Through trade journals and books, business writers helped to spread new ideas about selling and sales management. Publishers hosted conventions and trade shows, such as the World's Salesmanship Congress in 1916, which brought together businessmen and politicians from around the country and promoted the idea that selling had entered a new era of standardized and efficient procedures.

Sales-related publications also transformed selling into its own separate business function and identified sales management as a discipline with its own tools and vocabulary. Some business publishers, like Arch Shaw, pursued their study of selling even further, establishing connections with the universities and small business colleges that were popping up around the country.

Sales Management at the Academy

In the late nineteenth century, there were few schools of business, and most only taught bookkeeping and secretarial skills. The University of Pennsylvania's undergraduate Wharton School of Commerce and Finance, founded in 1881, was an exception, offering courses in commercial accounting and law. Around the turn of the century several more were founded: at the University of Chicago (1899), the University of California (1899), New York University (1900), Dartmouth (1900), and Harvard (1908).

Some universities began to offer courses on distribution, marketing, and sales management. In 1902, the University of Michigan offered "The Distributive and Regulative Industries of the U.S.," which discussed marketing, brand names, and wholesale and retail selling. The following year, the University of California presented "Techniques of Trade and Commerce: A Study of the Organization and Institutions of Commerce; Commercial Forms and Practices," and Ohio State University listed "The Distribution of Products" in its catalog. The major contributions to the study of marketing and sales management, however, were at the University of Wisconsin and Harvard.

Wisconsin, a seminal school for institutional economics, also originated methods of studying selling and distribution.[33] Much of the early work conducted there in those areas was on the distribution of agricultural products, and it was driven by concern about the low returns that farmers received from selling to wholesalers and retailers. Henry C. Taylor taught economic geography, studying where agricultural products were grown and consumed and how they were transported from one middleman to the next. He and his students published exhaustive studies of the sale and distribution of Wisconsin cheese and milk, complete with maps, statistics, and charts.[34] E. D. Jones also wrote extensively about the sale of agricultural products, publishing a series of articles on the role of advertising in product distribution. Benjamin H. Hibbard taught courses on the cooperative marketing of agricultural products in 1913 and published *Marketing Agricultural Products* (1921). And Theodore Macklin wrote *Effective Marketing for Agriculture* (1921).[35]

While Wisconsin was distinguished in the field of agricultural marketing, Harvard's Graduate School of Business Administration, founded in 1908, became the center for studying the marketing of manufactured goods. Because Frederick W. Taylor had made such inroads into analyzing manufacturing processes, Harvard emphasized distribution in its early research studies, rather than production. Dean Edwin Gay, an economic historian by training, decided to incorporate Taylor's principles of scientific management into the curriculum of the school, but he also dedicated resources to research on other subjects, including general management, distribution, and marketing.[36]

One of Harvard's most important figures in the study of sales and marketing was not a trained economist, but publisher and businessman Arch W. Shaw. Shaw's experience as a consultant had shown him the importance of branding and marketing.

During a year off from managing his company in Chicago, Shaw went to Harvard to learn from the renowned economist Frank W. Taussig and the faculty at the business school. He became a lecturer there in 1911 and worked closely with Dean Gay to plan the school's research agenda. Shaw's greatest intellectual contribution while at Harvard was his article "Some Problems in Market Distribution," published in the *Quarterly Journal of Economics* (1912).[37] In it, Shaw described the different functions played by middlemen and distributors over time: sharing risk, transporting products, arranging finance, repackaging and sorting

items, and promoting goods. He noted how the role of institutions varied over time and graphically displayed the way that manufacturers had
appropriated some of the activities previously performed by wholesalers—as exemplified by the tendency of manufacturers' sales agents to
replace drummers in many industries.

Shaw observed a general trend in distribution channels, reflecting a

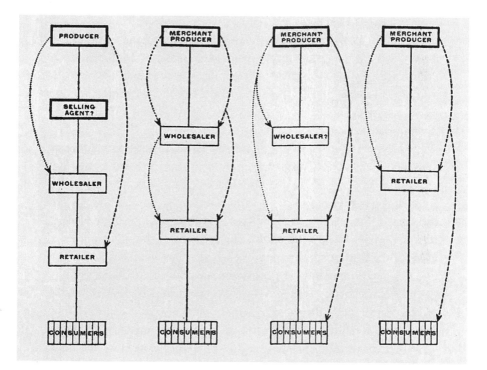

In this detail from "Some Problems in Market Distribution" (1912), Harvard
Business School lecturer Arch Shaw showed the variety of ways that manufactured products traveled from factory to consumer, with salesmen represented
by the curved lines at the left of each diagram and advertising by those at the
right. In the first diagram, producers hire salesmen to sell goods to wholesalers,
but aim advertisements at retailers. In the fourth, the producers are selling to
retailers and using advertising to reach both shopkeepers and consumers.

pattern of manufacturers selling directly to retailers and a diminished role for middlemen. Still, he found contemporary methods of distribution to be inadequate, even "chaotic," and in need of greater study and improvement. Historically, businessmen had paid little attention to distribution, Shaw argued, concentrating instead on improving production capacity and efficiency. Businessmen realized that the path to success lay in producing more goods at lower cost. They investigated methods of harnessing cheap energy sources and standardizing production, and they found a ready market for their staple articles. As a result, wrote Shaw, "We have built up a relatively efficient organization of production." But while production capacities increased dramatically and a new range of goods was produced, similar improvements in distribution had been neglected. The inefficient state of distribution was not only a "check upon further development of production," but also a "tremendous social waste."[38]

Businessmen needed to find better ways to calibrate demand, wrote Shaw. This was a tricky problem. Suppose an executive had a fixed sum of money to spend: "A salesman might make fifty calls at an expense of $100, and ten sales might result from his efforts," wrote Shaw. "Or for the same $100, 5,000 pieces of direct advertising might be mailed, resulting perhaps in only eight sales. Or, perhaps, if the same $100 were used for the insertion of a page advertisement in 100,000 of the circulation of a standard magazine, only six sales would result." Taking this example, Shaw explained, it seems obvious that using a salesman was the most effective method. But, he added, the story was not so clear: though the direct advertising did not result in an immediate sale, 4,992 people who did not buy immediately were now aware of the product and might buy someday; or, in the case of the magazine advertising, 49,994 people. Businessmen needed a way to judge these various shades of consumer demand. With the right access to information, businessmen could learn to create demand effectively. They could become "pioneer[s] on the frontier of human wants."[39]

The gathering of such information was necessary in order to improve the performance not just of individual companies, Shaw felt, but of the entire economy. Like others who studied marketing, Shaw believed that the magnitude of the new companies, and the efficiency of the transportation and communication systems, made adherence to laissez-faire principles counterproductive. Improved management, on both a business and governmental level, would make the economy more efficient.[40]

To begin the process of gathering information and analyzing practical business problems, Shaw donated $2,200 for the founding of Harvard's Bureau of Business Research. Its initial effort was to study, in great detail, the costs of a retail shoe store. In 1913 the bureau produced its first bulletin, *Object and History of the Bureau with Some Preliminary Figures on the Retailing of Shoes,* which cited data gathered from thousands of retailers. The following year, the researchers moved on to study costs in the grocery trade, among hardware dealers (1918), for department and specialty stores (1920), and in other businesses.[41] These bulletins were early examples of Harvard's tendency, most evident in the case studies that it now sells to business schools worldwide, to treat business as a series of practical, particular, problems, rather than as abstract models or theories.

Along with Shaw, Harvard employed other significant scholars of sales and advertising. Paul T. Cherington, a trained sociologist, wrote *Advertising as a Business Force* (1912) and *The Elements of Marketing* (1920). Melvin T. Copeland, an economist who had studied with Frank W. Taussig, served as director of Harvard's Bureau of Business Research and published *Problems in Marketing* (1920).[42] Harry R. Tosdal, another student of Taussig's, was the most productive in the field of sales management. He published a book of case studies entitled *Problems in Sales Management* (1921), in which he treated a range of issues, including price, predictions of future demand, motivation of the sales force, collection of data from the field, and organization of the sales force.[43]

Academics at business schools defined the field of selling from the viewpoint of management, and, for the first time, laid out the history of recent changes. Their main goal initially, until the early 1920s, was to collect and sort information and to come up with terms and taxonomies to describe aspects of selling. Their view of "science" was largely empirical: collecting and organizing data and making observations. While economists and other scholars at business schools looked at issues of sales management, cost, and organization, psychologists concentrated on the dynamics of the sales process—negotiations between sellers and buyers—and on motivating salesmen. They held a purer view of science as a series of basic principles stemming from their research.

The Psychology of Selling

Psychologists made many contributions to the field of selling and advertising in the early twentieth century. Among the more influential works were Harry L. Hollingworth's *Advertising and Selling: Principles of Appeal and Response* (1913), Edward Kellogg Strong's *The Psychology of Selling Life Insurance* (1922) and *Psychology of Advertising and Selling* (1925), Merrill Jay Ream's *Ability to Sell: Its Relation to Certain Aspects of Personality and Experience* (1924), and A. J. Snow's *Psychology in Personal Selling* (1926).

Like academics at business schools, psychologists adopted the perspective of managers in determining which research questions to pursue. Improving "efficiency" was their overall goal. This had been Taylor's main objective from the start and had set the direction and scope for the work done by the consultants and analysts who followed him.[44]

While much of the work undertaken by psychologists ultimately proved to be of little practical use to managers—and, indeed, revealed the limitations of applying basic research to selling—psychologists nonetheless influenced the professional development of selling. They changed the vocabulary of salesmanship, adding new terms like "suggestion," "instinctual wants," and "cognition" that had objective and experimental connotations. Shaw and other professors at Harvard, including Melvin T. Copeland and Harry R. Tosdal, were quick to incorporate these ideas in their sales and advertising texts.[45] Psychologists invented procedures for personnel selection and methods for investigat-

ing consumer behavior. They also elevated the status of selling and promoted the idea that salesmanship was becoming more efficient and
ethical, which for some businessmen was academia's most important
contribution.

One of the first—and most persistent—challenges psychologists
faced was distancing themselves from the pseudoscientific "character
analysts" who had gained a popular audience with their books on salesmanship. F. B. Goddard's *The Art of Selling: With How to Read Character*
(1889) was only the earliest of many books that relied on phrenology
and physiognomy to teach principles of selling.[46] Similar works showed
a surprising popularity in the 1910s and 1920s, shadowing the rise of
applied psychology. Edwin Morrell, an instructor at the Knox School
of Salesmanship, relied on physiognomy in his book *The Science of
Judging Men* (1917), which contained pictures of famous individuals
like Woodrow Wilson, Jane Addams, William Jennings Bryan, and John
D. Rockefeller, accompanied by instructions on how to sell to them:
Rockefeller, for example, had a "head measurement of more than
twenty-three inches in circumference" and could therefore best be persuaded with a "broadside of statistics, facts and profit values . . . [spo-
ken] with confidence and coolness of mind."[47] More troubling for psychologists, the 1923 edition of the six-volume *Ford Products and Their
Sale* contained instructions for selling cars to prospects according to the
size and shape of their foreheads. "*High head* leaves room for larger development at the very top," the manual instructed. "Thus we find the
high headed man comparatively idealistic and should be appealed to
with that thought in mind." Conversely, the low-headed prospect was
supposed to be approached with a "sense of the physical, through seeing
[the car], and through a grosser appeal."[48]

Psychologists rejected such techniques and turned away from examining outward physical qualities to testing inner abilities. They categorized men not by their physical features but rather according to their
instincts, wants, drives, and intellectual capacity, and they tried to understand the way people made decisions to buy. Just as academics at

business schools drafted lists of the functions of salesmen in the economy, so did psychologists outline human wants and speculate about how wants were formed. They created typologies of consumers and of salesmen: What types of consumers were there? How could these various types be "sold"? What were the most effective sales personalities?

Studies of sales and advertising were influenced by the work of German scientist Wilhelm Wundt, who founded a laboratory for psychological experimentation in Leipzig in 1879. Prior to the end of the nineteenth century, psychology had been associated with introspection, metaphysics, and moral philosophy.[49] Wundt was among the psychologists who helped to move the discipline toward one that used scientific methods, quantitative measure, and experimentation. He performed tests on sensation and perception, measuring in fractions of seconds the reaction times for various mental activities.[50]

The other leading influence was psychologist and philosopher William James, who introduced scientific experimentation into the study of psychology, establishing a research laboratory at Harvard. Like Wundt, James had a medical background. His massive work, *Principles of Psychology* (1890), contained chapters on habit, attention, memory, imagination, sensation, perception, and other functions of the brain. But James, who had written *The Will to Believe* (1897), *The Varieties of Religious Experience* (1902), and *Pragmatism* (1908), had also come to be seen as America's most brilliant philosopher.

James was not concerned with applying psychology to business, but some of his writings were reprinted in the new trade magazines and business books. His chapter "Habit" from *Principles of Psychology* was frequently reprinted in sales magazines and was called the "greatest ginger talk ever written" by *Salesmanship* magazine in 1905.[51] In it, James argued that individuals could inculcate desirable habits through the repetition of action and thought. "The great thing in all education is to make our nervous system our ally instead of our enemy," he wrote. This was best done in youth, he argued, for habits were hard to change once a person reached age thirty. James instructed his reader: "Seize the very first possible opportunity to act on every resolution you make, and on every emotional prompting you may experience in the direction of the habits you aspire to gain." The lesson, as sales managers chose to see it, was that young recruits could learn the habits of good salesmanship through hard work or by repeating a successful strategy.[52]

While Wundt and James did not analyze business, several of their students and followers were instrumental in developing the field of industrial psychology. Among the psychologists who took an early interest in studying business were Ernst Tisher, G. Stanley Hall, James McKeen Cattell, and Hugo Münsterberg.[53]

Münsterberg (1863–1916) is often referred to as the founder of industrial psychology. Like several other colleagues in this field, he completed his doctorate under Wundt in 1885, and he later established a laboratory in Freiberg. In 1892, James invited him to run the psychology laboratories at Harvard. Münsterberg visited there for three years, and then, after a two-year stay in Germany, returned to Harvard in 1897, where he remained until the end of his life (he collapsed and died while giving a lecture at Radcliffe in 1916). His career was marked by immense popularity, as he became one of the best-known psychologists in the country and made the acquaintance of Andrew Carnegie, Theodore Roosevelt, Bertrand Russell, and others; but, especially in his final years, he was ostracized due to his unwavering support for Germany during the early years of World War I.

Münsterberg envisioned a practical role for psychologists in assisting the study of crime, pedagogy, and business. In particular, he believed that psychologists could improve workplace efficiency and personnel selection. In *Psychology and Industrial Efficiency* (1913), Münsterberg expressed great hope that improved vocational guidance would promote harmony and efficiency; psychologists could sort out workers according to the jobs that best suited their skills.[54] This was, as Münsterberg's biographer pointed out, a romantic vision of an organic society, in which each person found his place and was eager to perform the functions that his betters selected for him.[55] He developed a program for the Boston Elevated Company to select railway-car drivers, and later, making use of mental tests developed by Alfred Binet, created a system for the American Tobacco Company to select salesmen.[56]

Other psychologists also established ties with commerce and took up the study of sales and advertising. Harry L. Hollingworth (1880–1956) studied psychology at Columbia under James McKeen Cattell, a leading proponent of educational testing. As a professor at Barnard, Hollingworth formed lasting ties with New York City's business community. In 1911 he was hired by Coca-Cola to study the effects of caffeine on the human mind and body as part of a legal defense of the soft drink; Hollingworth's research showed that caffeine was a mild stimulant with no lasting deleterious effects. He was later employed by other companies, including Beech-Nut, which sponsored research showing a connection between relaxation and gum chewing.[57] Hollingworth authored several books on selling, including *Advertising and Selling: Principles of Appeal and Response* (1913) and *The Psychology of Selling and Advertising* (1923). He also tried to defend psychology against the work of phrenologists—debating one at the 1916 World's Salesmanship Congress on the topic of selection.[58]

John Broadus Watson (1878–1958) was another psychologist who studied selling and advertising—though principally advertising. Watson, a student of John Dewey's at the University of Chicago and founder of behaviorism, took an early interest in vocational guidance, believing that his research with animals would be helpful in understanding learning processes and habit formation. After a highly successful academic career, Watson joined the J. Walter Thompson Company (JWT), which assigned him to work first as a traveling salesman and then as a retail clerk at Macy's in order to learn first-hand the rudiments of salesmanship. Afterward, he settled in at JWT as a vice president and account executive, where, among other things, he introduced the idea of blindfold comparison tests.[59]

But the psychologist who had the most sustained interest in the subject of selling was Walter Dill Scott. Scott, the subject of the next chapter, lectured on the subject of advertising and selling as early as 1901, and he conducted experiments to measure the efficacy of different sales and advertising approaches. He promoted the idea that human economic behavior was often based on emotion or sentiments, rather than rationality or logic, and worked to enhance the stature of psychology itself and its application to the problems of business.[60] He also headed the Bureau of Salesmanship Research at the Carnegie Institute of Technology, which engaged in the country's most elaborate effort to apply psychology to selling.

Instincts and Emotions

7

Walter Dill Scott and the Bureau of Salesmanship Research

Like other promoters of modern salesmanship—such as Saunders Norvell, Asa Candler, and John H. Patterson—Walter Dill Scott played an important role in the development of modern selling. Scott's experiences connect many of the elements of the professionalization of selling: an interest in gathering and analyzing large samples of data, an affiliation with a prominent business school, a belief that scientific insights could help businessmen make better decisions, and a reliance on the business trade press to circulate his ideas. His work proved enormously influential in making businessmen receptive to psychology.

Unlike economists at business schools, his focus was not on distribution and consumption but on the personalities, motivations, and capacities of the men and women involved in it. Scott used his research on the workings of the human mind to make sales appeals more effective, and created methods to help companies select the most promising sales personnel and train them to have positive mental attitudes. He promoted industrial psychology as the new frontier of scientific selling and participated in some of its formative debates: What creates and stimulates human wants? Is it something instinctual or environmental? Is it possible to alter human wants through

selling and advertising? What motivates salesmen to work and to succeed?

Applying Psychology to Sales and Advertising

Scott was born in 1869 in the rural town of Cooksville, Illinois, south-
west of Chicago. After spending his youth working on the family farm
and attending local schools, he won a scholarship to Northwestern
University. There he studied with religious educator and psychologist
George A. Coe, who introduced him to the work of William James on
the human mind and to the principles of hypnotism. Scott also pursued
a range of activities outside his studies: he played varsity football, was
on the University Settlement Committee, and taught Americanization

Walter Dill Scott, ca. 1895,
around the time of his graduation from Northwestern
University. A few years later
he traveled to Germany to
study psychology with
Wilhelm Wundt.

classes at the Northwestern Settlement House. He was also deeply religious and decided to become a missionary to China after finishing school. Scott enrolled at Chicago's McCormick Theological Seminary in 1895 for three years of study but was unable to secure a missionary position after graduation.[1]

Scott then pursued his interest in the growing field of psychology and traveled to Germany to study under Wilhelm Wundt at Leipzig, where he wrote a dissertation entitled "The Psychology of Impulses Historically and Critically Considered" that analyzed the nature of human drives, instincts, and desires. Scott returned to the United States in 1900 and improved his skills in laboratory research at Cornell under Edward B. Titchener, another student of Wundt's and America's leading advocate of experimental psychology. Scott then became an instructor in psychology and pedagogy at Northwestern in the fall of 1900.

His study of commerce began in 1901, when a Chicago businessman asked him to address an audience of advertising executives at the Agate Club. Two other psychologists, E. L. Thorndike and Hugo Münsterberg, had turned down the invitation, being reluctant at this early date to appear as though they were endorsing the advertising industry. Scott also had doubts, but he accepted. His talk, entitled "The Psychology of Involuntary Attention as Applied to Advertising," described contemporary psychological insights into the nature of attention, perception, and sensation. He spoke, for instance, of the Law of Habit ("The idea next to enter the mind is the one which has habitually been associated with the one present to the mind") and the Law of Recency ("If two things have been recently connected in the mind, when one is thought of again it suggests the other also").[2]

Scott argued that advertisers should appeal to consumer sentiment and passion, rather than logic. He emphasized the importance of using "suggestion," rather than rational argument, in efforts to influence potential customers. Suggestion was the "calling up" of an idea in another person without making a direct pitch. It was a subtle form of persuasion, intended to appeal to feelings and emotions. Advertisements showing pictures of women happily using Jap-a-Lac to polish their furniture, for instance, or of men proudly wearing bright white Arrow collars, would "suggest" a product to the readers in a less confrontational manner than "reason-why" ad copy. Advertisers should not try to "convince," Scott said. With the right form of suggestion, purchasing would become reflexive, almost without thought: "The idea is suggested by the advertisement, and the impulsiveness of human nature enforces the suggested idea, hence the desired result follows in a way unknown to the purchaser."[3]

Scott also discussed the workings of human memory and listed three keys to making advertisements more memorable: repetition, intensity, and association. Companies needed to repeat their advertisements frequently, often using the same image and slogan. They had to make sure the appeal was dramatic and attention-getting. And finally, they needed to link the appeal to the buyer's life. Advertisers could form an association through sympathy. An advertisement for a course in public speaking, he felt, could draw on sympathy for people with stage fright.[4]

Scott needn't have worried about his audience. The business trade press warmly received Scott's talks. John Lee Mahin, a Chicago advertising executive, offered to start a monthly magazine if Scott would contribute regular articles. The psychologist agreed and eventually published twenty-six articles in *Mahin's* magazine, several of which he collected in his books *The Theory and Practice of Advertising* (1903) and *Psychology of Advertising* (1908).[5] In 1910 Arch W. Shaw ran a series of eleven articles by Scott in *System*. According to Shaw, these articles gave Scott the opportunity "to help business men apply . . . proved principles of psychology to the management of their individual business."[6]

While gaining the approval of businessmen and publishers, Scott also began to find acceptance for his work among other psychologists, who had initially criticized his involvement with business.[7] He became director of Northwestern's psychology laboratory in 1905 and head of the Psychology Department in 1909. In 1912, he also secured an appointment in Northwestern's business school as professor of advertising—one of the first such posts in the nation.

Critical to Scott's understanding of the sales process was his view of the nature of human wants and how they are formed. Scott was initially influenced by the idea that perceptions, emotions, and behavior were based primarily on inborn traits, or instincts—a theory developed principally by William McDougall, who spent his early career at Oxford before going to Harvard. "Instinct" psychology claimed that the human mind operated through certain innate tendencies or feelings that were "the essential springs or motive powers of all thought and action."[8] Men and women possessed a set of primary instincts, each of which was accompanied by emotions. For instance, the instinct to flee was accompanied by feelings of fear, and the instinct to fight, by anger.

In *Psychology of Advertising*, Scott wrote, "An instinct is usually defined as the faculty of acting in such a way as to produce certain ends, without foresight of the ends, and without previous education in the performance."[9] Scott discussed the instincts to preserve and accumulate material goods, to obtain food, to wear clothes, to hoard and possess items, and to hunt. Men and women also had an instinct to construct, which was shown in nature, he wrote, "in a well-known manner in the bee and the beaver." Scott felt that the knowledge of these instincts had practical application. Advertisers and salesmen could, for instance, appeal to the construction instinct by depicting a product being used for building or making something, such as yarn being knit into a sweater.[10]

He was not the only one to take an interest in McDougall's work. To the sales and advertising press, McDougall's theories were useful, for they provided a way to make sense of, and even categorize, the variety of human wants. McDougall's *Introduction to Social Psychology* (1908) was reprinted year after year, eventually selling more than 100,000 copies.[11]

The influence of instinct psychology was evident in many books on salesmanship. Harvard Business School professor Harry R. Tosdal quoted McDougall at length in *Principles of Personal Selling*, even publishing a table of fourteen separate instincts and their attendant emotional qualities, including:

Instinct of escape (correlated with fear)
Instinct of combat (linked with anger)

Curiosity (tied to feelings of mystery, strangeness, the unknown, wonder)

Submission (connected with a feeling of subjection)

Assertion (accompanied by elation)

Tosdal felt that salesmen should consider the instincts and emotions they wanted to appeal to as they formulated their sales talks.[12] Such lists were common in the rash of books on salesmanship that appeared in the late 1910s and early 1920s.

Scott and other psychologists also performed tests to try to determine which types of visual and verbal appeals were most successful. He showed, for instance, that in printed ads people found rectangles more appealing to look at than squares. His tests also revealed that salesmen could gain an advantage by increasing a prospect's fear or anxiety, just as lightning-rod men had done, though Scott disapproved of such methods and presented results showing that positive appeals could also be effective.[13]

Rather than seeing man as purely rational, psychologists argued that although buyers were often irrational in their choices, consumer habits could be studied through rational experimentation. In many ways, the work of the psychologists confirmed the methods already in practice by sales managers, whose sales scripts revealed an awareness that people were motivated by a mixture of impulses to make purchases. Book canvassers knew that selling an "expectation" was much better than selling the real thing; that people are generally risk averse, especially when it comes to investing large sums of money; and that they are particularly fearful of being cheated or duped. Good salesmen needed to be aware of these tendencies.

The editors at *Printers' Ink* claimed that Scott was treading a path that advertisers had already cleared.[14] "Advertisers have reached all of the Professor's basic laws by the very serviceable kind of psychology called 'horse sense,' and his principles, while reduced to scientific facts, are all drawn from actual advertisements," the article claimed. The basic transformation that Scott called for—from explanatory or informational advertisements to emotional and evocative ones—was indeed underway when Scott began writing. From roughly the late 1880s through the early 1900s, most advertisers had conceived of advertising as a way of informing the public about products and their uses. But after the turn of the century, advertisers more often appealed to readers through both rational and irrational (or emotional) copy and through the use of pictures and illustrations.[15]

Scott admitted that he was not adding to the arsenal of advertising strategies. But while he was not saying anything that would change manufacturers' advertising methods, his theories at least seemed to confirm, and give justification to, their current strategies. His work, and that of other industrial psychologists, also gave businessmen a new vocabulary to discuss advertising and selling and, for those wanting to seem progressive and informed, allowed them to claim that they conducted their sales campaigns along "scientific" lines. The Franklin Mills Company, maker of Wheatlet cereal, wrote that it had successfully used the approach Scott had outlined in his article, "Direct Command as a Form of Argumentation." The publishers of the *Delineator* also claimed to have been inspired by Scott's ideas when they created their popular billboard advertisement, "Just get the *Delineator!*"[16]

Scott's work also provided "evidence" of the ethics of salesmanship. For Scott, selling and advertising were not about manipulation, but motivation. In *Influencing Men in Business* (1913), Scott debunked the idea, floated in some popular books, that aggressive advertisements and sales pitches had a hypnotizing effect on individual buyers, which he viewed as stemming from beliefs in superstition, magic, witchcraft, and astrology. Scott saw the work of the Austrian scientist and showman Franz Anton Mesmer as of particular importance in the persistence of those claims. He described how Mesmer, whose work was rooted in occult traditions, believed one could gain control over another by manipulating an internal magnetic fluid found in the body.[17] But such theories were antiquated, Scott wrote. It was impossible to gain control of an unwilling mind. The same was true for advertising. "A critical audience can not be moved by suggestion," Scott wrote, adding (in a statement similar to Melville's observation sixty years before, but with a positive spin): "Its *confidence* must first be secured."[18] In order to persuade, and to sell, advertisers and salesmen had to learn the customer's wants, rather than impose their own; they "must know [the customer's] habits of thought, for it is too difficult to attempt to get them to think along new lines."[19]

Despite Scott's efforts to distinguish his approach from that of phrenologists, "mind cure" experts, and assorted other character analysts, these esoteric consultants became increasingly popular in the 1910s and 1920s. The reception of their ideas revealed the thirst, among managers and salesmen, for quick solutions, especially those that invoked the mantle of science—even if it meant believing, as Patterson did, in the mystical power of pyramids, phrenology, and other phenomena. In an era in which Madison Grant's *Passing of the Great Race* was published and immigration restrictions were imposed, the resurgence of phrenology and similar beliefs also revealed the tendency of businessmen to see the commercial world as divided by ethnicity and race.[20] Perhaps the most significant exponent of physiognomy was Katherine Blackford, whose work analyzed the supposed differences between Nordic blondes and brunettes from southern Europe.[21] Her theory was that people with fair complexions and Nordic features could be sold with intelligent arguments; those with darker complexions required product features that could be touched and tested. Psychologist B. Von Haller Gilmer, who worked with Scott, recalled from his days as a consultant for Westinghouse that Blackford's system of character analysis was being used by executives at the company. Convincing them that it was all nonsense was not easy, he wrote. "One must use tact if not skill in attacking something like that when a vice-president believes in it."[22]

The success of the character analysts also revealed the blurry line between Scott's work and their own, a distinction made all the more difficult as popular writers appropriated scientific terms. William Walker Atkinson (1862–1932), a popularizer of New Thought and Eastern ideas who occasionally used the pseudonym Yogi Ramacharaka, published *Vim Culture* (1913), which emphasized the importance of living "the active life"; he also wrote *Psychology of Salesmanship*, which cited the work of William James and other psychologists.[23] In *Selling Things* (1916), the popular writer Orison Swett Marden included a chapter on "suggestion," in which he argued that salesmen had to be careful in using psychological methods, for they could, inadvertently, "overcome or dethrone the will" of a prospect if they acted too powerfully.[24]

Such passages aggravated Scott, who exclaimed: "The whole subject of suggestion has been rendered ridiculous and its true value obscured by a group of men who, with inadequate psychological learning, have been presenting suggestion as the *open sesame* to success in the business world."[25]

Questions about manipulation and motivation bothered Scott, for they brought to the surface issues about the role of salesmanship in the economy and society. To Scott, a former football player, a salesman was like an athletic coach, who encouraged people to buy things they wanted and to overcome feelings of inertia, or even fear, about purchasing new goods. Salesmen, like businessmen in general, were forward looking: "The typical business man is an optimist. For him the future is full of possibilities that never have been realized in the past."[26] They encouraged consumers to take action—and that action was volitional, just as the decision to purchase was a consensual, voluntary action.[27]

Bureau of Salesmanship Research

While Scott began his career by trying to uncover secrets of persuasion, he subsequently turned to examine the psychology of the persuaders— that is, the salesmen. He became increasingly interested in the mental and personal characteristics of successful sellers. In 1914 Scott undertook a survey of employee-selection processes for hiring salesmen and other types of workers at several companies, including NCR, General Electric, and New York Edison. In the following year, he began advising American Tobacco on its methods of selecting salesmen, just as Hugo Münsterberg had done before. Scott brought six managers and thirty-six sales applicants to Northwestern. There he observed the managers interviewing and ranking the candidates. Because the managers differed widely on their choices, Scott became convinced that a more systematic, objective method of selection was necessary. He began devising a series of procedures, which included physical exams, interviews, and tests of mathematical and verbal capacities. His great innovation was not to rely solely on the isolated scores of individuals, but to compare recruits against one another—and significantly, against existing, successful sellers. In order to do this, Scott asked the managers to rank sales applicants alongside their best salesmen to help choose the ones who had attributes similar to those of the top sellers. Scott experimented with this model at several other companies, including the Cheney Brothers Silk Company of Connecticut and the Clothcraft Shops of Ohio.[28]

In 1916, Scott became head of the Bureau of Salesmanship Research at the Carnegie Institute of Technology (now Carnegie Mellon), and undertook a large-scale effort to isolate the characteristics of successful salesmen. Edward Woods, president of the National Association of Life Underwriters, was the main spirit behind the formation of the bureau. Woods was an immensely powerful figure in the life insurance industry. His Pittsburgh office of Equitable Life Assurance Society was the largest single Equitable agency in the world.[29] He became interested in reforming life insurance and in improving the image of life insurance solicitation, still suffering from the Armstrong investigation of ten years before, which had exposed improprieties in the leading firms.[30]

Woods contacted psychologist Walter Van Dyke Bingham at the Department of Applied Psychology at Carnegie Tech. He wanted to create a Bureau of Salesmanship Research to "embrace all branches of salesmanship, including circularizing and advertising." Its first task would be to accumulate data—on contests, advertising plans, conventions, training methods, forms, and, especially, the personal characteristics of salesmen. The result, Woods hoped, would be a "different and better type of salesman."[31] The early contributors were preponderantly insurance companies, including John Hancock, Metropolitan Life, and Prudential, and manufacturers of technologically complex goods, such as Burroughs, Ford, and Westinghouse. H. J. Heinz and Norval Hawkins, manager of sales at Ford, each helped underwrite the organization.[32]

In 1916, Bingham recruited Scott to be the bureau's director. Along with his work in advertising, Scott had made a name for himself in the field of management with his book *Increasing Human Efficiency in Business: A Contribution to the Psychology of Business* (1911). In it, Scott explained that managers could make workers more efficient by eliminating "superfluous thinking," which would be achieved by choosing the employees who were best suited mentally for a specific job and by inculcating efficient habits. He merged Frederick W. Taylor's belief in simplifying the tasks of labor with William James's theory of "habit" formation—the idea that individuals could form good habits through the repetition of desirable thoughts and actions.[33]

Just as Scott had analyzed ways to "motivate" consumers to make purchases, he now wrote about motivating employees to work. Scott again turned to an analogy based on organized sports: "On the [athletic] field a player frequently finds himself unable to exert himself. His greatest effort is necessary to force himself to work. In such a mental condition a vigorous and enthusiastic appeal from the coach may supply the needed stimulus and stir him to [a] sudden display of all his strength."[34] Mental attitude was essential in achieving superior worker performance, in both manual and white-collar work. Most people had formed a habit of quitting when they felt tired, wrote Scott, when in fact they were capable of doing much more. With the right incentives and encouragement, the average man could increase his efficiency by 50 percent. Salesmen, whose self-esteem depended on their ability to sell, needed to be spurred on in the right way.

Scott laid out five clear aims of the salesmen's bureau: to "systematize" methods of selecting and training sales recruits; to use the methods of experimental and statistical psychology to determine the mental and personal traits of successful salesmen; to conduct experiments on the selection, training, and motivation of salesmen; to publish the findings of the bureau in academic journals and books; and finally, to offer courses to sales managers that would make use of the bureau's findings.[35]

His first effort was to systematize the methods of personnel selection. With a team of seven graduate students—among them Herbert Kenagy, Merrill Ream, and Henry C. Link—Scott developed a series of tests that companies could use to discover the best applicants for sales positions.[36]

The problem of selection was an important one, particularly in sales. At the Fuller Brush Company, canvassers were considered veterans after a year in the field. A leading insurance magnate estimated that of the 150,000 licensed insurance agents in the United States in 1915, half would leave the business before the end of a year. The Packard Motor Company had an amazing 112 percent turnover in the difficult year of 1920 to 1921, although that was unusually high; it had still been 45 percent in 1916. Thirty firms were involved in the bureau. Scott claimed that cumulatively they would have to employ 30,000 new salesmen per year to keep 48,000 positions filled.[37]

Managers tended to believe the problem lay with the salesmen, rather than with their methods of management. According to a survey conducted by the Dartnell Corporation on the subject of turnover, managers listed the reasons they felt their salesmen had "failed," or quit: 37 percent of salesmen failed due to lack of industry; the same number, 37 percent, due to discouragement; 12 percent because they did not follow instruction; 8 percent for being poorly informed about the product line; 4 percent for dishonesty; and 2 percent for poor health. Sales managers thus felt that roughly three-fourths of the salesmen who quit their jobs did so because of insufficient effort or because they became discouraged.[38] Following this line of thinking, managers believed they needed to select a better class of men.

Scott's *Aids in Selecting Salesmen* consisted of four basic parts: (1) the *Application Blank,* which collected personal data—the applicant's name, date of birth, marital status, languages, number of persons dependent on him, life insurance coverage, church and club affiliations, previous employment history—and instructed the applicant to write at least fifty words explaining "why you think you will succeed as a salesman for this company"; (2) the *Letter to Former Employers,* which asked the employers to rate the applicant's industry, personal habits and conduct, and fitness for a selling position on a scale ranging from "very good" to "very poor"; and (3 and 4) the *Interviewer's Scale* and *Sheet,* which required the interviewer to rate numerically the applicant on appearance (body build, facial expression, clothing, voice, cheerfulness, self-confidence, courtesy); convincingness; industry; character (loyalty, honesty, truthfulness, temperance—freedom from habitual drinking and gambling, economy); and value to the firm. Scott's tests stood apart from many others of the time in their reliance on the impressions and observations of businessmen, rather than on just an assessment of the applicant's mental ability. That is, he trusted the judgment of a group of experienced managers to complement his numerical analyses.[39]

Applicants also had to take five psychological tests, including a "mental alertness" test (which required applicants to specify the synonyms and antonyms of words, perform simple addition, and make sense of proverbs) and a test of "foresight" (which asked applicants to answer hypothetical questions). The answers were intended to show an applicant's creativity: "If because of climatic changes a year ago, your home territory had been brought into a zone of daily rainfall from 6 A.M. to 6 P.M., what might the inhabitants, who remained there, have done to meet this condition?"; "If each person flew about in a small flying machine whenever he pleased, what changes would occur in the daily life of individuals?" Finally, Scott gave applicants a test of general knowledge that asked salesmen to judge whether statements—such as "The breast stroke is used by all champion tennis players"—were true or false.

These psychological group tests were among the first to be developed for widespread use by business. They judged a variety of mental abilities. The questions of foresight and verbal dexterity determined whether salesmen could think quickly and respond to unanticipated questions. The tests of general knowledge were biased toward native-born, middle-class applicants, whose understanding of American history and culture was likely more detailed than that of newly arrived immigrants or the less well educated. Despite the long tradition of immigrant peddlers, Scott and his students assumed that a fair amount of cultural knowledge was necessary for salesmen working in sales departments.

Once Scott had finished administering all the tests to a particular candidate, he then combined the applicant's scores on the various parts, and the ratings from the interviews, into a single number, determining the candidate's potential value as a salesman on a scale from 1 to 10. This number could then be compared with that of other recruits to determine the top candidates.[40]

Scott promoted *Aids in Selecting Salesmen* in a variety of ways, presenting it at conferences and, with Woods's help, administering it to thousands of life insurance agents and other salesmen whose track records were already known—to see if the system sorted out the "successes" and "failures" sent to him. Scott also put his tests into practice at the World's Salesmanship Congress. In July 1916, he met with a group of twenty sales managers at the Statler Hotel in Detroit and asked each to test a group of applicants whose ability as salesmen was known. The managers were placed in separate rooms, and applicants were told to enter and "attempt to sell" something. The managers interviewed and rated them, and Scott gave them his mental tests. Four days later, Scott presented his results to a large audience and proclaimed success—he had even picked out the "ringers" that had been sent to fool him.

But Scott's tests did not always fare well in practice. At one convention, a manager who had tried to use the tests denounced Scott. "We took one of the tests . . . devised for salesmen [by the Bureau of Salesmanship Research, and gave it to] . . . some of our own men, whose production was known . . . [and we] found the . . . correlation . . . almost one hundred per cent in *inverse* relation to . . . production . . . The best men tested the lowest . . . and the poorest men tested the highest." Scott suggested the tests might have been misapplied—as well they might have been, for the complete tests, with all their parts and rankings, were cumbersome to administer.[41]

But more experienced administrators also found that the tests did not work well in practice. Herbert Kenagy and C. S. Yoakum, psychologists at the bureau, eventually claimed that the "mental activity" tests were of little value, except for the insight they provided that intelligent people tended to leave "low-level" sales jobs, like door-to-door canvassing, more quickly. Wrote Kenagy and Yoakum, "The salesman above the average in intelligence is unfitted for these lower grades of selling jobs. The job is not sufficiently complex to maintain his interest and, if the promotional opportunities are limited, he soon leaves the organization." Thus the best way to use the mental alertness tests was to screen out the people who were too intelligent.[42]

In spite of such problems, Scott's work on standardized personnel hiring policies, and his methods, caught on. His tests helped to orient the labor market toward personality, education, and the ability to present oneself and away from specific training and skills. Scott's exams for successful salesmen—and his identification of the qualities associated with selling—were adapted to numerous white-collar and even executive functions, especially after Scott's extraordinary involvement with the military.

An Economy of Wants

World War I was a boon to Scott and other psychologists, who gained credibility for their involvement in the war effort.[43] Harvard psychologist Robert Yerkes developed a general intelligence test under the surgeon general, known as the Army Alpha Test, which was given to 1.75 million soldiers; this work brought Yerkes prestige at the time, but since has gained him notoriety because of the prejudiced conclusions he drew from his summary data about different racial and ethnic groups.[44]

Scott created another series of tests for the army, tests whose results were translated into a ranking system to select officers. With the cooperation of the War Department, Scott quickly converted his *Aids in Selecting Salesmen* into a rating scale for selecting captains. The Salesman's "Personal History Record" became the "Soldier's Qualification Card"; the "Interviewer's Scale," the "Army Rating Scale."[45] Under

Scott's plan, thousands of soldiers were judged according to "appearance, military experience, influence over men, regard for authority, vigor, stability, judgment, and total value to the Regiment."[46] Just as with his tests for salesmen, Scott reduced the qualities of examinees to a single number. Scott was awarded the Distinguished Service Medal for his efforts.

The work of Carnegie Institute's applied psychologists also continued through the war, while Scott was in the military. In 1917, Edgar A. Kaufmann, a department-store magnate, persuaded six other businessmen to join him in founding the Research Bureau for Retail Training at Carnegie. The new organization devised training and merchandising manuals, selection tests, and other managerial tools.[47] Later in the decade, the salesman's bureau at Carnegie broadened its name and scope, becoming the Bureau of Personnel Research. Carnegie also formed a school for teaching life insurance salesmanship and a bureau for researching methods of selling life insurance.[48]

While Scott had spent his time at the bureau trying to identify the differences between salesmen—and between applicants to sales jobs—one of the psychologists there pulled together a portrait of an ideal salesman, based on characteristics of successful sellers. According to Merrill Ream, who worked under Scott, the ideal salesman was an extrovert who disliked "morbid things, such as funerals and spiritualism," was "intellectually uncritical," and cared not "to philosophize." He took "notice of little things" and had "more interest in details than his unsuccessful counterpart"; he was also "more flexible" and "able to modify his usual reactions when the social situation demands." He did not "care much for reading" and was "a stable conservative citizen" with "faith in the established order." He was antiradical and believed in religion, liking "ministers, bankers, conservative people" but not "gamblers and spendthrifts." He was married and opposed to easy divorce and believed in "individual thrift and individual responsibility for one's self and dependents." The ideal salesman was a high school graduate with perhaps one or two years of college, rather than a college graduate or the recipient of an advanced degree.[49] Such a portrait showed how the characteristics of successful salesmen, at least according to Ream, had changed from the days of peddlers and early drummers: salesmen were married and conservative, the allies of bankers and other established figures. They were white and native-born; they were also male. The processes of selection established at the Bureau of Salesmanship Research, which claimed to operate under the mantle of objectivity, only reflected and encouraged such trends.

In 1919 Scott opened an industrial consulting firm, the Scott Company, in Philadelphia, and signed up Sperry Gyroscope, Standard Oil, Westinghouse, and Strawbridge and Clothier as clients. He used the company to promote his man-to-man personnel ranking system.[50] Other prominent psychologists also founded consulting companies; in 1921, Robert Yerkes, James McKeen Cattell, J. B. Watson, and Walter Bingham created the Psychological Corporation in New York. Both Scott's company and the Psychological Corporation developed tests to help managers select employees and, in other ways, applied the principles of psychology to the problems of workplace efficiency and worker motivation.

Scott's postwar professional career flourished: the American Psychological Association elected him its president for 1919, and, in 1920, he became president of Northwestern University (a job he held until 1939). Scott disbanded his consulting company in 1923 but remained engaged in the work of psychologists at Northwestern. In the 1920s, he and other psychologists moved away from their original emphasis on instincts. They had seldom agreed on the number of instincts, or on their makeup.[51] Increasingly, psychologists perceived human wants to be dynamic, rather than fixed, and stressed that men and women were motivated not only (or perhaps not at all) through inherited instincts, but largely through interaction with the environment.

A. J. Snow's *Psychology in Personal Selling* (1925), written at Northwestern, claimed to be the first book on the "psychology of personal selling without recourse to the theory of instincts." Snow, whose book was deeply rooted in physiology, included a chapter entitled "The Mind of the Customer." He depicted the brain as being "an almost infinite variety of . . . interconnections upon which are built up everything in the way of habit, imagination, memory, and reasoning displayed by the individual"; the "interconnections," Snow argued, were shifted through advertising and salesmanship to create demand.[52]

In taking this approach, psychologists encouraged a view of the economy as one filled with undiscovered "wants" waiting to be formulated; salesmanship was about motivating consumers and overcoming their unhealthy inertia to buying. Publisher and Harvard Business School professor Arch W. Shaw described the country as a mass of consumers, whose wants and needs were complex, shifting, and malleable. "Today the more progressive business man is searching out the unconscious needs of the consumer, is producing the goods to gratify them, is bringing to the attention of the consumer the existence of such goods, and in response to an expressed demand, is transporting the goods to the consumer."[53] Economist Wesley C. Mitchell complained that the "great assumption" of classical political economy was that man was reasonable and sought, intelligently, his own good—that man was "guided in all his activities by enlightened self-interest." But the work of the psychologists had helped prove that "man is only a little bit reasonable and to a great extent very unintelligently moved in quite unreasonable ways."[54]

As marketing professors and economists produced some of the first syntheses of the subjects they had pioneered in the 1900s and 1910s, they included the work of Scott and other psychologists in discussions of consumer behavior and personnel selection. These topics were discussed, for example, in Paul T. Cherington's *The Elements of Marketing* (1920), Melvin T. Copeland's *Principles of Merchandising* (1924), and Harry R. Tosdal's *Problems in Sales Management* (1921) and *Principles of Personal Selling* (1925).[55] More important, by the 1920s businesses themselves, like Procter and Gamble and General Motors, were conducting research on consumers and their habits in the same way that psychologists and academics had done.

A Car for Her

Selling Consumer Goods in the 1920s

By the 1920s, American businesses recognized "salesmanship" as an essential component of modern strategy. Indicative of the rising importance of selling within corporations was that nearly one-quarter of the chief executives of the top two hundred industrial firms in 1917 had spent part, or all, of their careers in sales.[1] Arthur Vining Davis, who had figured out a way to sell aluminum to consumers in the form of pots and pans and numerous other items, became chairman of Alcoa. Edward Prizer, who became president of Vacuum Oil in 1918, made his reputation by organizing the firm's domestic and foreign sales operations. Clarence Mott Woolley, president of the American Radiator Company from 1902 to 1924, had similarly made his mark in selling. Woolley was, according to one popular magazine, "essentially a salesman," who succeeded so well in promoting his radiators and plumbing supplies that by 1935 the magazine's editors could conclude, "Every time you turn on the heat or draw yourself a glass of water or flush a toilet the chances are just about fifty-fifty that you are dealing with Mr. Woolley's machinery."[2]

Feats of salesmanship, both contemporary and historic, were recounted to the public as entertainment. While academics tended to describe selling in dry, quantitative terms, the *Saturday Evening Post* and *Colliers* portrayed

190

salesmanship dramatically, telling the story, for instance, of William Wrigley Jr. sending marching bands to China to sell his chewing gum there, or of Coca-Cola being sold in South America.[3] "Salesmanship" became shorthand for an aggressive, expansionist, highly "American" way of doing business that seemed to underlie the economic success of the decade. According to one historian, popular magazines around the turn of the century even wrote with a "salesmanship slant," adopting an editorial style that was more frank and direct than their predecessors had used. A story in the *Saturday Evening Post* proclaimed, "The history of America is in effect a saga of salesmanship." The "early pioneers who broke away from the settled life of the Atlantic Coast were traveling salesmen par excellence. They sold the Western country to the world as they went successively over the Alleghenies, the Mississippi, the Rockies; a continent was brought under civilization in a fraction of the time that such a task had ever been accomplished before."[4]

The figure of the salesman, as presented in popular books and magazines, was quickly parodied. Sinclair Lewis's portrait of the archetypal real estate salesman, George Follansbee Babbitt, was the most effective. Babbitt was the apotheosis of salesmanship. When he put on his spectacles, made of "the very best glass" with "thin bars of gold" for earpieces, he became a modern businessman, "one who gave orders to clerks and drove a car and played occasional golf and was scholarly in regard to Salesmanship."[5] His "faith" rested on the values of business, and correspondingly he often "reflected how hard it was to find employees who had his own faith that he was going to make sales."[6] He also expressed himself in the aggressive and manly idiom of salesmanship, with terms like "buck up," "knock him dead," and "he-man."

Babbitt was quite different from the fictional representations of peddlers and commercial travelers that had appeared decades before in the writings of Melville and Twain. Whereas peddlers and traveling salesmen of nineteenth-century fiction were usually marginal figures who used their wiles to fool ordinary citizens, Babbitt occupied a place at the very center of American society and culture. He was a member of the Good Citizens League, the Order of the Elks, and the Republican Party.

Babbitt was surrounded by items of the new consumer society: automobiles, skyscrapers, shaving razors, alarm clocks. He was intrigued, even defined, by business and profits. He viewed the logic of business as supreme and sanctified. He was up-to-date on business terminology, shunning the title "real estate salesman" in favor of the more professional-sounding "realtor" (a term that, in fact, had been promoted by the National Real Estate Association in its 1913 Code of Ethics).[7]

Lewis had researched the character, reading sales books, traveling in Pullmans, and visiting Midwestern cities. He was critical of the growing presence of salesmanship in everyday life and skeptical of the validity it claimed through academic study. The purpose or end of all this "selling" was hard to determine: Babbitt and his business friends had the "cosmic purpose of Selling—not of selling anything in particular, for or to anybody in particular, but pure Selling."[8] Nor was Lewis alone in his criticism. Economist Thorstein Veblen called salesmanship the "art of getting a margin of something for nothing" and saw modern selling as a branch of evangelism, rather than science; the sales agents who had promoted the business of the Kingdom of Heaven, wrote Veblen in his unique style, trafficked in the same "beneficial intangibles" as did salesmen on the "material plane."[9] But Lewis was so successful in capturing the language and manners of business that many businessmen who read the book were not offended by it. Instead, they tended to identify with Babbitt in a positive way. Newspapers in Minneapolis, Milwaukee, Duluth, Cincinnati, and Kansas City claimed that their home city had been the model for Zenith.[10]

Selling Consumer Goods

Interest in salesmanship among academics and popular writers was stimulated by salesmen's role in the increasing trade in consumer goods following World War I. After a recession from 1921 to 1922, the U.S. economy experienced general prosperity. During the 1920s, national per capita income rose from $7,495 (1919) to $8,939 (1929).[11] Manufacturing output increased by 60 percent overall.[12] And several major companies that had primarily made goods for industry, like General Electric and Westinghouse, now turned their attention to the consumer market and introduced products for the public.[13] While American households in the late nineteenth century tended to own few durable goods—some furniture, a horse carriage, or perhaps a piano—in the 1920s they began to purchase a variety of these items, including automobiles and appliances, such as vacuum cleaners, irons, electric toasters, and washing machines, all of which were sold by salesmen.[14]

Two types of salesmen were especially significant in the sale of consumer goods: automobile dealers and door-to-door salesmen of home products and appliances. The automobile industry quickly became famous for great salesmen, such as William C. Durant, Norval Hawkins, and Richard H. Grant. Durant, founder of General Motors, was, according to one source, "perhaps the 'hottest' personal salesman the country has ever known, who could sell anything—buggies, automobiles, stock, and faith in man's infallibility."[15] Hawkins, who headed the sales department at Ford from 1908 to 1917, was, in the words of a Detroit attorney, "perhaps the greatest salesman that the world ever knew . . . original in ideas, forcible in presenting them, a perfect dynamo for work, and a man who gets the quickest execution of any man I ever knew."[16] Grant, who started at Chevrolet in 1924, was the "Cicero" of the automobile industry; his "oratory has been known to reduce a meeting of 35,000 salesmen to tears, bright it with laughter, excite it to anger, and send it forth in a frenzy to make new sales of cars and trucks."[17]

The development of salesmanship in the automobile industry drew on John H. Patterson's work at NCR. Several industry executives had worked for Patterson at National Cash Register, including Hugh Chalmers, founder of Chalmers Motor Company, Alvan Macauley, president of Packard (after he left Burroughs), Joseph A. Fields, who was sales manager and vice president at Maxwell and later at Chrysler, and Richard H. Grant.[18] Grant had been a salesman at NCR before going to Delco, Frigidaire, and then Chevrolet. His special talent was training and motivating new recruits, transforming them into super salesmen.[19] He boiled down Patterson's teaching to seven laws:

1. Have the right product.
2. Know the potential of each market area.
3. Constantly educate your salesmen on the product, making them listen to canned demonstrations and learn sales talks by heart.
4. Constantly stimulate your sales force, and foster competition among them with contests and comparisons . . .
5. Cherish simplicity in all presentations.
6. Use all kinds of advertising (Patterson had 104).
7. Constantly check up on your salesmen, but be reasonable with them and make no promises you can't keep.[20]

Though Grant gleaned these seven points from Patterson, their implications for selling automobiles were different than for cash registers. Automobiles appealed to a wider variety of customers and markets, and sales executives in the auto industry pushed selling in new directions. Particularly at General Motors, selling entailed several new components, including the creation of sophisticated forecasting techniques that drew on government statistics and information from the field to link manufacturing schedules to predicted sales. GM also pioneered the sale of annual models and promoted them with great fanfare and aggressive sales campaigns. It brought salesmanship further "back" into the production process, by concentrating on style, color, and design features that would appeal to consumers—in a sense, thinking about the sales process beginning even with the initial design of new car models. It also, famously, elevated salesmanship within the company itself by dividing GM into separate divisions according to the brand sold. Each of the automobile divisions—Cadillac, Buick, Oakland (later Pontiac), and Chevrolet—served a different sales market.[21] Each one had its own house organ, its own dealer organization, and its own sales program.

Door-to-door salesmen also captured popular attention as more companies in the 1920s began selling their goods directly to the public. The Jewel Tea agent, the Hoover vacuum salesman, the Fuller Brush man, and the representative for the California Perfume Company (later known as Avon Products) all became familiar figures. Door-to-door salesmen became known for their ingenious persistence in selling. One *Saturday Evening Post* cartoon, for instance, showed a Fuller Brush agent hanging from a tree limb, keeping a ferocious dog at bay with a long-handled brush. The salesman was exclaiming to the dog's owner: "Notice how well it brushes the dog's back."[22]

In many ways, door-to-door salesmen were like the subscription booksellers of the nineteenth century. Whereas book canvassers brought self-help books and histories to farmers, door-to-door agents carried mass-produced appliances and small consumer items to suburban housewives. The strategy of the salesperson was similar. The seller came armed with a series of rehearsed arguments, hoping to make a quick one-time sale. Door-to-door salesmen, like canvassers, learned to navigate the culture of gender. With the notable exception of those who worked for the California Perfume Company and a handful of other firms that employed female agents, most door-to-door sales agents were men. Salesmen worked out different pitches for men and for women and were acutely aware of the advantages and disadvantages of flirtatious behavior. Alfred Fuller even referred to salesmanship as a form of courtship.

But there were also important differences between nineteenth-century canvassers and door-to-door salesmen. The door-to-door companies were far more systematically managed than canvassing organizations. They had large production facilities, and they sold expensive appliances as well as cheaper goods. Agents were given specific territories and sales routes, and managers assigned quotas and demanded accurate record-keeping from their sales force.

The promotion of consumer items had a great influence on the economy. From 1919 to 1929, the share of homes that had washing machines rose from 8 percent to 29 percent; vacuum cleaners, from 4 percent to 20 percent; radios, from 1 percent to 40 percent; and cars, from 26 percent to 60 percent.[23]

Advertising was central to the sale of these goods. As one historian commented, the advertising agent in the 1920s was an "apostle of modernity" who "introduced consumers to the newest in products and confided to manufacturers the newest in popular whims."[24] The total advertising volume in the United States increased from $1.409 billion in 1919 to $2.987 billion in 1929.[25] Advertisers took advantage of a range of outlets. The Associated Advertising Clubs reported that total advertising expenditures in 1920 were divided largely among newspapers ($600 million), direct mail ($300 million), and magazines ($150 million), with a smaller share going to business papers, novelties, electric signs, and window and store displays.[26] Moreover, there was growth during the decade of new advertising media, especially commercial radio, which spread rapidly after the founding of KDKA in Pittsburgh in 1920. Not only did the amount of advertising increase substantially, but its appearance also changed, becoming, as psychologists had encouraged, less informational and more suggestive.[27]

But salesmen were also essential in expanding demand for new consumer products, and they served a different role than advertising. They went door-to-door, even in the automobile trade, demonstrating products and speaking to "prospects" directly. These "mass salesmen" helped to create a market for specialty products like automobiles, radio, and vacuum cleaners, just as they had for brand-name goods like Coca-Cola and Ivory soap in the late nineteenth century.[28]

In particular, salesmen were instrumental in introducing two key elements of consumer culture: planned obsolescence and installment purchase.[29] Automobile salesmen encouraged customers to "trade up" to the latest products and models. They also pointed out the differences between their brands and those of competitors—something that advertisements could not accomplish in detail. In addition, appliance and brush salesmen demonstrated their products and highlighted the convenience of shopping at home rather than in stores.

Moreover, salesmen arranged terms of credit. Installment selling burgeoned throughout the decade. It had been used earlier to sell clocks and sewing machines and thus was not a new phenomenon, but it increased dramatically in the 1920s. Installment plans became common, particularly through the sale of automobiles. By 1930, 60 to 70 percent of automobiles were being bought on installment credit, and so was 80 to 90 percent of furniture, 75 percent of washing machines, 65 percent of vacuum cleaners, 75 percent of radio sets, and 80 percent of phonographs.[30]

Salesmen encouraged and enabled the "Consumer Durables Revolution" of the 1920s. While consumers purchased more "major" durable goods, such as autos and appliances (frequently sold by salesmen), they purchased relatively fewer "minor" durable goods, such as china, house furnishings, books, and jewelry.[31]

The experiences of automobile companies and manufacturers of products sold door-to-door reveal the extremes of consumer selling. The automobile companies operated with tremendous economic power and a high degree of analytic sophistication; the other manufacturers were relatively small players in the economy and adopted a distinctly antibureaucratic culture. The goal of the first was to make everyone a customer (and a repeat customer at that, by introducing annual model changes); that of the second, to make everyone a salesman, by hiring armies of canvassers. Moreover, automobile dealers and door-to-door salesmen had different strategies. At the automobile companies, salesmen explained the options available on cars and arranged credit and service; they also convinced consumers to choose one brand over another. They were critical, for instance, in the war between Ford and Chevrolet, as Chevrolet dealers targeted Ford customers who had owned their cars for a few years, hoping to persuade them to switch brands. In door-to-door companies, salesmen demonstrated products, tailoring their pitch to the specific needs of a housewife or family. Rather than competing against other brands, they often competed against retailers, in a sense setting one method of distribution against another.

Selling Appliances and Brushes Door-to-Door

Entrepreneurs developed door-to-door companies to work in cities and particularly in the expanding suburbs. Some companies, including Fuller Brush, had salesmen working overseas. They sold a number of products, including many household appliances that were intended to appeal to housewives. A Temple University survey of Philadelphia and its suburbs in 1930 found that among the people who purchased from door-to-door salesmen, 45 percent had bought brushes at least once. Others had purchased vacuum cleaners (23 percent), hosiery (10 percent), electric appliances (8 percent), aluminum ware (6 percent), apparel (3 percent), magazines and books (1 percent), and washing machines (1 percent).[32] There were also other salesmen and deliverymen who came to the door, including those selling ice, collecting insurance premiums, delivering milk, or offering to sharpen scissors and knives.

Many of the door-to-door concerns built armies composed of thousands of salespeople making daily rounds. Unlike the car companies, the number of distributors at door-to-door concerns, selling their wares, could be virtually unlimited. Often their most talented salespeople were the recruiters of new sales agents, rather than the actual sellers of the products. The ability to find new agents varied with the health of the economy. "When economic times are good and employment high, these door to door companies face much higher expenses in recruiting sales persons," observed Victor Buell in *Harvard Business Review*.[33]

In smaller firms, there was little initial communication between the manufacturer and the salesman; some advertised for salesmen in the back of magazines and communicated with them by mail.[34] *Opportunity* magazine carried advertisements for small concerns. In the premier issue in June 1923, "Master Salesman" H. L. Fogleman explained: "Every normal being is a Salesman. The Minister, the Doctor, the Lawyer—selling their knowledge of Religion, of Medicine, of Law. The President of the United States is a salesman—selling his time, his talent, his ability—trying to persuade the people of this Country to think as he thinks and get them to do as he wants them to do."[35] *Opportunity* in some ways resembled the scandalous *True Story* magazine, with many sentences ending in an exclamation point. It was a big, oversized magazine with a luridly colored cover. The front illustration of the January 1928 edition, for example, shows Baby New Year leaping out of a wallet, draped with banners reading "New Ways to Make Money" and "Make as Much

Opportunity, sometimes called *Salesman's Opportunity*, was founded by popular motivational writer Orison Swett Marden. In 1928, the year before the onset of the Great Depression, the magazine promised readers they could "make as much money" as they wanted by mastering the principles of salesmanship.

Money as You Want (see Page 22)." Each month *Opportunity* listed classified ads for agents and salesmen:

CALIFORNIA PERFUMED BEADS SELLING like hot cakes. Agents coining money. Big profits. Catalog Free. Mission Factory N, 2328 W. Pico, Los Angeles, Calif.

THIS IS THE GREATEST MONEY-MAKING house to house proposition ever known. N. R. G. tablets wash clothes in 10 minutes without rubbing. Free samples. N. R. G. Co. F232 W. Superior, Chicago.

SUPERKEEN! AMAZING NEW PATENTED Magnetical Blade Sharpener! Sharpens All Razor Blades Instantly, Magically, By Powerful Magnetic Force! New! Absolutely different! Sensational Demonstration! Whirlwind Seller! Write for Pocket Sample! Superkeen, Dept. B-35, Salisbury, N.C.[36]

Opportunity also highlighted several new products each month. These were usually small, unpromising-looking items. One was a Novelty Nut Cracker, a bronze or nickel-finished, squirrel-shaped device that cracked nuts in its mouth when its formidable tail was depressed. Another was a "Fork with Knife Blades"—a typical fork whose leftmost prong had been replaced by a thin, serrated knife, to be inserted into the mouth with care.

More highly structured door-to-door companies developed branch offices that recruited and trained salesmen. Branch managers were sometimes salaried employees of the company, but at other times they received a commission on all the sales in the branch area.[37]

Accurate accounting information was important for these companies, for despite pushing many costs onto the salesman, they faced numerous expenses—including the cost of advertising for new sales agents. They also had to pay sizable commissions to give sales agents an adequate incentive to sell. Most had to ship all their goods, sometimes thousands of small items, and maintain regional warehouses of inventory.[38] They also had to keep track of the installment payments made by thousands of consumers, a far more difficult task than that faced by organizations selling to industry and having to deal with, say, a few hundred retailers or wholesalers at most.[39]

"Direct selling" was useful for introducing new types of goods or new brands and enabled manufacturers to keep their products from losing to the competition at department stores.[40] The rise of door-to-door selling in the 1920s helped fuel the scientific homemaking movement, which provided housewives with new labor-saving devices.[41] The electric iron, first sold in 1893, sold extremely well in the 1920s. In one Ohio town, where a market research study was conducted, 82 percent of the households had electric irons in 1926.[42] Hoover sold its vacuums (patented in 1908) through stores, but used salesmen to do "missionary" work by canvassing neighborhoods and making house-to-house demonstrations.[43] Electrolux, which made the first canister-style vacuum, also sold its product door-to-door in the 1920s.[44] Electric washing machines appeared for home use by 1914, and by the end of the 1920s, could be found in more than a quarter of nonfarm households equipped with electricity.[45]

Some firms used door-to-door selling only to introduce their products and then sold them through retail shops. The Allister Electric Company, for instance, sold its vacuum cleaners door-to-door for one year (1923) and then, figuring that canvassers had familiarized the public with the product, turned entirely to retail selling and newspaper advertisements.[46]

There were other advantages to hiring agents who sold directly to consumers. Door-to-door companies tended to maintain their sales volume in times of recession. Even though consumers had fewer dollars to spend, many more recruits were willing and available to go out and sell.[47]

Some of the companies that got started around the turn of the century became well known, including the California Perfume Company (which was renamed Avon Products Company in 1939), Jewel Tea, and Fuller Brush.[48] And door-to-door selling offered opportunities to those who might have had difficulty finding work at larger bureaucratic corporations. For example, although women in the nineteenth century had worked as book agents and peddlers, most bureaucratic sales organizations of the early twentieth century would not hire them in the 1910s and 1920s (except for retail stores, which hired women for roughly one-quarter of sales positions in the early twentieth century).[49]

African American C. J. Walker came up with a treatment to counter thinning hair in women, along with a hair-straightening system and other products, which she began peddling in Denver in 1905. She toured the country extensively, recruiting and training agents. By 1910 she had established a factory in Indianapolis to manufacture her goods. Walker agents, who numbered in the thousands at this point, were distinctive for their long black skirts and crisp white shirts. Unlike the petty canvassers of the late nineteenth century, these women became models of respectability and industriousness.[50]

The longest lasting and best-known door-to-door sales agency employing women was the California Perfume Company. David Hall McConnell, a former book salesman, founded the company in 1886, in a single room in Brooklyn, New York. The use of "California" in the company name was intended to conjure images of floral landscapes. After establishing a production plant in Suffern, New York, McConnell concentrated on building several branch offices. By 1898, McConnell had a West Coast office in San Francisco and a Midwestern office in Kansas City, Missouri. In 1914, he expanded the company into Canada, opening an office in Montreal. In 1917 the company won a gold medal at the Panama Pacific International Exposition in San Francisco for its product quality and packaging. This proved to be a marketing bonanza for the company; depictions of the gold medal appeared on its bottles henceforth.[51] With the help of Mrs. Persis Foster Eames Albee, the company's first agent and principal recruiter, McConnell's company reached $1 million (about $9 million today) in annual sales by 1920, a figure that rose to $2.5 million (about $26 million today) by 1929. During the same period, the number of canvassers increased from 16,000 to 25,000.[52]

But door-to-door canvassing forces made up predominantly of women remained rare.[53] Even many firms that targeted housewives, such as the Fuller Brush Company, hired few women to sell their products. Alfred Fuller explained in 1922 that women had been hired only out of necessity. "During the war period we were obliged to put on a great many women. Men have proved more successful in our line, however, than women."[54] The fraternity of drummers had been ardently male, and salesmen for manufacturing concerns, such as those at the World's Salesmanship Congress, had trumpeted their own manliness with models of "Theodore Roosevelt, super salesman," and others.

One of the most successful door-to-door companies of the period was Fuller Brush, which, although it sold a simple product, succeeded not only in selling brushes but also in popularizing salesmanship. The Fuller Brush Company was much larger (in terms of sales volume) and more systematized in the early 1920s than the California Perfume Company. Alfred C. Fuller, a native of Nova Scotia, founded the company in 1906 in Hartford, Connecticut.[55] After working for a door-to-door brush-selling company in Somerville, Massachusetts, Fuller set out on his own. Moving to Hartford, he hired someone to help make the brushes, while he spent the mornings selling. Fuller canvassed exclusively in Hartford for a couple of years. He then began advertising in newspapers for agents to help him and expanded his sales into New York and Pennsylvania. By 1910, he had about twenty-five people selling brushes and six making them. Early that year, he placed an advertisement for salesmen in the nationally circulating *Everybody's Magazine*. This was the start of his success. He heard from about one hundred applicants in a month and offered nearly all of them a chance to sell. Salesmen, known as "dealers," were required to pay six dollars for a sample case, brushes, and a descriptive list of the wares; in return, they were given an exclusive territory to sell. By March 1910, Fuller had signed up 260 dealers. In 1913, the company started recruiting college students to work during their summer vacation—a practice the company continued for many years.[56]

Fuller Brush made a range of products, including mops, brooms, hairbrushes, toothbrushes, bathroom brushes, and combs. It manufactured brushes that performed specific tasks, such as cleaning Venetian blinds or radiators. Some, like those found inside vacuum cleaners, were marketed only to industry. The brushes—all produced in Hartford—were usually of high quality and somewhat expensive. Eventually the company also sold polishes, soaps, waxes, and creams.[57]

In 1925, there were 4,200 Fuller salesmen. They were expected to perform fifteen *demonstrations* per day—not just calls. Company statistics showed that a relatively high number of demonstrations, nearly half, resulted in some kind of sale.[58] When they did, Fuller salesmen earned a commission rate of about 40 percent.[59]

By the mid-1920s, Fuller had developed a fairly sophisticated sales organization to support, monitor, and motivate its sales force. The United States was divided into five divisions; Canada was a separate division. The divisions were themselves split into five districts, and each district was then subdivided into seven to ten branch offices. The branch territories were, finally, split into blocks, and each salesman (usually twenty to forty per branch office) was assigned specific blocks to work.[60]

The branch manager was the key figure. He hired, trained, and supervised salesmen. He assigned territory and issued an office bulletin each week. He held sales meetings, met personally with men to motivate them, and promoted the brand. Alfred Fuller also cultivated a homespun image—he called himself "Dad Fuller," a name that caught on throughout the organization. In fact, branch managers were encouraged to adopt the Fuller name as their own. "We like to have our branch managers establish a reputation in the territory so they may be known as Mr. Fuller," wrote vice president Frank S. Beveridge. "Some of our men are very proud because the people, their customers in the territory (and our salesmen have had the same experience), know them as Mr. Fuller." Unlike the supervisory staff of the automobile companies who tended to receive a salary, Fuller's branch officers earned a commission on the total sales of the branch. The company paid the branch-office rent and also some of the advertising expenses.[61]

In order to develop a large market, the company sent agents to work in smaller markets not well served by department stores or chains. In

1922, for instance, it hired African American agents to reach what it called the "colored" market. To secure agents, the Fuller Brush branch manager of Tulsa, Oklahoma, went to the principal of the local segregated high school and recruited teachers for summer sales work. The manager reported, "It has been a success, especially in servant quarters where Negroes feel proud to buy the same merchandise as their mistress does. The four salesmen sold $2,083 between June and July."[62]

The hardest part of the sale was getting in the door. Like other door-to-door companies, Fuller gave away a free premium—in this case a small "handy brush." If the prospect—often a housewife—said she wanted the premium but did not want to hear the demonstration, the salesman would mention that the free brush was buried in his sample case and that he needed to come inside the house to unpack it. This delay allowed him to launch into his talk.

Salesmen at Fuller were given a script. They asked "positive-response" questions throughout the demonstration. "The only thing I have against the Fuller brushes is that they wear too long, and to you or any one who uses them that is not a fault, but a virtue," said the salesman. "Am I not right?" To dramatize the effectiveness of Fuller's brushes, salesmen were supposed to use the body brushes on themselves while explaining their virtues. Like stage directions, the instructions next to the scripted words read, for instance: "Rub [brush] on hand briskly; *enthuse.*" Salesmen were then to "go through motions as if taking a bath."

Like patent medicine men, lightning-rod salesmen, and insurance solicitors, Fuller Brush men were supposed to exaggerate fear—fear of dirty brushes. "Do you know, Mrs. Brown, that if you could see what the back of a bath brush contains after it has been used a few times you would not have one in the house." The script contained instructions that read, "If possible carry old wooden-back bath brush. Look disgusted." Salesmen were then to "draw a picture so realistic of germs, etc., that she will throw away her old brush." Even the bathtub was depicted as dangerous: "This [shower] brush also does away with that old idea of getting into a tub of water and bathing with water that in five minutes' time is not clean. You will admit that the water stays clean only a very short time after you get into it. In a lot of the more modern homes they are doing away with the bathtub altogether."[63]

Selling was difficult, and Fuller had to cope with high turnover and increased competition from other canvassing organizations.[64] The company began the 1920s with great promise. Sales volume grew from just $30,000 in 1910 to $15 million in 1923 (about $160 million today). But in the mid-1920s sales began to decline. In 1925 they were at $13.5 million and, four years later, in 1929, they had dropped to $10.3 million (about $108 million today). With the economy of the 1920s strong, it was difficult to recruit new agents; at the same time, new door-to-door companies had entered the field and were competing for the housewife's dollar. Alfred Fuller did not turn the company around until the mid-1930s, when he changed the commission rate and the prices of his brushes.[65]

Motivation was critical at Fuller Brush. In his communications with employees, Alfred Fuller tried to give his salesmen a sense of mission. Wrote Fuller of his early years selling, "In the buoyant elation of my adventure, I considered myself a reformer, eager to attack the dirt and domestic labor of the city; destroying the one and alleviating the other."[66] This view of the sales process brought Fuller courage. "Too many salesmen are afraid to knock, lest the housewife be feeding the baby, cleaning, dressing to go out, taking a nap, or preparing her husband's supper," wrote Fuller. "I never hesitated to interrupt anyone, being convinced that my *mission* was to lessen the drudgery of domestic life."[67]

Fuller also claimed to draw strength from his religion, Christian Science, which he discovered early in his career. While prospecting in Scranton, Pennsylvania, Fuller had fallen ill. At one house, a woman handed him a copy of Mary Baker Eddy's *Science and Health* and told him to read a marked passage. Although the passage confused him, he began to feel better and afterward took an interest in the church. He reflected on the "confidence" of the woman who had given the passage to him and increasingly drew connections between the divine and his daily activities. Fuller began to write inspirational articles for sales magazines and published a book, *Out of the Rut,* in 1922.[68]

Fuller's history reveals that sales managers faced not only the difficult challenge of mapping out the best strategy to gain new customers, but also the arduous task of preparing salesmen for the marketplace. Motivational techniques based on "positive thought" were worked into the daily routine at Fuller Brush. Albert Teetsel, a motivational-technique success story, began selling brushes in Poughkeepsie, New York, before being elevated to district manager for New York City. He worked for the company from 1923 to 1945 and, according to Fuller, was "the best-known Fuller Brush Man of his day." A photograph of Teetsel shows him with a loud tie, diamond ring, and thick cigar. Teetsel was a relentless salesman, selling brushes even at the Macy's Thanksgiving Day Parade. He began a "Fine and Dandy" club at Fuller. Salesmen were instructed to answer every "How are you?" with "Fine and dandy." The club spread throughout his New York district. Teetsel boasted, "We have Fine and Dandy signs in hotels, restaurants, clubs, trolley cars, banks, Y.M.C.A.'s, . . . and are using every possible means to advance and advertise this wonderful spirit."[69] There were Fine and Dandy armbands, caps, pins, badges, and five degrees of pins (plain, red stone, green stone, blue stone, diamond).[70] Teetsel remarked: "The psychosocial effect of the words 'Fine and Dandy' or 'I'm Fine and Dandy, How are You?' is to impress the party spoken to with the enthusiasm and cheerful outlook of the speaker." This was, at least, the effect recalled by Fuller Brush vice president Frank Beveridge in 1925, though it is also easy to imagine how such a slogan could be grating:

> We once had a branch manager who made it a rule never to talk with a man until he said he was fine and dandy. It seemed a man went out one day and his automobile broke down, he had difficulties with deliveries, and when he came into the office he wasn't feeling very good. He came in gruffly, spoke with the branch manager and the branch manager didn't reply. He got a little angry and still the branch manager didn't reply. Finally, after the branch manager had asked how he was, and the man had

to reply, "Fine and Dandy," naturally he was in a better mood, and a good many of his problems vanished into thin air and it made it much easier to deal with that man and help him to solve his problems.[71]

Teetsel claimed that his inspiration for the Fine and Dandy clubs was a speech given by the Reverend Stanley LeFevre Krebs. Krebs wrote *The Law of Suggestion* (1906, later published as *The Fundamental Principles of Hypnosis*, 1957), and *Cries from the Cross* (1928).[72]

Exemplifying a theme of this book, Fuller's sales and management strategy suggests that the company did not view selling as an entirely logical or rational process. Nor did the company view the salesman as simply an information provider. Salesmen did not show up at the door and read a list of product specifications. Their task, instead, was to spark enthusiasm and influence the potential customer to buy.

Al Teetsel, founder of the Fine and Dandy Club and according to Alfred Fuller the "best-known Fuller Brush Man of the old era [1920s]," in his prime.

This did not mean that companies thought salesmen could sell just anything. After all, selling was difficult and salesmen often failed. Moreover, Fuller and many other companies spent time and money trying to improve their products, thereby making the salesman's task easier. But they depended on salesmen to persuade customers to choose their product, especially when their competitor's product was largely similar. Salesmen could make the difference, compensating for a product's relative weakness (say, its styling) by emphasizing its strength (say, its performance). If one company's sales force was stronger than another's, it might succeed in driving a competitor from the market, despite the similarity, or even slight inferiority, of its product. Once customers were persuaded to choose one company's product—or, as in the case of Fuller, became accustomed to buying brushes at home instead of in a store—they were more likely to continue buying it, rather than switch.

Automobile Salesmanship

Automobile companies were much larger than the door-to-door enterprises, but they too used salesmen to generate demand, relay information back to managers, battle the competition, and provide consumers with credit to purchase durable goods. But whereas door-to-door companies spent their time recruiting and motivating salesmen, automobile companies eventually developed a strategy designed to generate enthusiasm among new (and repeat) buyers each year with the introduction of annual model changes.

When Henry Ford introduced his Model T in 1908, the automobile market was fragmented, consisting of a number of competing entrepreneurs, including William C. Durant, Ransom E. Olds, and Alanson P. Brush. But Ford quickly dominated the market with his strategy of high-volume production and low price; due to his efficient methods of mass production, the price of the Model T dropped from $950 in 1909 (about $18,700 today) to $360 in 1916 (about $6,000 today).[73] He led the industry in the early twentieth century, holding a 56 percent share of the automobile market in 1921.[74]

Except for a single, short-lived retail sales facility in Detroit that closed in 1916, the Ford Motor Company did not sell cars directly to consumers. Like other automobile makers, Ford relied on semi-independent dealers. In that way, from 1903 to 1907, Ford's distribution system was somewhat similar to that of the McCormick Harvesting Company in the late nineteenth century. (Like the reaper, the automobile was largely a seasonal good at this time. Automobile sales tended to fall sharply in the winter, when the car proved unreliable.)[75]

Ford's distribution system was characterized by a relation between a large mass manufacturer and thousands of small, semi-independent dealers; this form of organization became the essence of car salesmanship in the United States. In the beginning, as GM president Alfred Sloan noted, the idea was to give the dealers great flexibility in how they went about selling. "The prevailing attitude of the industry [early on was] . . . that the manufacturer should attend to the product, the prices, the advertising and promotion, and leave the rest of the elements of distribution to the dealer to work out."[76] But as time went on, manufacturers took greater control over the affairs of dealers and, especially, advertising and sales strategies.

Because Henry Ford was not particularly interested in marketing and salesmanship—choosing instead to put his faith in low prices and an expanding market—the task of developing an effective sales and distribution organization for the company fell to others.[77] Norval Hawkins, Ford's sales manager from 1907 to 1918, devised much of the company's distribution system, including procedures for selling cars, monitoring dealers, and creating a common company culture through newsletters and conventions.

Hawkins was born in Ypsilanti, Michigan, and attended a local high school and nearby business college. After working for several years as an accountant, Hawkins took on a partner and, at age thirty-one, launched the Hawkins-Gies accounting firm. He did the first audit of the fledgling Ford Motor Company and, because of his careful work and strong personality, was hired to direct its sales operations.

Hawkins had a number of talents. As a professional accountant, he introduced standardized methods of reporting costs and kept careful watch over the prices of cars and car parts. He also formulated procedures for distributing automobiles that saved Ford money. For instance, Hawkins developed the idea of shipping the cars unassembled, to save money on freight; the cars were then reassembled at regional offices.[78]

Yet Hawkins was not a stereotypical "numbers" man. He was also a remarkable salesman, and he built up Ford's dealership network. Under Hawkins, the number of Ford dealers increased sharply from 215 in 1908 to 6,167 in 1917.[79]

Hawkins's office executed all the contracts with dealers. Dealers were expected to be familiar with technical aspects of the car and were required to give full demonstrations on their use and upkeep. They also had to maintain a supply of spare parts and engage a mechanic to make repairs.[80] Dealers purchased cars from Ford at a discount—which in the 1920s amounted to approximately one-quarter of the price of the car. They received income from the sale of new cars, parts, accessories, and service; they had expenses in all these areas (cost of new cars, of parts and services, and for service), and they also had to pay salesmen's commissions and salaries, automobile delivery charges, advertising costs, insurance, rent, and the salaries of administrators and other employees.[81]

Hawkins looked for ways to establish a common culture among Ford's network of dealers. In 1908 he started the journal *Ford Times,* which included motivational articles, portraits of successful dealers, jokes, and *do's* and *don'ts* for salesmen. In one article published in 1908, Hawkins reminded dealers to keep in touch with customers after the initial sale of an automobile—there was always money to be made on replacement parts and service. "Too much emphasis cannot be laid on the fact that when you have sold a car to a customer your acquaintance and business relations with that customer have only just commenced— not ended."[82]

To monitor dealers, Hawkins constructed a hierarchical sales organization run by salaried Ford employees. The organization rapidly stretched across the country and even around the globe. In 1917 Ford's sales organization consisted of six branch supervisors, sixty-nine branch sales managers, assistant branch sales managers (one per branch), and roadmen (one to eight per branch).[83] Roadmen toured the country and dropped in to inspect dealerships; they checked the showrooms and garages.[84] They then reported details about individual agents back to Detroit and also submitted information about the economic health of the region in general.[85]

Hawkins helped to recruit dealers himself. In 1909 William P. Young, a lawyer in Pottsdown, Pennsylvania, wrote Ford asking to become a dealer. He was told that he could have the agency for his hometown and the adjoining four towns by purchasing three cars at the wholesale price and agreeing to rent space for a showroom and repair shop, as well as by consenting to meet future sales quotas. He and two friends shared the costs and became partners in the dealership. The first year's contract called for Young to purchase ten cars and to forward $150 to a Philadelphia branch parts account. In his second year, he made arrangements with a local garage to store, service, and sell cars.

Young remembered getting a torrent of material from the company, including home-office departmental letters, branch-office memos, and the *Ford Times*. He also had frequent visits from Ford's roadmen. With his son in tow, Young attended a dealers' meeting in Philadelphia, where he heard Hawkins give the main address. Young wrote that Hawkins "sold us the idea of selling cars for a production to be stepped up from 20,000 to 40,000, to 75,000, on up to the then unbelievable number of 500,000 yearly; that the only limit to the dealer's volume and profit was the number of cars he could sell; and that in price and improvements the car would be paced with anything produced in the low priced class." Inspired, Young left the meeting "determined to cast my lot with Ford and make of it a career for myself and [my son]."[86]

Hawkins was a powerful motivator. Eventually he wrote two popular books on selling, *The Selling Process: A Handbook of Salesmanship Principles* (1918) and *Certain Success* (1920), which taught the idea that anyone could learn the skills of a master salesman. He supplemented his message with autobiographical details about how he had "recreated" himself into a success. From 1889 to 1894, Hawkins had worked as a bookkeeper and cashier for the Standard Oil Company in Detroit. In the fall of 1894, he was arrested for embezzling money (about $3,000), tried, and sent briefly to prison. His ability to rise to an important position afterward, he wrote, "demonstrate[s] how a man of character and brains, after a bad slip, could make an enduring success."[87]

Good selling took confidence and courage, but it brought a life of rewards. "Who of us who have chosen to live among the mountains of Salesmanship would be content to dwell on the dead level of men in other vocations?" he wrote.[88] Those born to disadvantage were more blessed than beaten, for valuable lessons were learned in overcoming hardship. Even physical unpleasantness could be cured by adopting the positive outlook of salesmanship. "The features are very mobile," Hawkins wrote. "The scowl lines between the eyes of a habitual 'crab' were cut there by his own claws. The sneering nose, the superciliously twisted mouth, have been acquired by *habit*."[89]

While Hawkins inspired dealers to aim high, he also kept careful watch on their progress. He wrote one dealer in Columbus who had fallen behind on his quota: "Are the men on your retail force real salesmen or mere canvassers? We are quite sure from information gathered from our records that C. F. McCall [and] C. O. Walker are in the latter class. Both of these men are considerably behind on their contract and we would suggest that you endeavor to see that the ten orders which they have obtained for future delivery are filled this month."[90] Dealers who did not perform well faced the ultimate consequence of losing their franchise. (Henry Ford himself was quick to use this threat. Unlike Hawkins, he showed little interest in maintaining the dealers' spirits or welfare. During the sharp, short depression of 1920 to 1921, Ford pressed his dealers to purchase their quota of inventory despite the hard times—which they did, for fear of losing their business. Ford was able to survive the period, but a rift began to grow between himself and several of his best executives over his idiosyncratic leadership.)

Though Hawkins, like many other talented executives at Ford, left the company in 1918 after a disagreement with Henry Ford, the sales network he developed—comprising a series of semi-independent franchised dealerships and a company-managed monitoring sales force—continued to grow through the 1920s.

Faced with increasing challenges from General Motors in the 1920s (and, after 1925, from Chrysler), Ford Motor Company outlined detailed instructions for selling its cars in manuals like *Ford Products and Their Sale* (1923) and *The Model T Specialist* (1925).[91] *Ford Products and Their Sale* was an achievement, running nearly 750 pages in six parts. It included an overview of the automobile industry, a history of the Ford Motor Company, a list of salesmen's responsibilities, instructions on salesmanship, and the specifications of Ford cars, trucks, and tractors. The book's "Forty Points to Observe in Selling" advised salesmen, among other things, to plan the day's work the night before, study the competition, research potential prospects, work on personal appearance, and eliminate "self-consciousness" in sales talks.[92]

The manual revealed the ways in which selling consumer-oriented goods contrasted with techniques for selling to business. The automobile salesman was supposed to establish himself as a well-known figure in the town—gaining public recognition by visiting shops and talking to owners and customers. He was instructed to be always looking for leads by keeping alert: scanning the newspaper for changes in management in local businesses; inquiring about turnovers of tenants in apartment houses (the person leaving may need a car to pack goods, while the one arriving may need a car to get to work); keeping in contact with people who purchased a used car from the dealership; and checking the local papers for births, marriages, deaths—all were opportunities. Salesmen were advised to conduct house-to-house canvasses and to remember the importance of selling to women. "Women do not only 85 percent of the retail buying at the stores, but probably have better than 51 percent of the say when the purchase of a car is decided," the manual reminded.[93]

In his autobiography, Henry Ford himself recognized the diffuse nature of the automobile market. "A dealer or a salesman ought to have the name of every possible automobile buyer in his territory, including all those who have never given the matter a thought," he wrote. "He

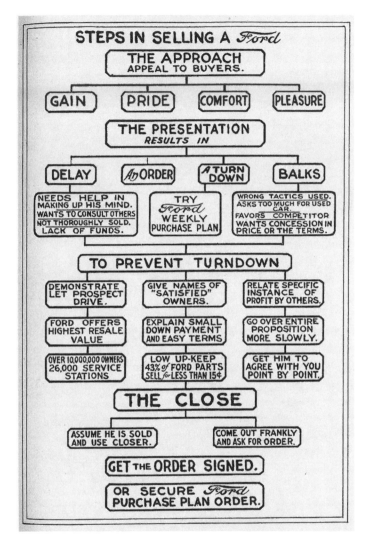

Ford further standardized its sales practices in the 1920s by producing the *Model T Specialist* (1925) for its dealers. The manual included a quick overview of the steps involved in selling a Ford.

DAILY REPORT ON PROSPECT CALLS

NO.	INTER-VIEWED	PHONED	OUT	PERSON INTERVIEWED	REMARKS: STATE MODEL SOLD OR GIVE REASON SALE OR ENROLLMENT NOT SECURED	DID YOU DISCUSS WPP	DEFINITE APPOINTMENT OR FOLLOW-UP DATE — DATE	TIME
	INDICATE BY CHECK MARK							
1	✓			Prospect	Secured Enrollment	✓		
2		✓	✓					
3	✓			Wife	Arranges Demonstration		March 7	4 pm
4	✓			Prospect	Wants Car appraised		Mar. 10	
5		✓		"	Appointment		Mar. 8	8 pm
6	✓			"	Sold Coupe			
7	✓			Daughter	Will visit Salesroom			
8								
9								
10								
11								
12								
13								
14								

NEW PROSPECTS SECURED

NAME	ADDRESS	NON-OWNER	OWNER
Dr. R. Donald	8081 Grand Blvd	✓	
M. B. Mott	24 Allegheny		✓
D. A. Boone	857 Hancock		✓

CANVASS CALLS MADE	NUMBER OF NON-CAR OWNERS	NO. OF ENROLL-MENTS	NEW PROSPECTS SECURED	REMARKS
10	1	1	3	

FORM FX1000 (ALL RIGHTS RESERVED) SALES EQUIPMENT CO., DETROIT, MICH.

A page from the *Model T Specialist* (1925) shows the proper way to fill out "prospect cards."

should then personally solicit by visitation if possible—by correspondence at the least—every man on that list."[94]

When meeting prospects—on the showroom floor, in the lot, or in their house-to-house canvassing—Ford salesmen had to be prepared to answer common objections. In response to comments that Ford's cars were too plain-looking in comparison with the stylish models of competing firms—what should the salesman say? "When the salesman sees a clouded brow on the prospect as he looks across the plain Ford instrument board, or if he anticipates a negative thought from that plainness, he should beat the prospect to the thought by sweeping his hand in front of the instrument board and saying: 'Just note the simplicity of that instrument board. Simple, plain and neat. Not one of those complex boards cluttered with instruments to watch, and to fuss with.'"[95] But this anticipated objection was just one of many listed in the manual that the salesman had to be prepared for. There were fifty-three in all, ranging from "I'll wait until spring" to "I must have immediate delivery," and "I can't afford a car" to "My wife does not want me to buy." (A complete list of objections by potential buyers can be found in the Appendix on p. 271.)

Answers to all of the objections were written out in detail in the manual. Responses tended to have a predictable format. The salesman began by agreeing with the prospect's objection, thereby deflating the tension, then redirected the conversation by asking a "positive-response" question to which the "prospect" would have to agree. In the first example, "Believe there will be another drop in price. I am going to wait," the salesman at first agreed: "We will admit, Mr. _____, that it has been Mr. Ford's policy to lower prices whenever he could. When those changes would come, or if they would come, no one has ever been able to definitely foresee. Business moves so fast at the Ford plant, well over a million cars a year, that we doubt if they even get much advance idea of when changes are coming." He would then add: "But we must admit that Ford prices are so extraordinarily low that not much change if any can be expected."[96] Handling the prospect's objections was a very delicate process, and although salesmen were not expected to memorize the answers to all the common objections, reading through enough examples in the manual provided a way to answer a prospect's complaints without seeming pushy or aggressive. Salesmen were supposed to act like a shortstop fielding ground balls: they caught the grounder, absorbing its punch, and then redirected it to first base.

Despite Ford's global dealership network, its sales began to lag during the 1920s, largely because of Henry Ford's rigid adherence to the "universal car"—the Model T. The more far-reaching changes in automobile salesmanship occurred at General Motors under the leadership of Alfred Sloan. Salesmanship at GM became defined in a more expansive way than at Ford. It was not something that happened only after cars were built but was a mission that permeated every aspect of the company's work, from initial design to the final sale. And unlike Ford, GM began to offer automobiles in a great range of colors, styles, and prices.

Sloan was much more concerned than Ford with the health of his dealership network. In the early 1920s, Sloan visited his dealers in much the same way that Patterson toured his sales offices during the depression of 1893. Traveling by private railroad car, Sloan visited between five and ten dealers a day, asking them for their suggestions about the business, their concerns, ideas about consumer trends, and their predictions for the future. "Our intention, naturally, was to penetrate the market as effectively as possible, and since in the end this had to be carried out by our dealers, it was necessary to have the appropriate number of dealers, each of [them] the appropriate size and in the appropriate location," wrote Sloan.[97]

Sloan also did more than Ford to assist the dealers, particularly in the area of credit. He set up the massive General Motors Acceptance Corporation (GMAC) in 1919, which financed purchases made by dealers as well as by consumers. Ford, by contrast, did not organize a finance company until 1928 to allow purchase of his cars on the installment plan. GMAC was a tremendous assistance to customers wanting to purchase cars; often their only other option was to borrow money from a bank or loan association.[98]

General Motors collected more statistical information than Ford, gathering data about population distribution, income, and the performance of individual dealers. A central inventory committee received sales estimates from dealers in each division, which became the essence of the division's financial planning. Purchases and production schedules were linked to these estimates. Dealers, too, became important for providing information. They reported on the number of cars delivered to consumers, new orders taken, total orders accumulated, and tallies of new and used cars on hand. These numbers were then compared with the prior forecasts in order to see if the estimate was too high or low; if too high, the production schedule was decreased. After 1923, Sloan demanded that sales estimates from each of the corporation's dealers be delivered every ten days. He also purchased data on new car registrations from R. L. Polk and Company to find out the share of the market enjoyed by each of the General Motors divisions and to disclose how this share was changing.[99]

In addition, GM began to survey consumers in the 1920s. Henry (Buck) Weaver, GM's customer research expert, compiled information through surveys: the magazines read by customers, the amount of time owners kept their cars, their degree of loyalty to brands, and their opinions about GM dealers.[100]

Much more than Ford, Sloan understood the changing market. In 1924, sales of new cars had begun to level off (at about 3.6 million cars per year) and remained stagnant until the end of the decade. Most Americans who wanted a car had already bought one, so the market seemed to be saturated.[101] Especially problematic for dealers was the growth of the used-car market, which forced salesmen to make spot estimates of the value of old cars and the costs of repairing and reselling them. This became a major concern early in the century. In fact, in 1916 H. H. Gordon's "The Problem of the Used Car in the Automobile Industry" won a prize for best thesis at Harvard Business School, no doubt in part because it was so timely.[102] By 1927, used-car sales exceeded new-car sales.[103]

Ford and GM had different policies for dealing with this problem. In the mid-1920s, Ford insisted that dealers get a profit (of 20 percent) on the sale of used cars, and each dealership was required to provide documentation on the dispensation of these used cars. GM, conversely, took the view that it was preferable for dealers to concentrate on the volume of new cars sold, recognizing that dealers, in trying to "move" used cars, might have to settle for a small profit or even a loss at times. The company encouraged dealers to maintain contact with the purchasers of used cars with an eye to selling them something else in the future.[104]

More important, GM helped spur the sales of new cars by introducing in the 1920s the concept of annual model changes. Each year the new model was celebrated with a sales push, an unveiling of the car, and sales conventions offering such luxuries as caviar, champagne, and brass bands. Along with the introduction of annual models, Sloan instructed his dealers to try to persuade car owners to trade up to more expensive models and to encourage people to buy a second car. GM also used the slogan "A car for her" to market the automobile to and for housewives. These marketing efforts helped GM overtake Ford before the end of the decade. By 1931, GM sales made up 41.3 percent of the market and Ford sales, 24.9 percent.[105]

GM's Chevrolet division was a particular challenge to Ford. After Norval Hawkins left Ford, he took his talents to General Motors. *Printers' Ink* speculated that Detroit businessmen expected "to see Mr. Hawkins invade on a comprehensive scale the territory of his former business associate, Mr. Ford."[106] In fact, Hawkins worked at GM only briefly, sitting in as a member of the executive committee that discussed sales and advertising policy. The growth of Chevrolet was accomplished largely by Richard H. Grant, who set out to challenge Ford directly and eventually developed the most extensive dealer organization in the world.[107] Grant built up the Chevrolet dealerships by offering a greater discount rate than Ford. In 1925, the discount rate on Chevrolets was increased to 24 percent; Ford was only giving dealers 17.5 percent.[108] There were 6,700 Chevrolet dealers in 1925 and 10,600 in 1929.[109]

Like Hawkins at Ford, Grant set up a sales organization to train and monitor dealers. He also developed a manual to teach dealers how to sell. Unlike the Ford manual, however, *Selling Chevrolets: A Book of Gen-*

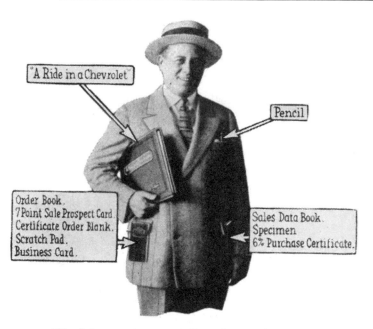

"A Ride in a Chevrolet"

Pencil

Order Book.
7 Point Sale Prospect Card
Certificate Order Blank.
Scratch Pad.
Business Card.

Sales Data Book.
Specimen
6% Purchase Certificate.

*All this equipment has been designed
so as to be easy to carry*

Chevrolet's sales manual, *Selling Chevrolets* (1926), encouraged dealers to take a scientific approach by carrying *A Ride in a Chevrolet* (a picture book showing Chevrolet models and options), as well as order forms, a pencil and scratch pad, and 6 percent purchase certificate order forms, which allowed customers to begin putting money away for their next Chevrolet.

eral Information for Chevrolet Retail Salesmen (1926) was filled with illustrations, charts, and cartoons to make the sales process seem simple and straightforward. It included a seven-point program that involved all levels of the GM organization in the sale—the salesman, the dealer, the zone manager, and the company itself.

The manual showed a picture of the ideal Chevrolet salesman: an eager-looking man in a double-breasted jacket and hat, with a pencil in his upper jacket pocket and a copy of the demonstration book *A Ride in a Chevrolet* tucked under his arm. In his lower pocket, his order book, seven-point sales prospect card, certificate order blank, scratch pad, and business card, all were packaged in a neat kit. In the other lower pocket were the sales data book and a sample 6 percent purchase certificate.[110]

Grant's manual paid particular attention to selling to women, though he did not hire them to sell cars. When women liked the car but seemed hesitant about buying it without consulting their husbands, the manual recommended confronting them with a barrage of information about the mechanics of the car that would, supposedly, allay their fears:

> Salesman—"Naturally, every woman will want to talk over so important an item as the purchase of the family automobile. Your husband will probably be even more interested than you are in many of Chevrolet's desirable features, especially its mechanical superiorities . . . He will be impressed by the dry disc clutch, which makes gear shifting easy; it starts the car smoothly, is fully enclosed and has no internal adjustments . . . Your husband will be thoroughly sold on the unit power plant construction which assures perfect alignment . . . He will heartily approve your choice when you tell him that Chevrolet uses a banjo type rear axle. You sign the order now and when I deliver your car tomorrow I can explain these quality features to him."[111]

Salesmen at Chevrolet played a similar role to salesmen of other durable consumer goods: they described the product, handled customer objections, gave demonstrations, and outlined terms of credit. Their job was to influence customers to purchase a Chevrolet rather than, say, a Ford. Here the salesman's intervention could be critical, for he could point out differences in largely similar products that buyers might not notice. This could have important consequences, for once a customer became accustomed to one brand, he or she was likely to stay with it for a long time. This tendency, which economists label a "path dependency" and marketers call "brand loyalty," helped to define the way companies competed against each other for the sale of consumer goods in the twentieth century.

Establishing this loyalty was a goal of the Chevrolet salesmen, as the manual made plain—for instance, in the following exchange, which occurred (or was supposed to occur) only *after* the customer had finished paying for the car. When the customer had completed all scheduled payments, the salesman was instructed to ride out to his or her home and deliver the canceled contract.

> Salesman—"I came out to deliver your cancelled contract from the General Motors Acceptance Corporation. You remember, you made the last payment on your car just a few days ago, so I thought I would bring you the cancelled contract." (Hands canceled contract to prospect.)
>
> Prospect—"Well, I am certainly glad that my payments have been completed. I won't have that amount to pay every month now."
>
> Salesman—"Since you purchased your car many new features have been added and improvements made. Why don't you get one of the new Chevrolets, Mr. Prospect?"
>
> Prospect—"I don't want a new car yet; I just paid for this one."
>
> Salesman—"Have you had a ride in one of the new IMPROVED Chevrolets?"

The salesman, in this script, wanted "Mr. Prospect" to buy GM's 6 percent purchase certificates, which could be used to purchase GM cars in the future. This way, the customer continued to pay the same amount to General Motors as before, even though the car itself had been paid for, and earned a return of 6 percent annually on the payments, which would eventually go toward purchasing his next GM car.

The strategies undertaken at General Motors in the 1920s revealed a new sophistication and complexity in managing the sale of consumer goods: building a range of products for consumers of different tastes and incomes, surveying consumer preferences, making careful forecasts to coordinate production and sales, and facilitating purchasing with installment plans.

Much of the interest in salesmanship in this period—at automobile companies as well as door-to-door enterprises and other concerns—developed during the rising expectations of the 1920s. But what would happen when the stock market crashed and the economy soured? Would large manufacturers have to change their sales strategy? Could salesmen maintain their day-to-day optimism through the Depression?

Selling Salesmanship

Public Relations
and the Great Depression

"A tremendous business machine now exists to satisfy human desires," wrote Charles W. Mears in his book *Salesmanship for the New Era* (1929), describing the whole of American commercial enterprise. Since the turn of the century, he explained, a vast, interconnecting institutional structure had been created, drawing together manufacturers, package designers, department-store owners, advertising copywriters, railroad engineers, truck drivers, and thousands of others in diverse occupations, to help move products from the shop floor to their final consumers. The modern salesman was a critical component of the new business machine. The salesman served not only as an "advance agent" for manufacturing companies, but also as "prosperity's ambassador," a "counselor who points out directions for our enjoyment of life."[1]

Writers, like Mears and others, remarked on the changed nature of the U.S. economy over the past several decades, from one of relative scarcity to one of material abundance. For the first time, it seemed, industry could produce enough wealth and goods to satisfy everyone. Economist Simon Patten argued, in several books written before his death in 1922, that Americans needed to rid themselves of their habits of savings and denial and learn to spend money and enjoy the pleasures of leisure.[2]

Statistics told the story of the nation's growth in production and distribution capacities. In 1929, just before the stock market crash, the U.S. economy had a wide range of retail outlets to serve consumers. It contained 1.5 million retail stores of various sizes: just over two thousand had annual sales of more than $1 million, while most, about three-fourths, were small, with annual sales of less than $30,000. Americans spent their money in various ways. Sales at retail stores totaled approximately $49 billion. There were also 7,061 chain-store organizations, operating 159,638 stores, with sales aggregating $11 billion. Catalog sales amounted to $515 million, and the country's 1,661 door-to-door companies had annual sales of around $100 million—though this figure was almost certainly an undercount.[3]

The number of people involved in distribution had greatly increased since the 1870s, when the hardware drummer Saunders Norvell and his traveling fraternity were kings of the road. Overall, about 6 million people worked in "trade" in 1930, including retail shop owners, auctioneers, newsboys, wholesale dealers, and salesmen. The United States contained 223,700 commercial travelers; 286,200 insurance agents and managers; 63,800 canvassers; and 1,988,300 salesmen and saleswomen, many of whom worked behind a counter. An additional 49,000 advertising agents wrote copy or designed advertisements to promote products. Taken together, the relative number of people involved in the distribution of products had grown much faster than those in production: for every 100 workers engaged in producing goods in 1870, there were 271 (or roughly three times as many) in 1930. The number of workers engaged in distribution, however, had increased much more, so that for every 100 workers in that category in 1870, 877 (or nearly nine times as many) were employed in 1930.[4]

Most of those working in distribution in 1930 were men, though women were better represented in sales-related jobs than in many other occupations. In the category of "agents," which included realtors and insurance agents, women accounted for just under 10 percent of the total, and in the classifications "commercial travelers" and "hucksters and peddlers," they were less than 5 percent. Women were best represented among retail sales workers, in department stores and elsewhere, making up 27 percent of that category.[5]

Calling the late 1920s the "Distribution Age," the business writer Ralph Borsodi noted that the "transformation in methods of salesmanship" at many of the largest firms was startling. "The happy-go-lucky salesmanship of the pre-McKinley era has been replaced by methods based upon scientific analysis of the psychology of the prospective buyer."[6]

Salespeople sold semifinished products to industry, office equipment and machinery to businesses, and vacuum cleaners, brushes, cosmetics, and appliances directly to consumers. They did "missionary" work, setting up promotional displays, giving away free samples, and explaining the differences between their line of goods and their competitors'. Salesmen scrambled to make their quotas, sat through training sessions, listened to motivational talks, and sang company songs at conventions.[7] "Selling yesterday / Selling the day before / Going to sell today as I never sold before / For when I'm selling / I'm happy as can be / For I'm a member of the Fuller family" went a song at Fuller Brush.[8]

Sales managers, working out of headquarters or branch offices, drew up maps of territories, checked statistics on wealth and population, and forecasted future sales. They tinkered with compensation programs in order to give salesmen the right motivation, while keeping costs down, and they relayed sales statistics and other information to their colleagues in production.

The Great Crash

While the scale and reach of American business supported Mears's idea that a "tremendous business machine" was now in place, any resemblance of the economy to a smoothly functioning mechanism quickly faded in the early 1930s, following the October 1929 stock market crash. Confidence in the economy did not evaporate overnight following the crash, and temporary upswings in economic activity in the early months seemed to promise recovery. But by 1933, the gross national product had fallen by 31 percent from its 1929 peak and unemployment had risen to a staggering 25 percent.[9]

Sales decreased at companies throughout the country. One indication of the impending crisis was a drop in sales at General Motors noted by Alfred Sloan in early October 1929, causing him to announce that the "end of expansion" had arrived.[10] Not all industries were affected to the same degree. Manufacturers of industrial goods fared worse than makers of consumer items. While consumption fell by 20 percent in the first four years of the Depression, investment declined by nearly 90 percent. People put off purchasing houses or cars but still spent money on food and entertainment, going to see movies like *Duck Soup* (1933), *Mutiny on the Bounty* (1935), and *Modern Times* (1936).[11]

To make matters worse for executives at large manufacturing companies like GM, the 1930s brought not only the nightmare of plummeting sales, but also a renewed criticism and scrutiny of their business. The "Depression sharply lowered the prestige of businessmen," observed noted writer Frederick Lewis Allen. The "worst sufferers were bankers and brokers," but "even business executives in general sank in the public regard to a point from which it would take them a long time to recover; and in this decline the conscientious and public-spirited suffered along with the predatory."[12]

The negative images of salesmen, which had turned to satire in the 1920s with *Babbitt*, also came rushing back. To the general public during the Depression, salesmen seemed not dynamos operating at the center of the economy but part of a bloated distribution system. In fiction they were weak, even tragic, figures. In Thornton Wilder's *Heaven's My Destination* (1935), the book salesman George Brush was a lost figure, continually falling for one self-improvement scheme after another. He lived, as one traveling companion pointed out, "in a foggy, unreal, narcotic dream."[13] Eudora Welty's "Death of a Traveling Salesman" (1941), which evoked many themes that were later taken up in Arthur Miller's play of a similar name, told the story of an elderly shoe salesman who had accidentally driven his car into a ravine in an unfamiliar countryside. Lost and confused, he begged to stay the night with a farm couple and in the morning suffered a heart attack on his way out to his car. Among his final thoughts were the mundane but unforgettable promises of commerce that were always on the tip of his tongue—musings about special deals on footware.[14] The rehearsed slogans of salesmanship became, in essence, the salesman's personality both on and off the job, leaving him incapable of dealing with the complexities of life for which there were no rehearsed answers.

More damaging to the image of business than these fictional accounts was a report written by the Twentieth Century Fund, a progressive foundation. *Does Distribution Cost Too Much?* (1939) explored the expense of sales and advertising, and asked, in its title, the central question of the period. Complaints about the wastefulness of distribution had their origins in earlier decades. Since the 1920s, one of the authors of the report, Stuart Chase, a trained accountant and follower of Thorstein Veblen, had published articles and books that described the ways in which consumers were defrauded or misled by sales and advertising campaigns.

The Depression brought such concerns to the forefront. In *Does Distribution Cost Too Much?* Chase and the other authors argued that competitive sales and advertising were inherently wasteful. Through numerous statistical tables, they documented the rising costs of selling, advertising, packaging, and shipping goods. Their analysis of distribution differed from writings about promotion and selling in the nineteenth century, like Harrington Bates's *How 'Tis Done* (1879), which railed against individual canvassers who stole from the pockets of working men. The authors of *Does Distribution Cost Too Much?* were not advocates for austerity, but for consumer rights. They were not critical of all forms of promotion; some advertising and salesmanship were necessary to inform and explain new products. But "not all costly advertising and promotion can be defended on the grounds that it is necessary to educate the consumer to new products," noted the authors of the book. "The consumer needs no education as to the qualities of cigarettes, toothpaste, canned goods, gasoline, and a multitude of other standard commodities."[15] Salesmen and advertising, therefore, had a legitimate informational role, but efforts to persuade people—which were at the heart of most sales scripts and sales strategies—were simply wasteful. If consumers were given accurate information, the report argued, economic markets would function effectively and consumers would make the right choices.

While the authors of *Does Distribution Cost Too Much?* believed that the persuasion, appeal, and evangelism of selling and advertising were damaging to economic efficiency, their book revealed an important new trend in economic thought: the idea that a high level of consumption was critical to the health of the economic and that, in fact, increased consumption, rather than increased production, was the surest route to prosperity. Traditionally, economists had viewed a depression as a product of fallen production. Increasingly in the 1930s, some began to perceive that the problem with the economy was not a lack of production of capital investment, but inadequate consumption. The key to recovery was to stimulate purchasing power: if people had more money to spend, stores would clear inventory from their shelves, and then factories would produce more. This was a major turn in economic thinking. What was new was not the idea that consumption was important, but that it was relatively more important to economic recovery in this instance than stimulating production.[16]

The rising interest in consumption was, in part, the result of a changed economy, one that had seen a tremendous growth in consumer spending in the 1920s, when national income rose dramatically. It also revealed the influence of John Maynard Keynes, whose work gained widespread attention during the final years of the Depression, and who argued that the economy was suffering from underconsumption. Keynes's principal idea, put forth in his *General Theory of Employment, Interest and Money* (1936), suggested that people did not automatically purchase enough to ensure economic prosperity.[17] Keynes argued that during a recession government could increase consumption through fiscal action. While Keynes saw a need for consumption to be stimulated, he did not envision private enterprise as having the power to increase consumption sufficiently to raise the economy out of difficulty.[18] His ideas, and those of like-minded American economists, eventually were welcomed by Roosevelt and his supporters, many of whom by the end of the 1930s and early 1940s believed that government intervention, rather than private promotion by businessmen, was necessary to stimulate consumption and bolster confidence and economic activity. This became the predominant thinking of the time and remained so for decades afterward.

During the Depression of the 1930s, therefore, salesmanship was at a crossroads. The context in which sales-oriented companies operated changed markedly: Public confidence and trust in corporate leadership had evaporated. Economists and policymakers had come to the idea that consumption was critical to economic well-being; yet they tended to deny that business was capable of reviving aggregate demand. They failed to concede that persuasion played a significant economic role, or, if they did, saw it as inimical and wasteful: salesmanship, in their view, was largely "wind" or "noise" in the economy. These developments— economic, cultural, and intellectual—led some business writers and executives to think about salesmanship in new ways. Not only did they try to solve questions about the "how to" of selling; they also looked for answers to the "why." That is, they were concerned not just about management and strategy, but also about justifying and explaining the social and economic role of salesmanship. The Depression forced executives to "sell" salesmanship.

The Pulling Power of Salesmanship

Leading businessmen and business writers were divided on how to respond to the Depression. Many, probably most, thought the problem stemmed from manufacturers' failure to invest due to the uncertainty of the times. Others criticized business for a lack of creativity and confidence in stimulating demand. In *The Sales Strategy of John H. Patterson* (1932), Russell W. Lynch and Roy W. Johnson used the life story of the NCR founder to argue that salesmanship was a potential weapon against the downturn. In order to survive the hard times, the authors claimed, companies needed to follow the lessons of Patterson, who, when sales slackened, had toured the country, visited agents, and held elaborate sales conventions. "If business men in general, and salesmen in particular, had a clear understanding of the sales strategy underlying Mr. Patterson's success, it would enable them to beat the present depression just as Mr. Patterson had been able to beat the depressions of 1893, 1907, and 1921," they believed.[19]

Norval Hawkins, who had left GM in 1923 to become an instructor of salesmanship and business efficiency, agreed with the necessity for a rejuvenated sales effort. In May 1931, he addressed a meeting in Ohio of the American Society of Sales Executives. Hawkins recommended a twelve-step program for the country's recovery. The gist of the "steps" was that each business had to lower manufacturing costs, study its methods of distribution, and pay more attention to salesmanship—including the selection of salesmen and the refinement of compensation plans. The key to recovery was individual initiative and imaginative selling: "All that distinguishes America in the power to absorb goods, in the luxury of her living, in the extravagance of her habits—all that distinguishes her as the active, virile, spending nation is—*imagination*."[20] Hawkins, who like many other business executives had suffered losses in the stock market crash, did not live to see his plan put in place. He died bankrupt in 1936.[21]

Dale Carnegie's *How to Win Friends and Influence People* (1937) also expressed a conservative faith in salesmanship. The book found a receptive audience among those who wanted to master sales skills to survive the Depression. Carnegie, who had worked as a salesman for Packard Automotive and for Armour, published one of the best-selling books of all time. Following in the tradition of popular books on salesmanship in the 1920s, Carnegie quoted from well-known Americans who had reinvented themselves, such as Benjamin Franklin, who rose up from poverty, Theodore Roosevelt, who was a child weakling, and William James, who "willed" himself out of emotional depression. Carnegie laid out twelve steps to gain influence, which were, in essence, sales steps. They instructed the reader to avoid arguing, get the other person to say "yes," and dramatize ideas. Addressing his lessons directly to agents in the field, Carnegie wrote, "Thousands of salesmen are pounding the pavements today, tired, discouraged, and underpaid. Why? Because they are always thinking of what they want . . . First arouse in the other person an eager want. He who can do this has the whole world with him. He who cannot walks a lonely way."[22] Carnegie's book contributed to the idea that "self-worth," as much as "product value," was determined by the marketplace, and that individuals, including customers, salesmen, and managers, related to one another through an endlessly shifting and calculated strategy.[23]

Perhaps the most thorough defense of salesmanship in the 1930s was Charles Bennett's *Scientific Salesmanship*. Bennett's book was a doctoral dissertation on the history of selling, begun in the late 1920s and published by the American Efficiency Bureau in 1933. Bennett traced the story of selling back to the Magna Carta, which, he argued, gave "merchants the privilege of going from place to place to buy and sell, free from unjust penalties" of the guild system. The building of macadamized roads facilitated travel and allowed for the growth of stores and the travels of medieval bagmen, who carried samples of the work of craftsmen-merchants to neighboring towns. From there, Bennett narrated tales of the emergence of peddlers "who hawked pins, needles, books, combs, small hardware, cotton goods, and laces," retail salesmen, specialty salesmen, and finally "professional salesmen" who worked under managers.[24]

Bennett wanted to change the way the public perceived selling. He believed that the role played by salesmen was not appreciated: "It is lack of understanding as to the specific task of salesmanship and its functions in connection with effecting sales transactions that causes confusion in the minds of writers on marketing about the value of salesmanship." Bennett argued that while most people saw selling as crass and unproductive, salesmen, in fact, created "subjective values" for goods in the minds of buyers. They accomplished this, in part, by explaining the product's use, but also by building "enthusiasm," which Bennett defined as "an economic force which can create value." Salesmanship, he wrote, "is the science of the expansion of meaning of objects for the purpose of creating utility for them in legitimate commercial transactions."[25] Good salesmanship could change the way people experienced consumption, increase the intensity of their appreciation for goods, and get them to save less and spend more. He advocated better sales training, more studies of consumer behavior, and the application of psychology to selling.

More than just lowering the rate of saving (and thereby restoring aggregate levels of demand to their pre-Depression heights), Bennett thought aggressive salesmanship could even improve the performance of the economy overall by bringing about more large-scale production and therefore raising industrial efficiency. He began his book with a quote from economist Roger Babson: "Though our country has lost the driving power of pioneering, we can replace the old push by the new pull—the pulling power of salesmanship." Improved methods of salesmanship did not merely bring one company a greater share of the pie over another, but rather increased the size of the pie overall.[26]

But Bennett's theory of the "expansion of meaning" attracted little attention, and his lengthy book, *Scientific Salesmanship,* appeared more as a tombstone for the scientific sales movement than anything else. In some sense, it was. Business writers and scholars turned away from equating selling with a science. In the 1920s, many books had used the term "scientific" or "science" in their titles, including Wilson M. Taylor's *The Science of Approach in Selling, Directing and Employing Men and Women* (1920), George Edwin Robinson's *Scientific Salesmanship Course* (1923), and Herbert Glenn Kenagy's *The Selection and Training of Salesmen: Scientific Methods in Developing the Sales Organization* (1925). In the 1930s the terms "scientific" and "science" were largely absent from new books about selling. Companies were not eager to promote the idea that their sales methods were scientific—that is, based on the use of statistics and buyer psychology. While they were happy to emphasize their efficiency in production, they were less willing to advertise the effectiveness of their sales campaigns.

But despite a change in terminology, sales managers did not abandon the "science of selling" during the Depression—even though the term was heard less often. Systematic methods of sales management were a fixture of modern business enterprise. They continued to evolve through the 1930s as managers tried to create appropriate motivational systems to weather the crisis. Managers adjusted compensation schemes and increased sales-contest prizes. Some reorganized the structure of their sales force. In response to the Depression, sales managers altered their product-marketing policy, balancing advertising and selling, increasing the range of products offered, and changing the prices of products. These were strategic calibrations using existing tools of sales management, rather than fundamental changes.

Managers tinkered with sales pitches, showing their persistent belief in the ability to influence consumers with the right approach. Salesmen, one survey noted, increased their use of visual aids, turning to photographs, miniature models of products, and illustrative diagrams of product features.[27] More important, managers veered away from straight salary, offering either straight commission, or more commonly, some mixture of salary and incentive-based pay.[28] In a survey conducted by the Dartnell Corporation of one hundred companies in different lines of selling, 86 percent of those paying salaries had reduced salary levels; at the same time, most either had kept commissions at the same level (77 percent) or increased them (17 percent), reflecting the goal of executives to lower fixed costs and to push salesmen harder.[29] Some managers changed their mix of promotional lures—shifting more of their resources to advertising and spending less on their sales forces; others, particularly in the office-machine industry, did the opposite, increasing spending on selling relatively more than on advertising. Manufacturers in some industries, such as automobiles, added more options to existing products or, as in the case of canned goods or prepared foods, introduced entirely new items in order to stimulate sales.

Manufacturers in several industries increased their investment in advertising as they tried to improve the recognition of brand names through ads in national magazines or on the radio. The National Broadcasting Company (NBC) took in $20 million in advertising income in 1930, and $26 million the following year. The Columbia Broadcasting

System (CBS) reported an increase from $8 million to $12 million during the same period. And radio spots became more aggressive in their efforts to promote, mentioning prices on the air for the first time.[30] Many firms similarly altered the nature of their advertisements in national magazines, adopting more attention-grabbing images and spicing up their copy.[31]

Companies continued to consult psychologists on their hiring practices and to gather insights about consumers. Henry C. Link (1889–1952), a graduate of Yale University and a former student of Walter Dill Scott at the Bureau of Salesmanship Research, worked as an employment psychologist at Winchester Repeating Arms, U.S. Rubber, and the department stores Gimbel's and Lord and Taylor. In 1931 he became secretary-treasurer of the Psychological Corporation, a consulting company, and later its director. Link invented the Psychological Barometer, known informally as the Link Audit, a semiannual survey of popular opinions about products, brand names, and manufacturers. He gathered information by sending teams of interviewers throughout the country to visit individual households. He then summarized the data and presented it to clients such as General Motors, Du Pont, Ford, General Electric, U.S. Steel, Alcoa, Eastman Kodak, and AT&T.[32] The Link Audits, he believed, provided a way to validate effective marketing strategies; improved advertising, he explained in *New Psychology of Selling and Advertising* (1932), would help stimulate consumption and end the Depression.[33] Others, like the sociologist and psychologist Paul Lazarsfeld (1901–1976), also became known for conducting empirical surveys. At the University of Vienna and at Columbia, Lazardsfeld produced startling and insightful analyses of consumer motives and opinions. One report involved interviewing roughly nine hundred shoe shoppers in Zurich about their buying experiences, asking shoppers how it felt to remove their shoes in public or how they grabbed the salesperson's attention.[34] His work influenced George Katona, who founded a large market-research institute at the University of Michigan, and other prominent consultants later in the century.

Overall, the same industrial patterns of investment in sales and advertising in the late 1920s remained at the end of the Depression. Manufacturers who sold raw materials and semifinished products had relatively low selling and advertising expenses per dollar of sales (less than 5 percent total). Makers of branded food products, cigarettes, and cereals had moderate to high selling and advertising expenses per dollar of sales (from 5 to 20 percent). And manufacturers of office machines and sewing machines had among the highest selling costs per dollar sales (from 25 to 35 percent).[35]

Brand-Name Manufacturers Adjust to the Depression

Salesmen who sold food, detergent, and other branded goods to retail stores struggled to gain larger shares of shelf space and pushed retailers to display promotional material, such as clocks or posters bearing a brand name. Coca-Cola, for example, increased its sales and marketing efforts in the 1930s. It had achieved national distribution in the mid-1920s and looked for ways to raise the volume of consumption by individual customers. In the early 1930s, Coke had its name on 160,000 billboards and 5 million soda-fountain glasses; it placed advertisements in more than 400 million individual newspaper and magazine pages per year. The company also issued other items such as matchbooks, blotters, calendars, pencils, trays, fans, and metal signs.[36] Its advertising expenditures rose between 1930 to 1932 to reach $5 million, then fell in 1933 to $4.4 million, before increasing to $8 million in 1939.[37] Coca-Cola's consumer sales fell from $41.3 million in 1930 to $32.3 million in 1933, but began to improve after that year. By the late thirties, 230 Coca-Cola "servicemen" were calling on 100,000 soda fountains throughout the country. These salesmen did not take orders; they distributed promotional material and instructed fountain operators on how to prepare the drink. When visiting a pharmacy or soda shop, they ordered a glass of Coke and took its temperature to make sure it was not warmer than 40 degrees.[38]

The low consumer income of the period increased demand for cheap, nutritional processed foods, especially canned goods, whose production roughly doubled from 1931 to 1940. For example, during the 1930s there was a rise in the manufacture of bottled pickles, prepackaged ice cream, boxed breakfast cereals, and margarine. These products were available to consumers in large new "supermarkets," which were able to offer a great variety of goods at relatively low prices; the number of these stores increased from 300 in 1935 to 1,200 by 1939.[39] The demand for inexpensive and nutritious food helped the H. J. Heinz Company survive the Depression. Howard Heinz, the son of the founder, introduced new products, such as prepackaged baby food and instant soups. He also expanded the sales force and attempted to maintain the low prices of his goods by cutting production costs. Although sales decreased significantly, Heinz remained profitable.[40]

NCR and IBM

Salesmen who sold finished goods, such as office machines, to businesses tried increasingly to interest customers in complete office "systems," rather than individual, stand-alone products—thereby moving away from one-time sales. Two senior executives, Edward A. Deeds and Stanley Allyn, led NCR, which began the 1930s under the presidency of Frederick Patterson, the founder's son. The company sold large posting machines to banks and other financial institutions. The machines had several cash drawers and were used to take deposits and keep track of interest earnings and withdrawals on large internal notebooks and on individual passbooks.[41] NCR also built a new sales training school in the mid-1930s. The annual report for 1937 noted the need for training: "Selling has become increasingly a matter of intelligent presentation to prospective customers of the merits of the Company's products, and this, in turn, requires a type of representative who is carefully selected, and instructed in those technical and other qualifications for selling, needed to assist the customer in selecting and using a machine suitable to his requirements, whether of merchandising, accounting, or any one or more of the manifold uses to which the products of the Company are adapted."[42] NCR, which had become a public corporation in 1925, three years after John H. Patterson's death, saw its sales plummet from $57.6 million in 1929 to $16.5 million in 1932. In the following year, the company carried out an intensive new training program and "postgraduate" course. The sales force grew to over three thousand before the end of the decade, and the company rebounded somewhat to achieve sales of $37 million by 1939.

Russell W. Lynch and Roy W. Johnson's 1932 biography of John H. Patterson was the last one written about him for many years; his star

New York Yankee Babe Ruth helps to motivate the sales force at NCR's Japan office, 1934. All the salesmen are wearing baseball caps, and the walls display the results of an "NCR Base Ball" sales contest.

was fading as another's was rising. Thomas J. Watson had worked as a salesman for National Cash Register in Buffalo, New York. Within fifteen years he had become a sales manager in the company headquarters in Dayton, assisting Patterson himself. In 1912 Watson was indicted under the Sherman Antitrust Law, along with Patterson and other executives, though the case was eventually dismissed.[43] Despite Watson's many years with the company, he fell out of favor with Patterson and went to work as a general manager at the Computing-Tabulating-Recording Company in 1914; the following year he became president of the company, which, in 1924, changed its name to International Business Machines. IBM sold a great range of machines, including scales and time clocks, but became best known for its punch-card tabulating system for adding and sorting data, which had been used since 1890 in compiling the U.S. census.

At IBM, Watson responded to the hard times of the Depression by undertaking the most intensified sales effort in the company's history. Biographer William Rodgers claimed that Watson felt "there was not . . . much wrong that better salesmanship and more straight thinking couldn't repair."[44] IBM machines came into great demand by the federal government after President Roosevelt passed the Social Security Act of 1935 and other New Deal legislation that required massive amounts of data to be processed. During World War II, the military also began to rely on IBM punch-card machines. Particularly important to IBM's sales plan was the fact that its machines were leased; this made it easy for salesmen to visit customers and renew leases year after year. IBM's revenue went from $40 million in 1939 to $138 million in 1945. Watson's son, Thomas J. Watson Jr., joined the sales force in 1940, testifying to Watson Sr.'s estimation of the importance of experience in sales.[45]

Watson created a corporate environment that resembled NCR's. He observed Patterson's method of neat dress, as well as his practices of coining inspirational slogans and organizing exercise classes, lectures, and entertainment for workers. The IBM factory in Endicott, New York, had four thousand workers, who were instructed to keep themselves well groomed and to wear white shirts. Employees became members in the company's country club for only one dollar per year. Salesmen competed to join the "Hundred Per Cent Club" and, at company conventions, sang "You're our Leader Fine" to Thomas J. Watson. At one sales banquet Watson handed out a card announcing the five C's "that we must possess if we want to do our full share": Conception, Consistency, Cooperation, Courage, and Confidence.[46] In 1930, the *Wall Street Journal* reported that 400 of IBM's 1,200 salesmen convened at the Hotel New Yorker for the Hundred Per Cent Club; Thomas J. Watson Sr. was the principal speaker.[47]

Thomas Wolfe captured the hard-driving tendencies of a Watson-like character in his novel *You Can't Go Home Again* (1934). Paul S. Appleton III of Federal Weight, Scales and Computing stood before his sales force, swept his arm in front of an enormous map of the United States, and said: "There's your market! Go out and sell them!" Wrote Wolfe:

> What could be simpler and more beautiful than this? What could more eloquently indicate that mighty sweep of the imagination which has been celebrated in the annals of modern business under the name of "vision"? The words had the spacious scope and austere directness that have characterized the utterances of great leaders in every epoch of man's history. It is Napoleon speaking to his troops in Egypt: "Soldiers, from the summit of yonder pyramids, forty centuries look down upon you." It is Captain Perry: "We have met the enemy, and they are ours." It is Dewey at Manila Bay: "You may fire when ready, Gridley." It is Grant before Spottsylvania Court House: "I propose to fight it out on this line, if it takes all summer."[48]

IBM's blue-suited salesmen, traveling throughout the globe, became the embodiment of American salesmanship.

More than this, though, Watson was a philosopher of salesmanship. "Everything starts with a sale," he was fond of saying. One IBM executive recalled: "I'd come to work at nine in the morning and hear that song ['Ever Onward'] rolling through the hills of Endicott. A new class of salesmen would be singing it, so loud the people over in the factory could hear it. I remember how inspiring I found it."[49] The company's sales force established great trust among its customers. IBM salesmen became IBM executives, and the company remained dedicated to the "primacy" of the customer.

Canvassing in Hard Times

The Depression had mixed effects on door-to-door companies. The situation of the early 1930s posed numerous problems for door-to-door salespeople, because "prospects" had less money to spend and regional store owners increasingly resented the intrusion of direct sales agents, just as they had at the height of book canvassing in the 1880s. In 1932, local retailers in Wyoming succeeded in securing legislation, known as "the Green River ordinance," prohibiting salesmen from making solicitations without the prior invitation of the homeowner. The ordinance, and similar ones in other regions, continued the battle between "itinerant" and "stationary" sellers. Some companies, such as Encyclopedia Britannica, responded by sending their salesmen to visit only the homes of people who answered magazine advertisements asking for free information. Also troubling to direct-sales companies was New Deal legislation that forced employers to pay minimum wages. With high turnover, part-time workers, and great variations in the performance of salespeople, the enforcement of a minimum-wage standard would have been costly for employers. In 1935, direct-sales companies redefined their sales agents as "independent contractors" (and, hence, owners of their own businesses) to avoid minimum-wage legislation.[50]

But overall, the volume of sales of door-to-door companies increased, roughly doubling in size during the 1930s.[51] One reason was that it was much easier to recruit salespeople during these years. Canvassing, like agricultural work, became a fallback occupation for workers who could not find anything else to do.[52] As one contemporary study noted: "When workers are forced out of highly organized industry through incompetence, old age, or by the introduction of labor-saving machinery, they may turn to house-to-house canvassing or operating a roadside stand or gasoline station or—at their most abject stages—to passing out advertising cards or carrying a sandwich board."[53] The observation also applied to hard economic times; people turned to direct selling.

Refrigerators, washing machines, and vacuum cleaners sold relatively well and were heavily promoted by manufacturers and by electric-utility companies.[54] By the end of the 1930s, 56 percent of American households had electric refrigerators. The number of radios sold increased dramatically in the decade, too, so that by 1940 they were found in roughly 80 percent of American households.[55]

The California Perfume Company, with its flexible sales organization of part-time workers, fared relatively well. In 1930, David McConnell Jr., the son of the founder, became vice president of the corporation following his graduation from Princeton. The annual turnover in the company was tremendous during the Depression (400 percent), but there was more opportunity to recruit saleswomen. Sales and profits increased throughout the 1930s. CPC responded in several ways to the economic hard times of these years. The company created permanent district sales offices—eleven were opened in 1937, and twenty-three more the following year—with most located in relatively small cities west of the Mississippi. (The market for California Perfume Company cosmetics and perfumes was greater in towns that did not have either large downtown department stores or shopping centers that constantly displayed new products.) The new sales offices improved the flow of information from the company to distributors and provided instruction and guidance for the saleswomen. The informal nature of the door-to-door network of the California Perfume Company proved an advantage. Most saleswomen continued to work part-time, using the money they earned to supplement household income. Sales increased at CPC from $2.5 million in 1929 to $3.6 million in 1936. The company changed its name to Avon Products in 1939.[56]

It was a different story at Fuller Brush: total sales at the company fell from $13.8 million in 1927 to $4.8 million in 1933.[57] The company faced increased competition from other door-to-door companies, and Fuller's full-time sales agents, who hoped to earn enough to support themselves and their families, became discouraged and quit. "In spite of the fact that many men are out of work, it has not been easier during the past two years to enlarge our sales organization, because of the fact that it requires better salesmanship and more intensive effort on the part of the salesman to secure a fair income, due to existing economic conditions," noted the company's annual report.[58] In July 1932, the company began briefly to sell brushes through retail stores at branch locations to complement the efforts of its canvassing force.[59]

Alfred Fuller did not turn the company around until the mid-1930s, when he changed salesmen's compensation. Unlike many other executives, he daringly *lowered* the commission rate to salesmen from 40 percent to 25 and 30 percent—depending on the item—but at the same time he reduced prices on brushes by 25 to 33 percent, thereby increasing sales volume so salesmen could potentially raise their incomes.[60]

Fuller Brush also changed its sales philosophy, moving away from Albert Teetsel's "Fine and Dandy" methods of pressurized selling. C. A. Peterson, a district manager from San Francisco, advocated a new approach based on high-volume sales with low profit margins. Dealers were instructed to spend no more than ten minutes at each house. "A snappy call and a three dollar sale were more profitable than pressure selling," Peterson reasoned. He suggested that too much time was wasted by the Fine and Dandy Men "who refused to take 'no' for an answer."[61] In the mid-1930s, sales agents were asked to make twenty demonstrations daily, averaging $1.25 per demonstration in sales, and instructed to keep to the following work schedule:

6–7 A.M.   Shave and study.

7–8 A.M.   Breakfast and keep any early appointments.

8–12 A.M.   Sell. Give away 10 handy brushes.

12–1 P.M.   Luncheon.

1–5 P.M.   Sell. Give away 10 handy brushes.

5–6 P.M.   Place cards, set appointments
            (for next day).
6–7 P.M.   Dinner.
7–10 P.M. Evening calls, recreation, clean sample, study.

The Fuller Brush Company also increased its use of newspaper and magazine advertising and began a half-hour weekly radio program featuring the Fuller Brush Man.[62]

During the Depression a new type of "direct selling" began to be developed. In 1932 Frank Beveridge, a former vice president of Fuller Brush, founded Stanley Home Products, a competing door-to-door company. After finding out that one of his leading saleswomen sold products by inviting her friends to her house and hosting a party that included the sale of goods, Beveridge instituted the "party plan" of selling. This eventually became the most common type of direct selling.[63]

Automobile Salesmen

While the success of individual automobile companies varied widely during the Depression, the industry suffered miserably. The total number of passenger motor vehicles sold by all manufacturers fell dramatically from 4.6 million in 1929 to 1.6 million by 1933. People were less likely to trade in their cars, knowing they could hold on to them for another year or more; and automobiles were lasting longer due in part to better workmanship, improved roads, and better tire manufacture.[64]

Carmakers tried to stimulate sales by means other than price reduction. They did not produce low-cost, no-frills machines, but instead offered new styles with increased horsepower and more amenities. Depression-era cars offered automatic transmission, power steering, and radios and heaters.[65]

From 1929 to 1933, the number of automobiles sold by GM fell 42 percent; by Ford, 66 percent.[66] In the automobile industry, as in many others, the Depression revealed the importance of strong marketing and sales networks. The Big Three—GM, Ford, and Chrysler—increased their control over the automobile sector, producing almost 90 percent of the cars made in the United States in 1933.[67] GM's share of the market increased from 34 percent in 1929 to 38 percent in 1932. From 1927 to 1937, GM made money every year, accumulating a net profit for those years of almost $2 billion; during the same period, Ford had almost $100 million in losses.[68] In 1938, Ford introduced the V-8 engine but lacked the marketing structure of GM to make it a success.[69] William P. Young, who, as mentioned in the previous chapter, founded a Ford dealership in 1910, was forced out of business in 1931; he blamed competition from other Ford dealers placed too near his own.[70]

The Depression did not alter the overall characteristics of General Motors, but instead brought about a widespread contraction in the company. "We made an orderly step-by-step retreat in all matters, including wage and salary reductions," wrote Alfred Sloan.[71] GM revised its 1921 multidivisional policy, which had organized the company into five brand-name car divisions: Chevrolet, Pontiac, Oldsmobile, Buick, and Cadillac. In March 1932, the separate dealerships operated by Buick, Oldsmobile, and Pontiac were consolidated in a single new sales company, "BOP." These dealers were given more than one make of car to sell. As Sloan noted, "In effect, from a management point of view, General Motors for a year and a half was reduced from five to three car divisions."[72]

GM, like Ford and Chrysler, continued to make the most important selling decisions at the manufacturing level, rather than leave them to dealers. Headquarters decided on car styling, approximate prices, service arrangements, dealer sales quotas, dealer locations, national advertising, and the number of dealerships.[73] The company continued to host elaborate Hollywood-style shows, with brass bands, to reveal their annual models.[74] Following the great success of GM's Chevrolet division in the late 1920s, Alfred Sloan promoted Richard H. Grant, the former head of Chevrolet, to become vice president of sales for the entire corporation just before the onset of the Depression. Chevrolet salesmen began their employment with a five-day training course held at regional offices and directed by a team from Detroit; the course instructed trainees on the basic Chevrolet sales strategy, but it also contained motivational speeches, training films, and other devices to boost confidence and spirit.[75]

The More "Human" Science of Public Relations

As the image of salesmen, and more generally of businessmen, began to fall during what Edmund Wilson called the "American Earthquake," a number of large manufacturing companies began to improve their methods of public relations. One of the last lessons companies learned about the "science of selling" was to avoid appearing too "scientific" or "systematic"—that is, too calculating and mechanistic—and to encourage a "human" image of the company instead.

Public relations became increasingly sophisticated during the Depression. Ironically, big businesses, which had learned to sell their products, now had to master the art of selling themselves. Companies polished their image in an effort to improve the environment in which they operated, thereby not only refining the reputation of the product (through brand-name advertising and other appeals), but also creating what one historian called a "corporate soul." Rather than a single peddler seeking to overcome the objections of a farmer, this was a case of corporations trying to change society's perceptions of business itself, attempting to move away from the image of business as being cold and aloof.[76]

The idea of public relations was not new. Patterson, Heinz, and other late-nineteenth-century entrepreneurs had publicized their efforts to create a system of corporate welfare. Patterson built a beautiful factory in Dayton, a "sermon in steel and glass" according to one pamphlet, which he opened to the public. The Heinz Company celebrated its founder by relocating his childhood home on the factory grounds and building a museum and public gardens. But the campaigns of the 1930s were more expansive, because they were devised not only to respond to the criticism of President Franklin D. Roosevelt and other New Dealers, but also to reassure workers and managers alike of the beneficence of the corporation. In the first nine months of 1937, four hundred companies launched new employee magazines, many of which emphasized the common interests of worker, company, and society.[77]

In other public-relations efforts, Ford Motor Company hired the newspaperman William Cameron to give short talks on topics such as American individualism during a regularly scheduled radio music program. Fuller pushed its folksy "Fuller Brush Man" image, increased its use of newspaper and magazine advertising, and launched a half-hour weekly radio program. And Procter and Gamble hired hundreds of women to bake and do laundry and then give their feedback. The company also began to host radio "soap operas" in 1933 to improve the recognition of its brand names.[78]

Bruce Barton, who had written the best-selling *The Man Nobody Knows* (1925), which likened the charismatic qualities of Jesus Christ to those of a salesman, helped GM craft its public-relations strategy. "Business says to *itself*, we have created most of the comforts and satisfactions of modern life—but it does not say this to the 130,000,000 in [a] language they can understand," he remarked. Alfred Sloan also noted that business had forgotten to keep the public informed about the workings of the system.[79]

In the early 1930s, GM began hosting the radio program *Parade of States*, which featured orchestral music and a tribute to a different state each week. The company also increased its direct contact with the public through consumer surveys. GM's customer research staff mailed questionnaires to citizens throughout the country, asking their opinions on issues of style, pricing, and performance features. These questionnaires were distinguished by their informal tone and occasional, deliberate, typos. Over time, the questionnaires had more value as a public-relations tool than as a method for gathering information about consumer tastes.[80]

Public-relations campaigns became a fixture for large companies during the years after World War II. Corporations worked to present themselves as responsible "good neighbors," as one historian put it, made up of a cross-section of American citizens.[81] As companies labored to improve the image of their firms, academics and business writers also tried to explain and justify the economic and social role of sales and advertising—to their colleagues and to the public.

Redeeming the Salesman after World War II

Intellectual criticism of advertising and selling reached its apogee toward the end of the Depression and in the decade following World War II. In *White Collar* (1951), the sociologist C. Wright Mills complained that the entire American economy had degenerated into a "great salesroom" that was run by market researchers, personnel men, and sales managers who studied the "fine art of prompting men to 'go get 'em.'"[82] The economist John Kenneth Galbraith's *Affluent Society* (1958) argued that the American economy was built on an irrational strategy in which companies spent $110 billion annually on advertising to create "wants" for the products they themselves manufactured. "Production, not only passively through emulation, but actively through advertising and related activities, creates the wants it seeks to satisfy."[83] Journalist and social critic Vance Packard's *The Hidden Persuaders* (1957) attacked the increasing psychological sophistication of advertisements that made them more manipulative and insidious. "At one of the largest advertising agencies in America psychologists on the staff are probing sample humans in an attempt to find how to identify, and beam messages to, people of high anxiety, body consciousness, hostility, passiveness, and so on."[84]

These works highlighted many of the features that had defined the effort to make selling more systematic: the growth of market research, the linking of production and distribution schedules, the reliance on psychologists to inform sales campaigns, and the use of a variety of lures to promote goods to consumers—including salesmen, advertising, branding, and premium giveaways. This vision of society featured advertising and salesmanship in their many forms as ubiquitous and manipulative.

Criticism of this nature resonated with the popular fictional characterizations of salesmen, especially Arthur Miller's *Death of a Salesman* (1949). Miller's play told the now-familiar story of Willy Loman, a salesman of unspecified products, who had worked for over thirty years for the same firm and was, at the time, entering old age. He had chosen to be a salesman early in life after meeting a popular elderly drummer. "What could be more satisfying than to be able to go, at the age of eighty-four, into twenty or thirty different cities, and pick up a phone, and be remembered and loved and helped by so many different people?" thought Loman as a boy.[85] Now, in advanced age, Loman was an ineffectual salesman, unable even to keep his car on the road as he went out on a business trip. Distraught at his futility and at the problems confronting his family, Loman committed suicide to secure money from a life insurance policy for his wife and sons. The play revealed the cruelty of a system of capitalism based on the principles of salesmanship, one in which a person was treated like a commodity to be replaced as soon as it was no longer effective. In the play, Loman was fired by a young man who, as a child, had once sat on his knee. Says Willy: "You can't eat the orange and throw the peel away. A man is not a piece of fruit!"[86]

Such assaults were stinging to business writers and business-school academics who had spent their lives studying selling or writing about it for national magazines. William H. Whyte, a sociologist and editor at *Fortune* magazine, noted, "As the oddly self-accusatory reaction to Willy Loman suggests, the salesman is now in lower estate, perhaps, than ever before—and this is so not only in numbers, in how much he is paid, but in social status as well."[87] Harry R. Tosdal, who by the mid-twentieth century had taught sales management at Harvard Business School for over thirty years, was disturbed by Miller's portrait. "It has been declared that many persons looked upon Willy Loman . . . as typifying the salesman and his work, rather than as a weakling who happened to get a selling job and who failed to mature in a changing world," he wrote. Tosdal, seeing the play more narrowly than Miller intended, acknowledged that some salesmen were ineffectual or incompetent, or even worse, dishonest. But he felt that the other side of the story had never been told: good salesmen never got their due. People praised America's miracles of efficient production but criticized the abundance of salesmanship—not seeing that the two were, according to Tosdal, intimately connected. In his view, all who practiced selling "decently and honorably" should receive high public regard.[88]

In 1957, Tosdal sought to redeem the image of salesmen by publishing *Selling in Our Economy: An Economic and Social Analysis of Selling and Advertising*. In many ways, Tosdal shared ideas with the critics, especially Galbraith. He hoped to refute the "conventional wisdom" of economics, which ignored the role of selling and advertising in the economy. Classical laissez-faire economists, argued Tosdal, saw salesmen as irrelevant. Adam Smith "writes of consumption as being the sole aim and end of production but does not carry his thinking further." John Stuart Mill had hardly "any treatment of consumption" at all.[89] Economists worked under the illusion that consumers behaved rationally, ignoring the insights into human behavior provided by psychologists. Even John Maynard Keynes had neglected the importance of personal selling in the economy. He had not considered the possibility that salesmanship could affect overall demand.[90] Tosdal wrote, "Keynes and other economists pay little if any attention to the fact that in the statistical data that they use on consumption, there is included the expenditure for selling, for the dynamic influencing of demand." Such neglect of personal selling—that is, the work of salesmen rather than advertising—was particularly remarkable to Tosdal since, according to his calculations, the aggregate cost of this activity accounted for as much as 10 percent, and certainly over 5 percent, of America's gross national product.[91]

But Tosdal's years at Harvard Business School had led him to understand salesmanship differently than many critics. He recognized that only some industries used aggressive sales and advertising techniques, and that much expenditure for these efforts was in the area of industry-to-industry selling. Most salesmen visited the same customers repeatedly, rather than encountering first-time buyers. They did not spend time introducing themselves or trying to close a one-time sale. "A manufacturer of adding machines recently made the statement that 40% of his billing machine business was made up of sales to former buyers.

Even a manufacturer of heavy machinery, such as gas and electric cranes and shovels, advertises that every third order is a repeat order."[92] IBM, with its system of leasing large computer systems, was a perfect example. Selling follow-up orders, wrote Tosdal, was a more efficient process than "missionary" or transactional peddling. Such an emphasis on repeat orders, Tosdal argued, ensured that salesmen were aiming to satisfy customers, rather than just selling to them once and disappearing.

While Tosdal agreed with critics that salesmanship was persuasive— that is, their promotional efforts entailed more than simply providing information—he saw salesmen not as manipulative but as overcoming a buyer's inertia or hesitation to change or try something new. Creative selling motivated people to introduce new products, carry on consumer research, improve distribution processes, even open new branches or found new firms. "Selling is the energizing, dynamic force which enables all these to be brought about."[93]

Salesmanship was best regarded as a form of "leadership," Tosdal concluded, presenting a view not entirely unlike the psychologist Walter Dill Scott's, in the 1910s, that salesmen were like athletic coaches. Salesmen motivated people—both consumers and businesspeople—to purchase goods. They pushed manufacturers to install new machines, which would improve production methods or cut costs. Similarly, they convinced homeowners to invest in new inventions, such as the electric washing machine and the vacuum cleaner. The result was, according to Tosdal, improved industrial efficiency and a higher standard of living. In 1940, in every 100 homes there were 89 radios, 79 passenger cars, 68 bathtubs, and 40 telephones.[94]

All of this seemed obvious to Tosdal. But the problem was that few people believed it. Worse, even some businessmen failed to see the importance of selling, or to understand its function in the economy. Perhaps, Tosdal thought, something had been lost in the effort to view selling as a science. With the growth of bureaucratic organizations, people had forgotten the dynamism of selling. There was no substitute for "plain hard selling," wrote Tosdal. The appurtenances, such as marketing research, were tools to aid the salesman, but they were not selling.

By 1957, he had come to think that the equation of "selling" with "science" was hobbling the salesman's effort.

Tosdal was not the only one expressing such views. William H. Whyte, writing in the introduction to a series of essays published by *Fortune* entitled *Why Do People Buy?* (1956) agreed, seeing something antithetical to selling in the constant emphasis on management and procedure: "What kind of work does 'professionalization' picture? It pictures riskless activity in which the man is essentially a technician, working, often, as a sort of staff assistant to the customer." Professionalization and "science" concealed the dynamic nature of selling, thought Whyte. The concepts were too risk averse and also obliterated "almost totally the factor of conflict that was inevitable in personal selling."[95]

Whyte's sales experience helped to shape his views. After graduating from Princeton, he worked for the Vick Chemical Corporation and went through their sales-training program in the late 1930s. Whyte watched the company's main product, VapoRub, being mixed and received instructions in selling. He memorized sales spiels and learned ways to counter objections. He was then given a list of counties to visit in Tennessee, a delivery truck, samples, a ladder, and an order pad. Rising at 6:00 or 6:30 A.M., Whyte began the day by posting signs on barns or telephone poles. By 8:00 A.M. he was visiting merchants and trying to convince them to take a year's supply of Vick products. In the evening he filled out his report forms for two hours. Whyte remembered that, at Vick, salesmen were instructed to see the person on the other side of the counter as the enemy. The training program was a "gladiator" school; in the field, combat was the ideal. More often, however, Whyte had noticed that this type of training and spirit was receding as the "human relations" school, developed by Harvard Business School psychologist Elton Mayo and others, gained a foothold. The psychologists favored cooperation rather than competition, and they theorized that business did not merely entail money-making but also had to ensure satisfaction. Whyte saw that, in many ways, pure, hard "salesmanship" was in conflict with the bureaucratic science that had come to guide business operation by the mid-twentieth century.

He explained his ideas about the problems of a stifling bureaucracy in his masterpiece, *Organization Man* (1956). Big business, he wrote, had become too fascinated by system and bureaucracy. It idealized group decision-making and conformity. Whyte argued that companies needed to foster competition within their bureaucracies to keep employees, including sales workers, sharp and inventive. Personnel tests tended to promote the same types of people; they tended to screen for social associations, conservatism, and other tendencies that signaled acceptance by the group. He revealed his antipathy for "scientism" by including an appendix that explained how to cheat on personality tests. He hoped to reform the structure of American enterprise in order to foster contention and competition.[96]

The work of Tosdal, Whyte, and a few other academics and business writers attempted to explain selling and advertising in a way that emphasized the constructive role of persuasion and enthusiasm in the economy. They moved away from an overly scientific definition of selling, which they felt robbed salesmanship of its creative and essentially human qualities. They also tended to see salesmanship as an all-inclusive endeavor, which began with the earliest phase of product research and stretched to the final sale. Whyte's work, like Tosdal's, stressed different aspects of economic activity than traditional economists had considered. They both focused on confrontation, innovation, and change, rather than equilibrium, the status quo, and the stability of price levels. They emphasized the psychology of individuals and the ways in which human motives, including those for buying, varied by product and over time. Persuasion in business, like enthusiasm in politics or evangelism in religion, had in their view defined the American economy, bringing it rapid development and wealth. To Tosdal and Whyte, the true advances of sales management were in providing salesmen with tools to draw on. The rationalization of the mass market and collection of data gave salesmen the ability to expand demand in new directions. In the end, selling was not itself a "science," Tosdal wrote, but science (in the form of sales data, managerial policies, insights into consumer behavior, and in other ways) had armed salesmen as never before.

Beyond Willy Loman 10

American Salesmanship Today

People have been predicting the demise of salesmen since
the early twentieth century. "Are salesmen necessary?"
asked a reporter in the *New York Times* on June 18, 1916.
Advertising was more efficient, he wrote, now that the
"railroads had turned the farms into cities."[1] E. B. Weiss
made a similar argument in his book *The Vanishing Salesman* (1962), suggesting that the vast amount of presel-
ling, branding, and advertising had eliminated much of
the need for salesmen. Face-to-face selling was doomed
because it was simply too expensive and too inefficient.[2]

There was something to this argument, for advertising
grew at a tremendous rate in the late twentieth century,
changing the way many goods were sold. The reach of advertisers increased substantially throughout the century,
with the growth of national magazines in the 1910s, radio
in the 1920s, and television after World War II. There were
187,000 workers in the advertising industry at the end of
the twentieth century.[3]

More than this, advertising became increasingly sophisticated in the 1960s, as advertisers carved out market seg-
ments based on lifestyles or personality types and "psy-
chographic" groupings, and marketed consumer products
as "hip," aiming their messages at youthful—as opposed to
strictly young—audiences. Advertisers used the appeal of

255

youth to sell everything from cars to soda, still preaching the old messages of self-transformation, but in new forms.[4] Some of these campaigns had enormous commercial and cultural effects. As historian Richard Tedlow wrote, "There was no such thing as the Pepsi Generation until Pepsi created it."[5]

Technological changes enabled new methods of delivering ads, some of which, such as cable television, blurred the line between selling and advertising, as salesmen increasingly put themselves on the small screen. Ron Popeil, the head of Ronco Inventions, which manufactured the Veg-O-Matic and other kitchen products sold on late-night TV, had relatives who had been pitchmen selling small appliances along the Atlantic City boardwalk in the late nineteenth century. Popeil became a pitchman of sorts, selling to millions through infomercials in the late twentieth century and the early twenty-first.[6] Others joined him: former heavyweight boxing champ George Foreman sold a line of grills; Tony Robbins hawked his "personal power" videos, courses, and books; and other entrepreneurs sold steam cleaners, muscle massagers, abdominal machines, and cures for dry skin, wrinkles, and lethargy that harkened back to the days of patent medicine.

Although advertising grew in volume and sophistication throughout the twentieth century, it did not replace salesmen. As this book has shown, selling and advertising are different. Sales workers played a unique function in the nation's economy. This was true in the late nineteenth century and has remained so through the beginning of the twenty-first. Face-to-face sales pitches, confrontation, persuasion, and the exchange of information between buyer and seller remain at least as vital to capitalism today as in 1776, when Adam Smith noted man's propensity to "truck, barter, and exchange."[7]

Sales workers perform a range of different tasks: explaining and servicing products, collecting information, and pressuring people to make purchases by overcoming resistance. Sales agents are trained to master both "formal" elements of selling, such as legal constraints, methods of shipment, and so on, and "informal" elements, such as codes of human behavior. They answer specific questions about a product and its application, grant credit to buyers, and make arrangements for delivery. Sales workers in many industries establish long-standing relations with customers and develop deep insights into the customers' wants and needs, as well as their habits and peculiarities—thereby erecting significant barriers for salesmen from competing concerns to overcome.

Companies today invest in a sales force for many of the same reasons they did in the past. The industries that traditionally relied on salesmen—insurance, automobiles, office machines, branded foods, and pharmaceuticals—did so because they believed salesmen were effective in creating and sustaining demand. Companies devoted a great deal of time and money to training their sales forces. They investigated the best way for salesmen to talk about products and make "pitches." Salesmen were taught how to answer any type of objection. They learned to counter the typical maneuvers people use to avoid making a commitment about purchasing a product and to surmount their attempts to say "no" politely. Salesmen and sales managers felt that "prospects," whether consumers or businesspeople, could be influenced in their choices. They did not think that customers based their choices solely on the objective assessment of information. Salesmen did not simply read a list of a product's virtues, but instead asked open-ended questions and used techniques to handle objections.

The ability of salesmen to influence buyers should not be overstated. The sales transaction itself—the act of persuading someone to buy— proved difficult to systematize and rationalize. Some writers have exaggerated the power of companies to shape consumers' desires and have described the ability of firms to shape buying patterns as a manipulative "apparatus" borne uncomfortably by society. But even companies that used the full arsenal of salesmanship and advertising were in no way "hegemonic," as some historians like to say, in their control of consumer buying decisions.[8] Sales techniques were not simply manipulative or conspiratorial, if only because selling was so difficult. Most of the time salesmen failed at what they tried to do. Burroughs salesmen found that even in the few cases where a prospect eventually bought a machine, they averaged six calls to close the sale.[9] And most Burroughs sales efforts did not ever result in a sale. Even the percentage of sales following free trials of the machines, at only 14 percent, was fairly low.[10]

But sales managers and salesmen believed that economic behavior followed somewhat predictable patterns and that an awareness of these patterns was helpful in swaying consumers' buying behavior. Lightning-rod salesmen in the 1870s knew, as did cash-register agents in the 1880s, that people were more likely to buy out of the fear of a loss than the promise of a gain. John H. Patterson's salesmen, therefore, found their most effective sales argument for the cash register to be the "thief catcher" campaign (even though in official company documents NCR instructed agents against this appeal). Salesmen learned to sell expectations: Book canvassers found more success when they revealed only a portion of a book to a farmer, rather than the whole text, thereby heightening the prospect's curiosity. Further, people were more often persuaded to make a purchase if they believed that their neighbors, or some prominent people in town, had already bought the product being sold. They did not want to appear unable to keep up with the "Joneses." Research by psychologists tended to confirm the effectiveness of many of the approaches pioneered by salesmen. Moreover, salesmen learned ways of presenting goods. They knew that prospects were less likely to interrupt a sales spiel if it was accompanied by some simple, seemingly natural, gesture, like digging inside a bag for a free sample, or taking off rubber overshoes in anticipation of being let inside out of the rain—as Fuller Brush salesmen did in the 1920s and 1930s.[11]

Companies invested in their sales workers because they believed that a strong, inspired sales force was necessary to create demand. Though salesmen often failed in their efforts, they created demand in two ways. First, they persuaded customers to buy products or services that they might not have otherwise purchased. This is what Harry Tosdal meant when he wrote about sales "leadership" in the 1950s, and what Walter Dill Scott referred to when he compared salesmen to athletic coaches in the 1910s; salesmen were not manipulating customers, according to these two academics, but overcoming their inertia. The effort of salesmen to sell major consumer-durable goods, such as cars and appliances, was significant, for it affected the composition of demand among American consumers. The type of goods purchased by households in the 1920s shifted toward many items that were sold by salesmen (and usually purchased on credit), thus encouraging the further industrialization of the economy.[12]

Or salesmen could persuade customers to buy their company's product rather than a competitor's, as when homeowners heeded a salesman's suggestion and purchased an Electrolux vacuum cleaner rather than a Hoover. Salesmen could be effective in this regard, pointing out marginal differences between one product and another. If two cars or two refrigerators were similar in performance and design, salesmen might be able to sway the customer toward one brand or another.

This was not a trivial accomplishment. The consequence of this type of marginal ability to influence consumers could be great. Once "prospects" had purchased one company's product rather than another's, they became customers of that company and were often targeted for follow-up calls or for more promotional material. They also became familiar with the product and were likely, unless disappointed with it, to continue to purchase from the company again, because this was less risky than trying something new. They had become, as economists say, "path dependent," or as marketers say, "brand loyal."

If this product was truly the superior item, then the customer was well served. But if not, then the effect of this sales campaign was to make a marginally inferior good the standard of the industry. Companies can conquer one sale at a time, and not always with the best product. Large sales forces present a difficult barrier for new companies to overcome. IBM machines were not always regarded as technologically the best after the mid-twentieth century. Even Thomas J. Watson wrote, "We consistently outsold people who had better technology because we knew how to put the story before the customer."[13] Similarly,

Microsoft products were not considered to be superior to those of all competitors in the late twentieth century, but the company's sales force was unmatched.[14]

Sales Workers Today

Today there are more sales workers than ever before. The number of people in sales occupations in 2000 was 16 million, or about 12 percent of the total employed workforce. This figure includes all types of sellers, from pharmaceutical sales workers to counterpersons at department stores; it is up from about 5 percent in 1920 and 7 percent in 1960. Of the 16 million people working in sales in 2000, about 10 percent are the type of sales workers highlighted in this book—manufacturers' sales reps, business-to-business salespeople, and independent canvassers. About 41 percent of today's sales workers sell in retail stores.[15]

The modern American economy employs a great variety of salespeople. It still has "peddlers," such as boardwalkers and pushcart vendors, and "drummers," who travel for wholesale companies. The names for these sales workers have changed, and their relative place within distribution channels has declined. But the economy is flexible and varied, and the importance of different channels changes with time. Since the early twentieth century, as this book has shown, the trend in large companies has been to favor sales management, branding, consumer research, and careful personnel selection.[16]

The demographics of America's sales workers have changed. Nearly half (49.6 percent) of the total sales workers recorded in the 2000 census were women.[17] This has changed the vocabulary of selling. The word "saleswoman" was used in the late nineteenth century, usually to refer to a retail sales worker. In the 1970s, as the number of women in sales jobs increased, there were scattered, clever, references to "saleswomanship," but the word did not catch on.[18] The main tendency in the final decades of the twentieth century was to refrain from using the term "salesman" in favor of the gender-neutral word "salesperson," a verbal adjustment similar to the one that had led to the coining of "chairperson" and "anchorperson" at the time. This change was overdue. The development of sales forces at large companies, beginning in the late nineteenth century, not only favored the hiring of men for sales positions, but also equated good salesmanship with manliness. Part of the effort of sales managers had been to present selling as a masculine pursuit—to play up the "man" in "salesman," as a business executive said at the 1916 World's Salesmanship Congress. But women had long been prominent in retail sales; they had worked as book peddlers in the nineteenth century and insurance agents in the twentieth. In the late twentieth century, too, women gained entry to other forms of selling, especially service-centered industries, working for investment banks, credit-card companies, and other financial service organizations. Women were also prominent in the field of direct selling as the "party plan" method of distribution replaced door-to-door selling. In fact, they dominated in several of the largest direct-sales companies, including Avon, with a sales force of about 3 million worldwide, and Tupperware and Mary Kay with about 1 million each.[19]

Other changes have occurred in the composition of sales workers. Many more are employed by foreign companies in the United States than at mid-century. Some of these workers come from the host country, but many are born in the United States and work for a foreign-owned concern. The Japanese automaker Toyota, for instance, began to expand its dealership network at home in the early 1950s, sending salesmen door-to-door, just as American companies had done in the United States. After succeeding against intense domestic competition from Nissan, Toyota began developing North American dealerships in 1957.[20] In 2002, 1,740 Toyota dealers were at work in the United States.[21] In addition, the Toyota salesman, thanks to John Updike's Rabbit (rhyming with "Babbitt") Angstrom, is represented in fiction. Rabbit sold the highly efficient Toyotas during the oil shortage of the 1970s, when dealers hung flags that announced "Fuel Economy." Rabbit told his customers, "You've just put your hand on one super machine," when they noticed the Celica GT Sports Coupe, which, he added, came with many standard features, such as steel-belted radials, a quartz crystal clock, and an AM/FM stereo.[22]

Despite changes in the gender composition of the workforce, and increased competition from overseas, many aspects of salesmanship in America remain the same. With changes in demographics, culture, and technology, the methods, intentions, and uses of modern selling have persisted. The same industries that relied on face-to-face sales workers in the mid-twentieth century still rely on them today, and for similar purposes. Some of the largest sales forces among manufacturing companies are in the field of beverages, including Pepsico and Coca-Cola, and pharmaceuticals, including Johnson and Johnson, Pfizer, Novartis, and Procter and Gamble. The computer industry is another one that contains many firms with large sales forces, including Microsoft, IBM, Oracle, Hewlett-Packard, and Xerox. All these companies have sales forces with more than five thousand agents, and Pepsico's and Microsoft's exceed thirty thousand.[23]

Salespeople have been essential in the growth of high-tech businesses, ushering in the rise of computer hardware and software firms just as they had pushed the cash register and IBM's punch-card machines. Digital Equipment Corporation and Hewlett-Packard developed sales forces to sell their mid-range systems, as did Oracle and Computer Associates to sell software. Cisco Systems also had a strong sales team pushing its networking hardware. The high-tech companies of the late twentieth century tended to be combinations of charismatic "high-tech pioneers" and "pioneer salespeople," commented one business writer.[24]

There has also been rapid growth in sales forces working for companies in the financial services industries. These salespeople log many hours on the telephone, but they also visit clients, working out complex deals. Among the largest service-sector sales forces are American General and Citigroup, with over 100,000 sales representatives each.[25]

Methods of sales management are also similar in many ways to those used before. Most of the innovations in sales management were in place by the early twentieth century. Managers still attempt to align the incentives of sales workers with the goals of the company. They create compensation schemes, adjusting commission rates and salary. They train sales workers, sometimes through online programs, and hold conventions and motivational talks. They assign sales territories, sometimes by region and sometimes, as at Xerox, according to product lines.

Salesmen and managers remain hungry for information about customers. Just as salesmen had been quick to exploit the changing technology of the late nineteenth century, so too did companies throughout the twentieth century make use of new inventions to allow salesmen and managers to gather information about clients and customers. The amount of information collected by companies has increased dramatically in retail selling with the use of point-of-sale scanners, which give retailers instant sales data about individual items at the checkout counter. Internet shopping has also allowed retailers and manufacturers to collect information about an individual's credit-card debt, personal shopping tastes, sizes, and color preferences. Some companies use video footage of consumers to analyze their behavior in shops and malls to figure out how to display merchandise and control the flow of shoppers through their stores.[26] All these methods of gathering and analyzing data are extensions and enhancements of strategies used earlier in the century, rather than representing anything entirely new.

Studying Selling Today

The study of salesmanship has also followed trends established earlier in the century. Sales management at business schools now tends to be subsumed under the larger discipline of marketing. Sections of Philip Kotler's textbook *Marketing Management*—first published in 1980 and reprinted frequently afterward—cover familiar themes: sales-force strategy, sales-force size, compensation, recruiting and selecting sales representatives, training, and motivating sales representatives.[27]

As relations with customers have become more complex, the language of the study of salesmanship has changed as well. In the 1990s, academics such as Benson Shapiro at Harvard Business School talked not just about transactional selling (one-time quick sales, like those made by canvassers) and system sales (long-term relationships forged between salesperson and buyer, like those developed by NCR), but also strategic selling, in which buyers and sellers formed even closer bonds, by offering joint products or services.[28]

While business schools have continued to offer some type of sales management instruction—usually within a larger marketing course—they do not offer courses in salesmanship skills. The topic remains, just as it was in the 1910s, more suitable for popular how-to books and memoirs of successful salespeople than for academic classes.

Economists, for their part, still tend to ignore the role of salesmanship in the economy. In recent years, however, more have attacked neoclassical understandings of the marketplace, including analyses of the ways that consumers make decisions. They have questioned the idea that consumers consistently make logical and rational choices when they buy.

The 2001 Nobel Prize in Economic Sciences, for instance, went to A. Michael Spence, Joseph E. Stiglitz, and George A. Ackerlof, who studied the way that asymmetric information affected decisions made by buyers and sellers. They criticized the traditional idea that the only task facing buyers and sellers was to negotiate an agreeable price, which would signal to companies how much to produce in the future (with a high price telling sellers to produce more goods). Ackerlof was cited, in particular, for his 1970 paper "The Market for 'Lemons,'" which appeared in the *Quarterly Journal of Economics*.[29] Ackerlof wondered what happened on a used-car lot when the salesperson did not disclose all available information about the quality of the car to the buyer. The buyer worried about the condition of the vehicle and whether the price was too high. The dealer knew the condition of the car, but the buyer did not. This prevented the price mechanism from functioning effectively. Because of the lack of information about used cars, people who owned good cars were less likely to trade them. The example of the used-car salesman was simply one exploration of a larger theme: markets did not follow neoclassical rules when there was unequal access to information. (Such situations also call for government correctives, such as "lemon laws.")

The 2002 Nobel Prize for economics was also given to academics who studied market imperfections. But they looked at the problem from another angle, one with more relevance to buying and selling—and to the activities of salesmen. They attacked the idea of most mainstream economists that consumers make decisions systematically, based on their own personal preferences and the available information. These behavioral economists critiqued the idea that people made logical decisions; they have found that customers are motivated, for instance, by risk aversion and at other times by altruism.

Daniel Kahneman, a professor of psychology at Princeton University (who shared the Nobel with Vernon L. Smith) suggested that consumers often acted irrationally or illogically in their decision-making. Other economists have also pioneered this field, including Matthew Rabin of the University of California, Berkeley. Rabin described the importance of collaboration between economists and psychologists in his article "Economics and Psychology." Standard economic theory, wrote Rabin, assumed that "each individual has stable and coherent preferences, and that she rationally maximizes those preferences." By researching human judgment and behavior, the work of psychologists "can teach us about making [the utility function] more realistic than under standard economic assumptions."[30] For instance, Rabin's psychological research revealed that the displeasure of financial loss was greater than the pleasure of financial gain, and that people made systematic errors in analyzing the choices that confronted them and in evaluating their preferences.

The rules of salesmanship, practiced for generations, map out economic behavior along similar terms in sales scripts and strategies. This does not mean that sales workers or entrepreneurs theorized about the nature of rationality and irrationality in the marketplace, but rather that through their experiences, they collected stories and anecdotes about actual buyer behavior. The new perspective that economists are applying to the study of nonrational buying activity may provide a better understanding of economic behavior, including the interactions between salespeople and buyers.[31]

The Culture of Salesmanship

Today "salesmanship" seems omnipresent, influencing how Americans think about business, capitalism, and self-advancement. It appears such an integral part of the economy that people assume it has no history, or if it does, that it is merely the story of a "peddler's progress"—simply the saga of fast talking on a grand scale. But as this book shows, the invention of the sales personality and the construction over time of methods of modern salesmanship have a long and complex history. Modern salesmanship developed under specific economic and political circumstances, led by entrepreneurs in particular industries who wanted, or needed, to systematize selling. The buildup has been institutional, organizational, and cultural. The evolution of a science of selling has led to an economy of "rational exuberance," with calculated waves of products, announcements, inventions, improvements, and regularly generated promises by companies of "satisfaction guaranteed."

The effects of the growth of sales and advertising have been pervasive. They emphasize both the "creative" and "destructive" aspects of capitalism, to borrow words from the economist Joseph Schumpeter—one of the few economists whose writings about capitalism paid tribute to the energy of entrepreneurs. Schumpeter described capitalism as a process of continual change that replaced old products, traditions, and business organizations. The distinguishing aspect of capitalism, in his famous phrase, was that it was constantly swept by a "perennial gale of creative destruction."[32]

The rise of modern salesmanship was "creative" in ways that Harvard professor Harry R. Tosdal and *Fortune* editor William H. Whyte described in the 1950s: The coming of large sales forces was intimately connected with the development of mass production and the long upward trend in the American gross national product. Salesmen introduced new inventions and encouraged businesses and consumers to "trade up." They pushed the goods that defined the American economy, including new office machines, automobiles, vacuum cleaners, soft drinks, breakfast cereals, and computers. In 1931 Henry Ford remarked that product standardization had brought an abundance of choices. "Machine production in this country has diversified our life, has given a wider choice of articles than was ever before thought possible—and has provided the means wherewith the people may buy them," wrote Ford. "We standardize only on essential conveniences. Standardization, instead of making for sameness, has introduced unheard-of variety into our life. It is surprising that this has not been generally perceived."[33] Ford's statement is counterintuitive, but the advent of mass production, and mass salesmanship, brought lower prices and more products, fabrics, designs, and colors (despite Ford's own preference for black), and salesmen were essential to introducing these goods and options.

Modern salesmanship has also been a destructive process, sweeping out products, ideas, and companies. Highly managed sales forces have been relentless in their work. Some—at United Fruit, Standard Oil, National Cash Register, and Burroughs Adding Machine, to name a few— have at times engaged in inefficient and even unethical behavior in their efforts to crush competitors. "Salesmanship," with its element of confrontation, is an inherently unlikable process. There is something unsettling about the salesperson's telephone call for an appointment, approach on the car lot, or knock on the office door. People hate to be forced to make a decision, or to be talked into anything, and are especially fearful of being duped. Salespeople themselves are disliked. In a 1940 survey, middle-class mothers with young children ranked selling as the least desirable career choice for their sons—storeowner, teacher, dentist, and bank officer all finished above realtor and insurance solicitor.[34] Similarly, a 2001 Gallup poll of honesty and ethics in professions ranked car salesmen lowest; just above them on the list were advertising writers and insurance salesmen.

The logic of salesmanship is relentless, turning everything, including employees, into products. The image of Willy Loman, who was fired when he became unproductive, is "as pertinent today as ever," wrote a *New York Times* critic during the play's Broadway revival in 1999.[35] The hiring and firing of workers is uniquely easy in America, allowing the quick buildup and dismantling of factories, branch offices, and service centers. The *Economist* commented on the message of Miller's play: "Every country in Europe would kill to have a capitalism that spits out inefficient people like Willy as ruthlessly as America does. Willy's frantic desire to compete, his merry recital of the management clichés of the day ('It's not what you sell; it's how you sell'), his determination to imitate his legendary brother Ben: all these things are what keeps America ahead of its peers."[36] Yet, as the magazine also noted, the problem remains of what to do with those displaced by the changes in salesmanship.

The story of American salesmanship is part of the broader history of the country's unrivaled economic growth. Modern sales methods have been an essential part of the performance of America's production and service-related industries. Salesmanship, too, as critics and fictionwriters have demonstrated for decades, is entwined with the negative consequences of this growth: the uprooting of old businesses and technologies, the problems caused by swings in unemployment and in stock market valuation, the conspicuous consumption of products and foods, and the ecological disaster posed by piles of worn-out merchandise. Most of the tens of thousands of new products introduced in the United States each year fail even to reach the marketplace.[37] Modern salesmanship arose in America largely because of the country's scale of production, coupled with its Progressive Era culture of rationalization and system building; it has become an integral part of the global marketplace over the past decades, taking form as marketing research, branding, advertising, and personal selling carried out worldwide.

Yet most people do not have a good understanding of what salesmen and saleswomen do. They see salespeople—in stores, at work, or on the car lot—but do not recognize the institutional and administrative systems that have defined their roles. In popular culture, for example, sales workers are represented as transactional sellers—individuals who sell a single good and then move quickly on to the next prospect. For instance, the Maysles brothers' documentary *Salesman* features Bible salesmen; Barry Levinson's film *Tin Men,* aluminum-siding salesmen; and David Mamet's play *Glengary Glen Ross,* realtors. Popular culture does not recognize the "scientific" seller; the salesperson who makes use of data, works on large accounts over years, and is supported by a large corporation does not hold the same dramatic appeal.

An awareness of the modern salesmanship is crucial for understanding the history of American economic and social change. All countries throughout time have had charismatic individuals who possessed the ability to charm and persuade. With the development of sales forces at large firms, the United States became distinguished by having armies of individuals with "trained" enthusiasm, replicated sales pitches, and handy credit terms, backed by established organizations. Salesmen and saleswomen are at the center of the story of industrialization, innovation, and change. All their appointments, questions, objection-handling routines, goodwill work, missionary calls, and "closings" have pushed American capitalism, with its vices and virtues, into every corner of the globe.

Appendix: Common Objections to Buying a Ford

- Believe there will be another drop in price. I am going to wait.
- They will be making some improvements. I am going to wait.
- I promised to see another dealer before I bought.
- I do not want to buy on time. Will wait until I can pay cash.
- I don't want to pay interest.
- I object to borrowing.
- I am afraid of business conditions in my line.
- I'll buy when business picks up.
- I must have immediate delivery.
- It will be three or four months before we will have the money.
- I am not ready yet.
- I'll wait 'till spring.
- I'll wait awhile.
- I'd like to have a car, but I don't want to get it now.
- I want a larger car.
- I cannot afford a car.
- Too expensive for me to keep up.
- There is no hurry, you will be around again.
- I guess I can get along without a car (or truck, etc.)
- I don't want a car.
- I do not understand mechanics and I don't want to bother with a car.
- My wife does not want me to buy.
- I want to think it over.
- I guess I'll get a _____.

- I am not in the market now.
- I am not interested.
- There is no use going into it. I know in advance that I do not want to take it up.
- Crop conditions are too poor to buy now.
- We have decided to build a home before we buy a car.
- Any car but a Ford.
- I could hardly meet the payments and I haven't enough to pay down.
- I don't like to assume the obligation.
- I do not want to put the money into it.
- I have planned to put my money into other things.
- I could not meet the payments.
- Another Ford salesman!
- I'll wait until after the holidays.
- I am not interested now. You might come around later.
- I can't decide today.
- I know a man who bought a Ford who said it was no good.
- I need the money.
- I am too busy to talk with you now.
- I am satisfied with the car I have.
- You would be wasting your time on me.
- I'm satisfied with the savings bank.
- I can use my big car.
- We have plenty of large trucks.
- You are a clever salesman.
- Write us your proposition.
- You claim too much.
- It is your business to sell me and of course you will try to sell me.
- I don't believe I can go ahead with that.
- Ford upkeep is too expensive.

Source: Don C. Prentiss, *Ford Motor Products and Their Sale* (Detroit: The Franklin Press, 1923), p. 443–494.

Notes

Prologue, 1916

1. *Detroit Free Press,* July 10, 1916, p. 1.
2. Leonard W. Ferguson, *History of Industrial Psychology* (Hartford, Conn.: Finlay Press, 1965), vol. 7, p. 89.
3. *Salesmanship: Devoted to Success in Selling, the Official Organ of the World's Congress of Salesmanship* (Sept. 1916), p. 273.
4. Grant Nablo, "The Value of Character and Ability Analysis in the Selection of Salesmen," *Salesmanship* (Dec. 1916), pp. 448–451.
5. *Detroit Free Press,* July 10, 1916, pp. 1, 3.
6. Economist Joseph A. Schumpeter famously described capitalism as an evolutionary process of "creative destruction." See Joseph A. Schumpeter, *Capitalism, Socialism, and Democracy* (1942; New York: Harper Perennial, 1976), esp. pp. 81–86; also see Thomas K. McCraw, "Schumpeter Ascending," *American Scholar* 60 (Summer 1991): 371–392.

Introduction

1. See Thomas K. McCraw, ed., *Creating Modern Capitalism: How Entrepreneurs, Companies, and Countries Triumphed in Three Industrial Revolutions* (Cambridge, Mass.: Harvard University Press, 1997).
2. Quoted in Timothy B. Spears, *One Hundred Years on the Road: The Traveling Salesman in American Culture* (New

Haven, Conn.: Yale University Press, 1995), p. 205. The quote is from P. W. Searles, "The Handling of Salesmen," *System* 4 (June 1904), pp. 76–77.

3. On the parallel between "salesmanship" and "craftsmanship," see Spears, *One Hundred Years on the Road*, p. 110.

4. Dartnell Corporation, *Survey of Modern Sales Organizations: Describing Modern Methods and Tendencies in 259 Different Lines of Business* (Chicago: Dartnell Corp., 1921); *Special Report: Sales Method Investigation, Plans for Building Up a Spirit of Loyalty in a Sales Organization, Report 172* (Chicago: Dartnell Corp., 1924); *Special Report: Enlisting Cooperation of Salesmen's Wives and Families* (Chicago: Dartnell Corp., 1928).

5. See Loren Baritz, *Servants of Power: A History of the Use of Social Science in American Industry* (Middletown, Conn.: Wesleyan University Press, 1960); Michael M. Sokal, ed., *Psychological Testing and American Society, 1890–1930* (New Brunswick, N.J.: Rutgers University Press, 1990); and Richard Gillespie, *Manufacturing Knowledge: A History of the Hawthorne Experiments* (Cambridge, Eng.: Cambridge University Press, 1991).

6. Melvin T. Copeland, *And Mark an Era: The Story of the Harvard Business School* (Boston: Little, Brown, 1958), pp. 211–213.

7. A. J. Snow, *Psychology in Personal Selling* (Chicago: A. W. Shaw Company, 1926), pp. 13–14.

8. Charles Bennett, *Scientific Salesmanship* (St. Louis: American Efficiency Bureau, 1933), p. 17.

9. Historian Thomas Hughes has written about technological enthusiasts, whose energy and drive brought many innovations to American business and society. There were many enthusiasts at the salesmen's conference, but in this case, they were individuals who were enthusiastic about the possibilities of salesmanship. See Thomas P. Hughes, *American Genesis: A Century of Invention and Technological Enthusiasm, 1870–1970* (New York: Viking, 1989).

10. The growth of large sales and distribution networks is best discussed in Alfred D. Chandler, Jr., *The Visible Hand: The Managerial Revolution in American Business* (Cambridge, Mass.: Belknap Press of Harvard University Press, 1977), and Richard Tedlow, *New and Improved: The Story of Mass Marketing in America* (New York: Basic Books, 1990). On salesmen, see Spears, *One Hundred Years on the Road;* Susan Strasser, *Satisfaction Guaranteed: The Making of the American Mass Market* (New York: Pantheon, 1989); Olivier Zunz, *Making America Corporate, 1870–1920* (Chi-

cago: University of Chicago Press, 1990); and William Leach, *Land of Desire: Merchants, Power, and the Rise of a New American Culture* (New York: Pantheon, 1993).

11. The phrase "is sold" is used in this way by the editors of *Fortune* magazine, in *A Close Look at Selling, the Great Unsolved Problem of American Business* (New York: McGraw-Hill, 1953), p. 8.

12. "The Great American Salesman," *Fortune* 21, no. 2 (Feb. 1940), p. 74.

13. *The Fuller Bristler,* n.p., 1923.

14. Tedlow, *New and Improved,* p. 137.

15. Charles Wilson Hoyt, *Scientific Sales Management: A Practical Application of the Principles of Scientific Management to Selling* (New York: George B. Woolson, 1912), p. 26.

16. See a colorful description in William Faulkner's *The Hamlet* (1931; New York: Vintage, 1959), esp. pp. 28–47.

17. According to one scholar of pottery and glassworks manufacturers, "For the most part, [these companies] ignored the 'managerial revolution' taking hold of the companies that made soap, cigarettes, sheeting, cereals, and canned goods, the large corporations often described as the harbingers of modern marketing." Regina Lee Blaszczyk, *Imagining Consumers: Design and Innovation from Wedgwood to Corning* (Baltimore, Md.: Johns Hopkins University Press, 2000), p. 2.

18. Robert Wiebe, *Search for Order, 1877–1920* (New York: Hill and Wang, 1967).

19. See Kenneth Cmiel, "Destiny and Amnesia: The Vision of Modernity in Robert Wiebe's *The Search for Order,*" in Stanley I. Kutler, ed., *American Retrospectives: Historians on Historians* (Baltimore, Md.: Johns Hopkins University Press, 1995), pp. 294–310.

20. On international influences on progressivism, see Daniel T. Rodgers, *Atlantic Crossings: Social Politics in a Progressive Age* (Cambridge, Mass.: Harvard University Press, 1998).

1. Hawkers and Walkers

1. [James Guild], "From Tunbridge, Vermont, to London, England: The Journal of James Guild, Peddler, Tinker, Schoolmaster, Portrait Painter, from 1818 to 1824," *PVHS (Proceedings of the Vermont Historical Society)* 5, no. 3 (1937), p. 250. Original spellings have been kept. See also David

Jaffee, "Peddlers of Progress and the Transformation of the Rural North, 1760–1860," *Journal of American History* (September 1991), pp. 511–535. Jaffee's article is a tremendous resource on Guild.

2. He traveled to Rochester, Bennington, Troy, Salom, Halifax, Hatfield, Massachusetts, Albany, Canasherog, Casanova, Auburn, Geneva, Gorum, Bethel, Canandaigua, Bloomfield, Montpelier, Hartford, Hoosick Falls, Waterford, Schenectady, Utica, Buffalo, and then to other places, including New York City, Charleston, Boston, Liverpool, and London.

3. While Guild was perhaps atypical in the variety of experiences he had, other peddlers also tried a range of occupations during their wanderings. See, for instance, the story of Gustavus Hesselius, a Swede, traveling through Maryland in the mid-eighteenth century, in J. R. Dolan, *The Yankee Peddlers of Early America: An Affectionate History of Life and Commerce in the Developing Colonies and the Young Republic* (New York: Clarkson N. Potter, 1964), p. 134.

4. Guild, "Journal," p. 268.

5. See Joyce Appleby, *Inheriting the Revolution: The First Generation of Americans* (Cambridge, Mass.: Harvard University Press, 2000). See also Jaffee, "Peddlers of Progress," p. 527. Jaffee remarks that Guild's writings "show how a rising generation of men and women greeted the possibilities of consumerism with enthusiasm and amazement rather than connoisseurship and criticism" (p. 527).

6. On the rise of Jewish peddlers, see Rowena Olegario, "'That Mysterious People': Jewish Merchants, Transparency, and Community in Mid-Nineteenth Century America," *Business History Review* (Summer 1999), pp. 161–189.

7. Guild, "Journal," pp. 250–251.

8. Thomas K. McCraw, ed., *Creating Modern Capitalism: How Entrepreneurs, Companies, and Countries Triumphed in Three Industrial Revolutions* (Cambridge, Mass.: Harvard University Press, 1997), p. 306.

9. Guild, "Journal," p. 251.

10. Jaffee, "Peddlers of Progress," pp. 521–522.

11. Guild, "Journal," pp. 256, 279.

12. David Jaffee commented that Guild "constructed a self in the role of a Yankee trickster." See Jaffee, "Peddlers of Progress," p. 527.

13. Guild, "Journal," p. 279.

14. Susan Porter Benson, "'The Customers Ain't God': The Work Culture of Department-Store Saleswomen, 1890–1940," in Michael H. Frisch and

Daniel J. Walkowitz, eds., *Working-Class America* (Urbana: University of Illinois, 1983), pp. 188, 191.

15. Guild, "Journal," p. 268.

16. Ibid., p. 259.

17. Jaffee, "Peddlers of Progress." See also Constance Rourke, *American Humor: A Study of the National Character* (Tallahassee: Florida State University Press, 1931), pp. 3–32.

18. See Joyce Appleby, *Inheriting the Revolution.*

19. On canals, see Ronald E. Shaw, *Canals for a Nation: The Canal Era in the United States, 1790–1860* (Lexington: University Press of Kentucky, 1990).

20. On railroad growth, see Colleen A. Dunlavy, *Politics and Industrialization: Early Railroads in the United States and Prussia* (Princeton, N.J.: Princeton University Press, 1994).

21. Jaffee, "Peddlers of Progress," p. 514–515, 512.

22. Susan Strasser, *Waste and Want: A Social History of Trash* (New York: Metropolitan Books, 1999), p. 76.

23. Joseph T. Rainer, "The Honorable Fraternity of Moving Merchants: Yankee Peddlers in the Old South, 1800–1860," Ph.D. diss., William and Mary College, 2000, p. 72.

24. Dolan, *Yankee Peddlers,* p. 164.

25. Jaffee, "Peddlers of Progress," p. 517.

26. Rainer, "Honorable Fraternity," pp. 98–99.

27. John Joseph Murphy, "Entrepreneurship in the Establishment of the American Clock Industry," *Journal of Economic History* 26 (June 1966), pp. 174, 184.

28. Earl W. Hayter, *The Troubled Farmer, 1850–1900: Rural Adjustment to Industrialism* (Dekalb: Northern Illinois University Press, 1968), p. 201.

29. Robert W. Lovett, "The Cole Brothers Pump and Lightning Rod Company," *Bulletin of the Business Historical Society* 24, no. 2 (June 1950), pp. 53–64.

30. Hayter, *Troubled Farmer,* p. 199, quotation from pp. 203–204, fn. 26.

31. See Frank Lambert, *"Pedlar in Divinity": George Whitefield and the Transatlantic Revivals, 1737–1770* (Princeton, N.J.: Princeton University Press, 1994); and Harry S. Stout, *The Divine Dramatist: George Whitefield and the Rise of Modern Evangelicalism* (Grand Rapids, Mich.: Eerdmans, 1991).

32. Nathan O. Hatch, *The Democratization of American Christianity* (New Haven, Conn.: Yale University Press, 1989).

33. R. Laurence Moore, *Selling God: American Religion in the Marketplace of*

Culture (New York: Oxford University Press, 1994), p. 91. Moore wrote, "Although nineteenth-century Protestant ministers and many entrepreneurs of commercial culture on occasion furiously attacked each other, they had to learn to work the same audiences using a market model that compelled them to adopt techniques of persuasion rather than coercion" (p. 6).

34. Dolan, *Yankee Peddlers*, p. 216; Sydney E. Ahlstrom, *A Religious History of the American People* (New Haven, Conn.: Yale University Press, 1972), p. 373.

35. James Erwin, *Reminiscences of Early Circuit Life* (Toledo, Ohio: Spear, Johnson, 1884), p. 12. Emphasis in the original.

36. Ibid., p. 19. Erwin also noted how the preacher served as entertainment: "News traveled slowly, and in the new sections of the country, among the sparse populations, was brought by any passing traveler who might chance to come that way. It was therefore a Godsend when the preacher came along. His appearance awakened as much interest in one of those back settlements then, as the arrival of a large mail would now in time of some great public interest" (p. 13).

37. Ibid., p. 27.

38. Ibid., p. 23.

39. See David B. McCarthy, "Russell Salmon Cook," in *American National Biography* (New York: Oxford University Press, 1999), vol. 5, pp. 386–387.

40. Peter J. Wosh, *Spreading the Word: The Bible Business in Nineteenth-Century America* (Ithaca, N.Y.: Cornell University Press, 1994), p. 176.

41. American Bible Society, *Instructions of the Committee on Agencies* (New York: American Bible Society, 1853), pp. 11–13. Archives of the American Bible Society, New York City.

42. Wosh, *Spreading the Word*, p. 19.

43. Jackson Lears, *Fables of Abundance: A Cultural History of Advertising in America* (New York: Basic Books, 1994), pp. 64–65.

44. Jaffee, "Peddlers of Progress," pp. 519, 518.

45. Rosalind Remer, *Printers and Men of Capital: Philadelphia Book Publishers in the New Republic* (Philadelphia: University of Pennsylvania Press, 1996), p. 125.

46. Emily E. F. Skeel, ed., *Mason Locke Weems, His Work and Ways*, vol. 2 (New York: Richmond Mayo-Smith, 1929), p. xiii. See also R. Laurence Moore, "Religion, Secularization, and the Shaping of the Culture Industry in Antebellum America," *American Quarterly* 41, no. 2 (June 1989), p. 220.

47. Skeel, *Mason Locke Weems*, vol. 2, letter from Aug. 9, 1800, p. 136.

48. Quoted in J. Owen Stalson, *Marketing Life Insurance: Its History in America* (Cambridge, Mass.: Harvard University Press, 1942), p. 195. Emphasis in the original.

49. Max Lerner, ed., *The Portable Veblen* (New York: Viking, 1948), p. 499.

50. Quoted in Priscilla Carrington Kline, "New Light on the Yankee Peddler," *New England Quarterly* 12, no. 1 (Mar. 1939), pp. 80–98. The letter, written by John Bartholomew in 1837, appears on p. 86.

51. Lears, *Fables of Abundance*, p. 59.

52. See Lendol Caldor, *Financing the American Dream: A Cultural History of Consumer Credit* (Princeton, N.J.: Princeton University Press, 1999), p. 75.

53. Richard S. Tedlow, "Nineteenth Century Retailing and the Rise of the Department Store," in Alfred D. Chandler Jr., Thomas K. McCraw, and Richard S. Tedlow, eds., *Management: Past and Present* (Cincinnati, Ohio: Southwestern College Publishing, 1996), pp. 3.5–3.17. See also Neil Harris's excellent biography, *Humbug: The Art of P. T. Barnum* (Chicago: University of Chicago, 1973), p. 11.

54. Rainer, "Honorable Fraternity," pp. 40–41.

55. See *Hart v. Willets,* Supreme Court of Pennsylvania, 62 Pa 15 1869 (189 Pa. LEXIS 205).

56. See Kline, "New Light on the Yankee Peddler," esp. pp. 93–96.

57. Ebenezer Graves, "Journal of a Peddling Trip: Kept by Ebenezer Graves of Ashfield, Massachusetts," *Bulletin of the Society for the Preservation of New England Antiques* 56, no. 3 (Winter 1966), pp. 81–90, esp. pp. 81, 89.

58. Rainer, "Honorable Fraternity," p. 15.

59. See Olegario, "'That Mysterious People,'" pp. 180–181; Strasser, *Waste and Want,* p. 77. Jewish merchants working in American cities often hired fellow Jews to work as peddlers and carry goods to the countryside. Many Jews had experience peddling in Europe and took up the occupation in the United States because it required little capital investment.

60. Timothy Dwight, *Travels in New England and New York,* 2 vols. (1823; Cambridge, Mass: Harvard University Press, 1969), vol. 1, p. 233. For folklore, see B. A. Botkin, *A Treasury of American Folklore: Stories, Ballads, and Traditions of the People* (New York: Crown, 1944), pp. 363, 392.

61. Henry David Thoreau, *Walden and Civil Disobedience* (New York: Norton Critical Edition, 1966), p. 12.

62. Daniel Horowitz, *The Morality of Spending: Attitudes toward the Consumer Society in America, 1875–1940* (Baltimore, Md.: Johns Hopkins University Press, 1985), p. 5.

63. Thomas C. Haliburton, *The Clockmaker; or, The Sayings and Doings of*

Sam Slick of Slickville ([1835]; Toronto: McClelland & Stewart, 1958), p. 8. Emphasis in the original.

64. Ibid., pp. 9–11; see also Jaffee, "Peddlers of Progress," pp. 528–529.

65. See Lears, *Fables of Abundance*, p. 99.

66. See Herman Melville, "The Lightning-Rod Man," in *The Piazza Tales* (1856; New York: Modern Library Edition, 1985), pp. 175–184.

67. See Jean-Christophe Agnew, *Worlds Apart: The Market and the Theater in Anglo-American Thought, 1550–1750* (New York: Cambridge University Press, 1986), p. 201.

68. See *W. B. Kiler v. Frank Wohletz*, Supreme Court of Kansas, 79 Kan 716, 101 P. 474 (1909 Kan. LEXIS 274); *The State of Kansas v. Stub Crane*, Supreme Court of Kansas, 54 Kan. 251, 38 P. 270 (1894 Kan. LEXIS 192). See also Bates Harrington, *How 'Tis Done: A Thorough Ventilation of the Numerous Schemes Conducted by Wandering Canvassers Together with Advertising Dodges for the Swindling of the Public* (Chicago: Fidelity, 1879), pp. 204–208.

69. See Harrington, *How 'Tis Done.*

70. Abram Vossen Goodman's translation of Abraham Kohn's diary is in *American Jewish Archives* 3, no. 3 (June 1951), pp. 99, 108.

71. American Bible Society, *Instructions of the Committee on Agencies*, pp. 11–13.

72. Wosh, *Spreading the Word*, p. 185.

73. Quoted in Lears, *Fables of Abundance*, p. 65, fn. 47.

74. See Agnew, in *Worlds Apart*, p. 201.

75. Harris used the contemporary comments of Alexander Herzen in making this observation. See Harris, *Humbug*, p. 11.

76. See James Ross Moore, "P. T. Barnum," in *American National Biography* (New York: Oxford University Press, 1999), vol. 2, pp. 211–214.

77. See Harris, *Humbug*, esp. pp. 59–90. Harris called Barnum's elaborate technique an "operational aesthetic."

2. Selling Ulysses S. Grant

1. The census also listed other types of salesmen: agents (33,989), commercial travelers (28,158), and salesmen and saleswomen (32,279). *Census of the United States, Statistics of the United States at the Tenth Annual Census* (Washington, D.C.: Government Printing Office, 1883).

2. Bates Harrington, *How 'Tis Done: A Thorough Ventilation of the Numer-*

ous Schemes Conducted by Wandering Canvassers Together with Advertising Dodges for Swindling the Public (Chicago: Fidelity, 1879), pp. 14–15.

3. Most manufactured products in the nineteenth century were generic, un-branded goods that supplied the farming population. Hinges, textiles, barbed wire, furniture, and other items were sold to wholesalers, who then set about selling these goods to retailers. Like agricultural merchants, wholesalers of manufactured goods found their work facilitated by the growth of the railroad and improvements in the telegraph. Wholesalers created their own distribution networks to supply goods to country stores, and depended on the work of traveling salesmen, or drummers, to forge long-lasting trade connections with rural retailers. Some manufacturers, as noted, preferred to hire itinerant salesmen to sell directly to the farming public, rather than sell in bulk to wholesalers or retail shops.

4. On the importance of credit networks to peddlers, see Laurence Fontaine, *History of Pedlars in Europe* (Durham, N.C.: Duke University Press, 1996), pp. 121–139.

5. Alba M. Edwards, *Population: Comparative Occupation Statistics for the United States, 1870 to 1940* (Washington, D.C.: U.S. Government Printing Office, 1943), p. 104. This survey excludes figures for the extraction of minerals and for forestry and finishing.

6. Alfred D. Chandler, Jr., *Visible Hand: The Managerial Revolution in American Business* (Cambridge, Mass.: Harvard University Press, 1977), p. 209.

7. See *Jacob Monk v. Henry Beal,* Supreme Court of Massachusetts, Plymouth, 84 Mass. 585 1861 Mass. LEXIS 391.

8. John Tebbel, *A History of Book Publishing in the United States,* vol. 1 (New York: R. R. Bowker, 1972), pp. 238–240.

9. Madeline B. Sterne, *Books and Book People in Nineteenth-Century America* (New York: R. R. Bowker, 1978), pp. 166–167.

10. Tebbel, *A History of Book Publishing,* vol. 1, pp. 238–240.

11. Judy Hilkey, *Character Is Capital: Success Manuals and Manhood in Gilded Age America* (Chapel Hill: University of North Carolina Press, 1997), pp. 16–17.

12. Tebbel, *A History of Book Publishing,* vol. 2, p. 106.

13. Hamlin Hill, "Mark Twain: Audience and Artistry," *American Quarterly* 15, no. 1 (Spring 1963), pp. 28–29.

14. Historian Judy Hilkey wrote of the sale of these books that the "model sales pitch was designed to play on people's hopes for success and fears of failure. According to one guide to canvassing, the question a book agent

must ask a potential customer to consider was not 'Can I afford it?' but 'Can I afford to be without it?'" Hilkey, *Character Is Capital*, p. 18.

15. See Joe L. Norris, "Pioneer Marketing Associations of the American Book Trade," Ph.D. diss., University of Chicago, 1939, p. 103; see also *The Trade Circular Annual for 1871* (New York: Office of the Trade Circular and Literary Bulletin, 1871), p. 110.

16. John Walton Caughey, "Hubert Howe Bancroft, Historian of Western America," *American Historical Review* 50, no. 3 (Apr. 1945), pp. 461–470.

17. Keith Arbour, "Book Canvassers, Mark Twain, and Hamlet's Ghost," *Papers of the Bibliographical Society of America* 93 (Mar. 1999), p. 9.

18. Annie Hamilton Nelles Dumond, *Annie Nelles; or, Life of a Book Agent* (Cincinnati: Annie Nelles, 1868), p. 243.

19. Ibid., pp. 240–262.

20. Norris, "Pioneer Marketing Associations," p. 105.

21. *Publishers' Weekly*, Mar. 21, 1874, p. 291.

22. *Publishers' Weekly*, July 10, 1886, p. 38.

23. See Francis E. Clark, *The Mossback Correspondence* (Boston: D. Lothrop, 1889), p. 117. Clark wrote, "Suppose he does ring your door-bell, good housewife, when your hands are in the dough and your cakes are frying, he is at least worthy of a polite refusal, if you do not wish his wares, rather than a metaphorical slap in the face and an actual slam of the door" (p. 118).

24. See introduction by Keith Arbour, in Arbour, ed., *Canvassing Books, Sample Books, and Subscription Publishers' Ephemera 1833–1951 in the Collection of Michael Zinman* (Ardsley, N.Y.: Haydn Foundation for the Cultural Arts, 1996), pp. xiv, xv.

25. E. Hannaford, *Success in Canvassing; A Manual of Practical Hints and Instructions, Specially Adapted to the Use of Book Canvassers of the Better Class* (1875; rev. ed., New York: E. Hannaford, 1884), p. 2.

26. Arbour, *Canvassing Books*, xxi. "The canvassing book's lacunae . . . created doubt; and with this doubt publishers required book agents to work and, if need be, play the confidence man," wrote historian Keith Arbour. "Men and women who could charismatically spin their targets' doubts into positive daydreams had the makings of successful book agents."

27. Hannaford, *Success in Canvassing*, pp. 5, 6.

28. Ibid., pp. 13–14. Emphasis in the original.

29. Ibid., pp. 5, 6.

30. Hamlin Hill, "Mark Twain: Audience and Artistry," *American Quarterly* 15, no. 1 (Spring 1963), p. 25.

31. Samuel Charles Webster, ed., *Mark Twain, Business Man* (Boston: Little, Brown, 1946), p. 249.

32. See Hamlin Lewis Hill, *Mark Twain and Elisha Bliss* (Columbia: University of Missouri Press, 1964), pp. 156–157.

33. Joseph B. McCullough, "Mark Twain and the Hy Slocum–Carl Byng Controversy," *American Literature* 43, no. 1 (Mar. 1971), pp. 42–59.

34. See Ulysses S. Grant, *Personal Memoirs of U. S. Grant.* A helpful edition is edited by E. B. Long, with an essay by William S. McFeely, pp. xix–xxiv, and published by De Capo Press, Cambridge, Mass. (2001). Reference to Twain's quote is from Long's introduction, p. xxx.

35. Webster, *Mark Twain, Business Man,* p. 279.

36. Mark Twain, *Notebooks and Journals,* vol. 3, 1883–1891 (Berkeley: University of California Press, 1979), notebook 23, p. 101, fn. 112. Emphasis in the original.

37. Webster, *Mark Twain, Business Man,* p. 312.

38. Twain, *Notebooks and Journals,* vol. 3, 1883–1891, notebook 24, pp. 142, 131, fn. 16. Emphasis in the original.

39. *How to Introduce the Personal Memoirs of U. S. Grant* (Hartford, Conn.: Webster, 1885), p. 2, The Mark Twain Project, University of California, Berkeley; see also Gerald Carson, "'Get the Prospect Seated . . . And Keep Talking,'" *American Heritage* 9, no. 5 (Aug. 1958), pp. 38–41, 77–80.

40. *How to Introduce the Personal Memoirs of U. S. Grant,* p. 2.

41. Carson, "'Get the Prospect Seated,'" pp. 38–41, 77–80.

42. *How to Introduce the Personal Memoirs of U. S. Grant,* pp. 26, 30.

43. Ibid., pp. 16–19.

44. Ibid., p. 33.

45. Mark Twain, *Notebooks and Journals,* vol. 3, 1883–1891, notebook 24, pp. 141–142.

46. *Publishers' Weekly,* Dec. 5, 1885, p. 886.

47. Mark Twain, *Notebooks and Journals,* vol. 3, 1883–1891, notebook 25, p. 175.

48. D. M. Dewey, *Tree Agents' Private Guide: A Manual for the Use of Agents and Dealers* (Rochester, N.Y.: Dewey, 1876), pp. 17, 20. Emphasis in the original.

49. Harrington, *How 'Tis Done,* pp. 29–30.

50. Henry Baldwin Hyde Letters, Mar. 1, 1868, Equitable Life Assurance Society Archives, New York, New York.

51. R. Carlyle Buley, *The Equitable Life Assurance Society of the United States, 1859–1964,* 2 vols. (New York: Appleton-Century-Crofts, 1967), vol. 1, p. 70. According to Buley, in fn. 131, the leading publisher of these in the 1860s was Gilbert E. Currie of the *United States Insurance Gazette,* located at 79 Pine Street, New York, New York.

52. J. Owen Stalson, *Marketing Life Insurance: Its History in America* (Cambridge, Mass.: Harvard University Press, 1942), p. 509.

53. Burton Hendrick, *The Story of Life Insurance* (New York: McClure, Phillips, 1907), p. 244.

54. James Harvey Young, *The Toadstool Millionaires: A Social History of Patent Medicines in America before Federal Regulation* (Princeton, N.J.: Princeton University Press, 1961), p. 97.

55. Ibid., pp. 193, 110. Young wrote: "An observer reckoned that the value of cocoa and chocolate, blacking and bluing, flavoring extracts and axle grease, beet sugar and glue, castor oil and lard, kindling wood and cosmetics, could all be added together, and still the total sum would not bulk so large as the $74,500,000 which was the manufactured value of American patent medicines. At retail prices, the nostrum-taking American public paid many millions more."

56. Ibid., p. 42.

57. Lawrence M. Friedman, *Crime and Punishment in American History* (New York: Basic Books, 1993), p. 195.

58. Hannaford, *Success in Canvassing,* p. 3.

59. Ibid.

60. Ibid., p. 4.

61. Karen Halttunen, *Confidence Men and Painted Women: A Story of Middle-Class Culture in America, 1830–1870* (New Haven, Conn.: Yale University Press, 1982), p. 4.

62. La Roy Sunderland, *"Confessions of a Magnetiser" Exposed!* (Boston, Mass.: Redding, 1845). See also T. J. Jackson Lears, *Fables of Abundance: A Cultural History of Advertising in America* (New York: Basic Books, 1994), p. 60. Emphasis in the original.

63. Harrington, *How 'Tis Done,* preface, pp. 11, 98.

64. Ibid., preface.

65. See S. James Weldon, *Twenty Years a Fakir* (Omaha, Neb.: Gate City Book and Novelty, 1899); Dumond, *Annie Nelles;* J. H. Mortimer, *Confessions of*

a Book Agent; or, Twenty Years by Stage and Rail (Chicago: Co-operative Publishing, 1906); Jack Greenberg, *Confessions of an Industrial Insurance Agent: A Narrative of Fact* (New York: Broadway, 1911).

66. The development of methods for managing canvassers and the evolution of sales arguments into elaborate sales scripts was an essential step toward modern selling. The sales arguments found in scripts were precursors to what Roland Marchand called the "parables of advertising"—that is, they were simple, repeatable narrative arguments that could be used to sell a variety of items. See Roland Marchand, *Advertising the American Dream: Making Way for Modernity, 1920–1940* (Berkeley: University of California Press, 1985), pp. 206–234.

3. Forging a National Marketplace

1. For general information on drummers, see Timothy B. Spears, *One Hundred Years on the Road* (New Haven, Conn.: Yale University Press, 1995), which was an invaluable source for this chapter; Spears, "'All Things to All Men': The Commercial Traveler and the Rise of Modern Salesmanship," *American Quarterly* 45, no. 4 (Dec. 1993), pp. 524–557; Susan Strasser, *Satisfaction Guaranteed: The Making of the American Mass Market* (New York: Pantheon, 1989); Stanley C. Hollander, "Nineteenth Century Anti-Drummer Legislation in the United States," *Business History Review* (Winter 1964), pp. 479–500; Alfred D. Chandler, Jr., *The Visible Hand: The Managerial Revolution in American Business* (Cambridge, Mass.: Belknap Press of Harvard University Press, 1977).

2. Chandler, *Visible Hand*, pp. 215–217.

3. Ibid., p. 216; Spears, *One Hundred Years on the Road*, p. 56.

4. Thomas J. Schlereth, *Victorian America: Transformations in Everyday Life, 1876–1915* (New York: HarperCollins, 1991), pp. 143–145.

5. Gerald Carson, "Holiday Time at the Old Country Store," in Samuel Rapport and Patricia Schartle, eds., *America Remembers: Our Best-Loved Customs and Traditions* (Garden City, N.Y.: Hanover House, 1956), p. 220.

6. Chandler, *Visible Hand*, pp. 215–217

7. Lewis S. Atherton, "Predecessors of the Commercial Drummer in the Old South," *Bulletin of the Business Historical Society* 21, no. 1 (Feb. 1947), p. 18.

8. Figures given in Hollander, "Nineteenth Century Anti-Drummer Legislation," p. 482.

9. Edward D. Briggs, *Fifty Years on the Road: The Autobiography of a Traveling Salesman* (Philadelphia: Lyon and Armor, 1911), p. 33.

10. Lee M. Friedman, "The Drummer in Early American Merchandise Distribution," *Bulletin of the Business Historical Society* (Apr. 1947), p. 43.

11. For the source of this information and a discussion of the changes in the marketplace, see Nancy Koehn, *Brand New: How Entrepreneurs Earned Consumers' Trust from Wedgwood to Dell* (Boston: Harvard Business School Press, 2001), pp. 4–7.

12. William Cronon, *Nature's Metropolis: Chicago and the Great West* (New York: Norton, 1991), p. 310.

13. Society of Commercial Travellers [of New York City], *The System of Commercial Travelling in Europe and the United States: Its History, Customs, and Laws* (New York: Riverside, 1869), p. 4.

14. A. M. Edwards, *Population: Comparative Occupational Statistics for the United States, 1870 to 1940* (Washington, D.C.: Government Printing Office, 1943); Nicole Woolsey Biggart, *Charismatic Capitalism: Direct Selling Organizations in America* (Chicago: University of Chicago Press, 1989), pp. 28–29.

15. Spears, *One Hundred Years on the Road*, p. 68.

16. The data are from ibid., p. 55.

17. Strasser, *Satisfaction Guaranteed*, p. 19; Glenn Porter and Harold C. Livesay, *Merchants and Manufacturers: Studies in the Changing Structure of Nineteenth-Century Marketing* (Baltimore, Md.: Johns Hopkins University Press, 1971), p. 3.

18. Glenn Porter, "Marketing," in *Encyclopedia of American Economic History*, p. 390.

19. Charles Bennett, *Scientific Salesmanship* (St. Louis: American Efficiency Bureau, 1933), p. 44.

20. Lee M. Friedman, "The Drummer in Early American Merchandise Distribution," *Bulletin of the Business Historical Society* (Apr. 1947), p. 43. Timothy Spears wrote: "Whereas *canvassing* means to seek, solicit, and finally to secure a pledge, *making* connotes the commercial conquest of a place and anticipates its new condition—sold." Spears, *One Hundred Years on the Road*, p. 82.

21. See Walter A. Friedman, "The Tactics of Traveling Salesmen: Using Geniality to Master the Marketplace," Harvard Business School Working Paper no. 99-016 (1998).

22. Chandler, *Visible Hand*, pp. 219–220.
23. Ibid., p. 221.
24. Ibid., p. 221–222.
25. Thomas Clark, *Pills, Petticoats and Ploughs: The Southern Country Store* (Indianapolis: Bobbs-Merrill, 1944), p. 113.
26. Margaret E. Hale, "The Nineteenth-Century American Trade Card," *Business History Review* (Winter 2000), pp. 683–688.
27. Clark noted in *Pills, Petticoats, and Ploughs*, pp. 111–112: "For merchants who were already in business, drummers served as advisers on such matters as credit, prices, rates of interest, stock, and lines of goods which would boost trade. A storekeeper nearly always had one or two dependable drummers who advised him on the amount of stock he should buy. They also helped him to arrange counter displays, special bargains, and gave him advice on the produce-buying end of the business. In short, the more reliable drummers were often as much economic advisers as salesmen."
28. On the relationship of drummers to their employers, see Susan Strasser, "'The Smile That Pays': The Culture of Traveling Salesmen, 1880–1920," in James Gilbert et al., eds., *The Mythmaking Frame of Mind: Social Imagination and American Culture* (Belmont, Calif.: Wadsworth, 1993).
29. Briggs, *Fifty Years on the Road*, pp. 16–17.
30. "'Uncle George' Olney," *New York Times*, Jan. 25, 1914, sec. 5, p. 8.
31. Ibid.
32. *Commercial Travelers Magazine* 16, no. 1 (Mar. 1910), p. 3.
33. Abraham Cahan, *The Rise of David Levinsky* (1917; New York: Modern Library Edition, 2001), p. 315.
34. Harold Barger, *Distribution's Place in the American Economy since 1869* (Princeton, N.J.: Princeton University Press, 1955), pp. 198–215.
35. *Confectioners' Journal* 1, no. 4 (Mar. 1875), p. 9.
36. Gerald Carson, *The Old Country Store* (New York: Oxford University Press, 1954), p. 179.
37. George Marshall, *O'er Rail and Cross Ties with Gripsack* (New York: G. W. Dillingham, 1892).
38. *Confectioners' Journal* 4, no. 45 (Oct. 1878), p. 9.
39. William H. Becker, "The Wholesalers of Hardware and Drugs, 1870–1900," Ph.D. diss., Johns Hopkins University, 1969, pp. 250–251.
40. See Clara Maude Arny, *Scissors and Yardstick; or, All About Dry Goods* (Hartford, Conn.: C. M. Brown and F. W. Jaqua, 1872).

41. Chandler, *Visible Hand*, p. 218.

42. For an excellent summary of Marshall Field's career and business, see Koehn, *Brand New*, pp. 91–130.

43. Robert W. Twyman, *History of Marshall Field and Company, 1852–1906* (Philadelphia: University of Pennsylvania, 1954), pp. 21–23, 29.

44. Ibid., p. 94.

45. Ibid.

46. Hollander, "Nineteenth Century Anti-Drummer Legislation," p. 496.

47. Ibid.; see also F. B. [Frederick Bartlett] Goddard, *The Art of Selling: With How to Read Character, Laws Governing Sales, etc.* (New York: Baker & Taylor, 1889), p. 93.

48. "Grievances of the Salesman," *New York Times*, Mar. 1, 1914, sec. 8, p. 5.

49. Hollander, "Nineteenth Century Anti-Drummer Legislation," p. 485. Wrote Hollander: "The episode in many ways was similar to the earlier attempt to curb the auctions and to the later attempts to restrain department stores, mail order houses, and chain stores."

50. Ibid., pp. 486, 495, 499.

51. Society of Commercial Travellers, *System of Commercial Travelling*, pp. 4–8.

52. *The Sample Case of the Order of the United Commercial Travelers* (Jan. 1902), inside cover. Accidents brought the following returns: loss of one eye, $650; loss of one foot, $1,000; loss of one hand, $1,250; loss of both feet, or hands, or eyes, $5,000; death, $6,300.

53. Ibid., pp. 15, 17.

54. Ibid., pp. 8–13.

55. Robert J. Schofield, *Drummer's Yarns and Funny Jokes* (New York: Excelsior, 1913), p. 10.

56. See Mark C. Carnes, *Secret Ritual and Manhood in Victorian America* (New Haven, Conn.: Yale University Press, 1989); and Mary Ann Clawson, *Constructing Brotherhood: Class, Gender, and Fraternalism* (Princeton, N.J.: Princeton University Press, 1989).

57. *Sample Case of the Order of the United Commercial Travelers* (Jan. 1902), pp. 15–16.

58. N. R. Streeter, comp., *Gems from an Old Drummer's Grip* (Groton, N.Y.: N. R. Streeter, 1889), preface.

59. Becker, "Wholesalers of Hardware and Drugs," p. 115.

60. Edward R. Kantowicz, *True Value: John Cotter, Seventy Years of Hardware* (Chicago: Regnery Books, 1986), p. 13.

61. Becker, "Wholesalers of Hardware and Drugs," pp. 114, 119.
62. Ibid., pp. 120–121.
63. Saunders Norvell, *Forty Years of Hardware* (New York: Hardware Age, 1924), p. 24.
64. Kantowicz, *True Value*, p. 11.
65. Norvell, *Forty Years of Hardware*, p. 50.
66. Ibid., p. 49.
67. Ibid., p. 61.
68. Ibid., p. 56.
69. Ibid., p. 59.
70. Kantowicz, *True Value*, p. 15.
71. Norvell, *Forty Years of Hardware*, p. 76.
72. Ibid., p. 57.
73. Malone Wheless, *By the Sweat of My Brow* (Richmond, Va.: Outlook, 1953), pp. 20, 35.
74. Ibid., p. 47.
75. Ibid., p. 75.
76. Norvell, *Forty Years of Hardware*, p. 68. Emphasis in the original.
77. Ibid., pp. 188–189.
78. Ibid., p. 190.
79. "The Great American Salesman," *Fortune* 21, no. 2 (Feb. 1940), p. 72.
80. Norvell, *Forty Years of Hardware*, pp. 191, 200.
81. Chandler, *Visible Hand*, p. 222.
82. L. C. Breyfogle, *The Commercial Traveler, Being a Hotel Guide and Gazetteer of the United States* (Lockport, N.Y.: United States Hotel Register, 1881); noted in Spears, *One Hundred Years on the Road*, p. 84.
83. Linus Pierpont Brockett, *The Commercial Traveller's Guide Book, Being a Complete Manual for the Use of Commercial Travellers and Sellers of Goods by Sample* (New York: H. Dayton, 1871), preface.
84. [Anon.], *Twenty Years on the Road; or, The Trials and Tribulations of a Commercial Traveler, by One of Them* (Philadelphia: Baker & Hayes, 1884); Streeter, *Gems from an Old Drummer's Grip;* Charles S. Plummer, *Leaves from a Drummer's Diary; or, Twenty-five Years on the Road* (Chicago: Belford, Clarke, 1889); and Marshall, *O'er Rail and Cross Ties with Gripsack.*
85. [Anon.], *How to Succeed on the Road as a Drummer* (Boston: Oxford Press Co., 1891), pp. 7–10.
86. Briggs, *Fifty Years on the Road*, pp. 17–19.
87. *Confectioners' Journal* 4, no. 45 (Oct. 1878), p. 24.

88. Clark, *Pills, Petticoats and Ploughs*, pp. 112–113.
89. "'Uncle George' Olney Started on the Road Six Years before the Civil War and Had Just Retired," *New York Times*, Jan. 25, 1914, sec. 5, p. 8.
90. [Anon.], *New Drummer's Yarns* (New York: Excelsior, 1913).
91. Ibid., pp. 56, 22, 44. The drummer's humor was described in fiction. Ring Lardner's short story "The Haircut" featured a traveling salesman who sold prepackaged food and paid more attention to "playin' jokes than makin' sales." One Saturday, the salesman told a gathering of his friends that he had lost his job. "'Gentlemen, I got an important announcement to make. I been fired from my job . . . I been sellin' canned goods and now I'm canned goods myself.'" Ring Lardner, *The Best Short Stories of Ring Lardner* (1915; New York: Scribner's, 1957), pp. 24–25.
92. Spears discusses this aspect of Maher in *One Hundred Years on the Road*, pp. 80–81. See also William H. Maher, *On the Road to Riches* (Toledo, Ohio: T. J. Brown, Eager, 1876).
93. Karen Halttunen, *Confidence Men and Painted Women: A Study of Middle-Class Culture in America, 1830–1870* (New Haven, Conn.: Yale University Press, 1982). See also Ann Fabian, *Card Sharps, Dream Books, and Bucket Shops: Gambling in Nineteenth Century America* (Ithaca, N.Y.: Cornell University Press, 1990), and a review of Fabian's book by John M. Findlay in *American Historical Review* 97, no. 1 (Feb. 1992), pp. 292–293.
94. Goddard, *Art of Selling*, p. 47.
95. *Detroit Free Press*, July 10, 1916, p. 2.
96. Theodore Dreiser, *Sister Carrie* (1900; New York: W. W. Norton, 1991), pp. 3–4. The best treatment of the drummer in fiction is in Spears, *One Hundred Years on the Road*.
97. Dreiser, *Sister Carrie*, pp. 3–4.
98. Barger, *Distribution's Place in the American Economy*, pp. 70–71.
99. Spears, *One Hundred Years on the Road*, p. 57.
100. Koehn, *Brand New*, pp. 4–9.
101. Norvell, *Forty Years of Hardware*, p. 383.
102. Chandler, *Visible Hand*, p. 231.
103. Richard Ohmann, *Selling Culture: Magazines, Markets, and Class at the Turn of the Century* (London: Verso, 1996), p. 67.

4. Fifty-Seven Varieties

1. Alfred Chandler wrote, "As the experience of all the new mass-produced machinery companies emphasizes, they could sell in volume only if they

created a massive, multiunit marketing organization." Alfred D. Chandler, Jr., *The Visible Hand: The Managerial Revolution in American Business* (Cambridge, Mass.: Belknap Press of Harvard University Press, 1977), p. 308.

2. Anon., *The Story of Selling: Yesterday, Today and Tomorrow* (New York: Crowell-Collier, 1946), p. 31.

3. Charles W. Hoyt, *Scientific Sales Management: A Practical Application of the Principles of Scientific Management to Selling* (New York: George B. Woolson, 1913).

4. Olivier Zunz, *Making America Corporate* (Chicago: University of Chicago Press, 1990), pp. 176–179.

5. H. J. Heinz Corporation, *The 57*, ca. 1905, p. 13.

6. Metropolitan Life Insurance Co., "History of the Agency Force," unpublished report, ca. 1940, p. 13. The Metropolitan Life Insurance Company Archives, New York.

7. Walter B. Weare, *Black Business in the New South: A Social History of the North Carolina Mutual Life Insurance Company* (Urbana: University of Illinois Press, 1973), p. 134.

8. Harold Barger, *Distribution's Place in the American Economy since 1869* (Princeton, N.J.: Princeton University Press, 1955), pp. 71–72. Barger wrote: "Neither the drug trade nor the grocery trade was seriously disturbed until after World War I."

9. William Elijah Castelow, *Only a Drummer: A Short History of the Commercial Travelling Salesman's Life* (Meriden, Conn.: W. E. Castelow, 1903), p. 17.

10. Twentieth Century Fund, *Does Distribution Cost Too Much? A Review of the Costs Involved in Current Marketing Methods and a Program for Improvement* (New York: Twentieth Century Fund, 1939), p. 394.

11. Andrew B. Jack, "The Channels of Distribution for an Innovation: The Sewing Machine Industry in America, 1860–1865," *Explorations in Entrepreneurial History* 9 (1957), p. 118.

12. Ibid., pp. 123–124.

13. Robert Bruce Davis, *Peacefully Working to Conquer the World: Singer Sewing Machines in Foreign Markets, 1854–1920* (New York: Arno Press, 1976), p. 58.

14. Jack, "Channels of Distribution," p. 123.

15. Lendol Caldor, *Financing the American Dream: A Cultural History of Consumer Credit* (Princeton, N.J.: Princeton University Press, 1999), pp. 163–165.

16. Pamela Walker Laird, *Advertising Progress: American Business and the Rise*

of Consumer Marketing (Baltimore, Md.: Johns Hopkins University Press, 1998), p. 36. Laird wrote that "Singer's early centralized control over marketing and distribution resulted in commercial success that derived more from his marketing prowess and innovation than from technological innovation, despite advertisements proclaiming technological progress."

17. Andrew C. Godley, "Pioneering Foreign Direct Investment in Britain," *Business History Review* 73 (Autumn 1999), pp. 414, 416–423.

18. Ibid., pp. 394–429.

19. Ibid., 417.

20. Davies, *Peacefully Working to Conquer the World,* p. 58.

21. Singer Manufacturing Company Records, box 110, folder 2, Wisconsin Historical Society, Madison.

22. Singer Manufacturing Company Records, box 109, folder 4.

23. Fred V. Carstensen, *American Enterprise in Foreign Markets: Studies of Singer and International Harvester in Imperial Russia* (Chapel Hill: University of North Carolina Press, 1984), pp. 17–21. Carstensen wrote: "A major legal obstacle hindered Singer's American expansion. Numerous state regulations sought to protect local wholesalers, retailers, and in-state manufacturers from 'foreign' (out-of-state) producers and direct marketing systems such as Singer's. Singer had agents intentionally seek arrest and conviction under these state laws in order to bring a constitutional challenge to the U.S. Supreme Court. In 1875, in a dramatic reversal of established judicial doctrine, the Court supported the company's argument that state harassment of 'foreign' corporations violated the commerce clause and overturned most discriminatory state laws. Later, in a second Singer-initiated case, the Court expanded judicial protection of national marketing organizations" (p. 20). See also Stuart Bruchey, *Enterprise: The Dynamic Economy of a Free People* (Cambridge, Mass.: Harvard University Press, 1990), p. 310.

24. Bruchey, *Enterprise,* p. 310.

25. Carstensen, *American Enterprise in Foreign Markets,* pp. 17–23.

26. Chandler, *Visible Hand,* p. 405.

27. *Canvassers' Manual of Instructions, with Hints and Suggestions Concerning the Art of Canvassing,* pp. 12–14, box 109, folder 5, Singer Manufacturing Company Records.

28. See U.S. Federal Trade Commission, *Report on Distribution Methods and Costs,* part 5: *Advertising as a Factor in Distribution* (Washington, D.C.: Government Printing Office, 1944), following p. 10.

29. Chandler, *Visible Hand*, p. 289.
30. Ibid., pp. 249–250.
31. Anon., *Story of Selling*, p. 51.
32. Susan Strasser, *Satisfaction Guaranteed: The Making of the American Mass Market* (New York: Pantheon, 1989), p. 19. Strasser does a particularly good job of showing the evolution of Procter and Gamble's strategy from its first advertisement for Ivory in 1881 to its elaborate campaign to sell Crisco in 1912.
33. On Heinz's sales and branding strategy, see Nancy F. Koehn, "Henry Heinz and Brand Creation in the Late Nineteenth-Century: Making Markets for Processed Food," *Business History Review* 73 (Winter 1999), pp. 349–393, and Koehn, *Brand New: How Entrepreneurs Earned Consumers' Trust from Wedgwood to Dell* (Boston: Harvard Business School Press, 2001), pp. 43–90.
34. Robert C. Alberts, *The Good Provider: H. J. Heinz and His 57 Varieties* (Boston: Houghton Mifflin, 1973), p. 62.
35. Koehn, "Henry Heinz and Brand Creation in the Late Nineteenth-Century," p. 385.
36. Chandler, *Visible Hand*, pp. 505, 510.
37. Koehn, *Brand New*, pp. 73–75.
38. See William Weisberger, "Henry John Heinz," *American National Biography* (New York: Oxford University Press, 1999), vol. 10, pp. 520–521.
39. H. J. Heinz Company, *The 57* 8, no. 1 (Pittsburgh, 1904), pp. 1–7. See also Koehn, *Brand New*.
40. H. J. Heinz Company, *Pickles*, May 2, 1898, n.p.
41. Quoted in Koehn, "Henry Heinz and Brand Creation in the Late Nineteenth-Century," p. 385.
42. H. J. Heinz Company, *Pickles*, Mar. 1, 1898, p. 1.
43. H. J. Heinz Company, *Pickles*, June 2, 1898, n.p.
44. H. J. Heinz Company, *The 57* 8, no. 1, (Pittsburgh, 1904), pp. 1–7.
45. See Richard Tedlow, *New and Improved: The Story of Mass Marketing in America* (New York: Basic Books, 1990), pp. 22–112. For the sales figures, see pp. 28–29.
46. Ibid.
47. Ibid., p. 31.
48. Patrick G. Porter, "Origins of the American Tobacco Company," *Business History Review* 43 (Spring 1969), pp. 59–76.
49. Chandler, *Visible Hand*, p. 289.

50. Ibid., p. 313. See Charles Morrow Wilson, *Empire in Green and Gold: The Story of the American Banana Trade* (New York: H. Holt, 1947), pp. 99, 168–173.

51. See figures for branded cereals in Federal Trade Commission, *Report of the Federal Trade Commission on Distribution Methods and Costs*, part 5: *Advertising as a Factor in Distribution* (Washington, D.C.: Government Printing Office, 1944), between pp. 10 and 11.

52. Glenn Porter and Harold C. Livesay, *Merchants and Manufacturers: Studies in the Changing Structure of Nineteenth-Century Marketing* (Baltimore, Md.: Johns Hopkins University Press, 1971), pp. 141–142.

53. Harold C. Passer, *The Electrical Manufacturers, 1875–1900: A Study in Competition, Entrepreneurship, Technical Change, and Economic Growth* (Cambridge, Mass.: Harvard University Press, 1953), pp. 112–114.

54. Ibid. See also Thomas Parke Hughes, *Networks of Power: Electrification in Western Society, 1880–1930* (Baltimore, Md.: Johns Hopkins University Press, 1983); Paul Israel, *Edison: A Life of Invention* (New York: John Wiley, 1998).

55. Chandler, *Visible Hand*, p. 310.

56. It was originally the American Arithmometer Company in St. Louis, Missouri. In 1904, it moved to Detroit and the following year became the Burroughs Adding Machine Company.

57. See Stephen B. Johnson, "William Seward Burroughs," *American National Biography*, vol. 4, pp. 52–53.

58. *Sales Bulletin* [*of the Sales Department of the Burroughs Adding Machine Company*], Feb. 6, 1908, vol. 325, Collection: "Burroughs/Burroughs and Sales Bulletins (loose issues), 1907–1952," box 10, folder 1, Burroughs Corporation Records, Charles Babbage Institute, University of Minnesota, Minneapolis.

59. Burroughs Convention Minutes, Sales Convention of January 1905, p. 91, Burroughs Corporation Records.

60. *Sales Bulletin* [*of the Sales Department of the Burroughs Adding Machine Company*], Feb. 6, 1908.

61. Burroughs Convention Minutes, Sales Convention of 1907, p. 13, Burroughs Corporation Records.

62. Burroughs Convention Minutes, Sales Convention of July 1905, p. 135.

63. Burroughs Convention Minutes, Sales Convention of 1907, p. 182.

64. Burroughs Convention Minutes, Sales Convention of January 1905, pp. 132–133.

65. Susan Strasser, "Consumption," in Glenn Porter, ed., *Encyclopedia of Amer-*

ican Economic History: Studies of the Principal Movements and Ideas (New York: Scribner's, 1980), pp. 1022–1023.

66. Dartnell Corporation, *Special Report: Sales Method Investigation; The Experience of 162 Concerns in Setting Sales Tasks* (Chicago: Dartnell Corp., 1929), p. 6.

67. Dartnell Corporation, *Special Report: Sales Method Investigation; Plans for Building Up a Spirit of Loyalty in a Sales Organization, Report 172* (Chicago: Dartnell Corp., 1924), p. 5.

68. Tim Thrift, "A Sales Contest That Was Staged as a War Game," *Printers' Ink* (October 7, 1915), pp. 17–18.

69. "Three Problems of Sales Policy," *Printers' Ink Monthly* (Dec. 1921), p. 15.

70. William James, *Varieties of Religious Experience* (1902; New York: Macmillan, 1961), pp. 78–114.

71. As David Montgomery noted in his study of the application of scientific management to the production of steel, managers employed methods of scientific management to gain control over the process of production—to take this power away from skilled artisans and thereby dictate the pace of work. In the field of selling, salesmen experienced increased supervision and standardization of the sales process under management—especially in comparison with the commercial travelers for independent wholesalers, who were often on the road for long periods and received little managerial training. See David Montgomery, *The Fall of the House of Labor: The Workplace, the State, and American Labor Activism, 1865–1925* (New York: Cambridge University Press, 1987).

72. Dartnell Corporation, *Special Report, Sales Method Investigation; Plans for Building Up a Spirit of Loyalty in a Sales Organization*, p. 8.

73. Ibid., p. 5.

74. J. Owen Stalson, *Marketing Life Insurance: Its History in America* (Cambridge, Mass.: Harvard University Press, 1942), p. 584.

5. The Pyramid Plan

1. Thomas Wolfe, *You Can't Go Home Again* (New York: Harper & Brothers, 1940).

2. The standard biography of Patterson is Samuel Crowther, *John H. Patterson: Pioneer in Industrial Welfare* (New York: Garden City Publishing, 1926); see also Roy W. Johnson and Russell W. Lynch, *The Sales Strategy of John H. Patterson* (Chicago: Dartnell Corp., 1932). Charlotte Reeve Conover, *Builders in New Fields* (New York: G. P. Putman's Sons, 1939),

was a joint biography of Robert Patterson and John Henry Patterson, described as a "study in heredity" (p. vii); see also Judith Sealander, *Grand Plans: Business Progressivism and Social Change in Ohio's Miami Valley, 1890–1929* (Lexington: University Press of Kentucky, 1988). Sealander wrote: "The NCR pioneered systematic sales promotion and invented the guaranteed territory, the sales convention, memorized sales pitches, sales manuals, and mandatory training schools" (p. 20).

3. On mass production, see David A Hounshell, *From the American System to Mass Production, 1800–1932: The Development of Manufacturing Technology in the United States* (Baltimore, Md.: Johns Hopkins University Press, 1984). There are numerous studies of Frederick W. Taylor and the scientific management movement, including Daniel Nelson, *Frederick W. Taylor and the Rise of Scientific Management* (Madison: University of Wisconsin, 1980), and Robert Kanigel, *The One Best Way: Frederick Winslow Taylor and the Enigma of Efficiency* (New York: Viking, 1997).

4. See Richard S. Tedlow's discussion of Patterson and Thomas J. Watson in *Giants of Enterprise: Seven Business Innovators and the Empires They Built* (New York: HarperCollins, 2001), pp. 187–246.

5. "The Great American Salesman," *Fortune* 21, no. 2 (Feb. 1940), p. 170.

6. Sinclair Lewis, *Babbitt* (1922; New York: Penguin Books, 1996), p. 46.

7. Alfred D. Chandler, Jr., *The Visible Hand: The Managerial Revolution in American Business* (Cambridge, Mass.: Belknap Press of Harvard University Press, 1977), pp. 288–308, 403–404.

8. *NCR*, July 1, 1902, p. 409.

9. Richard L. Crandall and Sam Robins, *The Incorruptible Cashier: The Formation of an Industry, 1876–1890*, vol. 1 (Vestal, N.Y.: Vestal Press, 1988), pp. 27–29; Crowther, *Patterson*, p. 65. In 1889 Patterson would incorporate the company in the State of New Jersey. In 1906, the company became a corporation of Ohio. See also *Transcript of Record, Patterson et al. v. United States, Circuit Court of Appeals, Sixth Circuit, No. 2571, March 13, 1915*, vol. 1, p. 5 (hereafter *Patterson et al. v. United States*). The transcript is housed at the National Archives and Record Administration, Great Lakes Region, Chicago.

10. Crowther wrote, "Then a salesman on commission was looked upon purely as a gamble. Selling on commission was not entirely respectable because only canvassers and life-insurance agents worked on commission, and neither class was particularly responsible." Crowther, *Patterson*, p. 88. See also Johnson and Lynch: "The straight commission, in those days was the sign of lack of confidence in the goods or in the salesman. It was the

badge of the book agent, the lightning rod artist, the insurance solicitor—
the confraternity of door-bell pullers more or less tainted with the odor
of disrespectability. Or else it indicated the neophyte still on probation."
Johnson and Lynch, *Sales Strategy,* p. 58.

11. Crowther, *Patterson,* p. 83. See also "What They Said and Did at the NCR
Convention," *Sales Management* (March 1919), pp. 100–101. For conversion rates, see John J. McCusker, *How Much Is That in Real Money? A Historical Price Index for Use as a Deflator of Money Values in the United States*
(Worcester, Mass.: American Antiquarian Society, 1992).

12. See Crowther, *Patterson,* p. 21.

13. *Patterson et al. v. the United States,* vol. 1, p. 50. There is little information
about commission rates of salesmen, because they made contracts with
agents rather than the company and were sometimes paid a salary. In the
Dartnell Company's *Special Report: Sales Method Investigation. Subject:
Present Practice in Arranging Salesmen's Earnings* (Chicago: Dartnell Corp.,
1929), C. E. Steffey, general sales manager of NCR, reported on p. 6, "New
salesmen are generally employed first on a straight salary basis. Later, as
they learn something about our business and commence to make sales, the
sales agents give them the opportunity to change their selling basis if they
so desire. When a man finally becomes a real salesman, he is usually operated on a straight commission basis. In cities, the salesmen on a commission basis receive from one-half to four-sevenths of the sales agent's commission. The provincial salesmen generally receive from four-sevenths to
five-sevenths of the sales agent's commission, depending on the territory
in which the salesman operates, and the expense of operation."

14. Other agencies included Washington; Denver; Minneapolis; Albany;
Saginaw, Michigan; Louisville, Kentucky; Milwaukee; Cincinnati; St Louis;
Council Bluffs, Iowa; Atlanta; Newark, New Jersey; Grand Rapids, Michigan; Pittsburgh; Dallas; Buffalo; Kansas City; Bloomington, Illinois; Chat-
tanooga, Tennessee; Richmond, Virginia; Kalamazoo, Michigan; New Orleans; York, Pennsylvania; Trenton; Helena, Montana; and Birmingham,
Alabama. See *NCR,* May 1888. A few early copies of the *NCR* are included
in the legal papers of the U.S. Court of Appeals (1st Circuit) in Baker Library, Harvard University Graduate School of Business, Boston. In this
collection, see *National Cash Register Co. v. Boston Cash Register Co., 1886–
1896* [hereafter *NCR v. Boston*]. Most issues of the *NCR* from the 1890s
and early 1900s can be found at the New York Public Library.

15. *NCR,* Jan. 1, 1897, p. 24. See also *NCR,* June 15, 1894, p. 149. Patterson had
a personal connection to the New England area. He had gone to college

in New Hampshire, and when he borrowed money for the company in the late nineteenth century, it was first from a Providence, Rhode Island, financier, and then from a Bostonian. Also, he married a woman from Massachusetts. In 1888, at age forty-four, he married Katherine Dudley Beck of Brookline. The two had only been married six years when she died of typhoid fever in June 1894. They had two children, Frederick Beck Patterson, b. 1892, and Dorothy Forster Patterson, b. 1893. The children were raised largely by Patterson's sister, Mrs. Joseph Crane.

16. Fred V. Carstensen, *American Enterprise in Foreign Markets: Studies of Singer and International Harvester in Imperial Russia* (Chapel Hill: University of North Carolina Press, 1984), p. 4; Mira Wilkins, *The Emergence of Multinational Enterprise: American Business Abroad from the Colonial Era to 1914* (Cambridge, Mass.: Harvard University Press, 1970), p. 37. For a general history of Singer, see Robert Bruce Davies, *Peacefully Working to Conquer the World: Singer Sewing Machines in Foreign Markets, 1854–1920* (New York: Arno Press, 1976), preface, p. 18.

17. Wilkins, *Emergence of Multinational Enterprise*, pp. 45–46. See also *NCR*, Mar. 16, 1891; and Crowther, *Patterson*, p. 265.

18. "Foreign," *NCR*, Jan. 1, 1894, pp. 8–10.

19. Lower levels of sales had also been recorded in Holland, Norway, France, Mexico, Italy, and Cuba. See *NCR*, Jan. 1, 1897, p. 24.

20. *NCR*, Jan. 1, 1894, p. 17.

21. Crowther, *Patterson*, p. 91; Johnson and Lynch, *Sales Strategy*, p. 85.

22. *NCR*, June 20, 1888, front page. Patterson explained, "During the past year we have employed, at our own expense, inspectors whose business it has been to ascertain and report to us, in writing, whether or not the Registers in use have been properly operated by the clerks. Type-written copies of these reports have been mailed to the proprietor, showing the time the inspector entered the place of business, the time he left, and giving a description, as nearly as possible, of the transactions made during his presence, and whether all sales made were registered by the clerks." See *NCR*, Nov. 15, 1889, p. 1.

23. "Removing Temptation—E. B. Wilson," *NCR*, Nov. 15, 1900, p. 505.

24. *Hustler* 9, no. 75 (1893); *NCR v. Boston*, folder 3.

25. Crowther, *Patterson*, p. 106.

26. Quoted in NCR Corp., *Celebrating the Future* (Dayton, Ohio: NCR, 1984), vol. 1, p. 7.

27. Quoted in Johnson and Lynch, *Sales Strategy*, p. 178.

28. Ibid., p. 175.
29. *NCR*, Feb. 1, 1899, p. 72. The term "P. P." was used throughout NCR's early history to designate "probable purchaser" and was changed by the company in 1897 to designate "possible purchaser" for the "sake of accuracy." *NCR*, June 15, 1897, p. 260.
30. See "Work of the Convention," *NCR*, July 15, 1895, p. 436.
31. *NCR*, Nov. 1, 1891, pp. 408–409.
32. *NCR*, Jan. 1, 1894, p. 10.
33. E. D. Gibbs, "How NCR Gets 100 Percent Efficiency Out of Its Men," *Printers' Ink* 76, no. 4, July 27, 1911, p. 34.
34. *Salesmanship: The Journal of the World's Salesmanship Congress* (July 1916), p. 13.
35. Sales statistics were frequently printed in the *NCR*. In one instance, the magazine printed a list of every U.S. town with a population over 1,000 that had not been visited by salesmen in the previous three months. *NCR*, May 15, 1892, p. 582.
36. *Patterson et al. v. the United States*, vol 1., p. 50.
37. Crowther, *Patterson*, p. 117.
38. For quota numbers, see *NCR*, Feb. 15, 1899, pp. 95–99. See also Crowther, *Patterson*, p. 118, and Dartnell, *Sales Method Investigation*, for general information about compensation.
39. *NCR*, May 15, 1892, p. 577.
40. Dartnell, *Sales Method Investigation*. "Each one of the National Cash Register Agency Offices develops its own type of score board, but the general method of arriving at monthly quota is outlined by the general sales manager, C. E. Steffey, at the beginning of each year" (p. 10).
41. See Crowther, *Patterson*, p. 101.
42. *NCR*, May 15, 1893, p. 577. See Crowther, *Patterson*, p. 186, for information on NCR finances. Eventually Patterson borrowed substantial sums to finance expansion during the Depression. From 1895 to 1899, Patterson borrowed approximately $750,000 from Joseph and John Banigan of Providence, Rhode Island. He then turned to a Boston financier, A. C. Ratshesky, who helped him repay the Banigan loans through a stock issue; NCR became a New Jersey–chartered concern. In 1906 the company incorporated under the laws of Ohio at a capitalization of $10 million, with almost all of the stock held by Patterson and his brother, Frank. See also Isaac F. Marcosson, *Colonel Deeds: Industrial Builder* (New York: Dodd, Mead, 1947), p. 93.

43. See Nicole Woolsey Biggart, *Charismatic Capitalism: Direct Selling Organizations in America* (Chicago: University of Chicago Press, 1989), esp. pp. 130–135. See also Alfred C. Fuller, *A Foot in the Door: The Life Appraisal of the Original Fuller Brush Man* (New York: McGraw-Hill, 1960); and Mary Kay Ash, *Mary Kay* (New York: Harper & Row, 1981).

44. Crowther, *Patterson*, pp. 204–205.

45. E. D. Gibbs, "NCR Rates Factory Visits High in Advertising Value," *Printers' Ink* 77, no. 3, Oct. 19, 1911, pp. 17–20.

46. For example, much of the Feb. 1, 1902, issue of *NCR* was devoted to diet and health.

47. *NCR*, Aug.–Sept. 1905, p. 219.

48. Stanley Allyn, *My Half Century with NCR* (New York: McGraw-Hill, 1967), p. 20.

49. When Stanley Allyn went to work for NCR in 1913, he recalled his father saying that Patterson was a "lunatic." Allyn, *My Half Century*, p. 1.

50. See Biggart, *Charismatic Capitalism*. Biggart, a sociologist, was interested in "how organizations come to be and why they take the forms they do" (p. ix). By examining a single industry, she hoped to link the study of an organization to the social environment, as part of a new "economic sociology." Introducing the work of Weber, Biggart contends that "charisma" acted as a means of social control. Direct sales organizations were charismatic forms of organizations.

51. See ibid., pp. 152, 133, 134, 136, 141.

52. Allyn, *My Half Century*, p. 48.

53. *Patterson et al. v. the United States*, testimony of Hugh Chalmers, vol. 1, p. 491.

54. Quoted in Martin Gardner, *In the Name of Science* (New York: Putnam, 1952), pp. 178–179. Emphasis in the original.

55. "The Science of Selling," *NCR*, August 1, 1903, p. 529.

56. Crowther, *Patterson*, p. 104; see also Johnson and Lynch, *Sales Strategy*, p. 140. This was the first agents convention, though it was not designated as such. Patterson put five agents up in style at the Phillips Hotel and had a coach and four horses take them out to the Soldiers' Home.

57. *NCR*, Nov. 1, 1891, p. 408.

58. *Patterson et al. v. the United States*, vol. 1, p. 738.

59. *NCR News* 8, no. 4 (Apr. 1922), p. 3.

60. American Management Association, *Field Sales Organization: Sale's Execu-*

tive Series, no. 14 (New York: American Management Association, 1925), p. 12. Emphasis in the original.

61. Marcosson, *Colonel Deeds*, pp. 85–86.

62. "Don't Be Satisfied," *NCR*, May 1, 1899, p. 224. Patterson, in an interview with Crowther, said: "I am always dissatisfied; I preach dissatisfaction." Crowther, *Patterson*, p. 173.

63. NCR, *NCR Mottoes* (Dayton, Ohio: NCR, 1906).

64. *Patterson et al. v. the United States*, testimony of W. S. Courtright, p. 593.

65. Martin J. Sklar, *The Corporate Reconstruction of American Capitalism, 1890–1916: The Market, The Law, and Politics* (New York: Cambridge University Press, 1988).

66. Chandler, *Visible Hand*, pp. 332–333.

67. Crowther, *Patterson*, p. 150.

68. Samuel Benner, *Benner's Prophecies; or, Future Ups and Downs in Prices* (Cincinnati: Samuel Benner, 1884), p. 50. I am especially indebted to Peter Eisenstadt for introducing me to the writings of Benner.

69. E. D. Gibbs, "How NCR Gets 100 Per Cent Efficiency Out of Its Men, Part I" *Printers' Ink* 75, no. 13, June 29, 1911, p. 4; *NCR*, June 1, 1893, p. 898.

70. *NCR*, June 1, 1893, p. 898.

71. "Note from Mr. J. H. Patterson," in ibid., p. 896.

72. *NCR*, July 15, 1893, p. 922. See also "The Work of 1893 and the Prospects for 1894," *NCR*, Aug. 1, 1893, p. 2.

73. *NCR*, Oct. 1, 1900, cover.

74. Gibbs, "How NCR Gets 100 Per Cent Efficiency," pp. 1–7; Johnson and Lynch, *Sales Strategy*, p. 240.

75. *NCR*, Jan. 1, 1897, p. 16.

76. *NCR*, May 1, 1901, pp. 226–230.

77. *Patterson et al. v. the United States*, vol. 1, p. 748.

78. T. C. Henry, *Tricks of the Cash Register Trust* (Winchester, Ky.: Winchester Sun, 1913), pp. 8–9.

79. As the historian Judith Sealander has noted, "The all-male NCR sales force competed not for money prizes but for new dining tables, silver services, or china." Sealander, *Grand Plans*, p. 37.

80. Crowther, *Patterson*, pp. 355–358.

81. Conover, *Builders in New Fields*, p. 188.

82. John H. Patterson, "Wives: Assistant Salesmen," *System: The Magazine of Business* 34 (July 1918), p. 34.

83. Dartnell Corporation, *Survey of Sales Management Practices* (Chicago: Dartnell Corp., 1921), section 6, p. 12.

84. Dartnell Corporation, *Dartnell Company Special Report: Enlisting Cooperation of Salesmen's Wives and Families*, no. 280 (Chicago: Dartnell Corp., 1928), p. 11.

85. Dartnell Corporation, *Survey of Sales Management Practices*, section 6, p. 11.

86. "Three Problems of Sales Policy," *Printers' Ink Monthly* (Dec. 1921), p. 15.

87. Gibbs, "How NCR Gets 100 Per Cent Efficiency," pp. 17–20.

88. *Patterson et al. v. the United States*, vol. 1, pp. 737–738.

89. "What They Said and Did at the NCR Convention," *Sales Management* (Mar. 1919), p. 100.

90. *NCR*, Apr. 1, 1903, pp. 309–310.

91. See *NCR*, Jan. 1, 1901, pp. 6–7; *Patterson et al. v. the United States*, vol. 1, p. 122.

92. "A Parting Word," *NCR*, June 15, 1897, p. 1.

93. *NCR*, Jan. 1, 1899, p. 14.

94. *NCR*, Jan. 1, 1903, pp. 295, 311.

95. *NCR*, Jan. 1, 1897, p. 24. See also *World NCR*, July 1906, p. 5, available in Loeb Library, Harvard University; Wilkins, *Emergence of Multinational Enterprise*, p. 296, n. 12.

96. Crowther, *Patterson*, p. 268.

97. *British NCR* 1, no. 12 (Dec. 1899), p. 283. Available at the New York Public Library.

98. *NCR*, Sept. 1, 1904, p. 236.

99. *British NCR*, Mar. 1900, p. 30.

100. Ibid., pp. 30–37.

101. NCR Corp., *Celebrating the Future*, vol. 1, p. 29.

102. J. W. Campion, "Selling National Cash Registers in the Sandwich Islands," *NCR*, Apr. 1, 1901, p. 174.

103. *NCR*, Mar.–Apr. 1907, p. 17.

104. *NCR*, June 20, 1888, p. 2.

105. Ibid.

106. *Patterson et al. v. the United States*, vol. 2, pp. 9–10.

107. *NCR* described the expenses of one trip by National men to "knock out" competitors: "Crane & Corwin's expenses during their two month's trip on the coast amounted in round numbers to $250 per day. This is what it costs to hold a monopoly, hence, make hay while the sun shines and rush

in all the orders possible. This amount includes travelling expenses, salaries, lawyers and detectives' expenses and the loss on our machines in making exchanges. Add to this our expenses in knocking out and fighting Bensinger in other sections of the country and we have a total of over $500 per day." *NCR*, May 22, 1890, p. 2.

108. *NCR*, May 15, 1892, pp. 575–576.

109. *NCR*, Nov. 1, 1891, p. 415. It would later be named the "Competition Department."

110. One agent, J. A. Sundwall, recalled receiving around 1900 "$50 a week and $10 a day expenses money for the knockout business." See *Patterson et al. v. the United States*, vol 1, p. 296.

111. Ibid., p. 279.

112. *Patterson et al. v. the United States*, prosecutor's brief, p. 6.

113. *Patterson et al. v. the United States*, vol. 1, pp. 175–176.

114. *NCR v. Boston*, folder 11, letter of Nov. 26, 1892.

115. Salesman's Papers, 1910–1985, box 1, 27.I.5.D, folder: Dodge, F. H. (Director of Sales). Burroughs Corporation Records, Charles Babbage Institute, University of Minnesota, Minneapolis.

116. See *Patterson et al. v. the United States*, vol. 2. The buyouts were as follows. In 1893: The Kruse Cash Register Co. (for $23,500), and the Lamson Cash Register Co. ($325,000). In 1900: the Boston Cash Indicator and Recorder Co. ($30,000), the Osborn Cash Register Co. ($90,000). In 1902: the Toledo Cash Register Co. ($75,000), Henry Theobald Agency ($40,000), Luke Cooney Agency ($10,000). In 1903: the Ideal Cash Register Co. ($12,000). In 1904: the Brainin Cash Register Exchange ($30,000), Metropolitan Cash Register Co. ($8,000), Sun-Simplex Cash Register Co. ($4,855), the Globe and Century Cash Register Co. ($25,000). In 1905: Isaac Freeman Agency ($15,000), The Foss Novelty Co. ($8,000), the Chicago Cash Register Co. ($8,000), and the Weiler Cash Register Co. ($9,000). In 1906: the Southern Cash Register Co. ($12,364), A. J. Thomas Cash Register ($17,122), and the Union Cash Register Co. ($80,000).

117. *Patterson et al. v. the United States*, p. 3. Lee Counselman, head of the competition department from 1902 to 1905, estimated the "percentage of business in cash registers . . . carried on by the National Company" at 95 percent. "We knew how many cash registers were made by the National Company that were in use, and we knew approximately how many cash registers made by other companies were in use . . . as the salesmen . . . reported all competing machines." *Patterson et al. v. the United States*, p. 415.

118. *The United States v. Patterson et al.*, no 1, 215, Circuit Court, D. Mass. (1893), 55 *Federal Reporter*, pp. 605–607. The charges included many that pointed at the sales force: threatening, harassing, and intimidating competitors; inducing agents to leave competitors; employing spies to obtain information; inducing purchasers to break their contracts with competitors; and other actions that indicated an organized conspiracy.

119. Hans B. Thorelli, *The Federal Antitrust Policy: Origination of an American Tradition* (Baltimore, Md.: Johns Hopkins University Press, 1955), pp. 371, 594. NCR informed its agents through a house organ that a deal "has just been consummated in Boston, a consolidation of the leading cash register companies of the country, by which the bitter warfare and expensive litigation, which has heretofore existed between them, was brought to an end." The cash-register offices of the two companies would be consolidated, and the manufacture of the machines would be carried on exclusively in Dayton. See *Hustler* 9, no. 75 (1893), included in *NCR v. Boston*, folder 3.

120. See Thorelli, *Federal Antitrust Policy*, pp. 371, 594; and Eliot Jones, *The Trust Problem in the United States* (New York: Macmillan, 1921), pp. 477–479.

121. See *Brief for the Plaintiffs in Error, John H. Patterson et al., Plaintiffs in Error, v. United States, Defendant in Error*, U.S. Circuit Court of Appeals, Sixth Circuit, no. 2571, 2; see also *Federal Anti-Trust Decisions*, vol. 5, 1912–1914, 110. For the Dayton flood, see Charlotte Reeve Conover, *The Story of Dayton* (Dayton, Ohio: Greater Dayton Association, 1917), pp. 199–200.

122. Sealander, *Grand Plans*, p. 35.

123. Allyn, *My Half Century*, p. 43.

124. Interview with Senator William Benton, pp. 70–71, Oral History Research Center, Columbia University, New York.

125. Stanley Allyn noted, "He liked to fire his best men, especially if they began to crowd him at the top." Allyn, *My Half Century*, p. 15.

126. Ibid., p. 42.

127. Ibid., pp. 46, 54.

128. Historian Roland Marchand wrote of Patterson's corporate welfare program, "While no one described the NCR as soulless, still its welfare policies were too entangled with Patterson's imperious style and too suggestive of unbusinesslike indulgence in personal whims to offer a persuasive formula for the creation of a corporate soul." Roland Marchand, *Creating*

the Corporate Soul: The Rise of Public Relations and Corporate Imagery in American Big Business (Berkeley: University of California Press, 1998), p. 21.

129. All from *Printers' Ink:* "How N.C.R. Gets 100 Per Cent Efficiency Out of its Men: Part I," vol. 75, no. 13, June 29, 1911, p. 3; "Part II," vol. 76, no. 1, July 6, 1911, p. 3; "Part III," vol. 76, no. 2, July 13, 1911, p. 17; "Part IV," vol. 76, no. 4, July 27, 1911; "The National Cash Register Advertising Policy," vol. 76, no. 11, Sept. 11, 1911, p. 3; "The N.C.R. Advertising Methods," vol. 76, no. 13, Sept. 28, 1911, p. 29; "How N.C.R. Worked Out Its Window Displays," vol. 77, no. 2, Oct. 12, 1911, p. 26; "N.C.R. Rates Factory Visits High in Advertising Value," vol. 77, no. 3, Oct. 19, 1911, p. 16.

130. For laudatory accounts of Patterson's career, see Frank Crane, *Business and Kingdom Come* (Chicago: Forbes, 1912); Crowther, *Patterson;* and Lynch and Johnson, *Sales Strategy.*

131. Explaining the function of a Burroughs salesman in a trade magazine, G. A. Nichols wrote, "[He] is, first of all, an analyst. Whether he is undertaking to sell a bank, a public utility, a manufacturing concern, a mercantile enterprise or whatnot, his first task is to study in detail the customer's accounting situation. G. A. Nichols, "Hiring, Training and Directing 1,500 Salesmen: How Burroughs Increases Efficiency and Adds to Volume through New Centralized Control Plan," *Printers' Ink Monthly,* July 1923, p. 23.

132. For information on Burroughs, see the Burroughs Papers, esp. Ray Abele, *The Burroughs Story* (n.p., 1975).

133. Crandall and Robins, *Incorruptible Cashier,* p. 46.

134. E. St. Elmo Lewis, "The Sales Manual," *Salesmanship: The Journal of the World's Salesmanship Congress* (July 1916), p. 333.

135. Explained in Charles Bennett, *Scientific Salesmanship* (St. Louis: American Efficiency Bureau, 1933), p. 61.

136. E. K. Strong, *The Psychology of Selling and Advertising* (New York: McGraw-Hill, 1925), p. 25. See also E. St. Elmo Lewis, *Creative Salesmanship* (Chatam, N.Y.: Caxton, 1911).

6. Salesology

1. Richard S. Tedlow, *New and Improved: The Story of Mass Marketing in America* (New York: Basic Books, 1990), pp. 55–62.

2. See Robert D. Cuff, "Edwin F. Gay, Arch W. Shaw, and the Uses of History

in Graduate Education for Managers," *Journal of Management History* 2, no. 3 (1996), pp. 9–25.

3. See Geoff Jones, "Firms, Nations, and Globalization: Past, Present, and Future," Business History Seminar, Harvard Business School, Dec. 9, 2002.

4. On the merger movement, see Naomi R. Lamoreaux, *Great Merger Movement in American Business, 1895–1904* (New York: Cambridge University Press, 1985).

5. Thomas K. McCraw, "American Capitalism," in McCraw, ed., *Creating Modern Capitalism: How Entrepreneurs, Companies, and Countries Triumphed in Three Industrial Revolutions* (Cambridge, Mass.: Harvard University Press, 1997), pp. 322–323.

6. See Testimony of Haley Fiske in New York State Legislature (Joint Committee on Investigation of Life Insurance), *Testimony Taken before the Joint Committee of the Senate and Assembly of the State of New York to Investigate and Examine into the Business and Affairs of Life Insurance Companies Doing Business in the State of New York* (Albany, N.Y.: Bradnow, 1906), p. 3851. At the 1905 Armstrong investigations of the insurance industry, chief prosecutor Charles Evans Hughes asked Haley Fiske, president of the Metropolitan Life Insurance Company, about the social need of a product that required high-pressure selling. Fiske replied, "Many a man knows he needs something, but he won't get it unless he is asked . . . If a man wants fire insurance he goes after it, and he knows he wants it. Whereas life insurance he does not—why it is I do not know; I do not see any reason on earth for refusing the working classes the same freedom of contract that is afforded the rich people, and the same facilities for getting insurance." In Jack Greenberg's *Confessions of an Industrial Insurance Agent: A Narrative of Fact* (New York: Broadway, 1911), p. 25, the author recalled that he had "taken away nickels and dimes earned by rheumatic women over the wash tub; nickels that should have bought bread or coal."

7. A natural disaster proved to be Patterson's ally in winning reprieve. While Patterson had an appeal pending, Dayton suffered a terrible flood. NCR financed relief work, and opened its facilities to help the city. Leaders of Dayton, where NCR was a major employer, pressured the federal government to drop the case, resulting in a bargained consent decree and lenient settlement. See Stanley Allyn, *My Half Century with N.C.R* (New York: McGraw-Hill, 1967).

8. Hugh G. J. Aitken, *Scientific Management in Action: Taylorism at Water-*

town Arsenal, 1908–1915 (1960; Princeton, N.J.: Princeton University Press, 1985), pp. 22–24.

9. Amasa Walker, "Scientific Management Applied to Commercial Enterprises," *Journal of Political Economy* 21, no. 5 (1913), p. 388. See also Irving Ross Allen, *Personal Efficiency, Applied Salesmanship, and Sales Administration* (Chicago: La Salle Extension University, 1915); Arthur Dunn, *Scientific Selling and Advertising* (New York: Industrial, 1919); Charles Wilson Hoyt, *Scientific Sales Management: A Practical Application of the Principles of Scientific Management to Selling* (New York: G. B. Woolson, 1913); and James Samuel Knox, *Salesmanship and Personal Efficiency* (Cleveland, Ohio: Knox Business, 1917).

10. Hoyt, *Scientific Sales Management*, p. 26.

11. See Olivier Zunz, *Why the American Century?* (Chicago: University of Chicago Press, 1998), pp. xi–xii.

12. E. K. Strong, *The Psychology of Selling and Advertising* (New York: McGraw-Hill, 1925), p. 8.

13. *Salesmanship: Devoted to Advancing the Science of Salesmanship in Its Relation to the Art of Selling* 1, no. 1 (June 1903), cover.

14. Arthur Frederick Sheldon, *The Science of Successful Salesmanship* (Chicago: Arthur Frederick Sheldon, 1904); Edgar Alexander Russell, *Ethics and Principles of Salesmanship* (Philadelphia: Benjamin Emery, 1905); Anon., *Sales Promotion* (Detroit: Book-Keeper Publishing, 1906); Sylvanus Stall, *Successful Selling of the Self and Sex Series* (Philadelphia: Vir Publishing, 1907); W. A. Waterbury, ed., *Book on Selling: What Makes Up the Science of Salesmanship* (Chicago: System Company, 1907); and Hoyt, *Scientific Sales Management*.

15. Charles S. Plummer, *Leaves from a Drummer's Diary; or, Twenty-five Years on the Road* (Chicago: Belford, Clarke, 1889); George L. Marshall, *O'er Rail and Cross Ties with Gripsack: A Compilation on the Commercial Traveler* (New York: G. W. Dillingham, 1892).

16. See Harold Barger, *Distribution's Place in the American Economy since 1869* (Princeton, N.J.: Princeton University Press, 1955). Barger used census data and considered those engaged in both retail and wholesale trades as working in commodity distribution.

17. Quoted in Nicole Woolsey Biggart, *Charismatic Capitalism: Direct Selling Organizations in America* (Chicago: University of Chicago Press, 1989), p. 23.

18. John L. Fullmer, *Principles and Secrets of Advanced Modern Salesmanship* (San Francisco: Auto-Science Institute, 1926), p. 33.

19. Norval A. Hawkins, *The Selling Process: A Handbook of Salesmanship Principles* (Detroit: Norval A. Hawkins, 1918), p. 15.

20. Orison Swett Marden, *Selling Things* (New York: T. Y. Crowell, 1916), p. 63. Emphasis in the original.

21. Hawkins, *Selling Process,* p. 107.

22. *Salesmanship: The Journal of the World's Salesmanship Congress* (July 1916), p. 33; see also E. St. Elmo Lewis, *Getting the Most Out of Business: Observations of the Application of the Scientific Method to Business Practice* (New York: Ronald Press, 1917), p. 210. Lewis's description of a sale was similar to that in an article in *NCR:* "Following Up the 'Hustler': How Sales Agents Can Get the Most Benefit from the New 'Hustler,'" *NCR,* Sept. 15, 1899, p. 434: "A P. P. usually has to go through a series of mental operations, one depending on another, before he buys a cash register. Make it your business to understand precisely what these mental steps are, and how many he may have already taken. They might be divided into three general states: First, the conviction that he is losing *considerable* money through errors in store transactions; second, that a National Cash Register will stop these losses and pay for itself; third, that he must get one *immediately.*"

23. E. K. Strong, *The Psychology of Selling and Advertising* (New York: McGraw-Hill, 1925), pp. 350–355.

24. Edgar Alexander Russell, *Ethics and Principles of Salesmanship* (Philadelphia: B. Emery, 1905); Carl Horton Pierce, *Scientific Salesmanship* (New York: Holden & Motely, 1906); Norman Gallileo Lenington, *Seven Principles of Successful Salesmanship: Commercial Science Series* (Scranton, Pa.: Commercial Science System, 1908); Harlan Eugene Read, *Read's Lessons in Salesmanship* (Chicago: J. A. Lyons, 1910); Nathaniel Clark Fowler, *Practical Salesmanship: A Treatise on the Art of Selling Goods* (Boston: Little, Brown, 1911).

25. Hawkins, *Selling Process,* pp. 71–77. See also Strong, *Psychology of Selling and Advertising,* pp. 349–350.

26. See Walter H. Cottingham's edited collection *Book on Selling* (Chicago: System Company, 1907); E. H. Selecman's *The Specialty Salesman* (Chicago: Progress, 1909) and *The General Agent; or, Methods of Sales Organization and Management* (Chicago: Progress, 1910); *System* magazine's series *The Knack of Selling: System's New Method of Training Men to Sell*

(Chicago: System, 1913); John G. Jones's *Salesmanship and Sales Management* (New York: Alexander Hamilton Institute, 1917); and Harold Whitehead's *Principles of Salesmanship* (New York: Ronald Press, 1918).

27. James Samuel Knox, *Salesmanship and Business Efficiency* (Cleveland, Ohio: Knox School of Salesmanship, 1915), p. 9.

28. Quoted in Robert D. Cuff, "Arch W. Shaw, the Harvard Business School, and *An Approach to Business Problems*," *ASAC Proceedings* 16, no. 15 (1995).

29. Aspley himself wrote or edited several Dartnell books, including *What a Salesman Should Know about Credits* (Chicago: Dartnell Corp., 1919); *Modern Sales Management Practices* (Chicago: Dartnell Corp., 1919); and *Closing the Sale: A Few Suggestions That May Help Men Who Sell Things to Cut Down the Percentage of "Almost" Orders* (Chicago: Dartnell Corp., 1923).

30. Dartnell Corporation, *Effective Quota Plans of Three Hundred Notably Successful Concerns*, report no. 180 (Chicago: Dartnell Corp., 1924).

31. Dartnell Corporation, *Survey of Modern Sales Organizations: Describing Modern Business Methods and Tendencies in 259 Different Lines of Business* (Chicago: Dartnell Corp., 1920); *Special Report: Sales Method Investigation, Plans for Building Up a Spirit of Loyalty in a Sales Organization, Report 172* (Chicago: Dartnell Corp., 1924); *Special Report: Enlisting Cooperation of Salesmen's Wives and Families* (Chicago: Dartnell Corp., 1928).

32. Dartnell Corporation, *Survey of Modern Sales Organizations*, section 9, p. 7.

33. Don R. Webb and Donald L. Shawver, "A Critical Examination of the Influence of Institutional Economics on the Development of Early Marketing Thought," in Terence Nevett, Kathleen R. Whitney, and Stanley C. Hollander, eds., *Marketing History: The Emerging Discipline: Proceedings from the Fourth Conference on Historical Research in Marketing and Marketing Thought* (East Lansing: Michigan State University, 1989), pp. 22–39.

34. D. G. Brian Jones and David D. Monieson, "Early Development of the Philosophy of Marketing Thought," *Journal of Marketing* 54 (Jan. 1990), pp. 105–106. See also Henry C. Taylor, W. A. Schoenfeld, and G. S. Wehrwein, "The Marketing of Wisconsin Cheese," *Agricultural Experiment Station Bulletins* 231 (Apr. 1913), pp. 1–26.

35. Robert Bartels, "Influences on the Development of Marketing Thought, 1900–1923," *Journal of Marketing* 16, no. 1 (July 1951), pp. 1–17.

36. Jeffrey Cruikshank, *A Delicate Experiment: The Harvard Business School, 1908–1945* (Boston: Harvard Business School Press, 1987).

37. Robert Cuff, "Gay, Shaw, and the Uses of History," p. 12.

38. A. W. Shaw, "Some Problems in Market Distribution," *Quarterly Journal of Economics* 26, no. 4 (Aug. 1912), pp. 705–706.

39. Ibid., pp. 53, 708.

40. Cuff, "Gay, Shaw, and the Uses of History," p. 17.

41. Melvin T. Copeland, *And Mark an Era: The Story of the Harvard Business School* (Boston: Little, Brown, 1958), pp. 211–213.

42. Robert Bartels, "Influences on the Development of Marketing Thought, 1900–1923," *Journal of Marketing* 41 (July 1951), pp. 1–19.

43. Harry R. Tosdal, *Problems in Sales Management* (Chicago: A. W. Shaw, 1921), p. xix.

44. Loren Baritz, *Servants of Power: A History of the Use of Social Science in American Industry* (Middletown, Conn.: Wesleyan University Press, 1960), p. 31.

45. See Tosdal, *Problems in Sales Management*.

46. F. B. Goddard, *The Art of Selling: With How to Read Character; Laws Governing Sales, etc.* (New York: Franklin, 1889), p. 47.

47. Edwin Morrell, *The Science of Judging Men* (Cleveland, Ohio: Knox School of Salesmanship and Business Efficiency, 1917), p. 6.

48. Tedlow, *New and Improved*, p. 157.

49. Baritz, *Servants of Power*, pp. 22–23.

50. Edwin G. Boring, *A History of Experimental Psychology* (New York: Appleton-Century-Crofts, 1957), p. 318.

51. Timothy B. Spears, *One Hundred Years on the Road* (New Haven, Conn.: Yale University Press, 1995), p. 213.

52. Linda Simon, *Genuine Reality: A Life of William James* (New York: Harcourt Brace, 1998), p. 234.

53. Boring, *History of Experimental Psychology*, p. 533.

54. Hugo Münsterberg, *Psychology and Industrial Efficiency* (Boston: Houghton Mifflin, 1913).

55. Matthew Hale, Jr., *Human Science and Social Order: Hugo Münsterberg and the Origins of Applied Psychology* (Philadelphia: Temple University Press, 1980), p. xi.

56. Baritz, *Servants of Power*, p. 38.

57. Ludy T. Benjamin, Jr., "Harry Levi Hollingworth," in *American National Biography* (New York: Oxford University Press, 1999), vol. 11, pp. 66–67.

58. H. L. Hollingworth, "Selection of Salesmen," *Salesmanship* (Dec. 1916), p. 432.
59. Benjamin Harris, "John Broadus Watson," in *American National Biography*, vol. 22, pp. 795–797.
60. Edmund C. Lynch, "Walter Dill Scott: Pioneer Industrial Psychologist," *Business History Review* 42, no. 2 (Summer 1968), pp. 168–169.

7. Instincts and Emotions

1. The main works on Scott include J. Z. Jacobson, *Scott of Northwestern: The Life Story of a Pioneer in Psychology and Education* (Chicago: L. Mariano, 1951); Leonard W. Ferguson, *The Heritage of Industrial Psychology*, vol. 1: *Walter Dill Scott: First Industrial Psychologist* (Hartford, Conn.: Finlay, 1964); Edmund C. Lynch, "Walter Dill Scott: Pioneer Industrial Psychologist," *Business History Review* 42, no. 2 (Summer 1968), pp. 149–170; and Richard T. von Mayrhauser, "Walter Dill Scott," in *American National Biography* (New York: Oxford University Press, 1999), vol. 19, pp. 507–510.
2. Lynch, "Walter Dill Scott," pp. 151–153.
3. Walter Dill Scott, *The Psychology of Advertising: A Simple Exposition of the Principles of Psychology in Their Relation to Successful Advertising* (Boston: Small, Maynard, 1908), p. 83.
4. Ibid., p. 18.
5. Quentin J. Schultze, "An Honorable Place: The Quest for Professional Advertising Education, 1900–1917," *Business History Review* 54, no. 1 (Spring 1982), p. 20.
6. Ferguson, *Heritage of Industrial Psychology*, vol. 1, p. 6.
7. Schultze, "An Honorable Place," p. 18.
8. William McDougall, *An Introduction to Social Psychology* (1908; New York: Barnes & Noble, 1963), p. 23.
9. Scott, *Psychology of Advertising*, p. 53.
10. Loren Baritz, *The Servants of Power: A History of the Use of Social Science in American Industry* (Middletown, Conn.: Wesleyan University Press, 1960), p. 27.
11. Ibid. p. 25.
12. The complete table is reprinted in Harry R. Tosdal, *Principles of Personal Selling* (Chicago: A. W. Shaw, 1925), p. 102; it originally appeared in McDougall, *Introduction to Social Psychology*, p. 324.
13. Scott, *Psychology of Advertising*, p. 122.

14. The kernel of these ideas was known to P. T. Barnum and to patent medicine salesmen, though not, surely, in psychological terms. The difference was that the effort to make sense of selling was now undertaken by people at the center of the economy, in positions of power, using "scientific" methods and with great capacity for research; it was linked, further, to the sale of mass-produced goods, and therefore—with the size of sales campaigns—could influence demand in a way that these small canvassers or entrepreneurs could not.

15. Merle Curti, "The Changing Concept of 'Human Nature' in the Literature of American Advertising," *Business History Review* 26, no. 4 (Winter 1967), quotation on p. 343.

16. Ferguson, *Heritage of Industrial Psychology*, vol. 1, p. 5.

17. Walter Dill Scott, *Influencing Men in Business* (New York: Ronald Press, 1911), pp. 40, 43.

18. Ibid., p. 178. Emphasis in the original. Scott's sense of the term was similar to that of William James, who wrote, "*The theory of Suggestion* denies that there is any special hypnotic *state* worthy of the name of trance or neurosis. All the symptoms above described, as well as those to be described hereafter, are results of that mental susceptibility which we are all to some degree possess, of yielding assent to outward suggestion, of affirming what we strongly conceive, and of acting in accordance with what we are made to expect." See William James, *Principles of Psychology* (1890; Cambridge, Mass.: Harvard University Press, 1981), p. 1198. Emphasis in the original.

19. Scott, *Psychology of Advertising*, p. 131.

20. Madison Grant, *Passing of the Great Race; or, The Racial Basis of European History* (New York: Scribner's, 1918). See also Stephen Jay Gould, *The Mismeasure of Man* (1981; New York: Norton, 1986).

21. Baritz, *Servants of Power*, 69.

22. B. von Haller Gilmer, ed., *Walter Van Dyke Bingham Memorial Program*, March 23, 1961 (Pittsburgh, 1962), 3.

23. Clay Bailey, "William Walker Atkinson," in *American National Biography*, vol. 1, pp. 717–719.

24. Orison Swett Marden, *Selling Things* (New York: Thomas Y. Crowell, 1916), p. 76.

25. Scott, *Influencing Men in Business*, p. 46. Emphasis in the original.

26. Scott, *Psychology of Advertising*, p. 1.

27. Ibid., p. 94; see also von Mayrhauser, "Walter Dill Scott."

28. Lynch, "Walter Dill Scott," pp. 156–158.

29. Ferguson, *Heritage of Industrial Psychology*, vol. 4, pp. 37–39.

30. J. Owen Stalson, *Marketing Life Insurance: Its History in America* (Cambridge, Mass.: Harvard University Press, 1942), p. 581. In the wake of the trial, companies and insurance journals had voiced a strong and not always successful call for professional standards and the proper education for agents.

31. Ferguson, *Heritage of Industrial Psychology,* vol. 5, pp. 54–55.

32. Other contributors included the Aluminum Company of America, Armstrong Cork Company, The Carnegie Steel Company, Pittsburgh Steel Company, B. F. Goodrich Company, Crutchfield and Woolfolk, Eli Lilly and Company, and H. J. Heinz Company. See Ferguson, *Heritage of Industrial Psychology,* vol. 5: *Bureau of Salesmanship Research.*

33. Richard T. von Mayrhauser, "The Manager, the Medic, and the Mediator: The Clash of Professional Psychological Styles and the Wartime Origins of Group Mental Testing," in Michael M. Sokal, ed., *Psychological Testing and American Society, 1890–1930* (New Brunswick, N.J.: Rutgers University Press, 1987), p. 146.

34. Walter Dill Scott, *Increasing Human Efficiency in Business* (New York: Macmillan, 1911), pp. 9–10.

35. Ferguson, *Heritage of Industrial Psychology,* vol. 5, p. 56.

36. See von Mayrhauser, "The Manager, the Medic, and the Mediator," p. 132.

37. Lynch, "Walter Dill Scott," p. 158.

38. Dartnell Corporation, *Special Report: Sales Method Investigation, the Systematic Supervision of Salesmen* (Chicago: Dartnell Corp., 1922), p. 4.

39. Walter Dill Scott, *Aids in Selecting Salesmen* (Pittsburgh: Carnegie Institute of Technology, 1916).

40. Ibid.

41. Ibid., vol. 6, p. 97. Emphasis in the original.

42. H. G. Kenagy and C. S. Yoakum, *The Selection and Training of Salesmen: Scientific Methods in Developing the Sales Organization* (New York: McGraw-Hill, 1925), p. 271; Baritz, *Servants of Power,* p. 71. See also W. V. Bingham to O. R. Johnson, Jan. 6, 1922, Walter Van Dyke Bingham Collection, Carnegie-Mellon University, reel 9. Bingham wrote: "All the recent work of the Bureau of Personnel Research in the study of salesmen, has gone to show that intelligence, whether measured by the Spiral Omnibus Text (Scrambled Alpha) or by other tests, has only a very low correlation with salesmanship ability, which is better predicted by other means. Of these a carefully weighted evaluation of the items in a complete personal history record is the most predictive."

43. Richard Gillespie, *Manufacturing Knowledge: A History of the Hawthorne Experiments* (Cambridge, Eng.: Cambridge University Press, 1991), p. 31.

44. See Gould, *Mismeasure of Man*, esp. pp. 222–255. See also von Mayrhauser, "The Manager, the Medic, and the Mediator," pp. 131–132.

45. Lynch, "Walter Dill Scott," p. 164.

46. Von Mayrhauser, "The Manager, the Medic, and the Mediator," p. 145.

47. Baritz, *Servants of Power*, p. 40.

48. Kenagy and Yoakum, *Selection and Training of Salesmen*, p. vii.

49. Merrill Jay Ream, *Ability to Sell: Its Relation to Certain Aspects of Personality and Experience* (Baltimore, Md.: Williams and Wilkins, 1924), p. 43.

50. Baritz, *Servants of Power*, p. 47; Lynch, "Walter Dill Scott," p. 166.

51. Bartiz, *Servants of Power*, pp. 26–27.

52. A. J. Snow, *Psychology in Personal Selling* (Chicago: A. W. Shaw, 1925), pp. 13–14. Snow wrote, on p. 19, "As has been said, the action is mechanical and in some degree predictable. In the field of selling this is an important factor because by knowing how to produce some types of reflex action, through the proper control of environment and presentation of stimulus, we may be able to produce action of the type that the salesman is interested in."

53. A. W. Shaw, "Some Problems in Market Distribution," *Quarterly Journal of Economics* 26, no. 4 (Aug. 1912), p. 708.

54. Wesley C. Mitchell, "The Rationality of Economic Activity: I" *Journal of Political Economy* 18, no. 2 (Feb. 10, 1910), p. 100.

55. Paul T. Cherington, *The Elements of Marketing* (New York: Macmillan, 1920); Melvin T. Copeland, *Principles of Merchandising* (Chicago: A. W. Shaw, 1924); and Harry R. Tosdal, *Problems in Sales Management* (Chicago: A. W. Shaw, 1921) and *Principles of Personal Selling* (New York: McGraw-Hill, 1925).

8. A Car for Her

1. I am grateful to Richard S. Tedlow for this data from his project on the American CEO in 1917.

2. *Fortune* 11, no. 10 (Apr. 1935), p. 81.

3. See "The Great American Salesman," *Fortune* 21, no. 2 (Feb. 1940), p. 73. The *Saturday Evening Post* was edited by former salesman George Horace Lorimer, who felt there was "no finer product of modern civilization than

the American businessman." On Lorimer, see Christopher P. Wilson, "The Rhetoric of Consumption: Mass-Market Magazines and the Demise of the Gentle Reader, 1880–1920," in Richard Wightman Fox and T. J. Jackson Lears, *The Culture of Consumption* (New York: Pantheon, 1983), pp. 39–63.

4. Jesse Rainsford Sprague, "On The Road," *Saturday Evening Post* 202, no. 14 (Oct. 5, 1929), p. 3.

5. Sinclair Lewis, *Babbitt* (1922; New York: Penguin Books, 1996), pp. 7–8. See also the excellent introduction by James M. Hutchisson in that edition, pp. vii–xxviii.

6. Ibid., p. 29.

7. Pearl Janet Davies, *Real Estate in American History* (Washington, D.C.: Public Affairs Press, 1959), pp. 110–111.

8. Lewis is quoted by James M. Hutchisson in his introduction to *Babbitt*, p. xxiv.

9. Thorstein Veblen, *Absentee Ownership: Business Ownership in Recent Times* (1923; New York: Viking Press, 1965), pp. 291, 284–325.

10. Thomas S. Hines, "Echoes from 'Zenith': Reactions of American Businessmen to *Babbitt*," *Business History Review* 41, no. 2 (Summer 1967), p. 123.

11. Nancy Koehn, *Brand New: How Entrepreneurs Earned Consumers' Trust from Wedgwood to Dell* (Boston: Harvard Business School Press, 2001), pp. 4–11.

12. Alan Brinkley, *Unfinished Nation: A Concise History of the American People* (Boston: McGraw-Hill, 2000), pp. 630–633, 636–637.

13. Roland Marchand, *Advertising the American Dream: Making Sense for Modernity, 1920–1940* (Berkeley: University of California Press, 1986), p. 27.

14. Martha L. Olney, *Buy Now, Pay Later: Advertising, Credit, and Consumer Durables in the 1920s* (Chapel Hill: University of North Carolina Press, 1991), p. 1.

15. "Great American Salesman," p. 73.

16. Quoted in Allan Nevins, *Ford: The Times, the Man, the Company* (New York: Scribner's, 1954), pp. 342–343.

17. "Automobile Selling," *Fortune* 4, no. 6 (Dec. 1931), p. 38.

18. See ibid., p. 40. Macauley of Packard was "first to concern himself with dealer operations in any form . . . He . . . had worked with John Henry Patterson . . . [and] brought with him a system of dealer supervision when he came from Burroughs Adding Machine in 1910. This he has continually

perfected and, as a result, the Packard dealer body became the envy of everyone."

19. "Great American Salesman," p. 170.

20. "General Motors III: Sales," *Fortune* 19, no. 2 (Feb. 1939), p. 76.

21. See Alfred D. Chandler, Jr., *The Visible Hand: The Managerial Revolution in American Business* (Cambridge, Mass.: Harvard University Press, 1977), p. 457.

22. Alfred C. Fuller and Hartzell Spence, *A Foot in the Door* (New York: McGraw-Hill, 1960), plate after p. 184.

23. Koehn, *Brand New,* p. 168.

24. Marchand, *Advertising the American Dream,* p. 1.

25. Quoted in ibid., p. 6. See also Daniel Pope, *The Making of Modern Advertising* (New York: Basic Books, 1983), pp. 22–29; and Joseph Dorfman, *The Economic Mind in American Civilization,* vols. 4 and 5: *1918–1933* (New York: Viking, 1959), p. 59.

26. *Crain's Market Data Book and Directory of Class, Trade and Technical Publications* (Chicago: G. D. Crain, 1920), p. 25.

27. Olney, *Buy Now, Pay Later,* p. 135.

28. "Great American Salesman," p. 170.

29. Sally Clarke, "Managing Design: The Art and Colour Section at General Motors, 1927–1941," *Journal of Design History* 12, no. 1 (1999), p. 67.

30. Lendol Calder, *Financing the American Dream: A Cultural History of Consumer Credit* (Princeton, N.J.: Princeton University Press, 1999), p. 201.

31. Olney, *Buy Now, Pay Later,* pp. 1–2.

32. Temple University, *Survey of Direct Sales Methods* (Philadelphia: Temple University, 1931).

33. Victor P. Buell, "Door-to-Door Selling," *Harvard Business Review* (May–June 1954), pp. 113–123.

34. Nicole Woolsey Biggart, *Charismatic Capitalism: Direct Selling Organizations in America* (Chicago: University of Chicago Press, 1989), pp. 25–26.

35. *Opportunity* 1, no. 1, (June 1923), p. 23.

36. Ibid., p. 6.

37. Biggart, *Charismatic Capitalism,* pp. 25–26.

38. Buell, "Door-to-Door Selling," pp. 113–123.

39. Ibid., p. 118.

40. Biggart, *Charismatic Capitalism,* p. 22. Biggart claimed that a resurgence in direct selling was stimulated in part, surprisingly, by the rise of department stores in the late nineteenth century. According to Biggart, "A num-

ber of manufacturers did not want their products to have to compete with the cornucopia of goods in the big emporiums."

41. Ibid., pp. 29–30.
42. Susan Strasser, *Never Done: A History of American Housework* (New York: Pantheon, 1982), p. 78.
43. Frank G. Hoover, *Fabulous Dustpan: The Story of the Hoover* (Cleveland, Ohio: World Publishing, 1955), pp. 108, 112–114.
44. Strasser, *Never Done*, p. 79.
45. Ibid., pp. 117–119.
46. "Case Studies in Business: Reaching the Consumer through Direct Personal Selling," *Harvard Business Review* 4, no. 1 (Oct. 1925), pp. 103–105.
47. Buell, "Door-to-Door Selling," pp. 120–121.
48. Jewel Tea Company, *The First Thirty Years: 1899–1929* (Chicago: Jewel Tea, 1929), pp. 10–11. The Jewel Tea Company was founded in Chicago in 1899 by Frank Vernon Skiff with $700 capital; the company was incorporated in 1903 with a capitalization of $25,000. The company took orders for coffee and tea and made deliveries once every two weeks. It began sending salesmen outside of Chicago in 1904, at which point it was selling tea, coffee, spices, cereals, and laundry and toilet products. Salesmen called on housewives every two weeks, taking orders for delivery on the next scheduled visit. It offered premiums to its customers, in the form of china and other such gifts. In 1908 the company imported the largest ever single lot of coffee into the country until that time—1.6 million pounds worth, brought on a train of 42 cars. Annual sales reached $1 million in 1910. The company expanded in 1916, mapping 1,645 routes for salesmen to travel. In 1923, it began its own company magazine, *Jewel News.* In 1926, the company had its salesmen switch to using motorized wagons; at that time, sales per week per wagon were $300. And in 1929 the company had 1,230 motor delivery trucks, reaching 6,000 towns, traveling 1,190 preplanned routes, and serving 780,000 customers.
49. Susan Porter Benson, "The Cinderella of Occupations: Managing the Work of Department Store Saleswomen, 1900–1940," *Business History Review* 60, no. 1 (Spring 1981), pp. 5–6.
50. A'Lelia Perry Bundles, *On Her Own Ground: The Life and Times of Madam C. J. Walker* (New York: Scribner's, 2001).
51. Anna J. Figsbee, *My Company and Me* (n.p., 1958), p. 14, Avon Products Company Archives, Hagley Museum and Library, Wilmington, Del.

52. Katina L. Manko, "'Now You Are in Business for Yourself': The Independent Contractors of the California Perfume Company," *Business and Economic History* 26, no. 1 (Fall 1997), pp. 19–21.

53. Nicole Woolsey Biggart, *Charismatic Capitalism: Direct Selling Organizations in America* (Chicago: University of Chicago Press, 1989), pp. 49–54.

54. Alfred Fuller, "How We Use Advertising to Sell Our Products," *Printers' Ink* (May 25, 1922), p. 61.

55. "The Fuller Brush Company," *Fortune* 18, no. 4 (Oct. 1938), pp. 68–73.

56. See "Profiles: May I Just Step Inside?" *New Yorker*, Nov. 13, 1948, pp. 36–56.

57. See *Fortune* 43, no. 4 (Oct. 1938), p. 68.

58. These Fuller Brush statistics are from Don C. Prentiss, *Ford Motor Products and Their Sale* (Detroit: Franklin Press, 1923), p. 8. Prentiss also reported that new salesmen seldom average less than $30 per week, and as soon as they learn how to sell they earn $50 per week. Some who are very good earn $75 or even $100 per week.

59. "Fuller Brush Company," p. 70.

60. F. S. Beveridge, *Field Sales Organization of the Fuller Brush Company*, Sale's Executive Series no. 14 (New York: American Management Association, 1925), p. 12.

61. See "Fuller Brush Company," p. 68; ibid.

62. "Methods Found Successful in Selling to Colored Population," *Printers' Ink*, n.d., 1922. Fuller also attempted to sell on Indian reservations; see W. L. Mayhew, "Working in Northern California: Where an Ambitious Fullerite Finds a Varied and Interesting Setting for the Sale of Fuller Brushes," *Bristler* 7, no. 9 (Sept. 1923), p. 2.

63. Quoted in A. J. Snow, *Psychology in Personal Selling* (Chicago: A. W. Shaw, 1926), pp. 376–378. Emphasis in the original. Snow reprints the Fuller Brush Company's sales talk.

64. Dartnell Corporation, *Sales Survey for 1921* (Chicago: Dartnell Corp., 1922).

65. "Fuller Brush Company," pp. 68–104. *Fortune* estimated the breakdown in costs of a $1.95 shower brush. Roughly 25.2 percent went to manufacture; 58.7 percent to sales (including a dealers' discount of 38.4 percent, branch managers' commission of 8.5 percent, field managers' commission of 5 percent, unit manager's commission and salary of 2 percent, sales promotion of 2.8 percent, and branch-office rent of 2 percent). Other parts of the

total cost went to warehousing and distribution, administration and taxes. The remaining profit was 2 percent.

66. Alfred C. Fuller, *A Foot in the Door: The Life Appraisal of the Original Fuller Brush Man* (New York: McGraw-Hill, 1960), p. 87.

67. Ibid., p. 71. Emphasis in the original. See also Alfred C. Fuller, "Why Our Business Is Good Now," *Printers' Ink Monthly* 3, no. 1 (June 1921), p. 11. Fuller writes, "Our men are trained not in selling brushes, but in household efficiency."

68. Alfred Fuller, *Out of a Rut* (Hartford, Conn.: Fuller Brush Company, 1922).

69. "Fuller Brush Company," p. 104.

70. Ibid.

71. Beveridge, *Field Sales Organization of the Fuller Brush Company*, p. 12; Fuller, *Foot in the Door*, p. 202.

72. Stanley Le Fevre Krebs, *The Fundamental Principles of Hypnosis* (New York: Julian Press, 1957), p. 7.

73. Richard S. Tedlow, *New and Improved: The Story of Mass Marketing in America* (New York: Basic Books, 1990), p. 125.

74. See the chapter "Putting America on Wheels: Ford vs. General Motors" in ibid., pp. 112–181. Tedlow offers the most thorough analysis of the marketing strategies of the two companies. He posits that the automobile market, like that in a number of other industries, passed through three specific stages, from fragmentation (phase 1), to unification (phase 2), to, finally, segmentation (phase 3).

75. Thomas S. Dicke, *Franchising in America: The Development of a Business Method, 1840–1980* (Chapel Hill: University of North Carolina Press, 1992), p. 59. See also Glenn Porter and Harold C. Livesay, *Merchants and Manufacturers: Studies in the Changing Structure of Nineteenth-Century Marketing* (Baltimore, Md.: Johns Hopkins University Press, 1971), p. 195.

76. Alfred P. Sloan, *My Years with General Motors* (1963; New York: Doubleday, 1990), p. 279.

77. Tedlow, *New and Improved*, p. 122.

78. Nevins, *Ford*, pp. 342–346.

79. Tedlow, *New and Improved*, p. 137. The rise was not always steady, however. The number of dealers fell from 8,468 in 1916 to 6,326 in Sept. 1920.

80. Porter and Livesay, *Merchants and Manufacturers*, p. 195.

81. See "Automobile Selling," *Fortune* 4, no. 6 (Dec. 1931), p. 42.

82. *Ford Times,* May 15, 1908, p. 5, found at Henry Ford Museum and Greenfield Village Research Center, Dearborn, Mich.
83. Tedlow, *New and Improved,* p. 137.
84. "Norval Hawkins Tells How Ford Car Was Sold to World in First Boom Years," *New York Times,* Feb. 2, 1927, p. 1.
85. Tedlow, *New and Improved,* p. 143.
86. William P. Young, *A Ford Dealer's Twenty-Year Ride* (Hempstead, N.Y.: William P. Young, 1932), p. 61.
87. See *People v. Hawkins,* Supreme Court of Michigan, 106 Mich. 479, 64 N.W. 736 (1895 Mich. LEXIS 1032); Nevins, *Ford,* p. 342.
88. Norval Hawkins, *The Selling Process: A Handbook of Salesmanship Principles* (Detroit: Norval Hawkins, 1919), p. 36.
89. Ibid., p. 104.
90. Ford Archives, letter, March 12, 1914, accession 509, Henry Ford Museum and Greenfield Village Research Center.
91. Fordex Editorial Staff, *The Model T Specialist* (Detroit: Ford Sales Equipment Division, 1925). From the collections of Henry Ford Museum and Greenfield Village Research Center; see also Prentiss, *Ford Motor Products and Their Sale.*
92. Ibid.
93. Ibid., p. 269.
94. Alfred D. Chandler, ed., *Giant Enterprise: Ford, General Motors, and the Automobile Industry, Sources and Readings* (New York: Harcourt, Brace & World, 1964), p. 35. See also Henry Ford, *My Life and Work* (1922; Garden City, N.Y.: Doubleday, Page, 1926), p. 41. "There was something more than a tendency in the early days of the automobile to regard the selling of a machine as the real accomplishment and that thereafter it did not matter what happened to the buyer," wrote Ford. "That is the shortsighted salesman-on-commission attitude. If a salesman is paid only for what he sells, it is not to be expected that he is going to exert any great effort on a customer out of whom no more commission is to be made."
95. Prentiss, *Ford Motor Products and Their Sale,* pp. 441–442.
96. Ibid., pp. 445–446.
97. Sloan, *My Years with General Motors,* p. 284.
98. Chandler, *Giant Enterprise,* p. 146.
99. Chandler, *Strategy and Structure: Chapters in the History of Industrial Enterprise* (Cambridge, Mass.: MIT Press, 1962), pp. 145–150.

100. Sally Clarke, "Managing Design: The Art and Colour Section at General Motors, 1927–1941," *Journal of Design History* 12, no. 1 (1999), p. 69.
101. Chandler, *Giant Enterprise*, p. 95.
102. Jeffrey Cruikshank, *A Delicate Experiment: The Harvard Business School, 1908–1945* (Boston: Harvard Business School Press, 1987).
103. Tedlow, *New and Improved*, p. 156.
104. Chandler, *Giant Enterprise*, pp. 170–172.
105. Ibid., p. xi.
106. G. A. Nichols, "General Motors to Spend Five Millions in Advertising," *Printers' Ink* (Sept. 29, 1921), p. 10.
107. "General Motors III: Sales," p. 71.
108. Chandler, *Giant Enterprise*, p. 147.
109. "General Motors III: Sales," p. 78.
110. General Motors Corporation, *Selling Chevrolets: A Book of General Information for Chevrolet Retail Salesmen* (Detroit: Chevrolet Motor Company, 1926), pp. 31–39.
111. Ibid., pp. 163–164.

9. Selling Salesmanship

1. Charles W. Mears, *Salesmanship for the New Era* (New York: Harper and Brothers, 1929), pp. 1, 12. See also Roland Marchand, *Advertising the American Dream: Making Way for Modernity, 1920–1940* (Berkeley: University of California Press, 1985).
2. See Simon N. Patten, *The New Basis for Civilization* (New York: Macmillan, 1907) and *The Theory of Prosperity* (New York: Macmillan, 1902).
3. *Fifteenth Census of the United States: 1930, Distribution,* vol. 1 (Washington, D.C.: Government Printing Office, 1933), pp. 14, 15, 17–19.
4. Twentieth Century Fund, *Does Distribution Cost Too Much?* (New York: Twentieth Century Fund, 1939), p. 13.
5. See Alba M. Edwards, *Population: Comparative Occupational Statistics for the United States, 1870–1940* (Washington, D.C.: Government Printing Office, 1940), esp. pp. 104–121.
6. Ralph Borsodi, *The Distribution Age: A Study of the Economy of Modern Distribution* (New York: D. Appleton, 1927), part 2, chap. 14.

7. Anon., *The Story of Selling: Yesterday, Today and Tomorrow* (New York: Crowell-Collier, 1946), pp. 5–6.

8. "The Fuller Brush Company," *Fortune* 18, no. 4 (Oct. 1938), p. 100.

9. Twentieth Century Fund, *Does Distribution Cost Too Much? A Review of the Costs in Current Marketing Methods and a Program for Improvement* (New York: Twentieth Century Fund, 1939), p. 71.

10. Quoted in Edward Chancellor, *Devil Take the Hindmost: A History of Financial Speculation* (New York: Farrar, Straus and Giroux, 1999), p. 214.

11. Thomas K. McCraw, *American Business, 1920–2000: How It Worked* (Wheeling, Ill.: Harlan Davidson, 2000), p. 41.

12. Frederick Lewis Allen, *The Big Change, 1900–1950* (1952; New York: Bantam, 1965), p. 132.

13. Thornton Wilder, *Heaven's My Destination* (New York: Harper and Brothers, 1935).

14. Eudora Welty, "Death of a Traveling Salesman," in Welty, *A Curtain of Green and Other Stories* (New York: Harcourt, Brace & World, 1941), pp. 231–253.

15. Twentieth Century Fund, *Does Distribution Cost Too Much?* p. 20. See also Robert B. Westbrook, "Tribune of the Technostructure: The Popular Economics of Stuart Chase," *American Quarterly* 32, no. 4 (Autumn 1980), pp. 387–408.

16. Alan Brinkley, *The End of Reform: New Deal Liberalism in Recession and War* (New York: Random House, 1995), pp. 69, 71.

17. *Fortune* editors, *Why Do People Buy?*, p. 7.

18. Ibid., p. 16.

19. Russell W. Lynch and Roy W. Johnson, *The Sales Strategy of John H. Patterson* (Chicago: Dartnell Corp., 1932), preface.

20. Norval A. Hawkins, *Bringing Business Back* (Congress Lake, Ohio: American Society of Sales Executives, 1931), p. 21.

21. Lewis H. Carlson, "Norval Abiel Hawkins," *Encyclopedia of Business History and Biography* (May 1989), vol. 1, pp. 244–247.

22. Dale Carnegie, *How to Win Friends and Influence People* (New York: Simon & Schuster, 1937), pp. 20, 52, 47, 5.

23. Rosemary Frances Carroll, "The Impact of the Great Depression on American Attitudes towards Success: A Study of the Programs of Norman Vincent Peale, Dale Carnegie, and Johnson O'Connor," Ph.D. diss., Rutgers University, 1968, p. 103.

24. Charles Bennett, *Scientific Salesmanship* (St. Louis: American Efficiency Bureau, 1933), pp. 35, 39, 41, 46.

25. Ibid., pp. 18, 57.

26. The editors of *Fortune* use the analogy of the economy to a pie in describing the role of selling. See their *Why Do People Buy?* p. 2.

27. Dartnell Corporation, *Special Report: Sales Method Investigation: Increasing Sales Call Efficiency under Present Conditions,* report no. 36 (Chicago: Dartnell Corp., 1931), p. 1; Dartnell Corporation, *Special Investigation: Securing and Utilizing Sales Facts,* report no. 428 (Chicago: Dartnell Corp., 1934), p. 1.

28. Dartnell Corporation, *Special Report: Sales Method Investigation: Adjusting Salesmen's Compensation to Present Sales Volume* (Chicago: Dartnell Corp., 1932).

29. Ibid.

30. "Radio Advertising," *Fortune* (Sept., 1932), p. 37.

31. Marchand, *Advertising the American Dream,* p. 300.

32. Roland Marchand, *Creating the Corporate Soul: The Rise of Public Relations and Corporate Imagery in American Big Business* (Berkeley: University of California Press, 1998), p. 247.

33. Richard T. von Mayrhauser, "Henry Charles Link," in *American National Biography* (New York: Oxford University Press, 1999), vol. 13, pp. 708–710.

34. See also Daniel Horowitz, "The Emigré as Celebrant of American Consumer Culture: George Katona and Ernest Dichter," in Susan Strasser, Charles McGovern, and Matthia Judt, eds., *Getting and Spending: European and American Consumer Societies in the Twentieth Century* (Cambridge, Eng.: Cambridge University Press, 1998), pp. 149–166.

35. *Report of the Federal Trade Commission on Distribution Methods and Costs,* part 5: *Advertising as a Factor in Distribution* (Washington, D.C.: Government Printing Office, 1944), p. 8.

36. Frederick Allen, *Secret Formula: How Brilliant Marketing and Relentless Salesmanship Made Coca-Cola the Best-Known Product in the World* (New York: HarperBusiness, 1994), p. 206. See also Richard S. Tedlow, *New and Improved: The Story of Mass Marketing in America* (New York: Basic Books, 1990), pp. 22–111.

37. Tedlow, *New and Improved,* p. 85–86.

38. "The Coca-Cola Industry," *Fortune* 18, no. 6 (Dec. 1938), pp. 65–106; ibid., p. 85.

39. Michael Bernstein, *The Great Depression: Delayed Economic Recovery and Economic Change in America, 1929–1939* (Cambridge, Eng.: Cambridge University Press, 1987), p. 64.

40. Nancy F. Koehn, *Brand New: How Entrepreneurs Earned Consumers' Trust from Wedgwood to Dell* (Boston: Harvard Business School Press, 2001), p. 89.

41. "National Cash Register," *Fortune* 2, no. 2 (Aug. 1930), p. 69.

42. NCR, *Annual Report for 1937* (Dayton, Ohio: NCR Corp., 1938).

43. "International Business Machines," *Fortune* 21, no. 1 (Jan. 1940), p. 37.

44. William Rodgers, *Think: A Biography of the Watsons and IBM* (New York: Stein and Day, 1969), p. 107.

45. Rowena Olegario, "IBM and the Two Thomas J. Watsons," in Thomas K. McCraw, ed., *Creating Modern Capitalism: How Entrepreneurs, Companies, and Countries Triumphed in Three Industrial Revolutions* (Cambridge, Mass.: Harvard University Press, 1997), p. 358.

46. "International Business Machines," p. 36.

47. *Wall Street Journal,* Jan. 15, 1930, p. A7.

48. Thomas Wolfe, *You Can't Go Home Again* (1934; New York: Harper & Row, 1940), pp. 131–132.

49. Quoted in Olegario, "IBM and the Two Thomas J. Watsons," p. 372.

50. Nicole Woolsey Biggart, *Charismatic Capitalism: Direct Selling Organizations in America* (Chicago: University of Chicago Press, 1989), p. 128.

51. Ibid., p. 32.

52. Twentieth Century Fund, *Does Distribution Cost Too Much?*, p. 71.

53. Ibid., p. 21.

54. Lendol Calder, *Financing the American Dream: A Cultural History of Consumer Credit* (Princeton, N.J.: Princeton University Press, 1999), p. 275.

55. Susan Strasser, "Consumption," in Stanley I. Kutler, ed., *Encyclopedia of the United States in the Twentieth Century* (New York: Scribner's, 1995), p. 1024.

56. The best source on CPC is Katina L. Manko, "'Now You Are in Business for Yourself': The Independent Contractors of the California Perfume Company," *Business and Economic History* 26, no. 1 (Fall 1997), pp. 5–26; for further information on the discussion in this paragraph, see esp. pp. 19–22. (See also *California Perfume Company Bulletin* [Mar. 1937], p. 8, Avon Products Company Archives, New York. The Jewel Tea Company, which sold coffee, tea, and small groceries, saw sales fall from $16 million (1928) to $13.7 million (1931), but then rise to $17.2 million

(1934). *Annual Report for Jewel Tea Company* (Barrington, Ill.: Jewel Tea, 1935).

57. *Fuller Brush Company Annual Reports, 1927–1933* (Hartford, Conn.: Fuller Brush, 1928–1934).

58. *Fuller Brush Company Annual Report, 1933* (Hartford, Conn.: Fuller Brush, 1934).

59. "The Fuller Brush Company," *Fortune* 63, no. 4 (Oct. 1938), pp. 68–73.

60. Ibid., p. 70.

61. Alfred Fuller, *A Foot in the Door: The Life Appraisal of the Original Fuller Brush Man* (New York: McGraw-Hill, 1960), pp. 205–206. According to Alfred Fuller, at the 1936 Fuller Brush Convention, Peterson challenged Teetsel outright, saying that the old salesman should leave the organization. This caused Teetsel to rise out of his seat and storm down the aisle. He challenged Peterson to settle the issue out in the alley, but was kept at a distance.

62. A. R. Hahn, "How Fuller Brush Hires and Trains Its House-to-House Army," *Sales Management* (Oct. 10, 1935), p. 377.

63. Biggart, *Charismatic Capitalism*, p. 42.

64. Michael Bernstein, *The Great Depression: Delayed Economic Recovery and Economic Change in America, 1929–1939* (Cambridge, Eng.: Cambridge University Press, 1987), pp. 59–60.

65. Ibid.

66. Alfred D. Chandler, Jr., ed., *Giant Enterprise: Ford, General Motors, and the Automobile Industry, Sources and Readings* (New York: Harcourt, Brace & World, 1964), p. 3.

67. Allan Nevins and Frank Ernest Hill, *Ford: Decline and Rebirth, 1933–1962* (New York: Scribner's, 1963), p. 4.

68. Tedlow, *New and Improved*, p. 175.

69. "He Gets Them in Back of the Wheel of the Ford V-8," *Ford Dealers News*, Jan. 15, 1933. From the collections of Henry Ford Museum and Greenfield Village Research Center, Dearborn, Mich. The effort to sell the V-8 was strong among dealers. Sam Tuthill of Tuthill Motors of Stamford, Connecticut, launched a campaign to sell the new Ford V-8. When the cars arrived at the dealership, Tuthill sent out invitations and hosted a party: a carpet was laid out from the sidewalk to the showroom, the salesmen were in tuxedos, a canopy was erected. The following day salesmen made telephone calls to attendees to arrange test drives. Tuthill even allowed for people to take the cars for a short time, for social calls or taking a small

trip. He also launched an evening sales program. Every night at 6:30 eight salesmen met at the office and started out with the car, proceeding to the residential sections to contact home owners on both sides of the street, offering demonstrations.

70. William P. Young, *A Ford Dealer's Twenty Year Ride* (Hempstead, N.Y.: William P. Young, 1932), p. 56.

71. Alfred P. Sloan, *My Years with General Motors* (1963; New York: Doubleday, 1990), p. 176–177.

72. Ibid., p. 177.

73. "Automobile Selling," *Fortune* 4, no. 6 (Dec. 1931), p. 41.

74. See "General Motors III: Sales," *Fortune* 19, no. 2 (Feb. 1939), pp. 71–74.

75. Sloan, *My Years with General Motors*, p. 170.

76. Marchand, *Creating the Corporate Soul*, p. 205. Marchand wrote: "Having proffered their service to the public in the 1920s as 'business statesmen,' they were now being pressed to renounce their noble (if politically blind), stick-to-business insensibility to public opinion and to confess to impotence in a central quality of business performance—salesmanship."

77. Ibid., pp. 18, 28, 38, 216.

78. Thomas K. McCraw, *American Business, 1920–2000: How It Worked* (Wheeling, Ill.: Harlan Davidson, 2000), pp. 50–52.

79. Marchand, *Creating the Corporate Soul*, p. 204. Emphasis in the original.

80. Ibid., pp. 214, 220, 230–233.

81. Ibid., pp. 357–364.

82. C. Wright Mills, *White Collar: The American Middle Classes* (New York: Oxford University Press, 1951), p. 165. "The national market has become an object upon which many white-collar skills focus: the professional market research examines it intensively and extensively; the personnel man selects and trains salesmen of a thousand different types for its exploitation; the manager studies the fine art of prompting men to 'go get 'em.'"

83. John Kenneth Galbraith, *The Affluent Society* (1958; Boston: Houghton Mifflin, 1998), pp. 127–128.

84. Vance Packard, *The Hidden Persuaders* (1957; New York: Pocket Books, 1972), pp. 2–3.

85. Gerald Weales, ed., *Death of a Salesman: Text and Criticism* (New York: Viking Critical Library, 1977), p. 81.

86. Ibid., p. 82. The story of Willy Loman bore directly on the theme of the "science of selling." In an interview, playwright Miller commented that Loman expressed essentially human aspirations in an automated, mecha-

nistic society. "I think Willy Loman is seeking for a kind of ecstasy in life which the machine civilization deprives people of," wrote Miller. "He is looking for his selfhood, for his immortal soul, so to speak, and people who don't know the intensity of that quest think he is odd, but a lot of salesmen, in a line of work where ingenuity and individualism are acquired by the nature of the work, have a very intimate understanding of his problem" (p. 176).

87. Fortune editors, *Why Do People Buy?* p. 2.

88. Harry R. Tosdal, *Selling in Our Economy: An Economic and Social Analysis of Selling and Advertising* (Homewood, Ill.: Richard D. Irwin, 1957), pp. 173, viii.

89. Ibid., p. 267.

90. Fortune editors, *Why Do People Buy?* p. 8.

91. Tosdal, *Selling in Our Economy,* pp. 271, vii.

92. Harry R. Tosdal, *Principles of Personal Selling* (Chicago: A. W. Shaw, 1925), p. 8.

93. Tosdal, *Selling in Our Economy,* p. 130.

94. Figures are from "The Great American Salesman," *Fortune* 21, no. 2 (Feb. 1940), p. 176.

95. Fortune editors, *Why Do People Buy?* pp. 50–51.

96. William H. Whyte, *Organization Man* (1956; Philadelphia: University of Pennsylvania, 2002), esp. pp. 109–128.

10. Beyond Willy Loman

1. *New York Times,* June 18, 1916, p. E8.

2. E. B. Weiss, *The Vanishing Salesman* (New York: McGraw-Hill, 1962).

3. U.S. Department of Commerce, *Statistical Abstract of the United States* (Washington, D.C.: Government Printing Office, 2000), p. 417.

4. See Thomas Frank, *The Conquest of Cool: Business Culture, Counterculture, and the Rise of Hip Consumerism* (Chicago: University of Chicago Press, 1997).

5. Richard Tedlow, *New and Improved: The Story of Mass Marketing in America* (New York, Basic Books, 1990), p. 372.

6. See Malcolm Gladwell, "The Pitchman: Ron Popeil and the Conquest of the American Kitchen," *New Yorker,* Oct. 30, 2000, p. 64.

7. Adam Smith, *Wealth of Nations* (London, 1776), book 1, chap. 2, p. 1.

8. Stuart Ewen described the persistent marketing efforts of companies as a

manipulative "apparatus" borne uncomfortably by society. See Ewen, *Captains of Consciousness: Advertising and the Social Roots of the Consumer Culture* (New York: McGraw-Hill, 1976), p. 81: "With the development of an apparatus for the stimulation and creation of mass consumption, business assumed an expansionist and manipulative approach to the problem of popular consciousness."

9. Burroughs Convention Minutes, Sales Convention of July 1905, p. 91, Burroughs Corporation Records, Charles Babbage Institute, University of Minnesota, Minneapolis.

10. *Sales Bulletin [of the Sales Department of the Burroughs Adding Machine Company]*, Feb. 6, 1908, vol. 325, Collection: Sales Bulletins (loose issues), 1907–1952, box 10, folder 1, Burroughs Corporation Records.

11. Behavioral economists have recently been studying these subjects. See, for example, Matthew Rabin, "Psychology and Economics," *Journal of Economic Literature* 36 (Mar. 1998), pp. 11–46.

12. See Martha L. Olney, *Buy Now, Pay Later: Advertising, Credit, and Consumer Durables in the 1920s* (Chapel Hill: University of North Carolina Press, 1991).

13. Rowena Olegario, "IBM and the Two Thomas J. Watsons," in Thomas K. McCraw, ed., *Creating Modern Capitalism: How Entrepreneurs, Companies, and Countries Triumphed in Three Industrial Revolutions* (Cambridge, Mass.: Harvard University Press, 1998), p. 363.

14. See Dept. of Justice, *Twenty-first Century Complete Guide to the Microsoft Antitrust Justice Department Case with the Legal History of the Federal Case against the Company founded by Bill Gates: Settlement Information, Court Filings, Trial Exhibits, Public Comments* (Washington, D.C.: Core Federal Information Series, 2003).

15. U.S. Department of Commerce, *Statistical Abstract of the United States* (Washington, D.C.: U.S. Census Bureau, 2002), pp. 380–381; Nicole Biggart, *Charismatic Capitalism* (Chicago: University of Chicago Press, 1989), pp. 28–29; Alba M. Edwards, *Population: Comparative Occupational Statistics for the United States, 1870 to 1940* (Washington, D.C.: Government Printing Office, 1943).

16. See Glenn Porter, ed., *Encyclopedia of American Economic History* (New York: Scribner's, 1980), vol. 1, p. 395.

17. U.S. Department of Commerce, *Statistical Abstract of the United States: 2001*, pp. 380–381.

18. Martin Amis, *Rachel Papers* (London: Cape, 1973), p. 28. "Gloria held the assistant pet-food saleswomanship in, handily, a Shepherds Bush emporium."

19. Figures are from *Selling Power* (Oct. 2002), pp. 55–87.
20. See Jeffrey R. Bernstein, "Toyoda Automatic Looms and Toyota Automobiles," in McCraw, *Creating Modern Capitalism*, p. 438.
21. There were 1,740 Toyota, Lexus, and Toyota industrial equipment dealers in 2003. Numbers provided by Toyota Corporation.
22. John Updike, *Rabbit Is Rich* (New York: Knopf, 1981), p. 13.
23. *Selling Power* (Oct. 2002), pp. 55–87.
24. Geoffrey A. Moore, *Crossing the Chasm: Marketing and Selling High-Tech Products to Mainstream Customers* (1991; New York: HarperBusiness, 1999), pp. 167–168, 199.
25. *Selling Power* (Sept. 2002).
26. See also Paco Underhill, *Why We Buy: The Science of Shopping* (New York: Touchstone, 1999).
27. See Philip Kotler, *Marketing Management: Analysis, Planning, Implementation, and Control,* 9th ed. (Upper Saddle River, N.J.: Prentice Hall, 1997).
28. See Harvard Business School case no. 9–595–018, "Strategic Sales Management: A Boardroom Issue," Nov. 29, 1994.
29. George A. Ackerlof, "The Market for 'Lemons': Quality Uncertainty and the Market Mechanism," *Quarterly Journal of Economics* 84, no. 3 (Aug. 1970), pp. 488–500.
30. Rabin, "Psychology and Economics," p. 11.
31. Ibid., p. 13.
32. See Joseph A. Schumpeter, *Capitalism, Socialism, and Democracy* (1942; New York: Harper Perennial, 1976), esp. pp. 81–86; also see Thomas K. McCraw, "Schumpeter Ascending," *American Scholar* 60 (Summer 1991), pp. 371–392.
33. McCraw, *Creating Modern Capitalism*, p. 273. Much of my thinking in this chapter has been shaped by McCraw's chapter in that volume, "American Capitalism," pp. 301–348.
34. *Fortune* editors, *Why Do People Buy?* pp. 32–33.
35. *New York Times*, Feb. 21, 1999, sec. 2, p. 14.
36. "Why Willy Loman Lives," *Economist,* June 19, 1999, p. 28.
37. Thomas K. McCraw, *American Business, 1920–2000: How It Worked* (Wheeling, Ill.: Harlan Davidson, 2000), p. 10.

Acknowledgments

I got the idea for this book while a graduate student at Columbia University, when I noticed that *Babbitt* was assigned in history classes to teach early-twentieth-century business culture. I hoped to provide a nonfiction alternative by looking at "real life" salespeople during the 1920s, and the story crept both backward and forward in time from that starting point. Columbia proved to be a great place to do research, not only because of Butler Library's outstanding collection, but also because of the proximity of New York Public Library. Most important was the school's faculty, who introduced me to the large historical themes—progressivism, professionalism, and consumption—that shape the text. I benefited from the generous counsel of Elizabeth Blackmar, Alan Brinkley, David Cannadine, Andrew Delbanco, and James P. Shenton. I owe a special debt to Professor Kenneth T. Jackson, my advisor, and his graduate dissertation discussion group, which reviewed chapters of the manuscript. I was also fortunate to know a group of Columbia graduate students who offered me advice on the project and on history in general. I am grateful to Tami Friedman, Michael Green, Kevin Kenny, Jo H. Kim, Peter Maguire, Edward T. O'Donnell, and Vernon Takeshita.

After Columbia, I became a postdoctoral fellow at Harvard Business School and have remained there ever since. I am thankful for the help of Thomas K. McCraw, who edited the entire manuscript. I owe him a tremendous debt for his encouragement and for the opportunities he has given me, including the chance to edit the *Business History Review* and to teach an introductory course on modern capitalism. Like many other historians, I received excellent feedback on my project from the business history seminar that he runs each fall. I also want to thank Nancy F. Koehn for her support, as well as for making me feel part of the group of historians at Harvard and for reminding me of the essentially human aspects of history. The business school is an exceedingly collegial place, and I have benefited from the advice of Kim Bettcher, Laura Bureš, Alfred D. Chandler, Rafael Di Tella, Jeff Fear, Charles "Kip" King, Joseph Lassiter, Laura Linard, David A. Moss, Das Narayandas, Rowena Olegario, Courtney Purrington, Richard S. Rosenbloom, Benson P. Shapiro, Richard S. Tedlow, and Felice Whittum. Much of the material in Chapter 5 of this book appeared previously in the *Business History Review* ("John H. Patterson and the Sales Strategy of the National Cash Register Company, 1884 to 1922," Winter 1998, pp. 552–584), and I appreciate having permission to include it here.

I have been fortunate in having other friends and colleagues who read and commented on the entire book, including Sven Beckert, Daniel Horowitz, Pamela Laird, Alexis McCrossen, and Jason Scott Smith. Richard R. John read and commented on the whole manuscript and found a cartoon for me to use. He offered me extremely helpful advice, much in the way he has done for many other scholars. Margaret Willard sharpened the prose throughout and made this a better book. Others have helped to shape my thoughts about the subject, or have assisted me through this project in other ways, and I am extremely grateful to all of them: Regina Lee Blaszczyk, Peter Eisenstadt, Ann Fabian, Meg Jacobs, Julia B. Jacobson, Kenneth Kolber, Jackson Lears, Bethany Morton, Barbara Rifkind, Bruce Sandys, and Jonathan Silvers.

I would also like to thank the librarians and staff at Harvard Business School's Baker Library, Columbia's Butler Library, the New York Public Library, the Charles Babbage Institute at the University of Minnesota, the Historical Society of Western Pennsylvania, the Library of Congress, and Widener Library at Harvard. I was delighted that Harvard University Press was interested in this book and am thankful for the assistance of my editor, Kathleen McDermott. Susan Burgin made completing this project much more enjoyable and more meaningful for me. Finally, I am grateful for the support of my parents, Carl and Marjorie, my sister, Anne, and my brother, Lawrence.

Illustration Credits

Page 21:   Bates Harrington, *How 'Tis Done: A Thorough Ventilation of the Numerous Schemes Conducted by Wandering Canvassers Together with Advertising Dodges for the Swindling of the Public* (Chicago: Fidelity, 1879), pp. 201, 207.

Page 48:   *How to Introduce the Memoirs of U. S. Grant* (Hartford, Conn.: Charles Webster, 1885), pp. 26–27, Mark Twain Papers, Bancroft Library, University of California, Berkeley.

Page 58:   *Puck* 9, no. 219, May 18, 1881, back cover. Widener Library, Harvard University.

Page 81:   L. P. Brockett, *The Commercial Traveller's Guide Book* (New York: H. Dayton, 1871), p. 77. Baker Library, Harvard Business School.

Page 84:   Thomas Carey, *Drummer's Yarns: Fun on the "Road"* (New York: Excelsior, 1886). Warshaw Collection of Business Americana—Humor, Archives Center, National Museum of American History, Behring Center, Smithsonian Institution.

Page 98:   *Salesman* 2, no. 2, Oct. 18, 1890. Image WHi-6311, Singer Manufacturing Company Records, box 110, folder 11, Wisconsin Historical Society, Madison.

Page 106:   *Edison Business Builder* (May 1914), p. 26, New York Public Library.

Page 109:   Photographic Collection, Burroughs Corporation Records, Charles Babbage Institute, University of Minnesota.

Page 110:   Burroughs Adding Machine Company, Special All Star Convention Issue of the Burroughs Sales Bulletin, no. 1468, Aug. 3, 1917, cover. Burroughs Sales Conventions, 1905–1929, box 2 27.I.2.C, Burroughs Corporation Records, Charles Babbage Institute, University of Minnesota.

Page 121:   NCR Archive, Montgomery County Historical Society, Dayton, Ohio.

Page 125:   NCR Archive, Montgomery County Historical Society, Dayton, Ohio.

Page 131:   *NCR*, Sept. 15, 1893. NCR Archive, Montgomery County Historical Society, Dayton, Ohio.

Page 132:   *NCR*, Oct. 1, 1900. NCR Archive, Montgomery County Historical Society, Dayton, Ohio.

Page 134:   *NCR*, Jan. 1, 1903. NCR Archive, Montgomery County Historical Society, Dayton, Ohio.

Page 149:   NCR Archive, Montgomery County Historical Society, Dayton, Ohio.

Page 156:   *Salesology*, Feb. 1923, cover. New York Public Library.

Page 163:   A. W. Shaw, "Some Problems in Market Distribution," *Quarterly Journal of Economics* 26, no. 4 (Aug. 1912), pp. 703–765.

Page 173:   Northwestern University Archives, Evanston, Ill.

Page 199:   *Opportunity* (Jan. 1928), New York Public Library.

Page 208:   Alfred C. Fuller, *A Foot in the Door: The Life Appraisal of the Original Fuller Brush Man* (New York: McGraw-Hill, 1960), between pp. 120 and 121.

Page 215:   Fordex, *Model T Specialist* (Detroit, 1925), p. 43, New York Public Library.

Page 216:   Fordex, *Model T Specialist* (Detroit, 1925), p. 179, New York Public Library.

Page 221:   *Selling Chevrolets* (1926), p. 31. GM Media Archives, General Motors Corp., used with permission.

Page 239:   NCR Archive, Montgomery County Historical Society, Dayton, Ohio.

Index